T0325025

Modern Software Engineering Methodologies for Mobile and Cloud Environments

António Miguel Rosado da Cruz
Instituto Politécnico de Viana do Castelo, Portugal

Sara Paiva
Instituto Politécnico de Viana do Castelo, Portugal

A volume in the Advances in Systems Analysis,
Software Engineering, and High Performance
Computing (ASASEHPC) Book Series

An Imprint of IGI Global

Published in the United States of America by
        Information Science Reference (an imprint of IGI Global)
        701 E. Chocolate Avenue
        Hershey PA, USA 17033
        Tel: 717-533-8845
        Fax: 717-533-8661
        E-mail: cust@igi-global.com
        Web site: http://www.igi-global.com

Copyright © 2016 by IGI Global. All rights reserved. No part of this publication may be reproduced, stored or distributed in any form or by any means, electronic or mechanical, including photocopying, without written permission from the publisher. Product or company names used in this set are for identification purposes only. Inclusion of the names of the products or companies does not indicate a claim of ownership by IGI Global of the trademark or registered trademark.

Library of Congress Cataloging-in-Publication Data

Names: Cruz, Antonio Miguel Rosado da, 1970- editor. | Paiva, Sara, 1979-
  editor.
Title: Modern software engineering methodologies for mobile and cloud
  environments / Antonio Miguel Rosado da Cruz and Sara Paiva, editors.
Description: Hershey, PA : Information Science Reference, 2016. | Includes
  bibliographical references and index.
Identifiers: LCCN 2015046896| ISBN 9781466699168 (hardcover) | ISBN
  9781466699175 (ebook)
Subjects: LCSH: Cloud computing. | Mobile computing. | Software engineering.
Classification: LCC QA76.585 .M645 2106 | DDC 004.67/82--dc23 LC record available at http://lccn.loc.gov/2015046896

This book is published in the IGI Global book series Advances in Systems Analysis, Software Engineering, and High Performance Computing (ASASEHPC) (ISSN: 2327-3453; eISSN: 2327-3461)

British Cataloguing in Publication Data
A Cataloguing in Publication record for this book is available from the British Library.

All work contributed to this book is new, previously-unpublished material. The views expressed in this book are those of the authors, but not necessarily of the publisher.

For electronic access to this publication, please contact: eresources@igi-global.com.

Advances in Systems Analysis, Software Engineering, and High Performance Computing (ASASEHPC) Book Series

Vijayan Sugumaran
Oakland University, USA

ISSN: 2327-3453
EISSN: 2327-3461

MISSION

The theory and practice of computing applications and distributed systems has emerged as one of the key areas of research driving innovations in business, engineering, and science. The fields of software engineering, systems analysis, and high performance computing offer a wide range of applications and solutions in solving computational problems for any modern organization.

The **Advances in Systems Analysis, Software Engineering, and High Performance Computing (ASASEHPC) Book Series** brings together research in the areas of distributed computing, systems and software engineering, high performance computing, and service science. This collection of publications is useful for academics, researchers, and practitioners seeking the latest practices and knowledge in this field.

COVERAGE

- Parallel Architectures
- Metadata and Semantic Web
- Storage Systems
- Engineering Environments
- Software Engineering
- Performance Modelling
- Network Management
- Computer Networking
- Human-Computer Interaction
- Distributed Cloud Computing

IGI Global is currently accepting manuscripts for publication within this series. To submit a proposal for a volume in this series, please contact our Acquisition Editors at Acquisitions@igi-global.com or visit: http://www.igi-global.com/publish/.

The Advances in Systems Analysis, Software Engineering, and High Performance Computing (ASASEHPC) Book Series (ISSN 2327-3453) is published by IGI Global, 701 E. Chocolate Avenue, Hershey, PA 17033-1240, USA, www.igi-global.com. This series is composed of titles available for purchase individually; each title is edited to be contextually exclusive from any other title within the series. For pricing and ordering information please visit http://www.igi-global.com/book-series/advances-systems-analysis-software-engineering/73689. Postmaster: Send all address changes to above address. Copyright © 2016 IGI Global. All rights, including translation in other languages reserved by the publisher. No part of this series may be reproduced or used in any form or by any means – graphics, electronic, or mechanical, including photocopying, recording, taping, or information and retrieval systems – without written permission from the publisher, except for non commercial, educational use, including classroom teaching purposes. The views expressed in this series are those of the authors, but not necessarily of IGI Global.

Titles in this Series

For a list of additional titles in this series, please visit: www.igi-global.com

Emerging Research Surrounding Power Consumption and Performance Issues in Utility Computing
Ganesh Chandra Deka (Regional Vocational Training Institute (RVTI) for Women, India) G.M. Siddesh (M S Ramaiah Institute of Technology, Bangalore, India) K. G. Srinivasa (M S Ramaiah Institute of Technology, Bangalore, India) and L.M. Patnaik (IISc, Bangalore, India)
Information Science Reference • copyright 2016 • 460pp • H/C (ISBN: 9781466688537) • US $215.00 (our price)

Advanced Research on Cloud Computing Design and Applications
Shadi Aljawarneh (Jordan University of Science and Technology, Jordan)
Information Science Reference • copyright 2015 • 388pp • H/C (ISBN: 9781466686762) • US $205.00 (our price)

Handbook of Research on Computational Simulation and Modeling in Engineering
Francisco Miranda (Instituto Politécnico de Viana do Castelo and CIDMA of University of Aveiro, Portugal) and Carlos Abreu (Instituto Politécnico de Viana do Castelo, Portugal)
Engineering Science Reference • copyright 2016 • 824pp • H/C (ISBN: 9781466688230) • US $420.00 (our price)

Intelligent Applications for Heterogeneous System Modeling and Design
Kandarpa Kumar Sarma (Gauhati University, India) Manash Pratim Sarma (Gauhati University, India) and Mousmita Sarma (SpeecHWareNet (I) Pvt. Ltd, India)
Information Science Reference • copyright 2015 • 407pp • H/C (ISBN: 9781466684935) • US $255.00 (our price)

Achieving Enterprise Agility through Innovative Software Development
Amitoj Singh (Chitkara University, Punjab, India)
Information Science Reference • copyright 2015 • 349pp • H/C (ISBN: 9781466685109) • US $225.00 (our price)

Delivery and Adoption of Cloud Computing Services in Contemporary Organizations
Victor Chang (Computing, Creative Technologies and Engineering, Leeds Beckett University, UK) Robert John Walters (Electronics and Computer Science, University of Southampton, UK) and Gary Wills (Electronics and Computer Science, University of Southampton, UK)
Information Science Reference • copyright 2015 • 519pp • H/C (ISBN: 9781466682108) • US $225.00 (our price)

Emerging Research in Cloud Distributed Computing Systems
Susmit Bagchi (Gyeongsang National University, South Korea)
Information Science Reference • copyright 2015 • 446pp • H/C (ISBN: 9781466682139) • US $200.00 (our price)

www.igi-global.com

701 E. Chocolate Ave., Hershey, PA 17033
Order online at www.igi-global.com or call 717-533-8845 x100
To place a standing order for titles released in this series, contact: cust@igi-global.com
Mon-Fri 8:00 am - 5:00 pm (est) or fax 24 hours a day 717-533-8661

Editorial Advisory Board

João Pascoal Faria, *Universidade do Porto, Portugal*
João Miguel Fernandes, *Universidade do Minho, Portugal*
Manuel Ramos Cabrer, *Universidad de Vigo, Spain*
Carlos Serrão, *ISCTE-IUL, Portugal*

Table of Contents

Section 1
Mobile Cloud Computing

Section 2
Mobile Cloud Computing

Section 3
Mobile Design and Applications

Detailed Table of Contents

Section 1
Mobile Cloud Computing

This section provides insight on how Mobile Cloud Computing may be used to address mobile devices' scarce resources, particularly their limited battery capacity and processing capability. The first two chapters discuss approaches to augment mobile devices' capabilities. In the third chapter, Mobile Cloud Computing techniques are used in a mobile collaborative application. The fourth chapter presents the COSMIC method, a functional size measurement method especially adapted for estimating the development effort of mobile and cloud solutions.

Chapter 1

Mobile computing and Cloud computing are two of the most growing technologies in number of users, practitioners and research projects. This chapter surveys mobile technologies and applications, along with cloud computing technologies and applications, presenting their evolution and characteristics. Then, building on mobile devices limitations and mobile apps increasing need of resources, and on the cloud computing ability to overcome those limitations, the chapter presents mobile cloud computing, and characterizes it by addressing approaches to augment mobile devices capabilities. The chapter is settled after some views about future research directions and some concluding remarks.

Chapter 2

Mobile Cloud Computing (MCC) at its simplest form refers to an infrastructure where both the data storage and the data processing happen outside of the mobile device. In this chapter, a study on existing software architectures for MCC is outlined with their way of working. Also, a Nature inspired Artificial Bee Colony (ABC) based architecture has been proposed to provide reliable services from the cloud to the mobile requests. The proposed approach will definitely pave a way for timely services by using three different agents working in parallel, which mimics the behavior of honey bees namely Employed Bees, Onlooker Bees and Scout Bees. As the service discovery from the UDDI, Mobile profile Analysis and Allocation of Cloud resources for the requests are done by these software agents in a parallel execution, it achieves a green IT solution for MCC based software Development.

Chapter 3

Mobile devices have experienced a huge progress in the capacity of computing, storage and data visualization. They are becoming the device of choice for operating a large variety of applications while supporting real-time collaboration of people and their mobility. Despite this progress, the energy consumption and the network coverage remain a serious problem against an efficient and continuous use of these mobile collaborative applications and a great challenge for their designers and developers. To address these issues, this chapter describes design patterns that help modelling mobile collaborative applications to support collaboration through the cloud. Two levels are presented: the first level provides self-control to create clones of mobile devices, manage users' groups and recover failed clones in the cloud. The second level supports group collaboration mechanisms in real-time. These design patterns have been used as a basis for the design of a mobile collaborative editing application.

Chapter 4

Estimation of Cost, Effort and Schedule is a very important aspect in commercial software development. Effort is usually the predominant cost driver in software development. The dominant determinant for effort is the size of the software to be developed. There are various ways to determine the size of software. The best option is to use a standardized measure for the functional size. In this chapter the COSMIC method for functional size is introduced. Due to its basic principles, the COSMIC method enables determination of the functional size of mobile and cloud-based applications. This chapter demonstrates how the COSMIC method provides a good basis for the estimation of Cost, Effort and Schedule in mobile and cloud environments.

Section 2
Mobile Cloud Computing

This section focuses on important issues to consider when designing and developing applications for the web and the cloud. The first chapter discusses the need to test the cloud, and what to test, in order to assure the services in the cloud are appropriately delivered. The second chapter refers to the use of various programming languages, known as polyglot programming, in the context of web applications creation. The third chapter presents an approach to allow multiple stakeholders to work in a collaborative environment for domain-specific modelling.

Cloud computing is rapidly gaining significant attention in our day-to-day life. Cloud computing and software testing is one of the hot research areas for both industry and research. While one aspect of this merger, i.e. cloud testing (STaaS), is on real high and is receiving significant research attention, there is a lack of research addressing the other side, i.e. 'testing the cloud'. This chapter tries to differentiate between 'cloud testing' and 'testing the cloud' and explains why 'testing the cloud' is so crucial. In addition, it also explains what tests should be done in order to mitigate the challenges and risks of migrating our businesses to the cloud. This chapter provides a comprehensive tutorial to discuss the testing of cloud and also explains the need, objectives, requirements and challenges in 'testing the cloud'.

Different programming languages have been designed to solve problems efficiently in different domains. The goal of polyglot programming, a technique where several languages are used in the creation of a single application, is to combine and utilize the best solutions from different programming languages and paradigms in a seamless fashion. In this paper, the authors examine polyglot programming in the context of web applications, where it has been commonly used to create compelling applications, but where there is still considerable potential to improve development in various ways.

Chapter 7

Complex systems typically involve many stakeholder groups working in a coordinated manner on different aspects of a system. In Model-Driven Engineering (MDE), stakeholders work on models in order to design, transform, simulate, and analyze the system. Therefore, there is a growing need for collaborative platforms for modelers to work together. A cloud-based system allows them to concurrently work together. This chapter presents the challenges for building such environments. It also presents the architecture of a cloud-based multi-view modeling environment based on AToMPM.

Section 3
Mobile Design and Applications

This section covers essential aspects of mobile design and development, namely testing, refactoring, modeling and finished prototypes. The first chapter identifies and discusses relevant quality attributes for mobile applications development. The second chapter present results on how refactoring some anti-patterns can have impact on battery consumption. The third chapter presents a methodology to conduct usability tests in android based web applications. Finally, the fourth chapter in this section introduces a generic mobile solution to provide tracking and localization in any indoor environment.

Chapter 8

A mobile application is a type of software application developed to run on a mobile device. The chapter discusses the main characteristics of mobile devices, since they have a great impact on mobile applications. It also presents the classification of mobile applications according to two main types: native and web-based applications. Finally, this chapter identifies the most relevant types of quality attributes for mobile applications. It shows that the relevant quality attributes for mobile applications are usually framed in the Usability, Performance, and Maintainability and Support categories.

Ana Victoria Rodríguez, ISISTAN, Argentina

Cristian Mateos, ISISTAN, Argentina

Alejandro Zunino, ISISTAN, Argentina

Mathias Longo, UNICEN, Argentina

Mobile devices are the most popular kind of computational device in the world. These devices have more limited resources than personal computers and battery consumption is always under user's eye since mobile devices rely on their battery as energy supply. On the other hand, nowadays most applications are developed using object-oriented paradigm, which has some inherent features, like object creation, that consume important amounts of energy in the context of mobile development. These features are responsible for offering maintainability and flexibility, among other software quality-related advantages. Then, this chapter aims to present an analysis to evaluate the trade-off between object-oriented design purity and battery consumption. As a result, developers can design mobile applications taking into account these two issues, giving priority to object design quality and/or energy efficiency as needed.

Hina Saeeda, National University of Sciences and Technology, Pakistan

Fahim Arif, National University of Sciences and Technology, Pakistan

Nasir Mehmood Minhas, Pir Mehr Ali Shah Arid Agriculture University, Pakistan

For success of android applications working in cloud environments usability testing is vital as the user usability satisfaction is the leading point in market. Authors are testing usability of the learning management system of (National university of science and Technology Pakistan)ten usability factors system content visibility, system learn ability, accessibility, operability, consistency, feedback, error message production, error prevention, and ease to remember system operations are chosen on the basis of these key factors proper experimentation on users who access LMS by their smart phones using android applications in cloud environments is conducted .Pre-test was conducted for measuring the initial requirements of experimentation process after that the detailed experimentation was performed to measure the usability factors presence in android based web applications operated in cloud environment. The results are statistically summarized against.

João Paulo Quintão, Instituto Politécnico de Viana do Castelo, Portugal

Luís Pereira, Instituto Politécnico de Viana do Castelo, Portugal

Sara Paiva, Instituto Politécnico de Viana do Castelo, Portugal

In this paper we propose a domain independent Pedestrian Dead Reckoning System that can be applied to any indoor environment. We describe the entire solution and adopted architecture. The user can create new indoor spaces, define reference points in it, positions for future access and also track his current location. In order to track the user's position, we solve several walking detection false positives including a common problem with most pedometers. We present results of conducted tests that show a 98% accuracy of the system. Finally, we present the developed prototype.

Section 4
Model-Driven Approaches to Mobile Computing

This section presents model-driven development approaches to mobile applications' development. The first chapter presents a MDD approximation to generating Android native applications from models, and the second discusses producing mobile applications through partial code generation from existing Java desktop applications.

Increasing adoption of mobile smart devices demands a growing number of mobile applications (apps). Each of these applications must often be deployed to different mobile platforms, such as Android, iOS or Windows. Many of these applications are data-oriented, enabling the user to manage information, by creating, updating, deleting and retrieving data on his smart mobile device. By using a model-driven development approach, it is possible to generate a platform independent user interface model from a domain model, which represents the information structure of the application domain, and then have different code generators for each different target platform. This chapter presents such an approach together with a case study for Android apps.

Chapter 13

Software developers face several challenges in deploying mobile applications. One of them is the high cost and technical complexity of targeting development to a wide spectrum of platforms. The chapter proposes to combine techniques based on MDA (Model Driven Architecture) with the HaXe language. The outstanding ideas behind MDA are separating the specification of the system functionality from its implementation on specific platforms, managing the software evolution, increasing the degree of automation of model transformations, and achieving interoperability with multiple platforms. On the other hand, HaXe is a very modern high level programming language that allows us to generate mobile applications that target all major mobile platforms. The main contributions of this chapter are the definition of a HaXe metamodel, the specification of a model-to-model transformation between Java and HaXe and, the definition of an MDA migration process from Java to mobile platforms.

Within the model-driven engineering field, model execution consists in interpreting the model through a dedicated execution engine instead of executing a code based on, or generated from, the model. The class of modeling languages endowed with such executability is called i-DSML (interpreted Domain-Specific Modeling Language). This is an important development shift because a modeling effort seamlessly substitutes to a programming effort. This alternative way for building increasingly complex software is particularly beneficial to the mobile applications market where fast development and agility are recognized as key factors of success. This chapter illustrates how parts of an Android mobApp can be modeled and executed by leveraging a well-known i-DSML, namely UML 2 State Machine Diagrams and the PauWare engine thereof. Beyond this specific case, the proposed installation of PauWare on Android OS sets up the foundation for a whole range of mobApps, provided that they are modeled with the Statecharts formalism.

Section 5
Mobile Networks Design

This section discusses mobility management in different heterogeneous networks, and a SIP-PMIP Cross-Layer Mobility Management Scheme for providing seamless mobility support for terminal, personal, network and service mobility is proposed.

Chapter 15

Heterogeneous networks have attracted a lot of interest due to its support provision for a large number of networks at an effective cost. Mobility Management also plays an important role in the heterogeneous network in providing a seamless mobility support for both devices and users, which poses a serious challenge. In this chapter, the researchers propose SIP-PMIP Cross-Layer Mobility Management in order to provide a seamless mobility in heterogeneous wireless networks. In effect, the researchers design a Cross-Layer Mobility Management Scheme, which can handle terminal, network, personal and session mobility. To demonstrate, video conferencing is included in the modeling, simulation and implementation of the module using Riverbed Modeler.

Preface

It has been more than a decade that Salesforce and Amazon delivered the first on-demand services on the web, starting an age of metered IT services provided to consumers at the pace they need them. Cloud computing is defined by the U.S. National Institute of Standards and Technology (NIST) as a model to enable ubiquitous access, convenient and on-demand to a shared pool of configurable IT services (e.g.: networks, servers, storage, applications and services), and where services can be rapidly provisioned and released without intervention of the service provider and with minimal management effort (Mell & Grance, 2011). This definition entails the unilateral provision of computing services as needed by the client, without intervention of the service provider; the access to the provided services through standard mechanisms and by disparate client platforms; the elastic provision of services, which may scale up and down or in and out, depending on consumer's demand; the use of a metering capability at a level of abstraction appropriate to the type of service; and, the pooling of computing resources, by the provider, so that several consumers may be served, according to their needs, using a multi-tenant model.

To companies, the arrival of the cloud concept facilitated their internal organization and management as they no longer need to highly invest in resources to achieve their goals. The pay-as-you-go model and the utility computing concept of cloud computing allows companies to use resources as required, avoiding bad and unused investments. The fundamental attributes used to characterize the cloud correspond, at the same time, to the benefits it provides to its users: *on-demand computing model,* which delivers IT resources to end users in a similar way public utilities - electricity or water – are delivered eliminating the prerequisite of each company needing to have its own datacenter; *autonomous* services as they hide, from end users, their complexity or technology; *predefined QoS* to service usage are defined in service-level agreements (SLA) and made clear to clients when they contract them; *internet-based* meaning all services are delivered through the Internet and publicly accessible; services are *easy-to-use* through friendly interfaces and GUI forms for administrators; the resources contracted are *scalable* up and down, or in and out, depending on the organization needs at a given moment; *inexpensive* solution compared to having their own datacenters and *subscription-based model* that allows clients to choose what services they are interested in (Hassan 2011).

Likewise, less than a decade ago, the arrival of iOS and Android mobile operating systems, together with the massive deployment of mobile high-speed data networks, such as 3G and 4G, and the proliferation of mobile smart devices (Islam & Want, 2014), enabled the advent of an age where people may be always connected, carry computing power constantly, and IT services may be accessed from almost anywhere, anytime, for both personal and corporate purposes. Over time, mobile technologies have proven to be of great importance for organizations providing mobility, flexibility, reactivity and productivity increase. The wide range of mobile devices and associated technologies and features brought additional challenges to mobile development. Mobile programmers need to address several issues to ensure a reliable and trustable application including portability, CPU and memory consumption, battery usage, seize devices heterogeneity, data input mechanisms, Wi-Fi or 3G/4G communication and built-in storage. When creating new mobile applications, companies need to target at least the two major mobile operating systems currently in the market. The great disparity in the programming languages used, UI guidelines and the IDEs themselves, make companies face the challenge of choosing the best approach that allows them to have a mobile application targeting more than one platform with a minimum cost, raising the question of when to use native or cross-platform environments.

All these developments have brought mobile and cloud based applications to the fore. As these are gaining momentum, by getting more and more integrated with business process models and expanding in scope and usage, they also become more valuable to businesses. This amplification in business value, together with the corresponding increase in complexity, has led to the development of new software engineering approaches specialized for these kinds of software applications. Existing software engineering methods and techniques have been adapted, and new ones have seen the light of day, so that business processes can rely on mobile and Cloud applications and services, trusting in their ability to respond to business needs, their quality of service, availability and performance.

Modern Software Engineering Methodologies for Mobile and Cloud Environments address mobile and cloud applications and services design and development. They encompass a set of methods and techniques for modeling, constructing and validating mobile and cloud-based applications, analyzing and testing underlying networks and services, and studying and developing new approaches that try to cope with the limitations of one through exploring the opportunities leveraged by the other. These methods and techniques are mainly specializations of existing approaches for desktop and web applications, but also include new proposals specifically tailored for mobile and cloud applications and services. Examples of these latter are domain specific languages for modeling and describing mobile applications' user interface or access to location-based services, approaches to multi-tenancy adaptation of legacy applications redeployed to the Cloud, or new distributed architectures for mobile-cloud applications. These are amongst many other examples.

The mission of this book on Modern Software Engineering Methodologies for Mobile and Cloud Environments is to discuss and analyze current methodologies, techniques and practical solutions and trends related to this new field of knowledge, in a comprehensive way.

The overall objectives comprise:

- To discuss the importance and the challenges associated to software engineering methods and techniques for mobile and cloud environments;
- To analyze the state-of-the-art of existing software engineering methods and techniques for mobile and cloud environments;
- To propose emerging technological developments and practical solutions for engineering software for mobile and cloud environments;
- To present case studies of application of software engineering methods and techniques specialized for mobile and cloud environments.

Potential contexts of use of the present book include the scientific community (scholars and researchers) with research interests in these fields. Moreover, information technologies companies and practitioners, and graduate and post-graduate level students, can benefit from the advances presented in the book and apply them in real applications and scenarios.

This edited book comprises contributions from several authors focusing the most recent progressive research concerning software engineering methods and techniques applied to the development of mobile and cloud applications and of cloud services-based applications. The book intends to cover the following topics:

- Mobile and cloud technologies and characteristics
- Software architectures for mobile cloud computing
- Collaborative cloud and mobile applications
- Mobile and cloud design patterns
- Modeling of mobile and cloud applications
- Software Testing as a Service
- Polyglot programming
- Model-driven mobile development
- Native and web-based applications
- Energy efficiency in mobile development
- Usability in mobile applications
- Indoor tracking and localization
- Cross-platform mobile development
- Software sizing for mobile and cloud projects
- Mobility management and protocols

ORGANIZATION OF THE BOOK

The book is organized into fifteen chapters. A brief portrayal of each of the chapters follows:

Chapter 1 reviews Mobile computing and Cloud computing, two of the most growing technologies in number of users, practitioners and research projects. The chapter surveys mobile and cloud technologies and presents their evolution and characteristics. Then, building on mobile devices limitations and mobile apps increasing need of resources, and on the cloud computing ability to overcome those limitations, the chapter presents Mobile Cloud Computing (MCC), and characterizes it by addressing approaches to augment mobile devices capabilities. The chapter is settled after some views about future research directions and some concluding remarks.

Chapter 2 outlines existing software architectures for Mobile Cloud Computing, and presents Artificial Bee Colony (ABC) as a nature inspired architecture for providing reliable cloud services to mobile requests. The proposed approach intends to pave the way for timely services by using three different agents working in parallel, mimicking the behavior of honey bees namely Employed Bees, Onlooker Bees and Scout Bees. The approach also intends to be seen as a green IT solution for MCC based software Development.

Chapter 3 debates about the capabilities of mobile devices for supporting collaborative applications. Despite the enormous progress in the capacity of computing, storage and data visualization experienced by mobile devices, these still face some difficulties related to energy consumption and the mobile network coverage. This poses serious problems against an efficient and continuous use of mobile collaborative applications and a great challenge for their designers and developers. The author describes design patterns that help modeling mobile collaborative applications to support collaboration through the cloud. Two levels are presented: the first level provides self-control to create clones of mobile devices, manage users' groups and recover failed clones in the cloud. The second level supports group collaboration mechanisms in real-time.

Chapter 4 addresses estimation of cost, effort and schedule as very important aspects in commercial software development. The authors identify effort as typically being the predominant cost driver in software development, and the size of the software to be developed, as the dominant determinant for effort. Then, the COSMIC method is presented as a standardized technology independent measure for estimating the functional size of software. Finally, the authors argue that the COSMIC method provides a good basis for the estimation of cost, effort and schedule in mobile and cloud-based applications.

Chapter 5 reflects about Software Testing as a Service (STaaS) and the conditions offered by the cloud for supporting it. The authors consider the cloud-based hardware infrastructure and computing resources to perform traditional testing like performance, load, stress, security and compatibility testing for regular on-premises applications. Their opinion that software testing in the cloud (cloud testing) has the capacity to change the way software testing is performed, is however threatened by the fact that the cloud itself poses many issues related to security, compatibility, performance, scalability, functionality, third party dependencies and many more. And, according to the authors, these issues need also be tested. Testing cloud infrastructure and applications has its own peculiarities that demand for novel/tailored testing methods and tools. The chapter distinguishes between 'cloud testing' and 'testing the cloud', debates why 'testing the cloud' is so crucial, and explains the need, objectives, requirements and challenges of 'testing the cloud'.

Chapter 6 presents polyglot programming, a technique where several languages are used in the creation of a single application. Different programming languages have been designed to solve problems efficiently in different domains, and polyglot programming tries to combine and utilize the best solutions from different programming languages and paradigms in a seamless fashion. In this chapter, the authors examine polyglot programming in the context of web applications, where it has been commonly used to create compelling applications, but where, according to the authors, there is still considerable potential to improve development in various ways.

Chapter 7 debates the growing need for collaborative platforms for software modelers to work together. It also analyses the challenges posed to solutions for the collaborative model-driven development of complex systems, which typically involve many stakeholder groups working in a coordinated manner on different aspects of a system. The authors also present the architecture of their prototype of a cloud-based multi-view modeling environment, AToMPM.

Chapter 8 reflects on the main characteristics of mobile applications and mobile devices, since they have a great impact on mobile applications. It also presents the classification of mobile applications according to two main types: native and web-based applications. Then, the authors identify the most relevant types of quality attributes for mobile applications, and show that the relevant quality attributes for mobile applications are usually framed in the Usability, Performance, and Maintainability and Support categories.

Chapter 9 discusses the limited resources of mobile devices when compared to personal computers, especially energy. In mobile devices, battery consumption is always under the user's eye. The authors also argue that object-orientation, which is currently the main paradigm in applications' development, has some inherent features that consume important amounts of energy in the context of mobile development.

According to the authors, these are however needed features, which are responsible for offering maintainability and flexibility, among other software quality-related advantages. The chapter aims to present an analysis to evaluate the trade-offs between object-oriented design purity and battery consumption, so that developers can design mobile applications taking into account these two issues, giving priority to object design quality and/or energy efficiency as needed.

Chapter 10 presents the results of testing the usability of a web-based learning management system (LMS) within Android mobile devices. The authors claim that usability testing is vital as the user usability satisfaction is the leading point in market for mobile web applications. Ten usability factors have been chosen, on the basis of which proper experimentation by users accessing the LMS through their smart phones is conducted. Initial requirements for the experimentation were measured in a pre-test process, after which the detailed experimentation has been performed to measure the usability factors presence in the LMS when accessed through android based systems. The results are statistically summarized.

Chapter 11 proposes a domain independent Pedestrian Dead Reckoning System that can be applied to any indoor environment. The chapter describes the adopted architecture and the developed prototype. The authors state that within the proposed system, the user can create new indoor spaces, define reference points in it, positions for future access and also track his current location. The chapter presents some solutions for solving several walking detection false positives, in order to track the user's position. The results of conducted tests are also presented, and show a 98% accuracy of the system when tracking the user's current position.

Chapter 12 proposes a model-driven development approach for generating data-oriented mobile applications from a domain model, which represents the information structure of the application domain. The authors present an approach for generating a platform independent user interface model from a domain model, and then propose to have different code generators for each different target platform. The approach responds to the increasing adoption of mobile smart devices, the demand for a growing number of mobile applications, and the need to deploy each mobile application to different mobile platforms, such as Android, iOS or Windows. The approach presented is applicable to data-oriented mobile applications. A generator prototype for Android apps is also presented.

Chapter 13 also tries to respond to the increasing demand of mobile applications, and the need to deploy each mobile application to different mobile platforms. The authors propose to combine techniques based on MDA (Model Driven Architecture) with the HaXe language. The main ideas behind MDA are separating the specification of the system functionality from its implementation on specific platforms, managing the software evolution, increasing the degree of automation of model transformations, and achieving interoperability with multiple platforms. HaXe is a modern high level programming language that allows generating mobile applications that target all major mobile platforms. The main contributions of this chapter are the definition of the HaXe metamodel and the specification of a model-to-model transformation process between Java and HaXe. These contributions enabled also the definition of an MDA migration process from Java to mobile platforms.

Chapter 14 presents the notion of model execution within the model-driven engineering field. Model execution is about interpreting the model through a dedicated execution engine instead of executing code generated from the model. The modeling languages able to be executable are called i-DSML (interpreted Domain-Specific Modeling Languages). The authors assert that model execution tends to abolish the boundaries between modeling and programming. This chapter then illustrates how parts of an Android mobile application can be modeled and executed by leveraging a well-known i-DSML, namely UML 2 State Machine Diagrams and the PauWare engine. The proposed installation of PauWare on Android

OS sets up the foundation for a whole range of mobile apps, provided that they are modeled with State Machine Diagrams.

Chapter 15 surveys mobility management and protocols, which play an important role in heterogeneous networks in providing a seamless mobility support for both devices and users. The chapter then presents SIP-PMIP Cross-Layer Mobility Management in order to provide a seamless mobility in heterogeneous wireless networks. In effect, the authors propose a Cross-Layer Mobility Management Scheme, which can handle terminal, network, personal and session mobility. To demonstrate, video conferencing is included in the modeling, simulation and implementation of the module using Riverbed Modeler.

António Miguel Rosado da Cruz
Instituto Politécnico de Viana do Castelo, Portugal

Sara Paiva
Instituto Politécnico de Viana do Castelo, Portugal

REFERENCES

Hassan, Q. (2011). Demystifying cloud computing. *The Journal of Defense Software Engineering*, 16–21. Available at http://static1.1.sqspcdn.com/static/f/702523/10181434/1294788395300/201101-Hassan.pdf?token=EqoGiTUTRMhCYeQnv9v5TJb41sA%3D

Islam, N., & Want, R. (2014). Smartphones: Past, present, and future. *Pervasive Computing*, *13*(4), 89–92. doi:10.1109/MPRV.2014.74

Mell, P., & Grance, T. (2011). *The NIST definition of cloud computing*. NIST Special Publication 800 – 145, Computer Security Division, Information Technology Laboratory, National Institute of Standards and Technology. Available at http://csrc.nist.gov/publications/nistpubs/800-145/SP800-145.pdf

Section 1
Mobile Cloud Computing

This section provides insight on how Mobile Cloud Computing may be used to address mobile devices' scarce resources, particularly their limited battery capacity and processing capability. The first two chapters discuss approaches to augment mobile devices' capabilities. In the third chapter, Mobile Cloud Computing techniques are used in a mobile collaborative application. The fourth chapter presents the COSMIC method, a functional size measurement method especially adapted for estimating the development effort of mobile and cloud solutions.

Chapter 1
Cloud and Mobile:
A Future Together

Antonio Miguel Rosado da Cruz
Instituto Politécnico de Viana do Castelo, Portugal

Sara Paiva
Instituto Politécnico de Viana do Castelo, Portugal

ABSTRACT

Mobile computing and Cloud computing are two of the most growing technologies in number of users, practitioners and research projects. This chapter surveys mobile technologies and applications, along with cloud computing technologies and applications, presenting their evolution and characteristics. Then, building on mobile devices limitations and mobile apps increasing need of resources, and on the cloud computing ability to overcome those limitations, the chapter presents mobile cloud computing, and characterizes it by addressing approaches to augment mobile devices capabilities. The chapter is settled after some views about future research directions and some concluding remarks.

INTRODUCTION

A long time has passed since the first telephone by Alexander Graham Bell in 1876. From then, it has been possible for people to communicate from long distances. The first (analog) mobile phone appeared only almost 100 years later, in the 1960s, adding mobility to the possibility of making long distance calls. The 1960's device was too big to be transported personally, so it had to be installed in vehicles. Only in 1973 the first handheld mobile phone (analog) was created. And, the first digital cellular networks have seen the light of day in 1977 (Cruz, 2012).

Just a few years ago, when talking about mobile devices, what would come to one's mind were mobile phones. Today, mobile phone is just one feature of what is called smartphones. Smartphones and other smart devices have processing power, different operating systems and incorporate sensors, GPS, electronic compass, accelerometer, etc., having added the goal of mobile computing to the previous goals of distance communication and mobility.

DOI: 10.4018/978-1-4666-9916-8.ch001

Copyright © 2016, IGI Global. Copying or distributing in print or electronic forms without written permission of IGI Global is prohibited.

With the appearance of iOS and Android operating systems, around 2007, together with the massive deployment of mobile high-speed data networks, such as 3G and 4G, mobile smart devices have become part of every day's life, allowing for people to access the internet almost anytime, anywhere (Islam & Want, 2014). We live in a world where more smartphones are activated every day than babies are born (Waugh, 2012).

Despite its increasing features and capabilities, mobile devices aren't able to substitute personal computers for most working and domestic applications, especially when storing data or collaboration between users are a must. For aiding in these tasks Cloud Computing, another recently boomed technology, may come in handy by providing backend services to some mobile applications or providing an environment where to offload mobile apps execution.

Cloud computing is built on technologies like system or platform virtualization, distributed systems, and web services, some of which have been around for nearly 40 years (Pearce et al, 2013; Phaphoom *et al.*, 2013). It made utility computing possible, as it was conveyed by the MIT in the early 1960s. Currently it is possible for organizations to pay only for what they use, in computing power or storage capacity, as well as in electricity or other utilities. This makes possible to reduce corporate's investment amount in IT, because organizations need not invest in datacenters sized for the maximum capacity they think they will ever need, leading to the more efficient use of shared datacenters. This also enables organizations to focus on the IT services they need to hire, being confident that the hired IT services' capacity or resources will elastically grow or shrink according to their usage needs (Phaphoom *et al.*, 2013; Costa & Cruz, 2012).

This chapter presents an overview of mobile devices and associated technologies, identifying their limitations and recognizing their resource scarcity. Then, the chapter presents cloud computing, its characteristics, service and deployment models, and related technologies. Afterwards, and building on mobile devices limitations and on the cloud computing ability to overcome those limitations, the chapter presents mobile cloud computing, and characterizes it by addressing approaches to augment mobile devices capabilities. Finally, some directions for future research are presented and some conclusions are drawn.

BACKGROUND: MOBILE DEVICES, MOBILE APPS AND CLOUD COMPUTING

Characteristics of Mobile Technologies

Mobile technologies allow users to have anytime, anywhere access to information and applications, which provides benefits for both personal and corporate purposes (Sheng *et al.*, 2005). This is achieved with handheld IT artifacts that encompass hardware devices, software applications and communication (Jarvenpaa & Lang, 2005) where technological infrastructure for connectivity is included such as Wireless Application Protocol (WAP), Wi-Fi, Bluetooth, 3G, Global Positioning System (GPS) and General Packet Radio Service (GPRS). Over time, mobile technologies have proven to be of great importance for organizations providing (Ivanochko *et al.*, 2014):

- Mobility: information can be accessed from anywhere, which is fundamental when dealing with critical information;
- Flexibility: with the possibility to contact employees at any time and space the organization becomes more flexible;

- Reactivity: by having immediate access to information, immediate response is possible increasing the satisfaction of customers;
- Productivity: with the possibility of visualizing information and act upon it, each member of an organization becomes more productive.

The constant connectivity is a mandatory requirement to make the most of mobile technologies, and current mobile telecommunication services make this possible. But it hasn't always been like this. In the early 1970s pre-cellular phone mobile telephony, known as 0G (zero generation), consisted of radio telephones that some had in cars before the advent of cell phones. Mobile radio telephone systems preceded modern cellular mobile telephony technology (Abraham, 2012; Bhalla & Bhalla, 2010).

In the early 1980s we assisted to the first generation of cellular mobile telecommunications – the 1G. It was an analog cellular telephone system used for voice service only, with plenty of limitations. The main problem of 1G was that there was only one channel which carried the data from source to destination so the first caller would have to wait for a response from the other caller once the voice was received (Singh & K.S., 2012). Different 1G standards were used in different countries. Examples are NMT (Nordic

Mobile Telephone), used in Nordic countries, Eastern Europe and Russia, AMPS (Advanced Mobile Phone System) used in the United States, TACS (Total Access Communications System) in the United Kingdom, C-Netz in West Germany, Radiocom 2000 in France, and RTMI in Italy (Singh & K.S., 2012; Bhalla & Bhalla, 2010).

The second generation – 2G – launched in the 90s, introduced digital systems as a significant difference from its predecessors. Although 2G cannot normally transfer data, such as email or software, other than the digital voice call itself, and other basic auxiliary data such as time and date, data services for mobile also appeared in 2G in the form of text messages. Some 2G standards allowed SMS messaging as a form of data transmission. 2G cellular telecom networks were commercially launched on the GSM standard (Global System for Mobile Communications, originally Groupe Spécial Mobile) in Finland (Singh & K.S., 2012; Bhalla & Bhalla, 2010).

In the late 90s, the third generation - 3G - networks were introduced, based on a set of standards that comply with the International Mobile Telecommunications (IMT-2000). With higher data transmission rates and greater bandwidth cellphone users started to have mobile Internet access, multimedia applications, TV streaming, multimedia, videoconferencing, Web browsing, e-mail, paging, fax, and navigational maps. In 2008, driven by the emergence of new technologies and the growing number of users' demands (Mshvidobadze, 2012), a set of requirements for 4G standards were created – under the name International Mobile Telecommunications Advanced (IMT-Advanced) – that specified speed requirements of 100Mb/s for high mobility communications and 1Gb/s for low mobility communications. The speed increase has been the most significant improvement for end users, who saw the access to services made available by 3G become faster. While looking back at these four generations, we verify that each one persisted for over a decade. This is why 5G is already being discussed and expected around 2020, mainly to address the Internet of Things which will lead to an exponential increasing number of connected people and devices (Andrews *et al.*, 2014).

3G and 4G, however, are not the only current solutions for connectivity in mobile devices. The Wi-Fi technology is suitable for plenty of scenarios. Wi-Fi, proposed by the Wi-Fi Alliance, describes the underlying technology of Wireless Local Area Networks (WLAN) based on the IEEE 802.11 specifications. Although first designed to be used by laptops in LANs, Wi-Fi is now being used for more services such as Internet telephony, music streaming, gaming, and even photo viewing and in-home video transmission (Dhawan, 2007).

With its first release in 1999 the Wi-Fi Alliance points out interoperability, ease of use, and innovation as the main factors for the success behind the Wi-Fi technology (Wi-Fi Alliance, 2014). The data rate offered has significantly increased over the years and its original 11 Mbps in 1999 are very different from the 1 Gbps data rate achieved in 2014. Device-to-device connectivity was introduced with Wi-Fi Direct, easy-to-use display with Miracast, and seamless access to Wi-Fi hotspots with Passpoint. The future trends of this technology include:

- For 2016, WiGig CERTIFIED will deliver interoperable products supporting multiple-gigabit data rates for room-range connectivity in 60 GHz.
- Certification programs based on 802.11ah and 802.11af, for operation below 1 GHz to support longer-range, very-low-power connectivity.
- With the Internet of Everything emerging, there will be the possibility to connect new types of devices to each other and the internet, extending Wi-Fi´s reach to smart home, connected cars, sensing and control networks, to name a few.

Bluetooth technology (Bluetooth, 2015) has also a very well defined space in the wireless technologies and it defines a uniform structure for a wide range of devices to connect and communicate with each other. The Bluetooth technology is simple and secure, and ubiquity, low power, and low cost are some of the key features, to name a few. It is present in mobile phones, computers, home products and medical devices, enabling plenty of functionalities and applications. Devices with Bluetooth enabled and in a near range can connect to each other in a process called pairing. A main strength of this technology is the ability to simultaneously handle data and voice transmissions, which provides users with a variety of innovative solutions such as hands-free headsets for voice calls, printing and fax capabilities, and synchronization for PCs and mobile phones.

The GPS is also a very common functionality present in mobile devices through a proper hardware component responsible for receiving positions from the space-based satellite navigation system. Mobile devices make use of this functionality to provide location and tracking applications such as tourist applications to suggest city reference points, monitoring applications for children and elder people, driving support applications to calculate routes, to name just a few. The main drawback of GPS signal is the need for an unobstructed line of sight to four or more GPS satellites, which invalidates its use in indoor environments.

Characteristics of Mobile Devices

There is today a large number of electronic equipment available for computing and communications. Despite that, not all of them can be considered as mobile devices. For that, some characteristics should be present, such as:

- **Portability:** This is a key feature of mobile devices so their users have the ability to move wherever they want and be able to operate with the equipment. Portability also means not being dependent on a fixed wired power source or a physical Internet connection.

- **Less Power (CPU, Memory, and Battery):** Mobile devices are still less resourceful than desktop or laptop computers, as they have less memory, weaker CPUs and limited battery power (Flora *et al.*, 2014).
- **Small Size:** In order to be portable, a mobile device also has to be relatively small, so it can fit in an adult´s hand or pocket. Some mobile devices may fold or slide to a larger size to reveal a built-in keyboard or larger screen.
- **Input Mechanism:** Input in mobile devices makes use of touch screens or small keypads and is typically independent from external interface devices. The user input mechanisms in mobile devices are based on features such as touch, pinch, and swipe. Traditional keyboard typing input is more cumbersome and should be minimized (Flora *et al.*, 2014).
- **Wireless Communication:** Mobile devices should be able to communicate with similar devices or others such as laptops, desktop computers or servers. To achieve this, mobile devices are equipped with Wi-Fi, Bluetooth and data networks connections that provide Internet connectivity. Examples of the type of communication mobile devices should perform are sending and receiving emails, texting, telephony services, RFID or barcode readers.
- **Built-In Storage:** As most mobile devices have the need to store music, photos or other type of data, a non-removable built-in storage is a requirement.
- **Applications:** Mobile devices should be provided with some applications and allow others to be installed through the web browser, applications' stores or third parties'.

From Mobile Devices to Smartphones

The first mobile telephones, in the 1960s, were very big, heavy (almost 40 kilos), expensive (the price of a small car) and power consuming. They were used in cars, trucks and trains, though briefcase models were also made. With the emergence of the first generation of mobile cellphone systems, of which NMT, AMPS and TACS are example standard technologies, the first truly portable telephones appeared. In 1987 Nokia announced Cityman and Ericsson the Hotline Pocket. These equipments, as others similar that followed, supported in average 30 minutes of conversation and weighted approximately 1 kilo.

In the early 90s, IBM Simon was released, which is usually considered the first smartphone, as it incorporated, beside calls functionality, personal digital assistant (PDA) features, accessible via a stylus, such as send and receive faxes and emails, an address book, calendar, clock, scheduler and a notepad. The concept of smartphone appeared in 1995 by Pamela Savage to describe the AT&T's "PhoneWriter Communicator" (Savage, 1995). In the late 90s it was common to see users carrying a mobile phone and a PDA. This scenario changed with the appearance of smartphones that combined the two functionalities.

In 2007, the iPhone was launched to present a multi-touch interface that didn´t use a stylus or keyboard for user interaction. A year later, the first smartphone with an Android operating system was released.

Characteristics of Mobile Applications

To develop a successful mobile application, it is fundamental to understand the key differences between mobile and desktop development. When we are working at a desktop computer, our activities tend to be longer in duration when compared to the ones we perform in a mobile device. In a desktop computer, activities tend to be one of the following three (Salmre, 2005): browsing the Web, working on documents or communicating, which can be time consuming activities. On the other hand, in a mobile device usually we perform quicker activities such as making a phone call, send or reply to an SMS or an email or check the schedule.

Another characteristic of mobile applications is that the mobile user has a high probability of being interrupted while using them, which leads us to the first mentioned characteristic that refers to the short length of mobile applications activities.

Another key difference to be considered is the nature of the activities performed in desktop and mobile applications, directly related to the size of the equipment. The big screen of a desktop computer, the precision of a mouse click and the keyboard allows us to perform more exploratory activities when browsing the Web and easily changing to a document to make annotations or add an event to the calendar. In a mobile device switching activities and copy/pasting information from one application to another is not so easy so activities in mobile applications are more focused on a given purpose.

According to Flora *et al.* (2014), an important aspect regarding mobile applications is to understand its type and category. The authors distinguish four types of mobile applications (browser access apps, native apps, hybrid apps (web or mixed)). Table 1 summarizes the key factors of each type.

Browser access apps are the only ones that do not need to be installed on a mobile device, so the storage capabilities and memory of the device is not very important for this type of mobile applications. They are accessed through a browser so Internet connection is always required to obtain data from a remote server.

Native apps are installed on a device and can be used without any Internet connection. The size of the application tends to be bigger so the storage and device memory are relevant.

Regarding hybrid apps, what mainly distinguishes web from mixed hybrid apps is the fact that web hybrid apps need Internet to get updated data, such as in Facebook or Twitter. The application is installed on the device but needs to get updates from a remote server. Mixed hybrid apps do not mandatorily need Internet connection as a part of the app may also work offline.

Flora *et al.* (2014) also present the main 7 categories in which a mobile application can fit into, claiming that various mobile applications that are available on any apps' store these days can be categorized into the following categories: Communications (e.g.: email clients, internet browsers, news clients), Games (e.g.: puzzle, strategy, adventure), Multimedia (e.g.: audio/video players, image viewers, audio/video streaming players), Productivity (e.g.: calendars, memo/text processors, spreadsheets, call recording), Travel (e.g.: city guides, location based services, currency converters, weather forecasters), Utilities (e.g.: address books, task managers, mobile search) and Education (e.g.: alphabet, numerical).

Table 1. Mobile Application Types and its Key Factors

Key Factors	Browser Access Apps	Native Apps	Hybrid Apps (Web)	Hybrid Apps (Mixed)
Installed on the device	No	Yes	Yes	Yes
Access through native browser	Yes	No	No	No
Get data from remote server	Yes	No	Yes	Depend
Importance of device memory	Low	High	Depend	High
Require internet connection	Yes	No	Yes	Depend

Characteristics of Cloud Computing

Cloud Computing represents a paradigm shift in the way IT services are provided. Google, Yahoo, Amazon, and others have built large architectures to support their applications and taught the rest of the world how to massively scale architectures to support computing power, storage and application services (ACM, 2009).

Cloud computing refers to moving data, computing power, or other IT services, from the place where they were, inside the company's premises, to a transparent internal or external location in a centralized facility, in the organization or contracted (ACM, 2009).

Among several other definitions, cloud computing may be defined as a model for providing IT services and applications over the internet on a pay-as-you-go payment model (AWS, 2015), a model to enable ubiquitous access, convenient and on-demand to a shared pool of configurable IT services (e.g.: networks, servers, storage, applications and services), and where services can be rapidly provisioned and released without intervention of the service provider and with minimal management effort (Mell & Grance, 2011). This latter is the definition by NIST, the U.S. National Institute of Standards and Technology, which assumes a cloud model composed of five essential characteristics, three service models, and four deployment models. The five essential characteristics are (Mell and Grance, 2011):

- **On-Demand Self-Service:** The unilateral provision of computing capabilities (e.g., server time, network storage) as needed, without requiring intervention of the service provider.
- **Broad Network Access:** Capabilities are accessed through standard mechanisms and by heterogeneous client platforms (e.g., mobile phones, tablets, laptops, and workstations).
- **Resource Pooling:** Computing resources (e.g., storage, processing, memory, and network bandwidth) are pooled, by the provider, to serve multiple consumers using a multi-tenant model. Different physical and virtual resources are dynamically assigned and reassigned according to consumer demand. The customer generally has no control or knowledge over the exact location of the provided resources but may be able to specify location at a higher level of abstraction (e.g., country, state, or datacenter).
- **Rapid Elasticity:** Capabilities can be elastically provisioned and released, to scale depending on consumer's demand. The capabilities available typically appear to be unlimited, from the consumer's viewpoint.
- **Measured Service:** Cloud systems automatically control and optimize resource use by leveraging a metering capability at a level of abstraction appropriate to the type of service (e.g., storage, processing, bandwidth, and active user accounts).

Service Models define the kinds of services provided by the service provider. NIST considers three cloud service models (Mell & Grance, 2011):

- **Infrastructure as a Service (IaaS):** The user runs its own operating system software and applications on the compute capacity provided by the cloud provider. The consumer does not manage or control the underlying cloud infrastructure but has control over operating systems, storage, and deployed applications.
- **Platform as a Service (PaaS):** The provider provides a platform, such as programming languages, libraries, tools or services, for the user to use to develop, install and deploy its applications.

The consumer does not manage or control the underlying cloud infrastructure including network, servers, operating systems, or storage, but has control over the deployed applications and possibly configuration settings for the application-hosting environment.

- **Software as a Service (SaaS):** The provider provides software applications for the users to subscribe and use. The applications may typically be accessed from various client devices through either a thin client interface, such as a web browser, or a program interface. The consumer does not manage or control the underlying cloud infrastructure including network, servers, operating systems, storage, or even individual application capabilities, with the possible exception of limited user-specific application configuration settings.

Other service models are always appearing, which originated the term Everything-as-a-Service (XaaS), in which everything may be acquired as a service, and where clients have a full control to customize the computing environment to best fit their unique demands by composing varieties of cloud-based services (Phaphoom *et al.*, 2013). Other service models can, however, typically be framed within the three service models referred above (SaaS, PaaS, IaaS).

Cloud services' deployment models have to do with the ownership and management of the cloud infrastructure, and are related to the consumers' privacy requirements for cloud adoption. NIST considers four main cloud deployment models: public, private, community and hybrid (Mell & Grance, 2011). Amazon introduced the concept of virtual private cloud as an alternative solution that balances the flexibility of public clouds and the security of private clouds (Phaphoom *et al.*, 2013). This is today also available from other cloud providers, such as Microsoft Azure.

Considered cloud deployment models are (Mell & Grance, 2011; Borko, 2010; Phaphoom *et al.*, 2013):

- **Private Cloud:** The cloud infrastructure is thought of for exclusive use by a single organization. The infrastructure may exist on or off premises, and its ownership, management and operation responsibility may be of the organization, a third party, or some combination of them.
- **Public Cloud:** The cloud infrastructure is aimed at the general public, and exists on the premises of the cloud provider. It is owned, managed, and operated by a cloud service provider organization.
- **Virtual Private Cloud:** The cloud infrastructure is aimed at the general public, and exists on the premises of the cloud provider. Virtual private cloud removes security issues caused by resource sharing of public clouds by adding a security platform on top of the public clouds. Virtual private network (VPN) technology is used and some resources are provided in a dedicated manner, allowing consumers to customize their network topology and security settings.
- **Community Cloud:** The cloud infrastructure is aimed at a specific community of consumers from organizations or groups with shared concerns. Its ownership, management and operation may be the responsibility of one or more of the organizations in the community, a third party, or some combination of them, and it may exist on or off premises.
- **Hybrid Cloud:** The cloud infrastructure is a combination of two or more distinct cloud infrastructures (private or public) that are bound together by standardized or proprietary technology that enables data and application portability (e.g., cloud bursting for load balancing between clouds).

Cloud computing is built on existing overlapping technologies, such as grid computing, virtualization or Service Oriented Architecture (Phaphoom et al., 2013; Sriram & Khajeh-Hosseini, 2010).

Grid computing is a distributed computing paradigm that enables resource sharing among organizations in order to solve a common computational problem. It is composed of heterogeneous and physically distributed resources, which are typically unified under standard protocols and middleware that mediate accesses to a range of physical resources and organizing functionalities (e.g.: resource provisioning, catalogue, job scheduling, monitoring and security assurance) (Foster, 2001; Phaphoom et al., 2013). Grid computing evolved to cloud computing and both share the common objective of achieving optimization of resource usage, being the main difference the fact that the cloud infrastructure is owned and managed by a single organization, while that is not the case with grid computing. This makes cloud computing a rather more homogenous platform, and enables cloud management to focus on managing a shared resource pool, while grid management is focused on coordinating resources (Foster *et al.*, 2008; Phaphoom *et al.*, 2013; Sriram & Khajeh-Hosseini, 2010).

Virtualization involves providing an abstraction of a computing system, which offers interfaces to hardware including a processing unit and its registers, storages, and I/O devices (Smith & Nair, 2005; Phaphoom et al., 2013). Virtualization at a system level allows multiple virtual machines to operate on the same physical platform. At a process level, virtualization is managed by an operating system, multiplexing processing cycles and resources to support multiple processes. Virtualization is used by all cloud computing providers for enabling the capability of resource pooling by allocating and deallocating virtualized resources in terms of a virtual machine to a client's system on demand (Smith & Nair, 2005; Phaphoom et al., 2013).

Service Oriented Architecture (SOA) is commonly considered as essential for cloud computing, as it enables software architecture for designing distributed and loosely coupled systems, which addresses many quality attributes that potentiate cloud services, such as component composability, reusability, and scalability (Bianco *et al.*, 2007; Erl, 2009; Phaphoom *et al.*, 2013).

Cloud computing architecture may be represented through the aforementioned service and deployment models. Cloud computing architecture captures the interrelationships among relevant entities and activities in that environment (Phaphoom *et al.*, 2013). A reference architecture model is an abstract view of such an environment, representing the interrelationships among entities in that environment, while abstracting away from the underlying standards, technology, and implementation details (Phaphoom *et al.*, 2013). Several organizations have proposed cloud reference architecture models, having the most important ones been gathered by NIST in a report (NIST, 2011). Their main objectives include cloud interoperability, including interfaces standardization and the creation of open standards to enhance interoperability among providers; and, security assessment, besides the general purpose of presenting relationships and dependencies among cloud entities (e.g.: resources, services). Architectural elements common to several of these models include (Phaphoom *et al.*, 2013):

1. A layered model (stack model), that combines key components and their relationships;
2. Actors, including their role and responsibilities (each actor may take more than one role at a time; e.g.: an customer of IaaS may develop and provide SaaS for its customers); and
3. Management domains, which facilitate basic operations of data centers and services on top of it. Management and operational activities to maintain cloud production environments could be grouped into five domains including physical resources and virtualization, service catalogues, operational supports, business supports, and security.

Cloud Security Alliance (CSA) proposes an abstract layered model of the cloud consisting of four-layers with seven sublayers (Phaphoom *et al.*, 2013):

1. Fabric, which is further subdivided into facility and hardware sublayers;
2. Unified resource, which is further subdivided into abstraction and core connectivity and delivery sublayers;
3. Platform, which is additionally divided into infrastructure's APIs and middleware sublayers; and,
4. Application layer, which involves elements of cloud applications (or SaaS), is subdivided into a number of application components, comprising data, metadata, contents, applications, APIs, modality, and a presentation platform.

This model proposed by CSA explicitly defines an APIs layer which mediates communication between an operation system and integrated virtual resources. It also illustrates dependency of relevant SaaS components.

Interoperability between cloud providers, and open standards, are key issues to prevent vendor lock-in, i.e. tying consumers into one cloud services vendor and make it hard for consumers to switch to competitors. Interoperability and open standards are also essential for creating an open market of providing and consuming resources (Sriram & Khajeh-Hosseini, 2010).

There are several groups currently working on standards for cloud computing including the *Cloud Management Initiative* (http://dmtf.org/standards/cloud) of the Distributed Management Task Force (DMTF), *Open Grid Forum* (OGF) (http://www.gridforum.org/), *Open Cloud Computing Interface* (OCCI) (http://occi-wg.org/), *Cloud Data Management Interface* (CDMI) (http://www.snia.org/cloud/newcontent) of the Storage Networking Industry Association (SNIA), *Open Group* (http://www.opengroup.org), and the *Open Cloud Consortium* (http://opencloudconsortium.org/).

Furthermore, there is an Open cloud manifesto that expresses why open standards may benefit cloud computing (Sriram & Khajeh-Hosseini, 2010).

Cloud computing portability and interoperability categories that may be considered include (Open-Group, 2013):

*   **Data Portability:** Enables reusing data components across different applications (mainly at SaaS level);
*   **Application Portability:** Allows reusing application components across cloud PaaS services and traditional computing platforms;
*   **Platform Portability:** Facilitates the re-use of platform components across cloud IaaS services and non-cloud infrastructure (Platform source portability); or, the re-use of bundles containing data and applications together with their supporting platforms (Machine image portability);
*   **Application Interoperability:** Relates to interoperability between application components deployed as SaaS, as applications using PaaS, as applications on platforms using IaaS, in a traditional enterprise IT environment, or on client devices. An application component may be a monolithic application, or may be part of a distributed application;
*   **Platform Interoperability:** Relates to interoperability between platform components. These may be deployed as PaaS, as platforms on IaaS, in a traditional enterprise IT environment, or on client devices. Platform interoperability requires standard protocols for service discovery and information exchange;

- **Management Interoperability:** Relates to interoperability between cloud services (SaaS, PaaS, or IaaS) and programs concerned with the implementation of on-demand self-service;
- **Publication and Acquisition Interoperability:** Relates to interoperability between platforms, including cloud PaaS services, and marketplaces (services' marketplaces and cloud app stores).

Cloud computing services are provided bound to a contract known as service level agreement (SLA). This contract is established between the provider and the consumers, and defines the needed level of service for the services provided, in term of quality of services such as performance and availability. For the consumers, it is important to ensure that the agreed level of service is respected, and any violation is reported accordingly. For the providers, it is important to manage dynamic infrastructure to meet the SLA and to maximize the profit and resource utilization (Phaphoom *et al.*, 2013).

Quality attributes relevant to cloud services are (Phaphoom *et al.*, 2013):

- **Scalability and Elasticity:** Refer to the capability to scale up or down the computing resources (scalability) and to scale with minimum overheads in terms of time and operation supports (elasticity).
- **Performance/Response time:** Are critical quality attributes for latency sensitive applications and introduce high impact for user experiences.
- **Security and Trust:** Security relies on each layer of the cloud infrastructure. Mechanisms to handle cloud security must be adopted by cloud providers and should be clarified before cloud services adoption by customers. Trust has to do with the cloud provider's reputation, and requires positive experiences and positive feedback from customers.
- **Availability:** Refers to the percentage of time that the services are available for use. Availability is one of the key constraints typically defined in SLA contracts, although some SLAs define availability as the percentage of time that the services are available for use at a specified quality level.
- **Reliability:** Is the capacity the services have to perform at a specific level overtime. This may be measured by the number of verified faults, the degree of fault tolerance, the capability to recover from failures, and so on.
- **Portability:** Is the ability to move deployed artifacts between different cloud providers. Deploying artifacts in the cloud, such as virtual machines, databases or service APIs typically entails a dependency between those deployed artifacts and the service providers. This dependency should be minimized to prevent system and data lock-in.
- **Usability:** Refers to the ability of understanding, learning and using services, and the degree of comfort that users have when using the service. Usability is especially important for SaaS to retain customers by easing the switching process from the old application to the new one.
- **Customizability:** Is the capability of services to be customized. As sharing resources are key to cloud computing, it is impossible to provide unique solutions for each user. Thus, service customization must be built-in each service architecture enabling its personalization for and by each service customer.
- **Reusability:** Refers to the ability of using service components for building other services or software components. Cloud computing opens new ways of reusing components.
- **Data Consistency:** Is a key characteristic of cloud services, especially in SaaS. Data services typically rely on storage replicas to ensure higher availability and network partition tolerance. This may cause data inconsistency if not handled appropriately.

Cloud fundamental technologies, such as virtualization, distributed storages, and web services, directly affect these quality attributes (Phaphoom *et al.*, 2013). Availability and reliability enable fault tolerance, which is taken as a mandatory requirement as partial network failures and random server crashes, are common for systems of the internet scale (Phaphoom *et al.*, 2013).

Characteristics of Cloud Applications

To fully take advantage of the cloud potentialities, applications and services built for being deployed in the cloud must have certain characteristics, namely (Fehling & Leymann, 2013):

- **Isolated State:** The majority of the application should be stateless, in what concerns to the session state, i.e. the state of communication between different parts of the application, and the application state, i.e. the data handled by the application.
- **Distribution:** The application should be decomposed into several components, which may be easily distributed through different cloud resources, supporting the fact that cloud services are large globally distributed systems.
- **Elasticity:** The application should be able to be scaled out dynamically, that is the application performance should increase when new resources are added. This adds to the scaling up feature that every application shall have, i.e. the capacity to increase performance by increasing the existing resources capabilities.
- **Automated Management:** The application's runtime tasks should be able to be handled quickly. This allows to exploit pay-per-use advantages by dynamically changing the number of resources, or to increase the application resiliency, by reacting to resource failures.
- **Loose Coupling:** The influence of each application component on its other components is limited. This limits the impact of a component failure, and simplifies the addition or removal of components.

In addition to building the enumerated characteristics into new applications being deployed in the cloud, also existing applications need to be restructured with these characteristics in mind when they are migrated to the cloud (Costa & Cruz, 2012). Besides allowing to better exploit cloud advantages, these desired characteristics of cloud applications enable the support of new types of applications (Golden, 2014). Indeed, applications of unknown size and unpredictable load or number of users, or applications accessed by many different users through different devices, may benefit from the cloud applications' characteristics enumerated above.

MOBILE CLOUD COMPUTING

Despite their increasing features and capabilities, mobile devices still have lack of resources, frequent disconnections, and mobility issues, as mentioned above. Moreover, mobile applications are increasingly resource demanding and communications dependent. For helping work around these issues, Cloud Computing can come along and, together, Mobile Cloud Computing (MCC) can address these problems by relying on Cloud services for providing backend services or data storage capabilities or by offloading and executing mobile applications on resource providers external to the mobile device (Fernando, Loke & Rahayu, 2013).

The term Mobile Cloud Computing (MCC) has several definitions. Sanaei *et al.* (2014), based on the accepted definitions of mobile computing, cloud computing and ubiquitous computing, propose the following definition for Mobile Cloud Computing: "a rich mobile computing technology that leverages unified elastic resources of varied clouds and network technologies toward unrestricted functionality, storage, and mobility to serve a multitude of mobile devices anywhere, anytime through the channel of Ethernet or Internet regardless of heterogeneous environments and platforms based on the pay-as-you-use principle."

Preston Cox (2011) uses a definition found in a 2010 blog entry in the Open Gardens blog, where MCC is defined as "the availability of cloud computing services in a mobile ecosystem". The blog entry continued stating the main elements that it considered as being incorporated into a mobile ecosystem, namely consumer, enterprise, *femtocells* (small cellular base stations), transcoding, end-to-end security, home gateways, and mobile broadband-enabled services.

Before these definitions, and paving the way for them to be established, Satyanarayanan (2001) proposed to offload mobile applications, entirely or partially, from the mobile devices to resource-rich-non-mobile devices (servers), as a way to overcome mobile devices' resource limitations and conserve energy. This approach, called *cyber foraging*, consisted in dynamically augment the mobile device computing resources by creating local cloudlets that exploited the computing resources (*surrogate*) connected to the available nearby networks, especially public networks. However, this surrogate-based approach raises several safety and reliability issues by migrating code and data to the surrogates in the absence of authorities supervising functionality, performance, and the reliability of surrogates (Sanaei *et al.*, 2014).

Cloud computing, as a distributed computing paradigm, has also been used for augmenting mobile devices resources. MAUI (Cuervo *et al.*, 2010), CloneCloud (Chun *et al.*, 2011), Elastic Applications (Zhang *et al.*, 2011) and Hyrax (Marinelli, 2009) are some of the efforts that exploit cloud infrastructures to mitigate resource scarcity of mobile devices.

The main difference between surrogate-based and cloud-based approaches for augmenting mobile devices resources is that surrogates offer free services based on local cloudlets without pledging to complete assigned tasks, whereas cloud based approaches provide paid services bound to a negotiated Service-Level Agreement (SLA) assuring to the mobile client an agreed level of availability and quality (Sanaei *et al.*, 2014).

Sanaei *et al.* (2014) present a taxonomy of approaches for augmenting the capabilities of mobile devices (Figure 1).

Figure 1. Taxonomy of Smartphone Augmentation Approaches (taken from (Sanaei et al., 2014)).
Source: (Sanaei et al., 2014)

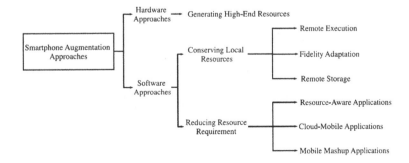

These approaches may be categorized as hardware approaches, which consist of generating better high-end smart mobile devices, and software approaches, which aim at conserving local resources or reducing resource requirements on the mobile devices.

Conserving local resources aims at preserving resources such as storage capacity, CPU time and, especially, energy consumption. Energy is, indeed, the only resource in mobile devices that cannot be restored spontaneously and requires external resources to be renewed (Satyanarayanan, 2005; Sanaei *et al.*, 2014). Current technologies can increase battery capacity by about 5% per annum, being current efforts for energy harvesting based on external resources, such as human movement, intermittent and not available on-demand (Sanaei *et al.*, 2014). Conserving local resources may be approached by application offloading, executing code and/or storing data remotely (refer to Figure 1), or fidelity adaptation, which consists of altering application-level quality metrics to exchange quality of service for local resources (Abolfazli *et al.*, 2012).

Reducing resource requirements involves consideration in the design phase of development with focus on developing resource-efficient applications (Abolfazli *et al.*, 2012). This can be done through resource-aware algorithms, which may promote considerable resource usage reduction; Cloud mobile applications, which minimize smartphones' resource usage by leveraging rich cloud resources with no quality degradation; or, Mobile mashup applications, which create mobile applications by aggregating available services and contents offered in ubiquitous environments leveraging Mobile Service Oriented Architecture (Mobile SOA) as the backbone or backend services (Abolfazli *et al.*, 2012).

Table 2. compares the mobile augmentation approaches represented in the taxonomy proposed by Abolfazli *et al.* (2012) and Sanaei *et al.* (2014) depicted in Figure 1.

Table 2. Mobile Augmentation Approaches Metrics Comparision (taken from (Abolfazli et al., 2012))

Metrics	Local Resource Consumption	Implementation Cost	Implementation Complexity	Device side Maintenance	Quality of Experience	Net-work Delay	Execution Delay	Security	Data Safety
Generating High-End Hardware	NA	High	High	Low	High	Low	Low	High	Low
Remote Execution	Low	Med	Med	High	Med	High	Low	Low	NA
Fidelity Adaptation	Low	Low	Low	Med	Low	Variable	Variable	Variable	Low
Remote Storage	Med	Med	Med	Med	Med	High	NA	NA	High
Resource Aware Algorithm	Low	Med	Med	Low	Med	Low	Med	Med	Low
Mobile Cloud Application	Low	Med	Med	Low	High	Med	Low	Med	High
Mobile Mashup Application	Low	Med	Med	Low	High	Med	Low	Med	High

FUTURE RESEARCH DIRECTIONS

Islam and Want (2014) identify six major trends affecting future smartphone design and use:

- **Personal Computing:** Smartphones are becoming the main computing platform. They will dock with nearby I/O devices and be the main way to access computing power, storage and network;
- **Internet of Things (IoT):** Smartphones will be the main interactors with the IoT, allowing us to interact with the world around us;
- **Multimedia Delivery:** Smartphones will rival traditional platforms to watch streaming video or listen to music, and for storing and accessing multimedia content;
- **Low Power Operation:** Low power hardware accelerators and new software structuring techniques will make batteries last longer;
- **Wearable Computing:** Smartphones will merge into a diverse set of wearable technologies, giving rise to new applications;
- **Context Awareness:** Smartphones will be more context-aware, being able to adapt to the surrounding environment, people and things.

These trends increase the pressure over smartphone resource scarcity. As hardware approaches for augmenting mobile devices capabilities involves technological advances in manufacturing, they are slower and more expensive than the growing expectations of smart devices' users driven by the growing resource requirements of mobile applications. Thus, software approaches are needed for providing resource capabilities at the user expectations' level (Sanaei *et al.*, 2014). This opens several opportunities to new and improved Mobile Cloud Computing techniques and approaches. MCC is still an emerging technology that has to deal with heterogeneity of mobile devices and cloud services, and also with safety, reliability and supervision issues, requiring lots of research and development for being ready to augment mobile devices capabilities in real scenarios (Sanaei *et al.*, 2014; Fernando, Loke & Rahayu, 2013).

The mobile augmentation approaches overviewed before allow conserving local mobile resources, such as processor and memory capability, storage capacity and energy. Conserving local resources may be approached by application offloading, executing code and/or storing data remotely, or fidelity adaptation, by altering application-level quality metrics (Abolfazli *et al.*, 2012).However, application offloading is risky and a resource-intensive approach, and needs further research and development to be deployed in real scenarios (Abolfazli *et al.*, 2012). Fidelity adaptation solutions, although conserving the device's energy, compromise quality while trying to preserve local resources. This promotes a poor user experience. Some researchers attempted to mitigate application offloading challenges by exploiting secure, reliable, elastic cloud resources instead of insecure, limited surrogates resources. However, cloud based application offloading cannot always save energy with current developments and demands further efforts (Abolfazli *et al.*, 2012). Therefore, the energy constraint of mobile nodes remains a challenge in MCC. Energy is, indeed, the only resource in mobile devices that cannot be restored spontaneously and requires external resources to be renewed (Satyanarayanan, 2005; Sanaei *et al.*, 2014).

MCC will still face greater challenges because of converged heterogeneous domains of mobile and cloud computing.

Open standards and cloud providers' interoperability, are crucial to prevent vendor lock-in, i.e. tying consumers into one cloud services vendor and make it hard for consumers to switch to competitors.

Interoperability and open standards are also essential for creating an open market of providing and consuming resources (Sriram & Khajeh-Hosseini, 2010).

CONCLUSION

This chapter characterized mobile and cloud computing technologies, and presented Mobile Cloud Computing, which allows augmenting mobile devices capabilities. MCC boosts mobile devices in a way that mobile computing by itself cannot do. MCC promotes virtual services that perform the most mobile resource demanding operations, allowing for mobile operating systems and/or apps to rely on them to save mobile devices scarce resources. This allows the mobile user to have an enhanced user experience by operating a device that performs high above its "pay grade". The virtual services that allow this to happen, are based on cloud computing services that provide computing resources, storage or network connectivity almost without limitations.

REFERENCES

Abolfazli, S., Sanaei, Z., & Gani, A. (2012). Mobile Cloud Computing: A review on smartphone augmentation approaches. In *Proceedings of the 1st International Conference on Computing, Information Systems, and Communications (CISCO12)*.

Abraham, J. (2012). *Generation of mobile communication systems*. Retrieved from: http://www.slideshare. net/jincy-a/generation-of-mobile-communication-systems

ACM. (2009). Cloud Computing: An Overview. *ACM Queue, 7*(5). Available at http://doi.acm. org/10.1145/1538947.1554608

Andrews, J. G., Buzzi, S., Choi, W., Hanly, S. V., Lozano, A., Soong, A. C. K., & Zhang, J. C. (2014). What Will 5G Be? *International Journal on Selected Areas in Communications, 32*(6), 1065–1082. doi:10.1109/JSAC.2014.2328098

AWS. (2015). *What is Cloud Computing?* Retrieved February 18, 2015, from http://aws.amazon.com/ what-is-cloud-computing/

Bhalla, M. R., & Bhalla, A. V. (2010). Generations of Mobile Wireless Technology: A Survey. International Journal of Computer Applications, 5(4), 26-32. doi:10.5120/905-1282

Bianco, P., Kotermanski, R., & Merson, P. (2007). *Evaluating a Service-Oriented Architecture*. Tech. Rep. CMU/SEI-2007-TR-015. Software Engineering Institute of Carnegie Mellon University.

Bluetooth. (2015). *A look at the basics of Bluetooth technology*. Retrieved June 30, 2015 from http:// www.bluetooth.com/Pages/Basics.aspx

Borko, F. (2010). *Cloud Computing Fundamentals. Handbook of Cloud Computing*. Springer Science Business Media, LLC.

Chun, B. G., Ihm, S., Maniatis, P., Naik, M., & Patti, A. (2011). CloneCloud: Elastic execution between mobile device and cloud. In *Proceedings ACM The European Professional Society on Computer Systems (EuroSys'11)*. doi:10.1145/1966445.1966473

Costa, P. J., & Cruz, A. M. (2012). Migration to Windows Azure – Analysis and Comparison. In *Proceedings of CENTERIS 2012 - Conference on ENTERprise Information Systems, Procedia Technology*. Elsevier.

Cox, P. A. (2011). Mobile cloud computing: Devices, trends, issues, and the enabling technologies. DeveloperWorks. IBM Corporation. Retrieved from ibm.com/developerWorks

Cruz, A. M. (2012). *Mobile Computing – Evolution and Current Status*. Retrieved January 18, 2015, from http://practicalsw.blogspot.pt/2012/08/mobile-computing-evolution-and-current.html

Cuervo, E., Balasubramanian, A., Cho, D., Wolman, A., Saroiu, S., Chandra, R., & Bahl, P. (2010). MAUI: Making Smartphones Last Longer with Code Offload. In *Proceedings of ACM 8th Annual International Conference on Mobile Systems, Applications and Services (MobiSys'10)*. doi:10.1145/1814433.1814441

Dhawan, S. (2007) Analogy of Promising Wireless Technologies on Different Frequencies: Bluetooth, WiFi, and WiMAX. *International Conference on Wireless Broadband and Ultra Wideband Communications*. doi:10.1109/AUSWIRELESS.2007.27

Erl, T. (2009). *SOA Design Patterns*. Upper Saddle River, NJ: Prentice Hall PTR.

Fehling, C., & Leymann, F. (2013). *Cloud Computing Patterns Fundamentals to Design, Build, and Manage Cloud Applications*. Tutorial at SummerSoC 2013, Hersonissos, Greece.

Fernando, N., Loke, S. W., & Rahayu, W. (2013). Mobile cloud computing: A survey. *Future Generation Computer Systems*, *29*(1), 84-106. 10.1016/j.future.2012.05.023

Fling, B. (2009). Mobile Design and Development – Practical concepts and techniques for creating mobile sites and web apps. O'Reilly Media.

Flora, H. K., Wang, X., & Chande, S. V. (2014). An Investigation on the Characteristics of Mobile Applications: A Survey Study. *International Journal of Information Technology and Computer Science*, *11*(11), 21–27. doi:10.5815/ijitcs.2014.11.03

Foster, I. (2001). The anatomy of the grid: enabling scalable virtual Organizations. In *Proceedings of the 1st IEEE/ACM International Symposium on Cluster Computing and the Grid*. IEEE.

Foster, I., Zhao, Y., Raicu, I., & Lu, S. (2008). Cloud Computing and Grid Computing 360-Degree Compared. In *Grid Computing Environments Workshop (GCE '08)*. doi:10.1109/GCE.2008.4738445

Golden, B. (2014). *The New Cloud Application Design Paradigm*. Retrieved from http://www.cio.com/article/2379480/cloud-computing/the-new-cloud-application-design-paradigm.html

Islam, N., & Want, R. (2014). Smartphones: Past, Present, and Future. *Pervasive Computing, IEEE Computers & Society*, *13*(4), 89–92.

Ivanochko, I., Urikova, O., & Gregu, M. (2014). Modern Mobile Technologies for Collaborative e-Business. In *Proceedings of International Conference on Intelligent Networking and Collaborative Systems*, (pp. 515 – 520).

Jarvenpaa, S. L., & Lang, K. R. (2005). Managing the Paradoxes of Mobile Technology. *Information Systems Management, 22*(4), 7–23. doi:10.1201/1078.10580530/45520.22.4.20050901/90026.2

Marinelli, E. E. (2009). *Hyrax: Cloud Computing on Mobile Devices using MapReduce.* (Master of Science Thesis). School of Computer Science, Carnegie Mellon University, Pittsburgh, PA.

Marston, S., Li, Z., Bandyopadhyay, S., Zhang, J., & Ghalsasi, A. (2010). Cloud computing — The business perspective. *Journal Decision Support Systems, 51*(2011), 176–189.

Mell, P., & Grance, T. (2011). *The NIST Definition of Cloud Computing.* NIST Special Publication 800 – 145. Computer Security Division, Information Technology Laboratory, National Institute of Standards and Technology, Gaithersburg, September 2011. Retrieved from: http://csrc.nist.gov/publications/nist-pubs/800-145/SP800-145.pdf

Mshvidobadze, T. (2012). Evolution mobile wireless communication and LTE networks. In *Proceedings of the International Conference on Application of Information and Communication Technologies.* doi:10.1109/ICAICT.2012.6398495

NIST. (2011). Cloud Architecture Reference Models. US National Institute of Standards.

Open Group. (2013). Cloud Computing Portability and Interoperability. Document Number: G135. The Open Group.

Pearce, M., Zeadally, S., & Hunt, R. (2013, February). Virtualization: Issues, Security Threats, and Solutions. *ACM Computing Surveys, 45*(2), 17. doi:10.1145/2431211.2431216

Phaphoom, N. & Wang, X. & Abrahamsson, P. (2013). Foundations and Technological Landscape of Cloud Computing. *ISRN Software Engineering.* 10.1155/2013/782174

Rahimi, M.R., Ren, J., Liu, C.H., Vasilakos, A.V. & Venkatasubramanian, N. (2014). Mobile Cloud Computing: A Survey, State of Art and Future Directions. *Mobile Networks and Applications, 19*(2), 133-143.

Salmre, I. (2005). Writing Mobile Code: Essential Software Engineering for Building Mobile Applications. Addison-Wesley.

Sanaei, Z., Abolfazli, S., Gani, A., & Buyya, R. (2014). Heterogeneity in Mobile Cloud Computing: Taxonomy and Open Challenges. *IEEE Communications Surveys & Tutorials, 16*(1), 369-392.

Satyanarayanan, M. (2001). Pervasive computing: vision and challenges. *IEEE Personal Communications, 8*(4), 10-17.

Satyanarayanan, M. (2005). Avoiding dead batteries. *IEEE Pervasive Computing / IEEE Computer Society [and] IEEE Communications Society, 4*(1), 2–3. doi:10.1109/MPRV.2005.5

Savage, P. (1995). Designing a GUI for business telephone users. *Interaction, 2*(1), 32–41. doi:10.1145/208143.208157

Sheng, H., Nah, F., & Siau, K. (2005). Strategic implications of mobile technology: A case study using Value-Focused Thinking. *The Journal of Strategic Information Systems*, *14*(3), 269–290. doi:10.1016/j.jsis.2005.07.004

Singh, B. & K.S., J. (2012). A Comparative Study of Mobile Wireless Communication Networks and Technologies. *International Journal of Computer Networks and Wireless Communications*, *2*(5).

Smith, J. E., & Nair, R. (2005). The architecture of virtual machines. *Computer*, *38*(5), 32–38. doi:10.1109/MC.2005.173

Sriram, L., & Khajeh-Hosseini, A. (2010). *Research Agenda in Cloud Technologies*. LSCITS Technical Report. Retrieved from: http://arxiv.org/abs/1001.3259

Waugh, R. (2012). Resistance is futile! More Androids are activated every day than babies are born. *Daily Mail*. Retrieved January 18, 2015, from http://www.dailymail.co.uk/sciencetech/article-2086144/CES-2012-More-Androids-activated-day-babies-born.html

Wi-Fi Alliance. (2014). *15 Years of Wi-Fi*. Retrieved June 30, 2015, from https://www.wi-fi.org/discover-wi-fi/15-years-of-wi-fi

Zhang, X., Kunjithapatham, A., Jeong, S., & Gibbs, S. (2011). Towards an Elastic Application Model for Augmenting the Computing Capabilities of Mobile Devices with Cloud Computing. *Mobile Networks and Applications*, *16*(3), 270–284. doi:10.1007/s11036-011-0305-7

KEY TERMS AND DEFINITIONS

Backend Service: Backend Service is a web service that augments the capabilities (e.g.: computing power, temporary or permanent storage capacity) of a mobile application, or adds sharing capabilities to a mobile application. Backend services are typically deployed in the cloud.

Cloud Computing: Cloud computing is a model for providing IT services and applications over the internet on a pay-as-you-go payment model (AWS, 2015). Cloud computing enables ubiquitous access, convenient and on-demand to a shared pool of configurable IT services (e.g.: networks, servers, storage, applications and services), and where services can be rapidly provisioned and released without intervention of the service provider and with minimal management effort (Mell & Grance, 2011).

Mobile Cloud Computing (MCC): Mobile devices still have lack of resources, when compared to desktop or laptop computers. Additionally, due to their type of use, they are affected by frequent disconnections, and mobility issues. Moreover, mobile applications are increasingly resource demanding and communications dependent. Mobile Cloud Computing (MCC) is "a rich mobile computing technology that leverages unified elastic resources of varied clouds and network technologies toward unrestricted functionality, storage, and mobility to serve a multitude of mobile devices anywhere, anytime through the channel of Ethernet or Internet regardless of heterogeneous environments and platforms based on the pay-as-you-use principle" (Sanaei et al., 2014). MCC can save or augment mobile devices resources by relying on Cloud services for providing backend services or data storage capabilities or by offloading and executing mobile applications on resource providers external to the mobile device.

Mobile Device: A mobile device is an electronic equipment available for computing and communications that is portable – has the ability to move and is able to operate independently from a fixed wired power source or a physical Internet connection –, is typically less resourceful than a desktop or laptop computer – has less memory, weaker CPUs and limited battery power –, is relatively small, so it can fit in an adult's hand or pocket, and makes use of touch screens or small keypads for input and is typically independent from external interface devices. The user input mechanisms in mobile devices are based on features such as touch, pinch, and swipe. Mobile devices should be able to communicate with similar or other devices, and so they are typically equipped with Wi-Fi, Bluetooth and data networks connections that provide Internet connectivity. Most mobile devices also have built-in storage in order to store music, photos or other type of data. Mobile devices are typically provided with some applications and allow others to be installed through the web browser, applications' stores or third parties'.

Utility Computing: Utility computing, firstly mentioned at MIT in the early 1960s, is the provision of computing services as a utility, similarly to what happens with electricity, gas or water. Utility computing makes it possible for users or organizations to pay only for what they use, in computing power or storage capacity, as well as in electricity or other utilities.

Chapter 2

A Study on Software Development Architectures for Mobile Cloud Computing (MCC) for Green IT:
A Conceptual Mobile Cloud Architecture Using Artificial Bee Colony-Based Approach

D. Jeya Mala
Thiagarajar College of Engineering, India

ABSTRACT

Mobile Cloud Computing (MCC) at its simplest form refers to an infrastructure where both the data storage and the data processing happen outside of the mobile device. In this chapter, a study on existing software architectures for MCC is outlined with their way of working. Also, a Nature inspired Artificial Bee Colony (ABC) based architecture has been proposed to provide reliable services from the cloud to the mobile requests. The proposed approach will definitely pave a way for timely services by using three different agents working in parallel, which mimics the behavior of honey bees namely Employed Bees, Onlooker Bees and Scout Bees. As the service discovery from the UDDI, Mobile profile Analysis and Allocation of Cloud resources for the requests are done by these software agents in a parallel execution, it achieves a green IT solution for MCC based software Development.

INTRODUCTION

There are several reasons that motivate Mobile Cloud Computing (MCC), as the Mobile devices (e.g., smartphone, tablet pcs, etc.) are increasingly becoming an essential part of human life, and the dream of "Information at your fingertips anywhere anytime". But Mobile devices still lack in resources compared

DOI: 10.4018/978-1-4666-9916-8.ch002

Copyright © 2016, IGI Global. Copying or distributing in print or electronic forms without written permission of IGI Global is prohibited.

to a conventional information processing device such as PCs and laptops. It has been attracting the attentions of entrepreneurs as a profitable business option that reduces the development and running cost of mobile applications, of mobile users as a new technology to achieve rich experience of a variety of mobile services at low cost, and of researchers as a promising solution for green IT.

Nowadays, the market of mobile phones has expanded rapidly. By the end of 2014, the number of mobile cellular subscriptions worldwide reached approximately 6.25 billion, 500 times the 1990 number. The widely use of mobile phones lead to the prosperity of mobile services. Dream of "Information at your fingertips anywhere, anytime" has become true. However, mobile devices still lack in resources compared to a conventional information processing device such as PCs and laptops.

Also, the limitation of battery restricts working time. The strategy to augment the capability of mobile phones has become an important technical issue for mobile computing. The paradigm of cloud computing brings opportunities for this demand. Cloud computing provides new supplement, consumption, and delivery models for IT services. Cloud-based services are on-demand, scalable, device-independent and reliable. Thus, there comes Mobile Cloud Computing, which aims at using cloud computing techniques for storage and processing of data on mobile devices, thereby reducing their limitations.

BACKGROUND

According to the white paper of Aepona (2010), MCC is described as a new paradigm in which the data processing and storage are moved from the mobile device to powerful and centralized computing platforms located in clouds. These centralized applications are then accessed over the wireless connection based on a thin native client or web browser on the mobile devices.

Some of the typical applications of MCC are: Yang et al. (2010) and Dai and Zhou (2010), proposed a 3G E-commerce platform based on cloud computing. This paradigm combines the advantages of both 3G network and cloud computing to increase data processing speed and security level based on PKI (public key infrastructure).

For practical system, a telemedicine homecare management system proposed by Tang et.al.(2010) is implemented in Taiwan to monitor participants, especially for patients with hypertension and diabetes. The system monitors 300 participants and stores more than 4736 records of blood pressure and sugar measurement data on the cloud.

Doukas et al. (2010) proposed '@HealthCloud', a prototype implementation of m-healthcare information management system based on cloud computing and a mobile client running Android operating system (OS). This prototype presents three services utilizing the Amazon's S3 Cloud Storage Service to manage patient health records and medical images.

Zhao et al. (2010) presented the benefits of combining m-learning and cloud computing to enhance the communication quality between students and teachers. In this case, smartphone software based on the open source JavaME UI framework and Jaber for clients is used. Mobile game (m-game) is a potential market generating revenues for service providers. Here, the m-game can completely offload game engine requiring large computing resource (e.g., graphic rendering) to the server in the cloud, and gamers only interact with the screen interface on their devices.

MeLog proposed by Li and Hua (2010) is an MCC application that enables mobile users to share real-time experience (e.g., travel, shopping, and event) over clouds through an automatic blogging.

From the concept of MCC, the general architecture of MCC has mobile devices connected to the mobile networks via base stations (e.g., base transceiver station (BTS), access point, or satellite) that establish and control the connections (air links) and functional interfaces between the networks and mobile devices. Mobile users' requests and information (e.g., ID and location) are transmitted to the central processors that are connected to servers providing mobile network services. Here, mobile network operators can provide services to mobile users as AAA (for authentication, authorization, and accounting) based on the home agent (HA) and subscribers' data stored in databases.

After that, the subscribers' requests are delivered to a cloud through the Internet. In the cloud, cloud controllers process the requests to provide mobile users with the corresponding cloud services. These services are developed with the concepts of utility computing, virtualization, and service-oriented architecture (e.g., web, application, and database servers).

The details of cloud architecture could be different in different contexts. For example, four-layer architecture is used to compare cloud computing with grid computing. Alternatively, service oriented architecture, called Aneka, is introduced to enable developers to build .NET applications with the supports of application programming interfaces (APIs) and multiple programming models. Also, architecture for creating market-oriented clouds, and an architecture for web delivered business services is also proposed by several researchers.

In this chapter, the different types of existing architectures of mobile based cloud computing is going to be discussed and a proposed MCC architecture using nature inspired Artificial Bee Colony (ABC) based approach in resource selection and allocation is provided to demonstrate the effectiveness of the cloud computing model in terms of meeting the user's requirements to achieve mobile cloud computing.

Layered Architecture of Mobile Cloud Computing

According to the definition given by Techopedia (Techopedia), Mobile Cloud Computing (MCC) is a distributed working model in which the mobile applications are accessed from the cloud. This approach helps the software engineers to develop the applications for mobile devices irrespective of the limitations imposed by the mobile operating system or the configuration constraints of mobile devices. Whenever, some service or an application is needed, the cloud which provides such service or application will be accessed using a mobile browser from a remote web server without the need to install the application on the mobile device.

According to Prasad et al. (2012), the Mobile Cloud Computing Forum defines MCC as "Mobile Cloud computing at its simplest refers to an infrastructure where both the data storage and the data processing happen outside of the mobile device. Mobile cloud applications move the computing power and data storage away from mobile phones and into the cloud, bringing applications and mobile computing to not just smart phone users but a much broader range of mobile subscribers".

The general objectives of mobile cloud computing (MCC) are to provide simple APIs to access the services from the cloud on need basis, to deploy the commercial applications over the cloud to be accessed by the mobile devices through an agreement with mobile service providers, easy handling of network policies with respect to the independent management principles of subscribers.

In Figure 1, a layered view of MCC is given. The cloud computing layer provides services such as IAAS, PAAS, SAAS and TAAS with principles of on-demand access, device specific applications, and pay as you go. The mobile computing layer is provided by mobile service providers with reliable communications, customer analysis and billing for the service used by the customers and so on. Now, the

Figure 1. Layered view of Mobile Cloud Computing

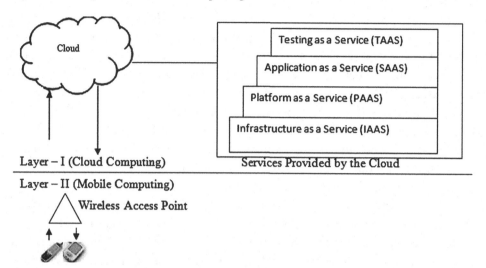

enterprise application providers and application developers try to combine these two layers to provide enterprise solution to the mobile users through the cloud by means of the service providers. In early days, the use of enterprise solutions through online via simple mobile browsers has various technology barriers and hence, the third parties try to have a cloud based solution to remove the technology barrier and to provide a complete satisfaction for the customers for the application they access.

As stated by Techopedia (Techopedia), the solutions such as Microsoft Corp.'s SharePoint, IBM Corp.'s Lotus Live suite, and more recently Chatter from Salesforce.com, all aim to make it easier for employees to collaborate, whether they are producing a document, managing project tasks or simply wishing to communicate in real time as a group. This way of cloud based enterprise solutions combined with mobile based network provides additional value so that, the application becomes portable across various platforms.

Generally, a mobile cloud service namely 'Intelligent Cloud', offers mobile marketers, app developers, enterprises, and content providers; the services such as carrier billing, discovery and mobile intelligence services, cross-network messaging, and location capabilities – all in conjunction with existing services such as barcode clearing, digital content locker, and short code campaign management.

Study on Existing Mobile Cloud Computing (MCC) Architectures

In the mobile cloud computing architecture proposed by Dinh et al. (2013), the mobile devices are connected to the mobile networks via base stations which establish and control the connections and provide required interfaces between networks and mobile devices. The information of mobile users such as ID, Location along with their requirements is transmitted to wireless access point of mobile network servers. The mobile network service providers then provide authentication, authorization and accounting and then store the mobile subscribers' data in the database servers. Once this is over, the requests given by the mobile user/subscribers are sent to the cloud through the internet and in cloud, the requests are processed by the cloud controllers to provide the requested cloud services to the mobile users.

According to the white Paper on Mobile cloud computing – The value-added role for service providers (RCR Wireless News, 2011), the Mobile Solutions on Google Cloud Platform provide services such as Resource Sharing, Storage of Data, Optimizing memory access via caching, Task processing with task queues, Push notification, Static Content Provider, Image Processing, Location based search, Jobs scheduling and maintenance, Applications Log analyzer, External execution of code outside sandbox, Maps API, Analytics, AdMob.

As stated by Ku et al. (2014), Software-Defined Networking (SDN) is an emerging technology, which brings flexibility and programmability to networks and introduces new services and features. However, most SDN architectures have been designed for wired infrastructures, especially in the data center space, and primary trends for wireless and mobile SDN are on the access network and the wireless backhaul. Their solution is on enabling SDN in wireless networks can bring the programmability and flexibility that is lacking in today's distributed wireless substrate while simplifying network management and enabling new services. While mobile and wireless deployment of SDN has recently begun, its scope has been primarily focused on carrier backbones and access networks.

The goal is to provide a framework for SDN-based Mobile Cloud that includes the components required by SDN in an Ad hoc environment. Each SDN wireless node has an optional local SDN Controller. This local SDN controller can either be the backup controller when connection to the global SDN controller is lost or the primary SDN controller when wireless communication to a global controller is not practical. Traditional Ad hoc routing protocols (e.g., AODV, DSDV, or OLSR) are supported as fallback mechanisms, to allow the SDN network to revert back to Ad hoc network operation even in the case where SDN controller communication is unavailable. In scenarios where the connection to a global SDN controller is stable, this device SDN controller can be removed.

One distinct characteristic of Ad hoc networks is that the nodes act both as Hosts (sending/receiving traffic) and Routers (forwarding traffic on behalf of other nodes). An SDN wireless node is therefore both an SDN data plane forwarding element and an end-point for data. Traffic from any wireless node will run through its own SDN module before being sent, which allows the SDN controller to determine the access of user traffic into the network. In this setup, the SDN controller can directly control the transmission frequency of a wireless interface. This flexibility is provided by a more advanced architecture which requires radio frequency to be part of the SDN control message component. The radios themselves must also be able to accept external commands to change the frequency, such as cognitive radios.

In MCC with Private Virtual Infrastructure (PVI) Management and Provisioning architecture, there is a PVI management and Provisioning module to take care of the different kinds of requests passed by the different mobile clients. The cloud infrastructure gets the information for processing and provides appropriate storage for the requested mobile service.

Rahimi et al. (2008) proposed both online and offline architectures for pervasive image computation application in MCC. The first one, called online architecture, the user sends the picture to the server and server sends the picture information directly back to him. In the second one, which is called offline architecture, the user uploads the image in one public image database such as Flickr and sends the ID of the image in this database to the server. The server processes the image and adds the information of the image in the database, and finally the user can connect to the database and download the image information.

The security architecture proposed by Bahar et al. (2013) for MCC has agents for consumer and requester. If a requester tries to access the access restricted cloud storage, the cloud identity service provider checks for authentication and provides access to the valid requesters. If a person is a valid person, then the encrypted data received from the consumer agent is then forwarded by the cloud service provider (CSP) in the form of decrypted data to the requester. The access control, encrypted text retrieval and sending of decrypted text to the requester are done by the cloud.

Satyanarayanan et al. (2009) have introduced a strategy of leveraging transiently customized proximate infrastructure which is cloudlet-based thus leads to resource-rich, mobile computing. In their architecture, the crisp interactive response, which is essential for seamless augmentation of human cognition, is easily achieved because of the cloudlet's physical proximity and one-hop network latency. Using a cloudlet also simplifies the challenge of meeting the peak bandwidth demand of multiple users' interactively generating and receiving media such as high-definition video and high-resolution images. Rapid customization of infrastructure for diverse applications emerges as a critical requirement, and by means of a proof-of-concept prototype, they have suggested that VM technology can indeed help meet such a requirement.

Enterprise Mobile Cloud Architecture by Amazon is able to provide processes, storage and load balancing operations in a seamless manner to the mobile users. MCC with Firewall at both Mobile Client Side and Server Side, a firewall is provided between client and the server side of the mobile device to have secured access of the services provided by the cloud over the internet.

In MCC Architecture with Multiple Clouds, the middleware blocks have the responsibilities such as admission control, mobile profile monitoring, mobile profile analysis, scheduling, QoS monitoring, Service discovery and QoS analysis. Among these services, the admission control accepts or rejects client requests based on the resources available and mobile profile. The mobile profile monitoring will monitor the mobile profile. The location pattern, power level for optimal scheduling is taken care by mobile profile analyzer. The scheduler helps to schedule the requests and design a plan by means of a schedule queue to work with the different cloudlets. The discovery of the appropriate cloudlets and registration of services and middleware business on UDDI are done using QoS monitoring and service discovery components. The cloudlets' services are analyzed and finding suitable cloudlets are done by QoS analyzer.

PROPOSED MCC ARCHITECTURE FOR GREEN IT: NATURE INSPIRED ARTIFICIAL BEE COLONY BASED ARCHITECTURE

Artificial Bee Colony (ABC) is one of the most recently defined algorithms by Dervis Karaboga (2005), motivated by the intelligent behavior of honey bees. It is as simple as Particle Swarm Optimization (PSO) and Differential Evolution (DE) algorithms, and uses only common control parameters such as colony size and maximum cycle number.

ABC as an optimization tool provides a population-based search procedure in which individuals called foods positions are modified by the artificial bees with time and the bee's aim is to discover the places of food sources with high nectar amount and finally the one with the highest nectar (Karaboga (2005,2008); Pham (2005); Karaboga & Basturk (2007,2008)).

In ABC system, artificial bees fly around in a multidimensional search space and some employed and onlooker bees choose food sources depending on the experience of themselves and their nest mates, and adjust their positions. Some scouts bees fly and choose the food sources randomly without using experience. If the nectar amount of a new source is higher than that of the previous one in their memory, they memorize the new position and forget the previous one.

In ABC model, the colony consists of three groups of bees: employed, onlookers and scouts. It is assumed that there is only one artificial employed bee for each food source. In other words, the number of employed bees in the colony is equal to the number of food sources around the hive.

Employed bees goes to their food source and come back to hive and dance on this area. The employed bee whose food source has been abandoned becomes a scout and starts to search for finding a new food source. Onlookers watch the dances of employed bees and choose food sources depending on dances.

ABC Algorithm

The steps of the basic ABC algorithm are given below:

- Initial food sources are produced for all employed bees.

    REPEAT
    - Each employed bee goes to a food source in her memory and determines a neighbor source, then evaluates its nectar amount and dances in the hive
    - Each onlooker watches the dance of employed bees and chooses one of their sources depending on the dances, and then goes to that source. After choosing a neighbor around that, she evaluates its nectar amount.
    - Abandoned food sources are determined and then, they are replaced with the new food sources discovered by scouts.
    - The best food source found so far is registered.
    UNTIL (requirements are met)

In ABC which is a population based algorithm, the position of a food source represents a possible solution to the optimization problem and the nectar amount of a food source corresponds to the quality (fitness) of the associated solution. The number of the employed bees is equal to the number of solutions in the population.

At the first step, a randomly distributed initial population (food source positions) is generated. After initialization, the population is subjected to repeat the cycles of the search processes of the employed, onlooker, and scout bees, respectively. An employed bee produces a modification on the source position in her memory and discovers a new food source position.

Provided that the nectar amount of the new one is higher than that of the previous source, the bee memorizes the new source position and forgets the old one. Otherwise she keeps the position of the one in her memory.

After all employed bees complete the search process; they share the position information of the sources with the onlookers on the dance area. Each onlooker evaluates the nectar information taken from all employed bees and then chooses a food source depending on the nectar amounts of sources.

As in the case of the employed bee, she produces a modification on the source position in her memory and checks its nectar amount. Providing that its nectar is higher than that of the previous one, the bee memorizes the new position and forgets the old one.

The sources abandoned are determined and new sources are randomly produced to be replaced with the abandoned ones by artificial scouts.

Thus, ABC system combines local search methods, carried out by employed and onlooker bees, with global search methods, managed by scouts, attempting to balance exploration and exploitation process.

Our previous research works on applying ABC in software testing have yielded good results and based on that experience and its application in other real time system domains, have motivated us to apply it as an effective alternative for MCC architecture to achieve green IT (Mala et.al. (2009, 2010, 2013, 2014).

Working Procedure of Artificial Bee Colony in MCC Architecture with Multiple Clouds Selection

In the existing approach, there is a need to keep middleware blocks to have the responsibilities such as admission control, mobile profile monitoring, mobile profile analysis, scheduling, QoS monitoring, Service discovery and QoS analysis.

In the proposed approach, these responsibilities are distributed among the agents who perform the activities of bees. These agents are named as Search Bee, Selector Bee, and Replace Bee to simulate the behaviors of Employed, Onlooker and Scout bees in the Bee Colony. This has been illustrated in Figure 2.

Initially, the UDDI with services and cloudlets that are providing such services are provided. Then, this UDDI is then subjected for the search processes by the software agents such as Search Bee, Selector Bee and Replace Bee which reflects the operations of Employed, Onlooker and Scout Bees. The working procedure of each of these agents in the MCC architecture is given below.

Search Bees

The Search bees locate the services registered in the UDDI to find the relevant clouds to satisfy the client requests. Once it has identified the clouds, the bee analyses the mobile profile and QoS provided by the clouds.

Figure 2. Proposed ABC based MCC Architecture

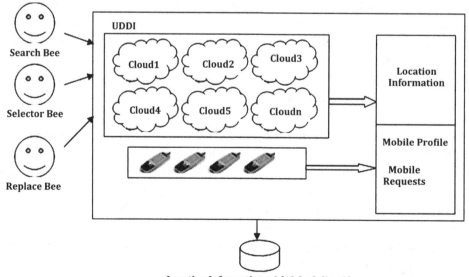

Location Information with Scheduling Plan

If the initially selected cloud does not provides the required level of service or the mobile profile does not satisfy the cloud resource usage, it makes a modification by discovering a new cloudlet.

If the newly identified cloudlet has higher QoS and mobile profile analysis also yields good results, the employed bee gathers the location information and stores in the mobile service repository. Otherwise the bees keep the previous location information.

To achieve this, the Search bees' responsibilities include: mobile profile monitoring, Mobile Profile Analysis, QoS monitoring, QoS analysis and optimal location identification. Then the location information of the appropriate clouds is shared with the Selector bees.

Selector Bees

On evaluating the location information of the identified clouds by the Search bees, the Selector bees identified the cloud depending upon the amount of resources. Similar to the Search bees, they also produce modification on the selection of cloud based on the availability of resources.

Then, these bees schedule the requests by formulating the fitness evaluation of nearest neighborhood of the mobile device and the cloudlet with highest availability to provide reliable non-breakable service.

Based on this, a scheduling plan will be prepared by these bees and the information is sent to the employed bees to allocate the client requests to the appropriate clouds.

If the Selector Bee could not find any such cloudlets or the mobile profile analysis does not yield the requested fitness value, the request will be rejected and it is intimated to the Scouts.

Scout Bees

The responsibility of scout bees include random selection of other mobile profiles based on service request and random selection of clouds purely based on its own decision and not based on previous experience.

Then this information is sent to the employed bees for further evaluation and selection.

This process will be repeated till the appropriate clouds have been selected to achieve QoS. Finally, the requests are optimally scheduled with the modified MCC architecture using a nature inspired approach ABC to achieve green IT.

IMPLEMENTATION OF BEES AS AGENTS IN MCC

As it is stated in the previous section, each bee in the proposed Artificial Bee Colony (ABC) based approach can be implemented as intelligent agents. As per Thangarajah et.al. (2014), the BDI (Belief-Desire-Intention) model of agency is a popular agent development paradigm for developing complex applications. Here, the agents are provided with cognitive resources such as goals, plans and beliefs. Hence, a BDI agent is provided with a set of plans to achieve the goals. The choice of achieving a goal is generally depending upon agent's beliefs. The plans provided in the agents normally contain several sub-goals which can be used to achieve the actual goal. Thus, to achieve a specific goal, the BDI agent generally achieves several intermittent sub-goals which are acting as mile stones.

During their decision making process, the agents can be provided with preferences which are nothing but the soft constraints that are preferred for a particular solution. These preferences help in improving the performance of an agent.

In MCC, each agent's work can be established by means of Belief-Desire-Intention (BDI) based architecture. This kind of BDI agent can achieve the goal in a number of different ways. In the case of MCC, the choice of using the appropriate cloud is done at runtime, depending upon the contextual information of resource availability, resource usage and the properties of goals to be achieved. Hence, a BDI kind of architecture can be used to implement such kinds of agents in MCC architecture.

In this proposed architecture, the BDI agent selects the appropriate cloud from the number of cloudlets based on its plans. Here, each plan is used to provide the sub-goals to reach. In the case of MCC, the intention is to get the service more quickly with higher resource availability. For instance, in the case of Patients health monitoring mobile app, the application needs to process a number of patients' records in terms of their health profile, images and videos to be processed simultaneously.

If we have separate clouds for profile matching application, image processing, video streamlining, the agent can then decide which clouds to choose based on the availability of the application, resource utilization and so on. Here users' preferences can also be used to achieve the sub-goals. For instance, if a Doctor uses this mobile app, and wants to do only image processing, that can be indicated as a preference so that the agent can start focusing on the appropriate cloud without reaching out the other clouds. Hence, runtime determination of selection of the cloud and providing the right outcome within less amount of processing time is possible with this kind of architecture. This further reduces the resources wastage to reduce power consumption and thus leads to green IT.

Competitive Advantages

- Data storage capability
    - As the agents work independently of the cloud platforms, the data can be stored in any of the cloudlets irrespective of their platform. This improves the storage capability of the MCC architecture without any dedicated platform oriented services.
- Processing Speed
    - Because of the parallel processing nature of the agents, the processing speed is high. As the Search, Selection and Scout bees are working in parallel in identifying the proper cloudlet to provide the service to the mobile client, this will definitely improve the processing speed.
- Reliability and availability
    - As the system works on parallel processing of the agents, the QoS will be high as it provides uninterrupted service to the requester.
    - Also, during peak time, the availability of the services will be assured as it finds the cloudlet with less requests.
- Dynamic Provisioning
    - Dynamic on-demand service is ensured as there is no dedicated cloud per mobile device.
    - As the services are provided based on the request, there is no need for advance reservation or resources being idle even when other devices are requesting them.
- Scalability
    - The proposed architecture can be scaled to any number of clouds as the processing is going to be done by the agents.
    - If the number of clouds is increasing, the number of agents can be increased to do the handling of requests. Even though it seems to be a slight overhead, when compared to the advantages we receive, this can be compensated.

- Ease of Integration
  - As it is completely platform independent, the ease of integration between various available resources with mobile devices will be improved.

CONCLUSION

In this chapter, a modified conceptual cloud architecture that can achieve requests allocation from several mobile devices to the appropriate cloudlets is proposed. Even though it is a comprehensive framework, the individual components that does the QoS operations can be easily implemented as intelligent agents which mimics the behavior of honey bees so that, parallel selection and optimization of resource allocation is done without compromising the QoS.

Thus, the proposed architecture not only achieves the required QoS but also Green IT as it consumes less time and not utilizing too much resources for a simple request and not utilizing multiple resources for a single request. Hence, the proposed nature inspired Artificial Bee Colony based architecture for Mobile Cloud Computing will really be a boon for the service providers and service requestors. As a future work, this research can be extended to evaluate the different parameters of QoS in mobile computing with existing architectures and other optimization approaches.

REFERENCES

Aepona. (2010). *Mobile Cloud Computing Solution Brief.* White Paper. AEPONA.

Bahar, H. (2013). Islam (2013). Security Architecture for Mobile Cloud Computing. *International Journal of Scientific Knowledge, 3*(3), 11–17.

Dai, & Zhou. (2010). A PKI-based mechanism for secure and efficient access to outsourced data. In *Proceedings of the 2nd International Conference on Networking and Digital Society (ICNDS)*, (vol. 1, pp. 640).

Dinh, T., Lee, C., Niyato, D., & Wang, P. (2013). Hong, Chonho Lee, Dusit Niyato, & Ping Wang (2013). A Survey of Mobile Cloud Computing: Architecture, Applications, and Approaches. *Wireless Communications and Mobile Computing, 13*(18), 1587–1611. doi:10.1002/wcm.1203

Doukas, T.. Pliakas, & Maglogiannis. (2010). Mobile Healthcare Information Management unitizing Cloud Computing and Android OS. In *Annual International Conference of the IEEE on Engineering in Medicine and Biology Society (EMBC)*, (pp. 1037 - 1040). IEEE.

Karaboga, D., & Basturk, B. (2008, January). On The Performance of Artificial Bee Colony (ABC) Algorithm. *Applied Soft Computing, 8*(1), 687–697. doi:10.1016/j.asoc.2007.05.007

Karaboga & Basturk. (2007). Artificial Bee Colony (ABC) Optimization Algorithm for Solving Constrained Optimization Problems. In Advances in Soft Computing: Foundations of Fuzzy Logic and Soft Computing (LNCS), (Vol. 4529, pp. 789-798). Springer-Verlag. doi:10.1007/978-3-540-72950-1_77

Ku, Lu, & Gerla. (2014). Software-Defined Mobile Cloud: Architecture, Services and Use Cases. *IC-WCM-2014*. IEEE.

Li, H., & Hua, X.-S. (2010). Melog: mobile experience sharing through automatic multimedia blogging. In *Proceedings of the 2010 ACM multimedia workshop on Mobile Cloud Media Computing (MCMC)*, (pp. 19-24). doi:10.1145/1877953.1877961

Mala, D. J., & Iswarya, R. (2014). A Multi Agent Based Approach for Critical Components Identification and Testing. *International Journal of Systems and Service-Oriented Engineering*, 4(1), 2014. doi:10.4018/ijssoe.2014010102

Mala, D. J., & Mohan, V. (2009). ABC Tester-Artificial bee colony based software test suite optimization approach. *International Journal of Software Engineering*, 2(2), 15–43.

Mala, D. J., & Mohan, V. (2010). Automated software test optimization framework - an artificial bee colony optimization-based approach. *IET Software*, 4(5), 334–348. doi:10.1049/iet-sen.2009.0079

Mala, S., Balamurugan, S., & Nathan, K. S. (2013). Balamurugan, & KS Nathan (2013). Criticality analyzer and tester: An effective approach for critical component identification & verification using ABC. *Software Engineering Notes*, 38(6), 1–12. doi:10.1145/2532780.2532811

Pham, D. T., Ghanbarzadeh, A., Koc, E., Otri, S., Rahim, S., & Zaidi, M. (2005). *Technical Note: Bees Algorithm*. Cardiff, UK: Cardiff University.

Prasad, G., & Murti, P. R. K. (2012). Mobile Cloud Computing: Implications and Challenges. *Journal of Information Engineering and Applications*, 2(7), 2012.

Rahimi, M. R., Hengmeechai, J., & Sarchar, N. (2008). Ubiquitous Application of Mobile Phones for Getting Information from Barcode Picture. In iCORE 2008.

RCR Wireless News. (2011). *Mobile cloud computing – The value-added role for service providers*. White Paper. Retrieved May 4, 2015, from http://www.rcrwireless.com/20110627/opinion/readerforum/reader-forum-mobile-cloud-computing-8211-the-value-added-role-for-service-providers

Satyanarayanan, M., Bahl, P., Caceres, R., & Davies, N. (2009, October). The case for VM-Based cloudlets in Mobile Computing. *IEEE Pervasive Computing / IEEE Computer Society [and] IEEE Communications Society*, 8(4), 14–23. doi:10.1109/MPRV.2009.82

Tang, W.-T., Hu, C.-M., & Hsu, C.-Y. (2010). A mobile phone based homecare management system on the cloud. In *Proceedings of the 3rd International Conference on Biomedical and Informatics (BMEI)*, (vol. 6, pp. 2442). doi:10.1109/BMEI.2010.5639917

Techopedia. (n.d.). *Mobile Cloud Computing (MCC)*. Retrieved May 4, 2015, from http://www.techopedia.com/definition/26679/mobile-cloud-computing-mcc

Thangarajah, J., Sardi~na, & Padgham. (2012). Measuring plan coverage and overlap for agent reasoning. AAMAS.

Yang, X., Pan, T., & Shen, J. (2010). On 3G Mobile E-commerce Platform Based on Cloud Computing. In *Proceedings of the 3rd IEEE International Conference on Ubi-Media Computing (U-Media)*, (pp. 198 - 201). IEEE.

Zhao, W., Sun, Y., & Dai, L. (2010). Improving computer basis teaching through mobile communication and cloud computing technology. In *Proceedings of the 3rd International Conference on Advanced Computer Theory and Engineering (ICACTE)*, (vol. 1, pp. 452 – 454).

Chapter 3
Designing Mobile Collaborative Applications for Cloud Environments

Nadir Guetmi
Poitiers University, France

Abdessamad Imine
Lorraine University, France & INRIA-LORIA Grand-Est, France

ABSTRACT

Mobile devices have experienced a huge progress in the capacity of computing, storage and data visualization. They are becoming the device of choice for operating a large variety of applications while supporting real-time collaboration of people and their mobility. Despite this progress, the energy consumption and the network coverage remain a serious problem against an efficient and continuous use of these mobile collaborative applications and a great challenge for their designers and developers. To address these issues, this chapter describes design patterns that help modelling mobile collaborative applications to support collaboration through the cloud. Two levels are presented: the first level provides self-control to create clones of mobile devices, manage users' groups and recover failed clones in the cloud. The second level supports group collaboration mechanisms in real-time. These design patterns have been used as a basis for the design of a mobile collaborative editing application.

INTRODUCTION

Recent statistics indicate that the world is evolving towards more connected mobile devices. Indeed, by the end of 2014, the number of mobile-broadband subscriptions reaches 2.3 billion globally (Brahima Sanou, 2014). Mobile devices enable users to manipulate powerful applications that take benefit of the increasing availability of built-in communication network and better data exchange capabilities of mobile devices. Accordingly, real-time data streams and web applications (such as mobile commerce, social networking and ad-hoc collaboration) are seamlessly incorporated in mobile applications.

DOI: 10.4018/978-1-4666-9916-8.ch003

Copyright © 2016, IGI Global. Copying or distributing in print or electronic forms without written permission of IGI Global is prohibited.

However, even though mobile devices hardware and network modules continue to evolve and to improve, mobile devices will always be resource-poor, less secure, with unstable connectivity, and with constrained energy. Resource deficiency is a main issue for many applications, and as a result, computation on mobile devices will always involve a compromise (Satyanarayanan, 2009). To overcome the mobile device resource limitations, one straightforward solution is to leverage cloud computing, which is an emerged model based on virtualization for efficient and flexible use of hardware assets and software services over a network. Cloud computing is a multi-purpose paradigm that aggregate several technologies such as virtualization, peer-to-peer networks and autonomic computing. Of course, a deeper user expertise is not necessary to benefit from all these technologies. Virtualization extends the mobile device resources by offloading execution from the mobile to the cloud where a *clone* (or *virtual machine*) of the mobile is running. Cloud computing allows users to build virtual networks "à la peer-to-peer" where a mobile device may be continuously connected to other mobiles to achieve a common task. The goal of autonomic computing is to provide self-configuration capabilities such as on-demand resources provisioning (e.g. memory size) without requiring user intervention.

The definition of design patterns is more challenging in new applications for cloud-supported mobile collaborative services, because the combination of mobile and cloud environments raises many design issues such as the management of real-time collaborative works (e.g. a collaborative editing works). These mobile collaborative applications involve many mobile users to manipulate shared data. So, they require suitable design patterns for modeling communication and synchronization services that are intended to be deployed in the cloud and several mobile devices, while delegating the maximum of inherent tasks to the cloud. Moreover, other processes such as installation, deployment, configuration, monitoring and management of software modules must be well modeled to fully provide the collaborative service to mobile users in the cloud.

This chapter provides a reusable design model of mobile collaborative applications in the cloud. It aims to meet the objective of providing pure decentralized synchronization mechanisms for preserving the consistency of the shared resources under constraints of mobile applications, namely the short-life battery and the connection instability. Accordingly, design solutions are illustrated for addressing the challenge of modeling the cloning and collaboration services in the cloud. The proposed design patterns concern two levels: the first level provides self-control to create clones of mobiles, manage users' groups and recover failed clones in the cloud. The second level presents group collaboration mechanisms in real-time, without any role assigned to the server.

The present chapter is structured in seven sections: Second section presents how mobile users collaborate via the cloud, and illustrates a use case example. Third section enumerates requirements to be satisfied when designing mobile collaborative applications. Fourth section describes two design patterns for managing the cloning of mobile devices and ensuring collaboration between these devices. Fifth section presents a mobile collaborative editing application designed according the proposed design patterns. Sixth section reviews the related work and seventh section concludes this chapter.

BACKGROUND

The area of mobile collaborative applications has experienced several published research works. Yet, few of these works have proposed a reusable design model. (Neyem, 2012) has presented a one, mainly based on coordination and communication services. However, mobile constraints such as short-life battery and connection instability were not considered by this design; this may negatively impact on such collaboration systems that are not intended for the cloud environments. Furthermore, there is no work that proposed a reusable model for mobile collaborative applications specifically designed for cloud environments. This section provides definitions around the two principal axes of this chapter's proposed design, mobile computation offloading and collaborative applications, and discusses their related works.

Mobile Computation Offloading

The battery limited lifetime is considered as a major concern for mobile devices. Computation offloading is a technique used for migrating intense computing tasks from limited-resources devices (i.e., mobile devices) to the cloud. This avoids taking a long time for mobile intense tasks processing and therefore extend the battery lifetime.

1. **Cloud Computing:** Cloud computing is a computing model which consists in proposing information processing services as services on demand, accessible from anywhere, anytime and by anyone. Several types of cloud can be distinguished. In the private cloud case all physical resources are fully supported by the company. The public cloud is managed by an external service provider and can be reached via internet (e.g. Amazon public cloud[1]). The hybrid cloud is a mix of the two previous. In general, when a company does not have enough physical resources, it can hire services of a public cloud provider.

2. **Virtualization:** Virtualization is a software mechanism for operating several systems, servers or applications, on a single physical server; it is a key technology component in the cloud computing. Virtualization is based on a multilayer system composed of a main operating system, called the "host system" which directly interacts with the hard layer of the physical server. Virtualization software, also called Hypervisor (e.g. VitualBox[2], Xen[3] and VMware[4]) is the second layer installed on the host system. It allows the creation of enclosed and independent environments on-which will be installed other operating systems: the "guest systems". These created environments are "virtual machines". Each virtual machine operates independently from others and has access to the physical server resources.

3. **Cloning:** In general, cloning is the operation which consists of copying an object instance. The new created instance will contain the same information. This chapter provides a self-mechanism based on virtualization techniques for creating virtual copies of mobile devices in a cloud environment. Clones will contain the same data and applications but will perform the mobile offloaded intense tasks for relieving their real devices.

Dealing with persistent problems related to limited mobile resources was the subject of several research works. The proposed solutions in (Chun, 2011; Cuervo, 2010; Liu, 2013; Xia, 2014; Shiraz, 2014; Park, 2014) are based on mobile computation offloading mechanisms of intense tasks parts to the cloud. (Flores, 2014) proposed the Mobile Cloud Middleware (MCM), an interface allowing an asynchronous migration of mobile tasks to heterogeneous cloud platforms through a dynamic resource allocation mechanisms.

However, offloading mechanisms are based on background process for continuously monitoring the use of different mobile resources by different applications. According to (Dinh, 2013) background monitoring processes and cloud workload can be as costly for mobile devices in time and energy consumption. Moreover, these approaches do not support the cloud mobile collaboration, since their offloading processes are dynamic and require constant mobile/cloud connection. In contrast, the cloning service proposed in this chapter enables offloading intense tasks through a static deployment of the collaborative application on the clone that is created in the cloud.

Fault tolerance is a major concern to guarantee the continuity of the smooth functioning of tasks offloaded in the cloud. This can be performed using two main directions: logical solutions such as replication (Marinelli, 2009) and hardware solutions (Palmer, 2009). For the logical solutions, two main works that use respectively, replication and migration can be cited. The work of Hyrax (Marinelli, 2009) uses replication techniques to allow the re-execution of tasks on a stable new node after the failure. In (Samimi, 2006), a dynamic instantiation of communication services at the distributed nodes in the cloud is proposed to meet different user requirement. To ensure continuity of communication between the various nodes, a proxy migration technique is used. It consists in creating and starting a new instance of the proxy service on a new node after the failure of the first host node. For the hardware solutions, (Palmer, 2009) proposes the use of a computing grid (called IBIS) to benefit from the enormous computing capacity resulting from the different nodes that compose it. Each user can integrate his/her mobile device to the grid in order to overcome the problems of limited resources. The fault tolerance is achieved through a resource-tracking model that uses a "JEL" (Join, Elect, and Leave) API.

The chapter's proposed solution for the failure tolerance is based on the heartbeat principle. The cloning middleware instantaneously monitors the clones smooth functioning in the cloud. In case of failure detection, it will recover states of the failed clones without affecting the collaborative works.

Collaborative Applications

Collaboration is a mechanism that allows multiple users/systems to process and manipulate shared data in order to achieve a common goal. Collaborative applications offer tools to create workspaces and add/ propose collaborative tasks. Thus, remote users can concurrently access/process shared resources and synchronization will be ensured by the collaborative applications. In particular, collaborative mobile applications are specifically intended for mobile environments where remote users are using their mobile devices (e.g. smartphones and tablets) to achieve collaborative tasks. Designing these particular applications must consider the requirements related to the mobile resources limitation and the network connections instability.

1. **Synchronization:** Data synchronization is a mechanism that aims to maintain the consistency of shared data as seen by various sites in collaborative and concurrent environments. In this chapter, a purely decentralized synchronization mechanism is presented. It is intended for preserving the consistency of shared resources through two levels, real mobile devices and their clones in the cloud.
2. **Replication:** Replication is a data sharing mechanism to ensure consistency between different sources of redundant data; in this case the same data are duplicated on multiple devices. This mechanism can be well adapted to distributed and decentralized systems to improve reliability, fault tolerance and availability. Should be noted that it is not to confuse replication with backup: the backed data does not change over time, while the replicated data are constantly changing.

Several research works have proposed collaboration systems specifically designed for cloud environments, where end users can simultaneously edit shared documents online.

(Feldman, 2010) proposed SPORC a real-time collaborative mechanism that allows end users (clients SPORC) to concurrently edit shared documents. SPORC is based on a remote server (in the cloud) that assigns a global sequence number to each edit concurrent operation received by different clients and manages their network broadcast. Each client SPORC uses a technique based on operational transformation (OT) approach to maintain the consistency of shared documents. Following the centralization of synchronization and intensity of the tasks executed by each client for maintaining consistency, SPORC is unsuitable for mobile devices under their constraints of limited resources.

(Kosta, 2013) proposed CloneDoc, a collaboration mechanism suitable for mobile devices. For the mobile relieving, CloneDoc delegates intense computing tasks towards clones of smartphones on a mobile cloud platform called Clonetoclone (c2c). The clones' collaboration is carried out across the same synchronization mechanism used by SPORC; the concurrent operations scheduling and their broadcast is based on a central server. Such a centralized synchronization can cause malfunction of the collaborative system in case of server failure. Furthermore inconsistencies views of the shared documents can occur in the clone and its real device; this is due to the offset of execution of the same operation in both sides. For reconciling the shared documents consistency, CloneDoc will perform additional treatments based OT in mobile side. Unfortunately, this can cause huge energy consumption.

(Xia, 2014) proposed HERMES a transparent approach providing cross-cloud interoperability mechanisms of heterogeneous collaborative editing services. This system acts as a broker to allow different users to collaborate through the cloud while preserving their own editing service providers. In this case it uses a synchronization mechanism based on operational transformation technology (OT) to maintain the consistency of shared documents.

(Guetmi, 2015) proposed a mobile collaborative editing service in the cloud resulting from the reuse of the design patterns presented (for the first time) in this chapter. This service consists in providing web services that allows users to clone their mobile devices within virtual networks in the cloud. On the other hand, it provides fully decentralized synchronization mechanisms for collaboratively editing shared documents in real time.

MODEL OF COLLABORATION

A model of collaboration is presented here to allow several geographically dispersed users collaborate (i.e. to achieve common task) at any time. The adoption of mobile devices for such a collaboration relies on critical factors such as computational power, battery life and network coverage. Further extending this collaboration in space and time will inevitably stumble across limits of these factors. For instance, collaboration may involve mobile users located in the same limited geographical area, yet connected via wireless channels, which can be less reliable and offer lower data rates than traditional wired ones. To overcome these limitations, the most of mobile device's computing tasks as well as the communication between these devices are delegated to the cloud. Indeed, virtualization extends the mobile device resources by offloading execution from the mobile to the cloud where a *clone* (or *virtual machine*) of the mobile is running. Cloud computing allows users to build virtual networks "à la peer-to-peer" where a mobile device may be continuously connected to other mobiles to achieve a common task. The goal of autonomic computing is to provide self-configuration capabilities such as on-demand resources provisioning (e.g. memory size) without requiring user intervention.

Thus, each user owns two copies of the shared data where the first copy is stored in the mobile device whereas the second one is on its clone (at the cloud level). The user modifies the mobile copy and then sends local modifications to her/his clone in order to update the second copy and propagate these modifications to other clones (i.e. other mobile devices). Moreover, the user can work even during disconnection by means of the mobile device's copy.

To well illustrate this collaboration model, here is a use case of collaborative editing application in the following situation:

A team of reporters, equipped with mobile devices, is collaborating to cover a large-scale event (e.g. concert, political meeting, and general strike) from multiple locations. Because of the large crowds, a permanent and stable communication network may be absent. That is why, the reporters can use a collaborative application and form a group over a mobile cloud network (with servers embedded in some special trucks or virtual mobile cloud computing provider (Huerta-Canepa, 2010 ; Pal, 2013) to share and update in real time a common data (e.g. news, images) on the ground. Moreover, the reporters must hide their location against some hostile persons in order to go unnoticed inside the crowd and covering freely and without any constraint the event. Such ad-hoc collaboration requires a safe and secure coordination to get consistent common data that enables the reporters to deliver credible corroborating information about the event. It is clear that the reporter tasks are high-consuming resources as synchronizing a shared data in a dynamic group is costly. Thus, cloning the mobile devices in the cloud enables reporters to better manage their battery-life and cover the events for a long time. The mobile device can be temporarily disconnected from the cloud but its clone remains operational. This reduces the network overhead. The reporters can work in offline and occasionally connect to their clones to disseminate data or receive new data from the group.

DESIGN REQUIREMENTS

The design phase of an application must consider both functional and non-functional requirements such as flexibility, performance, interoperability and security in order to increase the application usefulness (Chung & Prado Leite, 2009). Given that this is a rule, the context of mobile collaborative applications does not constitute an exception and must comply with this rule in its general form. But given the peculiarities related to mobile applications, a more detailed list of requirements is advisable. These requirements are listed as follows (Herskovic et al., 2011): user's interaction flexibility (or scalability), user's interaction protection, communication, heterogeneity and interoperability, autonomous interaction-support services, user awareness, and data consistency and availability. This list is extended by an important requirement, namely the failure recovery. It considers the capability of the mobile collaborative application to support fault tolerance mechanism for the auto detection / repair of failures. Note, due to space limitation, this chapter does not consider the user's interaction protection.

In the following, requirements related to the design of mobile collaborative applications for cloud environments are listed.

- **Data Availability:** The application should be responsive in online and offline works in such a way the shared data must be available forever. Even though the user loses her/his mobile device, she/he must able to recover data from the cloud. This situation can be addressed by explicit data replication between the mobile device and its clone.

- **Data Consistency:** Users are able to freely and concurrently modify any part of the shared data at any time (in online and offline works). These modifications typically generate inconsistency of the shared data. More precisely, this inconsistency is caused by concurrent updates in clone-to-clone and mobile-to-clone interactions. Therefore mobile collaborative applications must provide lightweight and decentralized synchronization mechanisms to preserve data consistency. The synchronization must be mainly performed at the cloud level in such a way the collaboration will decrease the energy spend on the mobile device. As for decentralized synchronization, it enables users to avoid a single point of failure.

- **Communication:** Communication between mobile users must be available and permanent. Indeed, it is the support of any form of collaboration (e.g. exchanging multiple data types to perform a common task) and synchronization to maintain data consistency. It is well known that the communication through mobile devices suffers from frequent disconnections. To address this situation, the proposed cloud-based collaboration model enables each mobile user to communicate directly with her/his clone that is always available in the cloud. Thus, any mobile user is accessible, via the clone, at any time.

- **Scalability:** Mobile applications must be adapted to dynamic environments where changes in collaborative group size are unforeseeable and frequent. Typically, events such as creating a new group or joining/leaving an existing group must not affect the availability and integrity of the shared data. Thus, on the one hand, users must participate on-demand to any collaborative work session. On the other hand, the management of user groups should be performed in transparent and consistent manner, and most importantly, computationally costless for mobile devices. As the reader will see in the next sections, the proposed cloud-based collaboration model is well suited to achieve highly scalable mobile collaborative applications.

- **User Awareness:** Each clone must be able to detect in real time and share with other clones (members of the same group) information related to state of their real devices. To establish this awareness, like (Herskovic et al., 2009), the following mechanisms are used: user's reachability (i.e. connected/disconnected), user's availability (i.e. available/busy) in which each user is notified via the clone of its real mobile device on the presence/availability of other users (members of the same group) in real time.

- **Heterogeneity:** The type of device (or operating system) used by mobile users must not be an obstacle to perform on-demand collaboration between them. The proposed conception is based on a cloning manager, a middleware composed of web services based on WSDL (Web Services Description Language) for mobile cloning and ad-hoc networks management in the cloud. This interface allows for creating clones with a unified operating system (i.e. Android). This will eliminate any problems related to mobiles' heterogeneity for the communication of their clones in the cloud. On the other hand, communication between clones and their non-android mobile devices is based on standard SOAP (Simple Object Access Protocol) through the web services provided by the cloning manager; but this is an exception, since android mobile devices can directly communicate with their clones. It also should be noted that at present, the current cloning system does not realize perfect clones for mobile devices with operating systems other than Android. In this case the cloning manager will only create an android virtual machine equipped with the collaboration protocol without the possibility of saving data and applications from non-Android mobile devices.

- **Failure Recovery:** Users have to recover easily all shared data when technical hitch (e.g. crash, theft or loss of mobile device, or clone failure) happens, and continue seamlessly the collaboration. To tackle this problem, a manager of the complete life cycle of clones is necessary. This manager will detect failed clones and restore their states without affecting collaborative tasks.

PROPOSED DESIGN PATTERNS

This section presents design patterns for mobile collaborative applications in the cloud. Figure 1 depicts the global architecture of the system that consists of two levels:

1. *Cloning Protocol* (CP) provides web services for: (a) creating clones of mobile devices in the cloud; and, (b) managing user groups through the creation and membership management of virtual networks in the cloud.
2. *Cloud Mobile Collaboration Protocol* (CMCP) supports synchronization mechanisms for manipulating shared data by multiple users in the cloud. This protocol must ensure in real-time the consistency of replicated shared data.

To illustrate the features of the proposed design patterns, *class diagrams* (see Figures 2 and 4) and examples of *java classes* will be given throughout this section.

Figure 1. The architecture of mobile collaborative applications in the cloud

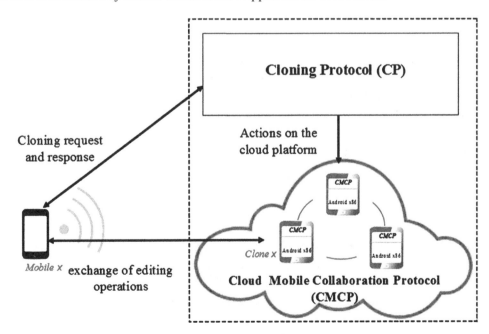

Figure 2. Design pattern for cloning

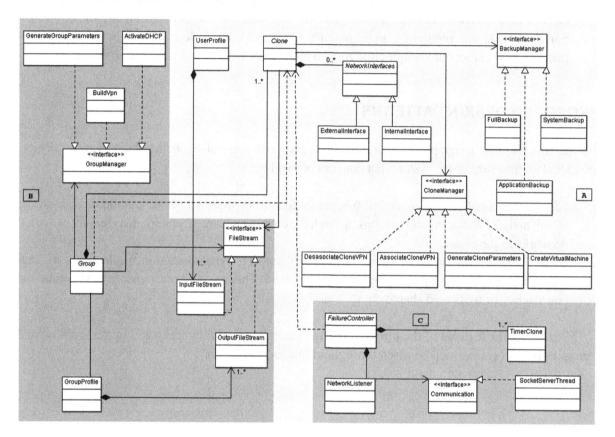

Design Pattern for Cloning

This pattern consists of web services acting on the cloud platform for cloning mobile devices, managing virtual networks and repairing seamlessly eventual clone failures. To illustrate the features of this pattern, this sub-section presents java classes that encapsulate actions applied on the virtualization environment VirtualBox (private cloud in this case) in order to implement different functionality of this pattern (creation of virtual networks and clone construction).

In the following, the three main components of the design pattern for cloning (see Figure 2) are described.

A. Cloning Engine

Context: With its treatments and data deployment services, the cloud is considered as a good solution that fits with insufficient resources of mobile devices (i.e. short-life battery and storage capacity). In this context a cloning process will enable the creation of clones (i.e. mobile virtual device) that will take charge the execution of all collaboration processes and networking tasks.

Figure 4. Collaboration pattern

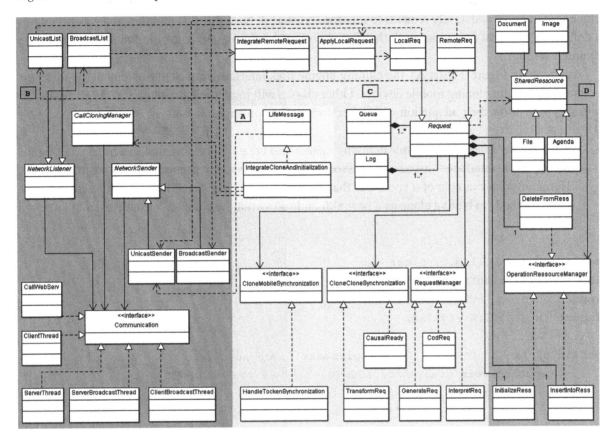

Moreover, the absence of users due to an intentional disconnection or occurrence of a wireless network failure will not be considered as an obstacle for the collaborative works, since its clone ensures the collaboration continuity acting.

Problem: Building mobile clones is not a simple task. The question arising at this stage is: how to realize an interface encapsulating a cloning actions automaton on the cloud platform? Moreover, it is necessary to equipping every new clone with network parameters needed to communicate with other clones and its mobile.

Solution: The proposed solution is the implementation of cloning engine as web service. The cloning process is triggered by a user request via a web interface and it includes the following actions:

The first action consist in creating a user profile using the registration information introduced through the web interface (user name, password, photo, mobile IP address) and other generated information as the identifier of the clone, the clone IP address and the group identifier. The cloning engine uses an *"Output File Stream"* in order to save user profile information. Next, user will be asked for backing mobile data and applications. Once the backup is finished, the creation of a virtual machine based on android operating system is launched. After this step it is necessary to settle the clone network configuration: it consists of activating at least one network interface and associates it with a previously created virtual private network (VPN). This virtual network is created by a user request and allows communication for clones of the same group in private mode (see next point). In addition, another network interface is activated and associated with an external network allowing communication with the mobile device. The clone is ready now and it only remains to rename and start it. Note that this cloning process also allows a default deployment (auto-start with the clone boot) of the distributed collaboration protocol with the required settings.

As shown in Figure 2 (part A), the cloning engine uses interface classes to implement the different actions required for cloning mobile devices. Other classes will implement these interfaces (grouped into a package) to allow their adaptation with several virtualization environments:

1. *The "CloneManager" interface* contains methods to create clones (virtual machines), configure the network interfaces (associate/disassociate clone VPN) and generate the clone parameters. Hereinafter an example of a java class that implements this interface. This allows redefining one of its methods to build a clone as a new x86-android virtual machine in VirtualBox.

```java
package Cloud.Collab.Cloning;
import java.io.BufferedReader;
import java.io.InputStreamReader;
import java.util.ArrayList;

public class CreateAndroidOnVB implements CloneManager{
        public void CreateAndroidOnVB () {
            //clone's creation parameters.
                String vbm="VboxManage", imp="import", f="CloneAndroid.OVA",
line;
            //process of creating a new Android Virtual Machine by importing.
                try {
                    String[] argVmCreate = {vbm, imp, f};
                    ProcessBuilder proc = new ProcessBuilder(argVmCreate);
                    Process pr4 = proc.start();
                    pr4.waitFor();
                    BufferedReader br2 = new BufferedReader(new
InputStreamReader(pr4.getInputStream()));
                    while ((line = br2.readLine()) != null);
                } catch (Exception e) {
                    System.err.println("Error");
                }
            }
}
```

2. *The "BackupManager" interface* consists of methods for mobile data and applications backup. This backup is optional: it can be complete or partial (applications, user data and system parameters). The following example of java class implements this interface. It redefines one of its methods to perform a total backup of data, system parameters and mobile applications:

```java
package Cloud.Collab.Backup;
import java.io.BufferedReader;
import java.io.InputStreamReader;

public class FullBackupOnVB implements BackupManager{
        public void FullBackup() {
            //Backup parameters
                String adb="adb", backup="backup", arg1backup="-f",
chemback="sauv.ab", arg2back="-apk", arg3back="-shared", arg4back="-all",
arg5back="-system", line;

            //Full backup process.
                try {
                        String[] argbackup = {adb, backup, arg1backup, chem-
back, arg2back, arg3back, arg4back, arg5back};
                        ProcessBuilder proc = new ProcessBuilder(argbackup);
                    Process pr = proc.start();
                    pr.waitFor();
                    BufferedReader br = new BufferedReader(new
InputStreamReader(pr.getInputStream()));
                        while ((line = br.readLine()) != null);
                } catch (Exception e) {
                    System.err.println("Error");
                }
        }
```

B. VPN Builder

Context: Mobile users form collaborative groups, share resources, and always want to protect their data relying on private communication modes. These groups are dynamic in the sense that users can create, change or leave groups at any time and participate on-demand in collaboration sessions (connection / disconnection).

Problem: The formation of real ad-hoc networks is expensive, limited by geographical restrictions and suffers from instability due to frequent disconnections. In addition, decentralized collaborative works in such mobile networks require intense communication tasks between peers (i.e. mobile devices). This leads to exhaust the batteries lifetime.

Solution: The use of the VPN builder component allows solving this problem. This VPN will group the clones that will take charge the total of network tasks instead of their real devices (user mobiles of the same group). Like the cloning engine, the process of creating cloud virtual networks is implemented as web service. Actions of this process are triggered by a user request via a web interface; this activates the virtualization hypervisor for building a new virtual network. Then other actions are applied to configure parameters of the created network by (i) activating the DHCP server with setting lower and upper limits of the IP addresses that will be dynamically allocated to clones network interfaces; and, (ii) providing a specific broadcast address to the VPN in order to facilitate the communication between the clones affiliated to the same group.

As shown in Figure 2 (part B), the VPN builder uses interface classes to implement the different actions required for building virtual private networks:

1. *The "GroupManager" interface* contains methods to create virtual private networks and their configurations. The following example is a java class that implements this interface. This class redefines one of its methods for building the host-only network in VirtualBox.

```java
package Cloud.Collab.Group;
import java.io.BufferedReader;
import java.io.InputStreamReader;

public class BuildVpnOnVB implements GroupManager{
        public void BuildVpn() {
                //VPN creation parameters.
                    String vbm="VboxManage", reseau="hostonlyif", allez="create",
line;
                //Creating VPN process.
                try {
                            String[] argbackup = {vbm, reseau, allez};
                            ProcessBuilder proc = new ProcessBuilder(argbackup);
                    Process proces = proc.start();
                    proces.waitFor();
                    BufferedReader br2 = new BufferedReader(new
InputStreamReader(proces.getInputStream()));
                            while ((line = br2.readLine()) != null);
                } catch (Exception e) {
                    System.err.println("Error");
                }
            }
}
```

C. Failure Controller

Context: Clones are virtual copies of real mobile devices deployed in the cloud. They act on behalf of them to perform the main collaboration tasks such as saving data, exchanging requests with other clones and performing protocols for maintaining shared data consistency. These virtual machines must be always online to report data changes performed by other clones and receive local requests applied by their mobile devices. However, autonomous mechanisms for detecting clone failures and their immediate repair are necessary to prevent the users' isolation from their collaboration groups.

Figure 3. Failure Controller

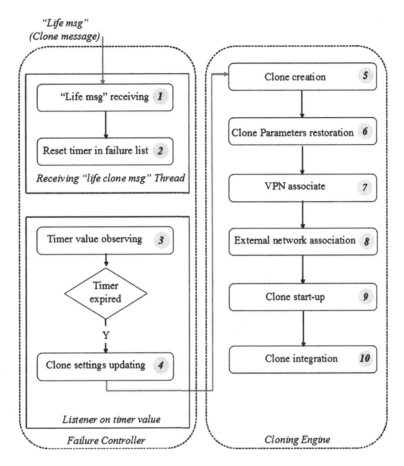

Problem: Two main questions arising at this stage are: (i) how to detect clone failures that are deployed in the cloud on remote servers? (ii) After clone failure detection, how to perform a full restoration of the clone status?

Solution: One solution to this problem involves the use of a failure controller that consists in addressing failures that can affect the smooth running of clones (see Figure 3). For that, it provides a mechanism for detecting failures in three situations:

1. Failure of the collaborative application: This problem will occur after generating software exceptions or errors. In this case, a possible shutdown of the collaborative application will interrupt all exchanged messages to and from the clone.
2. Failure of a clone: This failure comes from the virtualization software or the local OS; it stops the normal behavior of the clone that turns into unreachable for any interaction with either the mobile device or other clones.
3. Transient communication failure: This problem troubles the communication inside the network for a finite but arbitrary time. For instance, this failure may be due to the message loss.

As shown in Figure 2 (Part C), the failure controller instantiates the class "*NetworkListener*" to build a list of network listeners where each entry corresponds to a clone in the cloud. It will periodically receive life messages from different clones with equal time intervals through these listeners. Sending regular life messages indicates the smooth functioning of the sender clone.

The failure controller also uses a list that contains timers to compute the reception waiting-time of a life message for each clone. To do that, it must instantiate the "*TimerClone*" class for each created clone. Each timer is reset to zero after regular reception of a life message from the corresponding clone.

As depicted in Figure 3, when a timer expires, a failure event is generated; it will trigger the repair process that calls the cloning engine for creating a new instance of the failed clone in order to reintegrate it into its original group. Thus, all clone parameters saved before the failure must be restored using an "*Input File Stream*".

Collaboration Pattern

The collaboration pattern offers a management protocol for mobile collaborative works in the cloud. Thus, it supports synchronization mechanisms used by each clone to share resources in the cloud. These mechanisms enable reconciliation of divergent copies of resources in a decentralized manner (i.e. without the necessity of central synchronization hosted by a super clone). It is necessary to mention that the collaboration protocol uses an optimistic replication scheme to provide simultaneous access to shared resources. Thus, each user has two copies of the shared resource: the first copy is stored in the mobile device whereas the second one is on the clone. For maintaining the consistency of the shared resources in real time, each clone must be simultaneously synchronized with the other clones and its mobile device. The objective of this pattern is to delegate the maximum of intense tasks (synchronization and communication) to clones of mobile devices.

A. Clone Integration

Context: Newly created clones must be integrated into their collaborative groups. This integration involves acquiring identifiers and communication parameters necessary for clones identification and fulfilment of their collaborative tasks. Collaboration of clones is based on the exchange of requests for manipulating shared resources. Each request consists mainly of an identification part containing the clone and group identifiers and an operation part that is also composed of several fields (e.g. operation type). Additionally, diffusion primitives that are based on a broadcast address through Virtual Private Networks send these requests.

Problem: A deployed clone in the cloud will receive a dynamic IP address that will be assigned to its external interface from a DHCP server with its boot up. The clone and group identifiers and the group broadcast address are stored at the server hosting the cloning protocol. So the clone must be able to autonomously act for requesting these parameters.

Solution: A solution is available through the clone integration component (see Figure 4).

The deployed clone in the cloud is pre-equipped with the required configuration allowing an auto-start of the collaborative application (i.e. collaboration protocol) after the clone boot.

As shown in Figure 4 (part A), methods of the "*IntegrateCloneAndInitialization*" class are used to launch the first tasks performed by a new clone just after its start-up. This includes a call for the cloning manager, the launch of a thread for sending the clone life messages and the start of the network listening

Figure 5. Clone integration

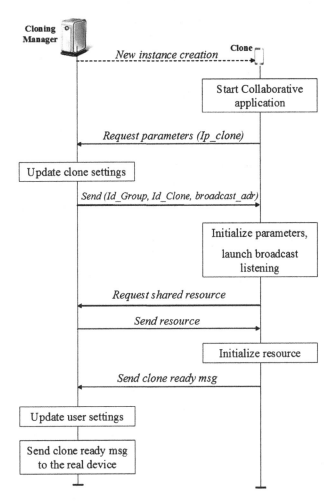

by respectively instantiating the "*CallCloningManager*", "*LifeMessage*", "*BroadcastList*", "*UnicastList*" classes. To better explain this self-mechanism, Figure 5 illustrates the required steps for integrating a new clone that are summarized as follows:

1. *Starting the collaborative application.* The collaborative application is launched automatically with the first boot of the created clone (the new android virtual machine). Then a call of "*Request parameters(IP clone)*" service of the cloning manager is performed. It will request the required parameters for performing different networking primitives. The clone IP-address (of external interface) is passed as parameter with this service call.
2. *Update clone settings.* Following the previous call, the cloning manager will update the Clone IP-address using the address provided by this calling clone. As a result of this call, the clone will receive its unique identifier (*clone-identifier*), the group identifier (*group-identifier*), the broadcast address and the current mobile IP address.
3. *Initialize parameters and launch broadcast listening.* Given the received data, the clone updates the parameters of the collaborative application. The broadcast address will be used to start a thread

for listening messages (containing remote requests) coming from other clones to store them in the request queue. Starting such a listening enables the clone to participate early in the group (by receiving all editing modifications in real-time) while it is fulfilling steps for its complete integration. Next, it will send a message to get the current state of the shared resources.

4. Accordingly, the cloning manager will send to the clone a copy of the shared resources as well as the logs of operation requests (containing all modifications performed on the shared resources before and during the integration of the clone).

5. *Initialize Resource.* After receiving the shared resources and their logs, the clone will integrate remote requests from the request queue to be in phase with the clones of the same group. At this time, the clone is ready to establish direct links that may be internal with other clones of its group or external with its mobile. It will send then a ready message for the cloning manager.

6. *Update user settings.* The cloning manager contacts the mobile user by sending a "*ready msg*" to complete the connection between the user and its clone. The user will call then an authentication service for logging in to its clone. After a successful authentication, the user will receive the clone IP-address. Using this IP address, the user can establish a direct mobile/clone connection to request the current copy of the shared resources.

B. Communication

Context: The collaboration of different users through clones of their mobile devices requires a mechanism for exchanging requests (messages) between the different components of the collaborative system. This communication is considered as a separate package in the collaboration protocol. Each clone uses the package methods for exchanging messages with other clones and with its mobile device and calling the cloning protocol services. Recall that exchanging messages between clones allows the integration of remote requests applied on shared resources. Whereas calling the cloning protocol services allows for clones to receive the required parameters for their collaborative works.

Problem: The collaboration protocol is based on a communication module that should enable a fully decentralized synchronization ("à la peer to peer") without any role assigned to a central server. Further, communication tasks must be optimized (e.g. messages broadcast) in order to avoid overloading of virtual networks and therefore improving response times.

Solution: The use of the communication component allows solving this problem (see Figure 4). This is achieved by implementing network primitives for listening and sending at the same time. As shown in Figure 4 (part B), these communication primitives are provided by implementing the "Communication" interface across the "*NetworkListener*", "*NetworkSender*" and "*CallCloningManager*" abstract classes.

1. Network Listener: using these primitives, clones can continuously listen to the network for receiving messages in two modes:

    a. Broadcast mode, using the "*ClientBroadcastThread*" class for receiving remote requests applied and diffused by other clones. Hereinafter an example of the "*ClientBroadcastThread*" java class that implements the "*Communication*" interface. This allows redefining one of its methods (the "*NetworkBroadcastListener*" method) for listening and receiving in broadcast mode. It should be noted that networks tasks must be launched as thread with android.

```
package Cloud.Collab.Communication;
//Here, instructions to import required java packages
class ClientBroadcastThreadForAndroid implements Communication{

        int PORT; String adr;
     // The constructor
      public ClientBroadcastThreadForAndroid (String adr, int Port){
          //The broadcast listening parameters:
               this.adr=adr;          // Broadcast address
               this.PORT=Port;        // Listening port
      }
     //Redefining the " NetworkBroadcastListener" method of the "communica-
tion" interface
        public void NetworkBroadcastListener() {
           // instantiating the receiver thread
             BroadcastReceiverThreadForAndroid bra=new BroadcastReceiverThr
eadForAndroid(adr,PORT);
           new Thread(bra).start();
        }
    //A subclass for defining a Broadcast receiver thread for android
    class BroadcastReceiverThreadForAndroid implements Runnable{
                    public void run() {
           // Here, instructions for:
           // Initializing the network Broadcast parameters
           // Joining the Broadcast network
           // Define packet for receiving data
           // launching Listening loop
        }
      }
}
```

      b.   *Unicast mode*, using the "*ClientThread*" class for receiving local requests applied by the real device.

2.   Network Sender: allowing each clone to send messages in two modes:

      a.   *Broadcast mode*, using the "*ServerBroadcastThread*" class for broadcasting local requests applied by the clone (and its real device) to all other clones (members of the same group).

      b.   *Unicast mode*, using the "*ServerThread*" class for sending remote requests integrated by the clone to its real device. Bellow an example of the "*ServerThread*" java class that implements the "*Communication*" interface. This allows redefining one of its methods (e.g. "*NetworkUnicastSender*") for sending messages in unicast mode.

```
package Cloud.Collab.Communication;
//Here, instructions to import required java packages
 class ServerThreadForAndroid implements Communication{
        String ipdisp, s;
         int PORT;
        //Constructor
        public ServerThreadForAndroid (String IP, int Port, String str){
            //The sending parameters:
                this.ipdisp=IP;                 //destination ip
                this. PORT=Port;                //Sending port
                this.s=str;                     //message
            }
        //Redefining the "NetworkUnicastSinder" method of the "communication"
interface
        public void NetworkUnicastSender() {
            // instantiating the sending thread
                UnicastSenderThreadForAndroid sth=new UnicastSenderThreadFo-
rAndroid();
                new Thread(sth).start();
            }
        //A subclass for defining a tcp unicast sending thread for android
class UnicastSenderThreadForAndroid implements Runnable {
    @Override
    public void run() {
            // Here, instructions for:
            // Preparing a tcp connection;
            //Sending message.
    }
}
}
```

3. Call cloning protocol: this web service call is necessary for clones to acquiring the required parameters in two cases: integrating their groups after their first creation or following a restoration after failure.

C. Synchronization

Context: A user can at any time connect and manipulate shared resources through the replicas stored at his/her real device. Clones are always online in the cloud and exchange messages between them for integrating remote requests or with their real devices for applying local requests.

Problem: The concurrent accesses to replicas of shared resources may result in inconsistent views at different clones. Furthermore, an offset for applying requests between the clone and the real device is unavoidable; this is another concern for maintaining consistency of shared resources.

Solution: The solution to this problem is the use of any decentralized synchronization technique for maintaining consistency and reconciling the copies divergence (e.g. Operational Transformation approach (Ellis, 1989; Imine, 2009). The decentralization allows avoiding a single point of failure.

The next section will better illustrate a concrete synchronization protocol.

D. Resource Management

Context: Users collaborate to manipulate shared data in a simultaneous manner. These data are stored locally at the real device and its clone.

Problem: Mobile collaborative applications must provide mechanisms to share a variety of data types (resources or files). In addition, the proposed design must be reusable and easily extensible for allowing the integration of new data types with their editing tools.

Solution: Shared Resources Management component (see Figure 4) is used to solve the previous problem. This component allows for instantiating and editing multiple data types (e.g. document, image, table or agenda) through subclasses of an abstract class called "*SharedResource*". The super class uses an interface that includes methods to initialize or update data. As the interface is implemented by a set of classes (grouped in a package) for redefining different methods of this interface, the developer can adapt the redefined methods with the different data types.

Consider the example of a simple text editor. The simple instantiation of a "StringBuffer" variable within a class that implements the "*OperationResourceManager*" interface allows creating a document for containing a linear sequence of characters. Furthermore, the insertion of a character in the text can be done across the class "*InsertIntoDocument*" that implements this interface as follows:

```
package Cloud.Collab.ResourceManager;

class InsertIntoDocument implements OperationResourceManager {
        StringBuffer Doc;
        //constructor
        public InsertIntoDocument(StringBuffer s){
        this.Doc=s;
        }
        //insertion method
        public void Do (StringBuffer s1, int position, char c) {
        s1.insert(position,c);
        }
}
```

MOBILE COLLABORATIVE EDITING APPLICATION

This section shows how the proposed design patterns were reused for the design of a mobile application across a collaborative editing service in the cloud (Guetmi, 2015).

The implemented and validated system consists of two main levels:

1. **Cloning Protocol:** In the one hand, it provides web services that enable users to clone their mobile devices in the VirtualBox hypervisor. On the other hand, it furnishes a pure peer-to-peer virtual private network platform where users can form ad-hoc groups based on their clones to achieve a common goal. This platform is equipped with mechanisms to transparently manage the user departure, the arrival of new users joining the group, the management of failures and the collaboration spots. The two main components of the Cloning protocol are described as follow:

   a. *The Cloning engine*: When a user registers for the first time, the cloning engine builds a new clone for his/her mobile. As only Android-based mobile devices are handled, the cloning process consists of creating a new x86 Android virtual machine as well as its configuration and auto-start. This process consists in: (i) Saving clone parameters: It records information related to the user (username, password, email) and the clone (new clone identifier and IP address that will be provided as parameters for any subsequent use of the web service). Note that, during this step, the user can create a new group or be affiliated to an existing group. (ii) Clone Creation: For each mobile device, it builds a new Android x86 virtual machine using an IZO file by importing a pre-configured virtual machine. This choice is motivated by the fact that the deployment of clones will be easy and very quick. (iii) Clone startup and setting initialization: When the clone starts (i.e. the clone boot), it gets its IP address from a host server and calls the web service to receive the required data for any collaboration such as clone identifier, group identifier, multicast address of the group and the IP address of the mobile. This data is important for the communication and collaboration of mobile-to-clone and clone-to-clone.

   b. *The VPN Builder*: responsible for the preparation of the collaboration platform. To achieve this, two actions are required, namely: the preparation of a Virtual Private Network (VPN), and the integration/collaboration of clones that are members of this network. These actions are described as follows: (i) New group creation: it consists of assigning a new identifier (ID) and a multicast address to a new group and building a new *"Virtualbox host-only network"*. (ii) Clone interfaces configuration: To ensure the communication of clones, two interfaces are required. The first network interface of the created virtual machine (i.e., clone) is associated to a *"host-only network"* gathering clones of the same group. The second interface is associated to a network enabling the access to outside virtual machines (i.e., it handles functions like Network Address Translation and Port Forwarding). Note that a dynamic allocation of IP addresses is enabled on these interfaces.

2. **Cloud Mobile Collaborative Editing Protocol:** The shared document owns a linear data-structure (e.g. a list). This list is a sequence of elements from some data type, such as a character, a paragraph, a page, etc. Two editing operations are used: (i) Ins(p,e) to insert element e at position p; and (ii) Del(p) to remove the element at position p. Inspired from the protocol given in (Imine, 2009) for managing collaborative editing works, called *Optic* (Operational transformation with intensive concurrency), the proposed design patterns are reused in the development of this protocol for coordinating the same works in the cloud. Protocol *Optic* supports an unconstrained editing work. Using optimistic replication scheme (shared documents are replicated at mobiles and their clones), it provides simultaneous access to shared documents. Using operational transformation approach for maintaining consistency, reconciliation of divergent copies is done automatically in decentral-

ized fashion (i.e., without the necessity of central synchronization). Moreover, this protocol is well-suited for peer-to-peer environments as it supports dynamic groups where users can leave and join at any time. As the objective is to delegate the maximum consuming-resources tasks (such as operational transformation and communication) to the cloud, this protocol runs in split mode: the light computing task is executed on mobile device (as front-end) and the heavy computing task is performed on the clone (as back-end).

This protocol consists of three components: (i) the *local state* is the copy of the shared document stored in the clone. It must be the same than those of the mobile; (ii) *Operation log* contains the history of editing operations executed by the clone; (iii) *Operation queue* contains remote editing operations (coming from other clones) that are not causally ready for execution. These components are respectively represented by the "*SharedResource*", "*Log*" and "*Queue*" classes in the presented collaboration pattern (see Figure 4).

Two cases are considered: the receipt of local operation generated by the mobile device and the integration of remote operation coming from another clone.

1. **Receipt of Local Operation:** When the mobile device sends an editing operation to its clone, the editing operation is immediately executed on the clone's local state as if the clone itself generated it. After this step a backward computation is carried out on the operation log to determine the causal order (i.e. the operation that precedes it) for the local operation (*ApplyLocalRequest* class in the collaboration pattern). Note that this causal order must be preserved at all clones. Next, the clone produces a request by wrapping the local operation with some meta-information, such as a unique identifier and the precedent request according to the causal order. ("*GenerateReq*" class in the collaboration pattern). Finally, the request is sent to all other clones (of the same group) in order to be executed ("*CodReq*" and "*ServerBroadcastThread*" classes in the collaboration pattern).

2. **Integration of Remote Operation:** When the clone receives a remote request, it proceeds as follows: firstly, it stores the remote request in the operation queue. This request will be dequeued when it is causally ready ("*CausalReady*" class in the collaboration pattern). When the request is causally ready, a forward computation is carried out on the operation log to maintain the consistency of the shared document. More precisely, using an operational transformation function, the remote request is transformed against all concurrent (or not already seen) requests. The resulting request of the previous step is then executed on the local state and added to the operation log ("*TransformReq*" class in the collaboration pattern). Finally, this request is sent to the mobile device in order to be integrated on the local copy ("*ClientThread*" and "*CodReq*" class in the collaboration pattern).

    a. *Clone-Clone Synchronization:* As seen previously, to converge towards a consistent document, each clone transforms the remote requests against local ones before applying them on its local state. To better understand the role of operational transformation, let consider the following example: Given two clones, CLONE1 and CLONE2, starting from a common state of the document "XYZ". At CLONE1, a mobile user executes op-CLONE1 = Ins(2,A) to insert the character 'A' at position 2 and end up with "XAYZ". Concurrently, a user at CLONE2 performs op-CLONE2 = Del(1) to remove the character 'X' at position 1 and obtain the state "YZ". After the operations are exchanged among CLONE1 and CLONE2, if they are applied naively both clones get inconsistent states: CLONE1 with "AYZ" and CLONE2 with "YAZ". Operational transformation is considered as safe and efficient method for consistency maintenance. In general, it consists of application-dependent transformation algorithm, called IT, such that for every possible pair of concurrent operations, the application programmer has to specify how to integrate these operations regardless of reception order. Thus, at CLONE2, operation op-CLONE1 needs to be transformed to include the effect of op-CLONE2: op-CLONE1' = IT(op-CLONE1, op-CLONE2)=Ins(1,A). As for CLONE1, operation op-CLONE2 is left unchanged. Accordingly, both get the same state "AYZ".

b. *Clone-Mobile Synchronization:* Mobile and its clone are two entities that are physically separated. Therefore, a delay of applying the same operations on both sides with the same state is possible. This may lead to document inconsistency. To overcome this problem, a solution based on distributed mutual exclusion is used between the mobile and its clone ("*HandleTokenSynchronization*" class that implements the "*CloneMobileSynchronization*" interface in the collaboration pattern, see figure 4). The shared document will be considered as a critical section (CS) when the mobile tries to commit/synchronize w.r.t its clone. Only one of them will have the exclusive right to access in synchronizing mode to its document copy. This distributed mutual exclusion protocol is achieved by the exchange of messages (i.e., token). Initially, the mobile device has the right to be the first to commit/synchronize with its clone. Whatever where the exclusive access right is, the mobile device and its clone can edit independently their local copies. The clone continues to receive remote operations from other clones to integrate them later on the local state. At the meanwhile, the mobile user can work on its copy in unconstrained way. But, once she/he decides to synchronize with its clone, all local editing operations are sent to its clone and the exclusive access right is released to enable the clone to start the synchronization with the mobile device. Thus, the clone performs the received operations on its local state, includes by transformation their effects in its local (and not seen by the mobile) operations, and sends the resulting operations to the mobile device in order to integrate them.

APPLYING THE PROPOSED DESIGN PATTERNS

Search and rescue operations in disaster situations own a mobile and collaborative aspect. Mobile devices can play a crucial role in saving human lives. However, any mobile collaborative application usage in such situations must consider the mobile resources limitation and the network connections instability/unavailability.

This section presents a brief description of a real mobile collaborative application based on the proposed design patterns. The "*MobileMapCloud*" application falls within the scope of a project to develop a smart cloud based collaborative system for managing natural disasters and accidents (application under development). This system is intended to be used by structures that manage departments or regions frequently affected by natural disasters. "*MobileMapCloud*" is fully decentralized and allows sharing and manipulating textual and cartographic data as well as multimedia objects (e.g. photos and videos). The purpose is to provide assistance to decision-making in order to properly conduct search and rescue operations. Be noted that the main collaboration actors are not limited in the civil protection staff, any other person may participate but with different rights and roles.

Figure 6. MobileMapCloud application

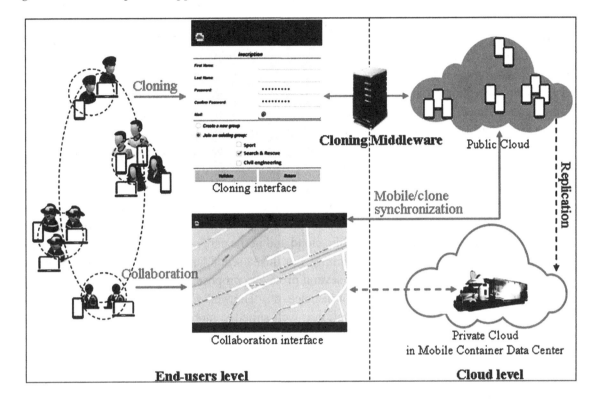

In accordance with the proposed architecture, the implementation of this application makes abstraction of two main services. Figure 6 shows the two main interfaces of the *"MobileMapCloud"* application: the cloning and collaboration services that are described in the following:

1. **Cloning Service:** It is intended to be used by an administrative body that manages a region or department. This service creates a cloud platform composed of virtual networks corresponding to different groups for performing collaborative tasks that requires mobility and displacement (e.g. search and rescue, security and public works). On the other hand, each virtual network consists of a set of virtual machines (clones of users' mobiles). A mobile collaborative application is provided for each group. The *"MobileMapCloud"* application is intended for the "search and rescue" group that is mainly composed of the civil protection, health and police personnel. However, any other person is invited to participate but with lesser roles. Cloning service is offered through a cloning web interface (see Figure 6).

2. **Collaboration Service:** It is accessed through the collaborative web interface of the *"MobileMapCloud"* application (see figure 6). For properly conducting the search and rescue operations, this service provides tools to create, view and share various types of data (e.g. image, text and geographic coordinates) in real time. As shown in figure 6 different tools are accessed through the collaborative interface tool bar. The display and editing tool of interest points (near the current site) is one of the most important.

These interest points can be fixed such as hospitals and police departments or mobile such as fire trucks and ambulances. In addition, another important tool for capturing and sending pictures can significantly improve search and rescue operations. Clones of mobile devices will collaboratively process and group the received photos on the basis of several information (e.g. location, user comments and similarity). These processed photos may be subject to decision-making by other actors. For instance, based on photos collection of an injured person, several doctors can collaborate for sharing and editing a text or even multimedia file for describing preliminary care for this injured person. In all these cited cases, the clones perform all intense tasks for maintaining the consistency of shared resources. This will greatly extend the batteries' life of real mobile devices, and therefore enable their effective and long use in such critical situations.

On the other hand it is important to mention that various telecommunication supports and media cannot be an exception of damages caused by disasters. This can cause a disconnection from the public cloud.

As shown in Figure 6, hybrid system architecture is used to address this problem. "*MobileMapCloud*" application is by default connected to the public cloud and in the case of connection unavailability, it is redirected to a mobile private cloud in the vicinity. For this, a secondary solution consists in acquiring a mobile data center. It should be noted that several providers propose private cloud solutions through data center included in mobile containers. For instance, the "Huawei" Company offers the "IDS1000-A All-in-One Container" Data Center[5], this solution is well-suited to mobile scenarios.

CONCLUSION

The development of collaborative applications is considered as a challenge, since mobile devices are constrained by insufficient resources that must be regarded during design and development phases. However, recent research works on mobile applications design models are not supported by cloud environments. Furthermore, other solutions are intended for the cloud environments without providing a reusable design patterns.

This chapter presented design patterns for modeling mobile collaborative applications in the cloud without neglecting mobile resource limitation constraints. The designed system makes abstraction of two main levels. The first level is the cloning protocol that allows for preparing a platform of mobile clones. This protocol offers web services, where end users can create and control clones of their mobile devices and manage their collaborative groups. The second level is the collaboration protocol that provides mechanisms for achieving collaborative works in the cloud; intense tasks are delegated to the clones of mobile devices.

The next job is to provide a reusable design pattern for security within mobile collaborative applications in the cloud. It consists in designing a model for managing distributed access rights and adding cryptographic mechanisms to ensure maximum security of shared resources.

REFERENCES

Chun, B. G., Ihm, S., Maniatis, P., Naik, M., & Patti, A. (2011, April). Clonecloud: elastic execution between mobile device and cloud. In *Proceedings of the sixth conference on Computer systems* (pp. 301-314). ACM. doi:10.1145/1966445.1966473

Chung, L., & do Prado Leite, J. C. S. (2009). On non-functional requirements in software engineering. In *Conceptual modeling: Foundations and applications* (pp. 363–379). Springer Berlin Heidelberg. doi:10.1007/978-3-642-02463-4_19

Cuervo, E., Balasubramanian, A., Cho, D. K., Wolman, A., Saroiu, S., Chandra, R., & Bahl, P. (2010, June). MAUI: making smartphones last longer with code offload. In *Proceedings of the 8th international conference on Mobile systems, applications, and services* (pp. 49-62). ACM. doi:10.1145/1814433.1814441

Dinh, H. T., Lee, C., Niyato, D., & Wang, P. (2013). A survey of mobile cloud computing: architecture, applications, and approaches. *Wireless Communications and Mobile Computing, 13*(18), 1587-1611.

Ellis, C. A., & Gibbs, S. J. (1989, June). Concurrency control in groupware systems. *SIGMOD Record, 18*(2), 399–407. doi:10.1145/66926.66963

Feldman, A. J., Zeller, W. P., Freedman, M. J., & Felten, E. W. (2010, October). SPORC: Group Collaboration using Untrusted Cloud Resources. In OSDI (Vol. 10, pp. 337-350). OSDI.

Flores, H., & Srirama, S. N. (2014). Mobile cloud middleware. *Journal of Systems and Software, 92*, 82–94. doi:10.1016/j.jss.2013.09.012

Guetmi, N., Mechaoui, M. D., Imine, A., & Bellatreche, L. (2015). *Mobile Collaboration: a Collaborative Editing Service in the Cloud.* ACM. doi:10.1145/2695664.2696021

Herskovic, V., Ochoa, S. F., & Pino, J. A. (2009, April). Modeling groupware for mobile collaborative work. In *Computer Supported Cooperative Work in Design, 2009. CSCWD 2009. 13th International Conference on* (pp. 384-389). IEEE. doi:10.1109/CSCWD.2009.4968089

Herskovic, V., Ochoa, S. F., Pino, J. A., & Neyem, H. A. (2011). The Iceberg Effect: Behind the User Interface of Mobile Collaborative Systems. *J. UCS, 17*(2), 183–201.

Huerta-Canepa, G., & Lee, D. (2010, June). A virtual cloud computing provider for mobile devices. In *Proceedings of the 1st ACM Workshop on Mobile Cloud Computing & Services: Social Networks and Beyond* (p. 6). ACM. doi:10.1145/1810931.1810937

Imine, A. (2009, January). Coordination model for real-time collaborative editors. In Coordination Models and Languages (pp. 225-246). Springer Berlin Heidelberg.

Kosta, S., Perta, V., Stefa, J., Hui, P., & Mei, A. (2013, April). CloneDoc: exploiting the cloud to leverage secure group collaboration mechanisms for smartphones. In *Computer Communications Workshops (IN-FOCOM WKSHPS), 2013 IEEE Conference on* (pp. 19-20). IEEE. doi:10.1109/INFCOMW.2013.6970704

Kosta, S., Perta, V. C., Stefa, J., Hui, P., & Mei, A. (2013, June). Clone2clone (c2c): Peer-to-peer networking of smartphones on the cloud. In *5th USENIX Workshop on Hot Topics in Cloud Computing (HotCloud13).*

Liu, F., Shu, P., Jin, H., Ding, L., Yu, J., Niu, D., & Li, B. (2013). Gearing resource-poor mobile devices with powerful clouds: Architectures, challenges, and applications. *Wireless Communications, IEEE, 20*(3), 14–22. doi:10.1109/MWC.2013.6549279

Marinelli, E. E. (2009). *Hyrax: cloud computing on mobile devices using MapReduce* (No. CMU-CS-09-164). Carnegie-Mellon University.

Neyem, A., Ochoa, S. F., Pino, J. A., & Franco, R. D. (2012). A reusable structural design for mobile collaborative applications. *Journal of Systems and Software*, *85*(3), 511–524. doi:10.1016/j.jss.2011.05.046

Pal, S., & Henderson, T. (2013, September). MobOCloud: extending cloud computing with mobile opportunistic networks. In *Proceedings of the 8th ACM MobiCom workshop on Challenged networks* (pp. 57-62). ACM. doi:10.1145/2505494.2505503

Palmer, N., Kemp, R., Kielmann, T., & Bal, H. (2009, February). Ibis for mobility: solving challenges of mobile computing using grid techniques. In *Proceedings of the 10th workshop on Mobile Computing Systems and Applications* (p. 17). ACM. doi:10.1145/1514411.1514426

Park, S., Chen, Q., Han, H., & Yeom, H. Y. (2014). Design and evaluation of mobile offloading system for web-centric devices. *Journal of Network and Computer Applications*, *40*, 105–115. doi:10.1016/j.jnca.2013.08.006

Samimi, F. A., McKinley, P. K., & Sadjadi, S. M. (2006). Mobile service clouds: A self-managing infrastructure for autonomic mobile computing services. In Self-Managed Networks, Systems, and Services (pp. 130-141). Springer Berlin Heidelberg. doi:10.1007/11767886_10

Sanou. (2014). *The World in 2014: ICT Facts and Figures*. Retrieved from http://www.itu.int/en/ITU-D/Statistics/Documents/facts/ICTFactsFigures2014-e.pdf

Satyanarayanan, M., Bahl, P., Caceres, R., & Davies, N. (2009). The case for VM-based cloudlets in mobile computing. *Pervasive Computing, IEEE*, *8*(4), 14–23. doi:10.1109/MPRV.2009.82

Shiraz, M., & Gani, A. (2014). A lightweight active service migration framework for computational offloading in mobile cloud computing. *The Journal of Supercomputing*, *68*(2), 978–995. doi:10.1007/s11227-013-1076-7

Xia, F., Ding, F., Li, J., Kong, X., Yang, L. T., & Ma, J. (2014). Phone2Cloud: Exploiting computation offloading for energy saving on smartphones in mobile cloud computing. *Information Systems Frontiers*, *16*(1), 95–111. doi:10.1007/s10796-013-9458-1

Xia, H., Lu, T., Shao, B., Ding, X., & Gu, N. (2014, May). Hermes: On collaboration across heterogeneous collaborative editing services in the cloud. In *Computer Supported Cooperative Work in Design (CSCWD), Proceedings of the 2014 IEEE 18th International Conference on* (pp. 655-660). IEEE.

ENDNOTES

1. https://aws.amazon.com/?nc2=h_ls
2. https://www.virtualbox.org/
3. http://www.xenproject.org/
4. http://www.vmware.com/
5. http://e.huawei.com/en/products/network-energy/dc-facilities/ids1000-a

Chapter 4
Estimation for Mobile and Cloud Environments

Frank Vogelezang
Ordina, The Netherlands

Jayakumar Kamala Ramasubramani
Amitysoft Technologies, India

Srikanth Arvamudhan
Amitysoft Technologies, India

ABSTRACT

Estimation of Cost, Effort and Schedule is a very important aspect in commercial software development. Effort is usually the predominant cost driver in software development. The dominant determinant for effort is the size of the software to be developed. There are various ways to determine the size of software. The best option is to use a standardized measure for the functional size. In this chapter the COSMIC method for functional size is introduced. Due to its basic principles, the COSMIC method enables determination of the functional size of mobile and cloud-based applications. This chapter demonstrates how the COSMIC method provides a good basis for the estimation of Cost, Effort and Schedule in mobile and cloud environments.

INTRODUCTION

Estimation of Cost, Effort and Schedule is a very important aspect in commercial software development, since it is used to allocate resources, plan product releases and negotiate payments between suppliers and contractors. In the Software Engineering Body of Knowledge, Estimation is specified as a sub area of Project Planning for the Software Engineering Management knowledge area (IEEE Computer Society, 2014). In software development effort is usually the predominant cost driver. Estimation of Cost and Schedule, however, depends on the estimate of Effort. The dominant determinant for effort is the size of the software to be developed.

DOI: 10.4018/978-1-4666-9916-8.ch004

Copyright © 2016, IGI Global. Copying or distributing in print or electronic forms without written permission of IGI Global is prohibited.

There are various ways to define size, which can be divided into technical and functional size measures. Technical size measures are easy to extract from the software itself, but have proven not to be very accurate predictors for effort estimation (Jones, 2013). In traditional software development a number of so called first generation functional size measurement methods have been developed such as Function Point Analysis, Feature Point Analysis and Use Case Points (Vogelezang, 2013a). These methods were developed empirically and were based on the paradigm of stand-alone applications with limited interactions with other software. This paradigm base leaves them not really suited for mobile and cloud software, with their layered architecture and multi-level interaction with other software components.

The COSMIC method is a second generation functional size measurement method that is based on the idea that software can exist in multiple layers and that moving data from one software component to another is the main predictor for the functional size of software (Vogelezang, 2013b). COSMIC is increasingly recognized for its applicability in estimating the development effort for mobile and cloud solutions involving multilayer and service oriented business applications.

BACKGROUND: FUNCTIONAL SIZE

Organizations engaged in software engineering have struggled for years in search of acceptable quantitative methods for measuring process efficiency and effectiveness, and for managing software costs, for the systems they acquire, develop, enhance or maintain. One critical, and particularly elusive, aspect of this measurement requirement has been the need to determine software size. In 1998, the concept of functional size was defined in an International Standard (ISO, 2007).

Functional size is a measure of the amount of functionality provided by the software, derived by quantifying the user practices and procedures that the software must perform to fulfill the users' needs, independent of any technical or quality considerations. The functional size is therefore a measure of what the software must do, not how it should work. This means that the functional size can be determined before the actual software has been built, and even before there is a final decision on what platform the software will be built and in which programming language.

The concept of functional size is therefore an ideal basis for comparison, either between software with similar characteristics or for cross-platform comparison. These different types of comparison can be useful for development or maintenance benchmarking or to support decisions on platform choices.

Functional Size Measurement

Functional Size Measurement deals with the measurement of functionality to be developed based on requirements for the software. Requirements describe the functionality to be built and certain characteristics of that functionality in order to deliver the software fit for the purpose. ISO has developed a meta standard for functional size measurement methods (ISO, 2007). All methods for functional size measurement must comply with this standard. ISO has recognized the COSMIC method, which is fully compliant with the meta-standard, as a standard for functional size measurement in 2003 (ISO, 2011).

Although the prime objective of the COSMIC method is to measure the functional size, a limited field trial on real-time applications was done to verify whether the COSMIC method was suitable for predicting Effort for specification, build and test, before submitting the method as an International Standard (Abran, 2001). More recently the International Software Benchmarking Standards Group analyzed performance data on 324 business application software projects, 40 real-time software projects and 22 projects that produced software components (ISBSG, 2012). Their conclusion was that the COSMIC benchmark data was self-consistent for all types of projects analyzed and well-suited for both external performance comparisons and for new project estimating. In comparing the data with IFPUG benchmark data the COSMIC method gives more differentiated figures for differing sets of project characteristics.

The COSMIC Method

The COSMIC method made a significant shift from the first generation methods by using a new paradigm and by making use of established software engineering principles. The COSMIC method is a second generation functional size measurement method that is based on the idea that software can exist in multiple layers and that moving data from one software component to another is the main predictor for the functional size of software. The new paradigm ensures that the method can be applied to all software where moving data is the main predictor for the functional size. This means that the COSMIC method can be applied to business application software and real-time software alike, making it a very powerful estimating resource in the mobile and cloud domain. The COSMIC method is maintained by the Common Software Measurement International Consortium.

THE COSMIC MODEL OF SOFTWARE

The COSMIC method regards software as a set of *functional processes* based on the functional user requirements. Users interacting with software across boundary through functional processes are referred as *functional users*. Functional processes do two things: they move *data groups* to and from the functional process and they manipulate data groups within the functional process. Data manipulation is assumed to be accounted for by the movement of the data groups associated with the manipulation.

The movement of a single unique data group to or from the functional process is called *data movement*. Based on the functionality of the process, data groups move between 'user and the software' as well as between the 'software and persistent storage'. The COSMIC method distinguishes four types of data movements (COSMIC, 2015a).

- *Entry* data movements move data into the software from functional users
- *Exit* data movements move data out of the software to functional users
- *Read* data movements move data from persistent storage to the software
- *Write* data movements move data from the software to persistent storage

This is depicted in figure 1.

COSMIC functional size measurement is based on the number of data movements related to functional processes executed by users (figure 2).

The sum of all data movements associated with all functional processes associated with the software is the size of software in *COSMIC Function Points* referred as *CFP*.

Figure 1. The four types of data movements

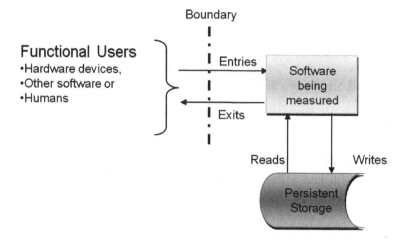

The COSMIC Measurement Process

In order to determine the functional size you need a repeatable process. The COSMIC method has a very well described measurement process (COSMIC, 2015a), consisting of three main steps:

First, it must be defined what will be measured. Therefore there must be agreement on the purpose and the scope of the measurement. This determines who or what are defined as functional users of the software. The next step is to transform the functional description into functional processes and data movements of the COSMIC generic software model.

The final step is the actual measurement. The size of the software is determined by identifying all the data movements (Entries, Exits, Reads and Writes) of each functional process and adding the number of data movements over all the functional processes.

Figure 2. COSMIC generic software model

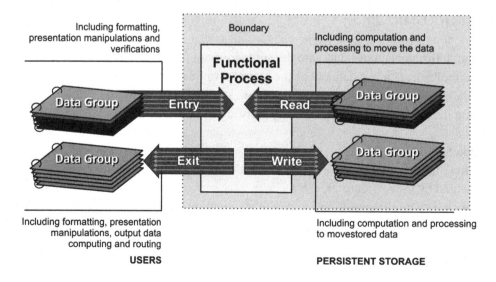

Figure 3. COSMIC measurement process

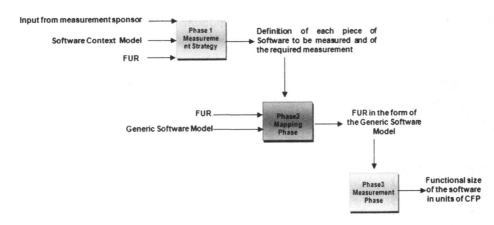

Figure 3 illustrates these steps of COSMIC Measurement process with inputs to and outputs from each of the stages.

The COSMIC Concept of Functional User

One of the key concepts of the COSMIC method is the functional user (COSMIC, 2015a). Functional users can be human beings, software or engineered devices that interact with the software being measured. In general, functional users can be identified as the senders and/or intended recipients of data to and from the software. This can be human users, engineered devices, and peer components on the same platform or external applications on a different platform (figure 4).

Different types of users may require different functionality and therefore functional sizes will vary with the choice of functional users. This is why the measurement strategy is an important step in the measurement process. Thus, COSMIC measure is based on functional user requirements (FUR) as opposed to implementation artifacts or objects. Although COSMIC is the only method that describes such a process, this process is applicable to all kinds of measurement processes.

Figure 4. Functional Users of Software

Figure 5. Three views of Layers

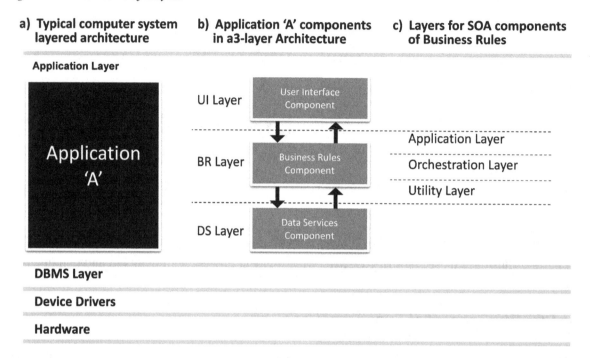

The COSMIC Concept of Layer

COSMIC is the only functional size measurement method to recognize layers according to the standards of software architecture. Functional requirements can be mapped to any layer based on the nature of services provided. Figure 5 provides three views of layers as addressed by (COSMIC, 2015a).

In the first view the application is considered to be a monolith that contains all functionality, with the exception of the database management system, the device drivers and the operating system. This type of architecture is becoming very rare and mostly used for 'quick and trivial' small business software solutions, like temporary MS Access programs.

The most common architecture for software for the networked world using the Internet as back bone is the three layered architecture in which the functional process logic, data access, computer data storage and user interface are developed and maintained as independent modules on separate platforms. Layering is a software design pattern and is well-established software architecture (Janssen, 2014) for building complex software. This architecture allows any one of the layers to be upgraded or replaced independently.

- The user interface component is implemented on the user device and uses the standard graphical user interface of that device.
- The business logic component can be either on the user device (this is very common in mobile applications) or on an application server of a cloud solution or business administrative system.
- The data services component contains the computer data storage logic and is usually located on a data server in the cloud or as a separate part of a business administrative system.

In service oriented architecture, the business logic is split up into services that perform a specific task. The business logic layer itself is divided into multiple-layers. Service oriented architecture, adopted in cloud environment uses this paradigm (COSMIC, 2010).

- The application layer provides specific, limited operations as services. Such services may be regarded as a request/reply mechanism that feeds the user interface or orchestration layer with reusable functionality. Common examples in the application layer are services to create a booking or services to verify the authentication or authorization of the functional user of the user interface component.
- The orchestration layer calls and controls other services to implement a complete (business) process. It handles the communication with multiple application services and/or business services that process a part of the (business) process. Examples of an orchestration are a risk analysis in a mortgage application or a location-based travel advice from a public transportation app.
- The utility layer provides common functionality (business or non-business) independently of, but available to, the other layers or even other applications. Common examples of services in the utility layer are logging and a file parsing API.

Most of the current first generation functional size measurement methods can only deal with the first view presented in the above figure, where the application is considered to be a monolith that contains all functionality. This makes them less powerful for estimating mobile or cloud software. Cloud and mobile software are usually constructed with a design pattern from the second or third view. The different layers are usually developed and maintained as independent modules on separate platforms by separate teams, so they need to be estimated separately (Janssen, 2014).

In COSMIC, sizing and estimation can be performed specific to a layer and hence provides more accurate and useful measures. As the technology for implementing different layers can vary, concerned productivity factors can be used to measure the development effort accurately than using a single productivity factor for the entire application.

The COSMIC method contains a guide that provides a mapping of the COSMIC principles to service oriented architecture. It describes how services and their interactions can be measured to determine the functional size (COSMIC, 2010). The COSMIC method is equipped to measure functional processes that reside in different layers, but use the same stored data, as shown in the figure 6. This is a concept that is not present in any of the first generation functional sizing methods, but very common to cloud and mobile software.

APPLICATION OF THE COSMIC METHOD FOR MOBILE ENVIRONMENTS

Mobile Computing Characteristics

Software operating in Mobile environment can be classified as a hybrid of both real-time and business application types. Operating system and critical components are driven in real-time like any other real-time systems. Mobile Apps built on the top behave like business applications with characteristics specific to mobile environment. Although Mobile apps could be regarded as a modern type of client-

Figure 6. Mapping of COSMIC data movements in a service oriented architecture

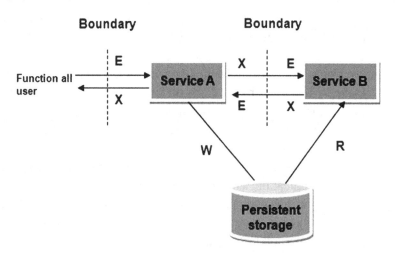

server architecture, they are different from traditional applications, in a number of ways (van Heeringen & van Gorp, 2014).

- The user can interact with the apps in more ways than in traditional applications. For instance, the app can react to changing the position (toggling) of the mobile device, to shaking the mobile device and some apps can accept voice messages.
- Some apps respond to real-time events as well, like moving of the mobile device, switching from Wi-Fi to cellular and back or when the network is out of reach.
- Apps must have functionality that handles interruptions, like an incoming call.
- There are usually important non-functional requirements to which an app should comply, e.g. security, performance, minimum data traffic, space occupied on the device and consumption of battery power.

Mobile Architecture Context

The concept of functional user in COSMIC addresses interactions by users of all types that is present in a mobile environment. Functional Users can be human users, engineered devices, and peer components on the same platform or external applications on a different platform.

In the COSMIC method all functional processes respond to events in the real world. An event is sensed by a functional user. Functional user triggers a functional process. When a sensor detects a condition to which the software must respond sensor becomes the functional user and the triggering event is the condition that the sensor is designed to detect. The triggering entry data movement is the message from the sensor to the software announcing that the event has occurred. The message may also carry data about the triggering event. This is depicted in figure 7 (COSMIC, 2015a).

While the processes in business application software mostly deal with data inputs and outputs, there is significant amount of internal processing in case of mobile applications that is not directly related to the processing of the inputs and outputs, like visualizing in graphs or images or highlighting of certain data, based on processing rules. Any process that has a significant amount of internal processing but little external visibility will not be accredited for the full functionality it delivers, when measured using first generation methods such as IFPUG FPA.

Figure 7. The relationship between events, functional users and functional processes

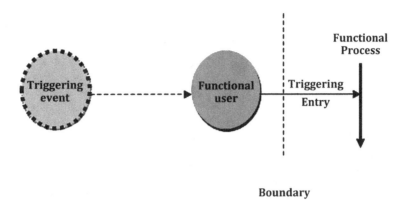

Mobile applications do not have the same emphasis on stored and maintained data as business application software. They connect to cloud or back-office systems and retrieve only the results of the data processing. Internal processes often use real-time information to present the retrieved data in the right context. The data input to the process is not always permanently stored but retrieved externally and used during the concerned process requiring the data. Even when it comes to non real-time applications such as business apps, some data may be stored on the mobile device, but most of the data will be in the cloud or on back-office servers. The exact architecture may vary for each app, but as a general rule mobile apps do not have much emphasis on stored data.

The first generation functional size measurement methods heavily rely on functionality around stored and maintained data. It is not possible to map these first generation methods such as IFPUG function points to a mobile architecture in a natural way where the concept of internal and external files have to be explicitly identified. The COSMIC method directly fits into the needs for sizing and estimation in mobile environment for developing both real-time components and business apps. The COSMIC method only has to know that there is a data source somewhere to retrieve data from. This idea is illustrated in figure 8.

In a mobile app human users communicate with the app by means of Entry and Exit data movements. Typically the app will communicate real-time with peer components on the mobile device also via Entry and Exit data movements. If data needs to be stored on the device the app will communicate with the permanent storage via Read and Write data movements. The app can communicate with an administrative back-end system or with a cloud service via Entry and Exit data movements.

Example of a Banking App

To illustrate the COSMIC method we show a common function of a banking app (figure 9), the transaction overview. This is a basic view functional process:

E Triggering entry
X Request for transaction data to the Orchestrator
E Reception of transaction data
E Reception of Orchestrator error messages
X Show transactions
X Show application error message

Figure 8. Example of data movements in a mobile app

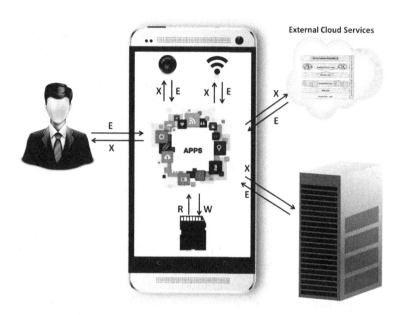

Figure 9. Banking app

This functional process consists of six data movements and thus the functional size of the transaction overview is 6 CFP. This functional process includes the view of all data attributes of a data group that belongs to one object of interest. When tilting the mobile device, more data attributes are shown. This is considered to be the display of the same data group and does not lead to a new functional process. Tilting the device is considered to be a control command within this functional process that is not counted as a separate data movement. For the measurement of the functional size this is similar to the ability to change the view of the displayed data (e.g. by filtering or sorting the data) which also does not lead to the identification of additional data movements (van Heeringen & van Gorp, 2014).

The transaction overview is only the app functionality. To be able to present the user of this app with his or her financial transactions this is not the only functionality that needs to be developed to make the app work. As stated before, COSMIC functional size is counted per architecture layer. In this case the relevant part of the full architecture of the bank is shown in the figure below (Figure 10).

The app sends the request to the Mobile Request Orchestrator component in the Business Rules layer. The Orchestrator verifies with the Mobile Authorization component that the mobile device is authorized to receive financial transactions. When the device is authorized, the Orchestrator requests the transaction data from the Mobile Transaction Data Engine and sends them back to the App. When either the authorization fails, or there is no transaction data available. The Mobile Transaction Data Engine is an exact copy of the financial transactions in the Private Accounts Administration that only holds the data attributes that will be used on mobile devices. The Private Accounts Administration is not capable to service the number of requests from mobile devices, therefore the Data Engine component is introduced in the bank's architecture.

For the transaction overview, functional processes in all components shown in the figure above are necessary:

Figure 10. Essential elements of the banking architecture that support the Mobile App

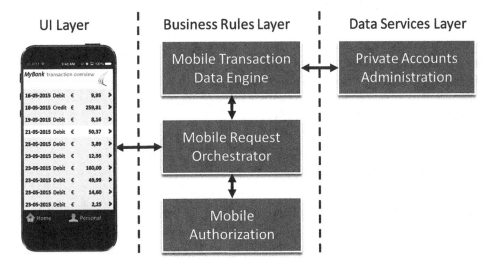

Mobile Request Orchestrator

Generate Transaction Overview Functional Process

E Request for transaction data from the Transaction overview*(triggering Entry)*
X Authorization request to the Mobile Authorization component
E Reception of Mobile Authorization information
E Reception of Mobile Authorization error message
X Request for transaction data to the Mobile Transaction Data Engine
E Reception of transaction data from the Mobile Transaction Data Engine
E Reception of Mobile Transaction Data error message
X Send transaction data to the App
X Send error messages to the App
9 CFP

Mobile Authorization

Authorize Requesting Device Functional Process

E Authorization request from the Mobile Request Orchestrator *(triggering Entry)*
R Verifying whether the requesting device is authorized
W Storing the timestamp of the authorization request *(when authorized)*
X Send authorization message to the Mobile Request Orchestrator
X Send error message to the Mobile Request Orchestrator
5 CFP

Mobile Transaction Data Engine

Transaction Overview Functional Process

E Transaction Data request from the Mobile Request Orchestrator *(triggering Entry)*
R Retrieving transaction data from the Data Engine
W Storing the timestamp of the latest retrieved transaction
X Send transaction data to the Mobile Request Orchestrator
X Send error message to the Mobile Request Orchestrator
5 CFP

Mobile Transaction Data Engine

Transaction Data Update Functional Process

E Transaction data update file from the Data Service layer *(triggering Entry)*
W Storing transaction data to the Data Engine
W Storing the timestamp of the latest retrieved transaction

X Send completion message (error or OK) to the Data Service Layer
4 CFP

Private Accounts Administration

Transaction Data Extract Copy Functional Process

E Completion message from the Business Rules layer *(triggering Entry)*
R Reading the latest timestamp (on OK) or the previous (on error)
R Retrieving transactions after the latest timestamp for the extract copy
W Storing the timestamp of the latest retrieved transaction
X Send transaction data extract copy to the Business Rules layer
5 CFP

The 6 CFP functional process of the Transaction overview in the App, thus makes use of four functional processes in the Business Rules layer of 23 CFP in total and one functional process in the Data Services layer of 5 CFP. Functional size measures from different layers should never be combined (COSMIC, 2010).

This example illustrates that it is important to know whether the infrastructure to supply the required data for the App is already available. The App functionality is only 6 CFP, but the infrastructure in the Business Rules layer and Data Services layer is an additional 23 and 5 CFP, respectively. This does not only increase the functional size, but different layers usually require different skills to implement the functionality.

The example works with a 3-layer architecture (figure 5b) in order to be able to meet the requirements for the transaction volume. In case a SOA architecture would have been chosen (figure 5c) the *Generate Transaction overview* functional process would have been in the Orchestration layer, the *Transaction overview* functional process in the Application layer and the *Authorize requesting device* and the *Transaction data update* functional processes in the Utility layer.

This illustrates that the choice for a layer structure does not influence the total functional size, but only the distribution over the different layers. This is not only relevant for Mobile environments, but also for cloud environments, because when you look at the complete architecture, you can see that there is a large overlap between the Mobile environment shown in the example and a basic cloud architecture (see also figure 8).

APPLICATION OF THE COSMIC METHOD FOR CLOUD ENVIRONMENTS

Cloud Computing Characteristics

Cloud computing is a model for enabling ubiquitous, convenient, on-demand network access to a shared pool of configurable computing resources (e.g., networks, servers, storage, applications, and services) that can be rapidly provisioned and released with minimal management effort or service provider interaction. This cloud model is composed of five essential characteristics, three service models, and four deployment models. (NIST, 2011). Cloud resources are usually not only shared by multiple users but are also dynamically reallocated per demand. With cloud computing, multiple users can access a single server to retrieve and update their data without purchasing licenses for different applications. Cloud computing allows enterprises to get their applications up and running faster, with improved manageability and less maintenance, and enables IT to more rapidly adjust resources to meet fluctuating and unpredictable business demand. The present availability of high-capacity networks, low-cost computers and storage devices were the essential preconditions that have led to the emergence of cloud computing (figure 11).

The cloud environment is characterized by the following:

- High speed network access promoting use of heterogeneous platforms.
- Resource pooling building economies of scale.
- Multi-tenancy enables sharing of resources and costs across a large pool of users.
- On demand self-services provided without requiring human interaction.
- Elasticity allowing applications to scale rapidly, based on actual demand of service.
- Reliability by using multiple sites, providing business continuity and easy disaster recovery.
- Measured service enabling transparency in IT expenditure based on actual usage.
- Can be linked to large data warehouse solutions for big data applications.

Figure 11. COSMIC measurement patterns for cloud software

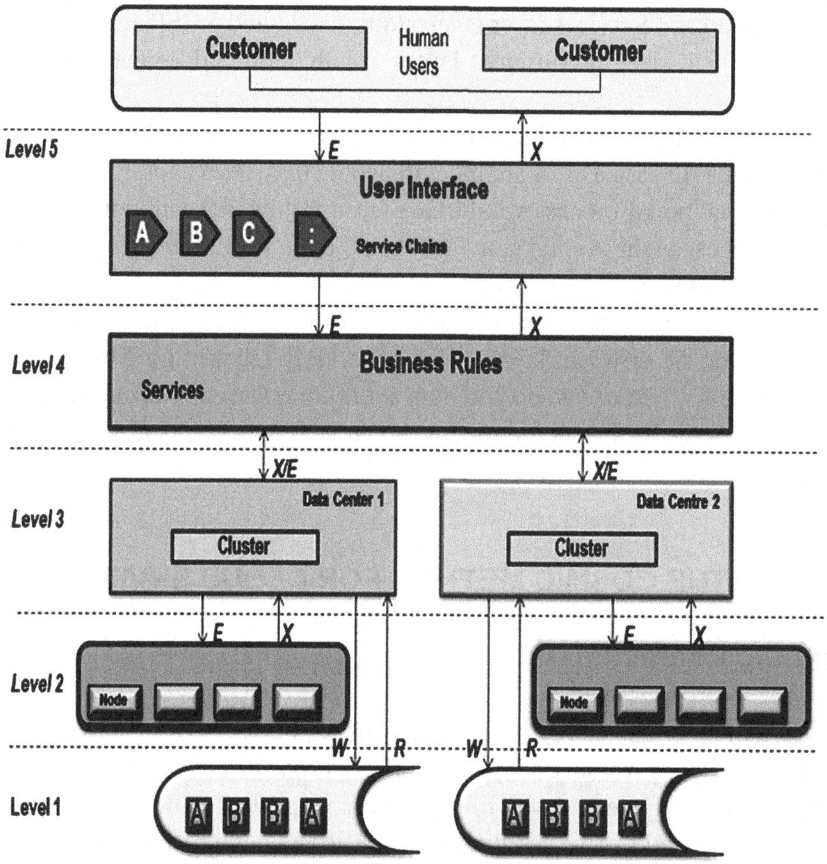

The computing stack of cloud software is made up of the following software paradigms:

- Virtualization, the main enabling technology to make cloud software independent of the actual hardware platforms behind.
- Service oriented architecture, to break the business processes into services that can be wired together and consumed according to the need.
- Programmable API's, to provide the ability to interact with the available cloud services, independent of the connecting device of the user (PC, tablet or mobile phone).
- Management layer, providing real-time insight in the actual use of services for management and billing.

In 2013 German researchers proposed an architecture to describe the different levels of functionality involved in cloud software (Schmietendorf, 2013). This Cloud Systems Architecture consists of five levels of functionality:

Level 1: represents the different machines (whether virtualized or not) producing a service. These machines have a priority corresponding to the criticality of the outage.
Level 2: maps the factor of clustering on a machine level while not all machines and role types are necessarily clusterable. On these both levels different severities of events and incidents (log, replication, capacity information etc.) can occur.
Level 3: consolidated the datacenter level representing the aspects of multiple redundancies on physical hosting level (such us twin or triple core datacenter approaches) where services are produced in full redundancy. Is one datacenter fully - or a service hosted there partially failing - a failover in real-time is initiated without any service and user impact. For these three levels providers set certain Operation Level Agreements to ensure their Service LevelAgreements.
Level 4: finally constitutes the Service Level over all complex alignment underneath where only a well-founded Customer Business Impact can be determined. In addition this determination will be automatically on a sound model and algorithm instead of manual interpretation.
Level 5: shows the layer of service chains which is an important level for customers if business is distributed through the cloud and different service providers for example.

From a user's point of view, there may not be much difference in functionality between on-premise traditional software and similar cloud functionality. Cloud applications function in the above ecosystem and their functionality needs to be designed and built accordingly, especially on the levels below the top level. Many functional requirements for the traditional computing models need to be examined and reformed for deployment on a cloud. Therefore, the Functional User Requirements of the cloud system can be characterized in the following general manner (Schmietendorf, 2013):

Level 1: The physical services constitute the functional processes by SOA architecture, including their Business Impact constraints (infrastructure (de-)provisioning request, withdraw of Virtual Machines, storage, network bandwidth / IO, CPU, memory)
Level 2: The clustered services constitute the functional processes by SOA architecture, including their Business Impact constraints (service (de-) provisioning and requests (CRUD (Create, Read, Update, Delete) and incident, problem, and change requests)

Level 3: The hosted services that build the functional processes by SOA architecture, including the constraints by the Operation Level Agreement to ensure their Service Level Agreements

Level 4: The provided services constitute the functional processes by SOA architecture including their Business Impact constraints (Sarbanes-Oxley Audit & Log Requests)

Level 5: The required services are the functional processes by users including their Service Level Agreement constraints of usability and kind of paying (Live, Realtime Information of fulfillment KPIs)

The following figure describes the generic COSMIC software model for the proposed Cloud Systems Architecture using the appropriate COSMIC patterns above.

Applications in the cloud range from simple personal applications, that can be accessed by mobile apps for instance, to very complex enterprise class applications with users across the globe. Applications often combine real-time and business applications data as generated by internet of people, things and machines thus requiring engineering methods to scope and model the functional data across domains and devices in a standardized manner.

Many types of cloud applications evolve very rapidly with the continuous discovery of new use cases based on usage patterns/feedback by functional users or often through social media across the globe. This requires scientific methods that can quickly map the scope and measure the changes in a consistent and practical manner which is acceptable to and understandable for all stakeholders, from customer super users and management sponsors to technical software engineering staff. This is where a functional size Measurement method as the COSMIC method can play a vital role.

Figure 12 depicts a typical cloud application and its SOA ecosystem on the Internet. The COSMIC data movements E – Entry, R – Read, W – Write and X – eXit that contribute to "FUR" in different layers and interfaces are clearly identifiable using the Measurement Strategy and COSMIC Generic Software Model. It is important to recognize that these "data movements" are functional in nature and visible to the functional user in that scope of sizing.

Cloud Architecture Context

Cloud applications use distributed service-oriented architectures with functional requirements crossing one or more application boundaries to use web services in specific ways required by different users/applications. The architecture typically involves multiple components communicating with each other over a loose coupling mechanism such as a messaging queue. Because of the elastic provision, the architecture must contain intelligence in the coupling mechanisms. Theyalso use different data exchange formats across different layers of the solution. Software components process different data types and data entities at different layers. Multi-tenancy brings in software requirements that are unique to cloud-solutions.

Often cloud application development teams consist of multiple distributed sub-teams focusing on some layer, component or specific service. Productivity of different teams working on different layers/ component using different technologies will vary and thus require estimation of efforts at any layer/ level of components. Quick reliable estimation of small enhancements to very big enhancements across distributed service oriented architecture should be possible.

Figure 12. Context of cloud applications

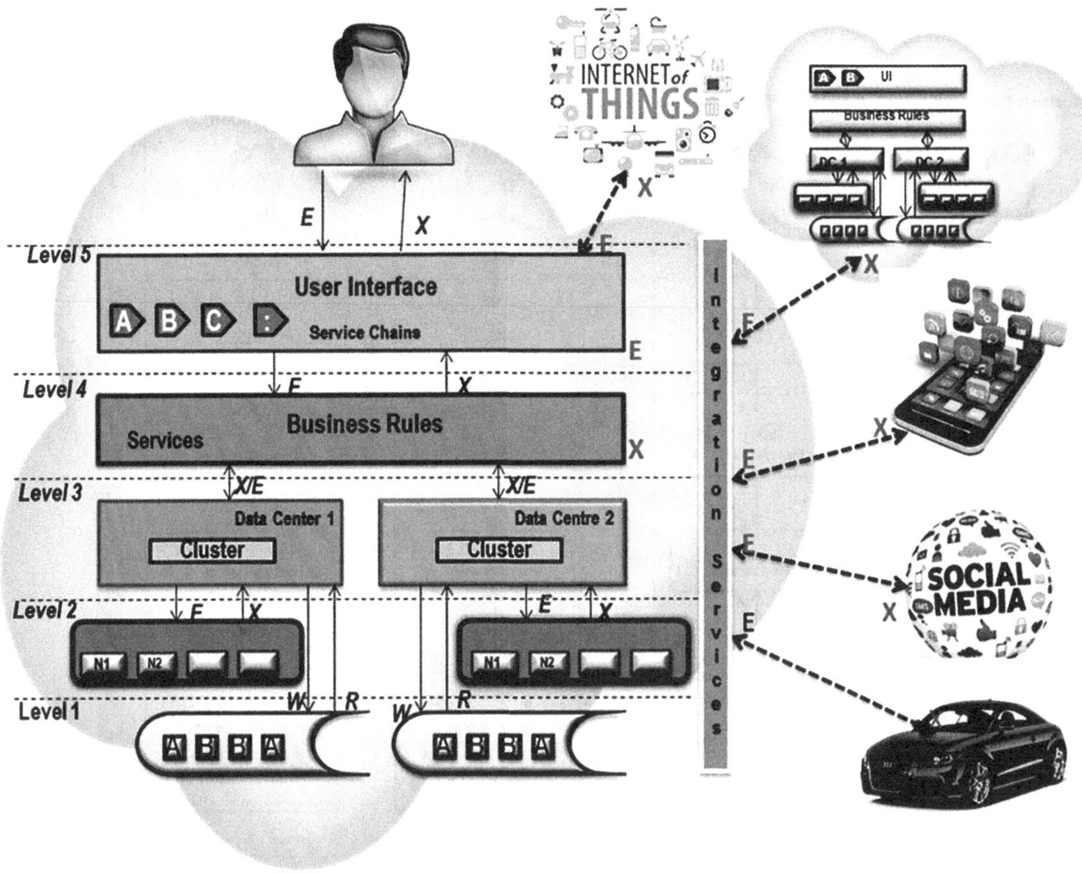

Applying COSMIC in Cloud Usage Contexts

There can be multiple scenarios that can be visualized for cloud applications as illustrated in figure 13 and corresponding data movements can be measured using COSMIC for the purpose of sizing.

Context A: UR within the scope of business process A. This particular interaction does not require any functionality from any other layer or component. Though it may have its mini data-store with work-flow rules, parameters and settings.

Context B: FUR generated at the application user level involves implementing functional changes to hosted service "2" and clustered service CS 2 This enables the measurer(s) to clearly scope out the sizing instance applicable to their functional changes at their level in the cloud stack, and draw interaction boundaries to identify triggering events and functional users at different levels.

Context C: FUR includes intra component data-movements between CS2 and CS3 as well as the related Business Process B, Hosted Service 3 and Data Component D5. This illustrates the application of COSMIC to horizontal movements between components (on two nodes) within the same Cluster

Figure 13. Example of data movements in cloud software

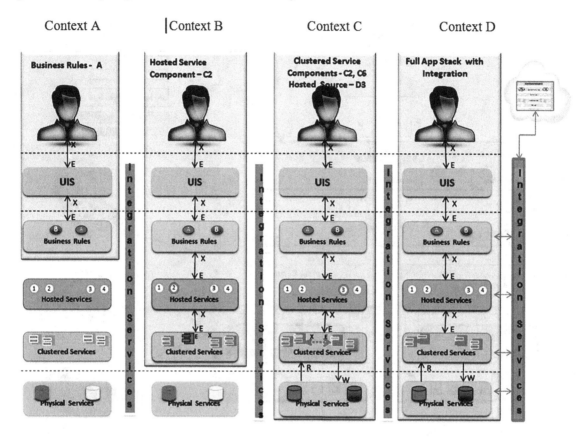

CS. These cluster service components may be developed by different teams using different technologies at the same level of abstraction.

Context D: FUR involves the user using an external cloud application thru the Integration Service component I6 and the related data movements of the full application stack where each layer interacts independently with the integration layer. This illustrates the application of COSMIC in various hybrid-cloud Enterprise applications integration scenarios.

ESTIMATION OF COST, EFFORT AND SCHEDULE

As already mentioned, the estimation of cost, effort and schedule is a very important aspect in commercial software development projects, since it is used to allocate resources, plan product releases and negotiate payments between suppliers and contractors. In software development projects, effort is the most dominant parameter for determining cost and schedule. Therefore, estimation of cost, effort and schedule are very closely linked. The most significant input for the estimation of effort, and thus cost and schedule, is the size of the software to be developed.

The relation between size and effort is the productivity. Productivity is the number of size units that can be produced per unit of time, for example CFP/person day. Productivity is dependent on a number of factors, like the programming language, development platform, team experience and organization maturity. The factors that determine or influence productivity have been extensively studied and have led to the COCOMO family of models that predict productivity in various areas of software engineering (Boehm, 1981). Most of today's estimating tools use some descendent of the COCOMO family. Because of the more convenient numbers often the inverse of productivity, product delivery rate, is used to report on productivity figures. The most common unit for product delivery rate is hr/CFP. Note that a higher number of hours per COSMIC function point means worse productivity. For a given productivity, the relationship between size, effort and schedule is governed by Brooks' law (Brooks, 1995). Brooks was the first to describe that productivity was not a fixed figure, but in fact a function of time pressure. Brooks' law is therefore also known as the time/effort trade-off.

In figure 14, this trade-off is depicted from the top left, to the bottom right (Ross, 2005). Each point on the line represents a situation where all factors determining and influencing productivity are the same, except for the required schedule (Putnam & Myers, 2003). When the productivity increases, the trade-off will shift towards the lower left corner. When the productivity decreases, the trade-off will shift towards the upper right corner. Brooks' law explains that projects that are put under time pressure (moving to the left in the figure) require more effort, and hence cost more. This effect is caused by the fact that activities that ideally are executed by the same person in sequence now must be done by different people in parallel. This increases the amount of people needed to staff the project and increases the time to coordinate the parallel activities (Galorath & Evans, 2006).

Brooks did not define any boundaries to this effect. In theory that would mean that when we can wait long enough, projects would require almost no effort. In reverse, when we have enough resources, projects could be finished in a day. Paul Masson developed a function that determined for every project the minimum time in which a project can be finished (Jensen, 2006). The point where the Masson function intersects with Brooks' law is the minimal time in which a project of a given size with a given

Figure 14. Relations governing parametric estimation of cost, effort and schedule

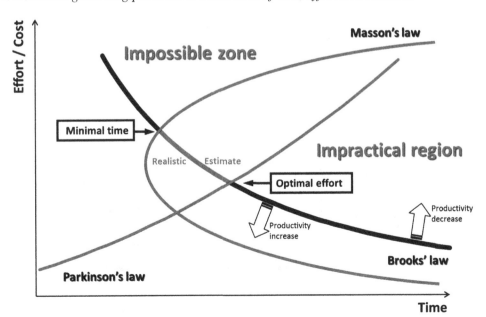

productivity setting can be realized. The area outside the Masson function is known as the impossible zone. This is consistent with the analysis done on 6,300 projects a few years earlier, where no project was found that was finished before the minimum development time (Putnam & Myers, 2003). Finishing the project earlier than that intersection is only possible when a higher productivity can be achieved, or when the scope of the project is decreased significantly.

There is also a maximum to the economically realistic schedule for a project to finish. Beyond a certain point a project will not require less effort. This point is governed by Parkinson's law. Parkinson's law was first stated by Cyril Northcote Parkinson as a part of a humorous essay published in The Economist in 1955: *Work expands so as to fill the time available for its completion*. A few years later the essay was expanded to a full book and the law entered the world of serious economic principles (Parkinson, 1957). Creating a schedule beyond the intersection of Brooks' law and Parkinson's law will not lead to less effort for the project to complete. So the intersection of these laws is the point where the project can be realized with the economically optimal amount of effort. Any point between the intersection of Brooks' law with the laws of Paul Masson and Parkinson is considered a realistic estimate.

The effect of this trade-off was demonstrated in an experience report in 2011 for a 500 CFP Java project (van Heeringen, 2011).The productivity to build this application can be anything between 0.11 CFP/hr and 0.20 CFP/hr, depending only on the chosen duration of the project, all other variables remaining constant (figure 15).

The size of software in COSMIC FP can be used to estimate the cost, effort and schedule by building parametric models based on the above rules. Best practice for building such parametric models is to build them based on internal data of the organization (Abran, 2015). As a quick start, benchmark reports based on COSMIC FP from the International Software Benchmarking and Standards Group can be used to populate the first version of an estimating model (ISBSG, 2012). COSMIC measures have been successfully used with estimation models based on Regression Analysis, Estimation by Analogy, COCOMO and Putnam Norden Rayleigh. COSMIC size based estimation models can be used to estimate efforts for full life cycle of software development or any major life cycle activities such as Testing (Kamala Ramasubramani & Abran, 2013).

Figure 15. Time-effort trade-off for a 500 CFP Java project

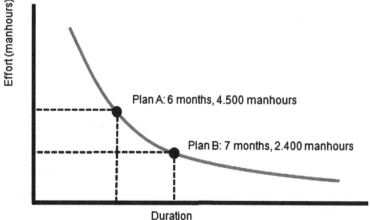

COSMIC can also be used in software development projects using Agile approaches (COSMIC, 2011). In 2014 PhD research in the remote surveillance industry showed that the inaccuracy of effort estimation for Agile projects could be reduced from 58%, based on the Planning Poker technique, to 16.5%, based on COSMIC (Commeyne, 2014). Similar results, although more qualitative in nature, have been reported by an Australian risk broker (Dekkers, 2014).

The most important application of the COSMIC method is (supplier) cost management for software development and maintenance. The COSMIC organization maintains a list of known users of the method (COSMIC, 2015b). Most of the companies on that list use the method for cost management. Only a few of them have reported their success in the use of the COSMIC method in detail, for example in the financial (Vogelezang & Lesterhuis, 2003) and automotive industry (Stern, 2010 & Oriou, 2014).

Another application of the COSMIC method is the estimation of software code size. This application is particularly useful for embedded mobile applications that must be fit on ROM memory into products with high cost pressure, like in-car software systems and electronic control units (Lind & Heldal, 2011). Researchers from the Swedish car industry showed that it is possible to estimate the code size within 15% accuracy. This makes it possible to implement the software into the smallest possible memory product.

FUTURE RESEARCH DIRECTIONS

The COSMIC method is getting wider recognition and its usage for various environments is evolving. The original basic principles of the COSMIC method have remained unchanged since they were first published in 1999. Due to various refinements, clarifications and additions the method has now progressed up to version 4.0.1 (COSMIC, 2015a). The documentation structure of the method is such that guides are issued to provide special guidance for specific topics. The guidance that may be needed to apply the COSMIC method on mobile and cloud software is currently addressed in guides on service oriented architecture, real-time software and agile software development. Currently a number of case studies are under development from the mobile community.

One of the subjects that requires further research is early size estimation. Especially mobile and cloud software is evolving rapidly. Estimates of cost, effort and schedule are needed faster and earlier and thus it must be possible to produce the underlying size estimates based on global specifications. A number of approximation techniques have already been developed and a guide how to apply them is expected in 2015. Some of these techniques need to be fully tested in practice, some have not been tested yet in the mobile and cloud domain.

Another major subject, not only in mobile and cloud software, but in software development and maintenance in general, is the impact of non-functional requirements. Experience of IBM's Event-driven Decision & Smart Mobile Platforms department has shown that non-functional requirements in spatio-temporal aware services represent more than 50% of the effort to produce services (IBM Research, 2014). Late 2015, a joint initiative of COSMIC and IFPUG led to a classification of different types of non-functional requirements and project constraints that can be used to estimate Cost, Effort and Schedule (COSMIC & IFPUG, 2015).

CONCLUSION

The COSMIC method has proven its applicability in mobile environments and is gaining acceptance for estimating software development in cloud environments. The method has been accepted as International Standard, recognized as a technology independent measure for the functional size of software. The COSMIC method can be used by procurement and contract managers to select a supplier and control supplier performance. COSMIC can be used by investors to decide on the cost/benefit analysis for new projects and for valuing software assets. The COSMIC method is an independent size measure that can be used by Project Managers for estimating, project scheduling and controlling scope creep in projects. Response from the users of COSMIC reveal that requirements become unambiguous, traceable and testable when COSMIC is used for sizing, resulting in improved customer satisfaction.

Major Advantages of the COSMIC Method Are:

- Early size approximation, as a basis for the estimation of cost, effort and schedule early in the development lifecycle.
- Applicable in layered and distributed architecture.
- Applicable to different types of software (components) in different architectural layers.
- Suitable for different types of applications (transactional, real-time, data warehouse).
- Technology and platform independent.
- Applicable for linear, iterative and agile software development methodologies.
- Open standard, conformant to the ISO meta standard for functional size measurement.
- Supported by a world-wide community of volunteers.

ABOUT COSMIC

COSMIC is a voluntary, not-for-profit organization of software metrics experts, representing both industry practitioners and academics, from over twenty countries around the world. COSMIC was founded in 1998. All its publications are 'open' and available for free distribution subject to copyright and acknowledgement restrictions.

The principles of the COSMIC method were laid down in 1999 after which field trials were conducted during 2000 – 2001 with several international companies and academic institutions before announcing the method. ISO adopted COSMIC as an International Standard and announced it as ISO/IEC 19761 in 2003. Currently the Measurement Manual v4.0.1 serves as the reference for COSMIC Measurement (COSMIC, 2015a). A number of additional documents to support the method have been published and can be downloaded free of charge (COSMIC, 2014).

REFERENCES

Abran, A. (2015). *Software Project Estimating: The fundamentals for providing high quality information to decision makers*. Hoboken, NJ: John Wiley & Sons.

Abran, A., Symons, C. R., & Oligny, S. (2001). An overview of COSMIC field trial results. In *Proceedings of the 12th European Software Control and Metrics conference.*

Boehm, B. W. (1981). *Software Engineering Economics.* Upper Saddle River, NJ: Prentice Hall PTR.

Brooks, F. P. Jr. (1995). *The Mythical Man-Month.* Boston, MA: Addison-Wesley Longman Publishing.

Commeyne, C. (2014). *Établissement d'un modèle d'estimation a posteriori de projets de maintenance de logiciels.* (PhD thesis). École de Technologie Supérieure, Montréal, Canada.

Common Software Measurement International Consortium. (2010). *Guideline for Sizing Service Oriented Architecture Software.* Montréal, Canada.

Common Software Measurement International Consortium. (2011). *Guideline for the use of COSMIC FSM to manage Agile projects.* Montréal, Canada.

Common Software Measurement International Consortium. (2012). *Guideline for Sizing Real-time Software.* Montréal, Canada.

Common Software Measurement International Consortium. (2014). *Publications.* Retrieved May 20, 2015, from http://cosmic-sizing.org/publications

Common Software Measurement International Consortium. (2015a). Measurement Manual (version 4.0.1). Montréal, Canada.

Common Software Measurement International Consortium. (2015b). *Usage of the COSMIC method.* Retrieved May 20, 2015, from http://cosmic-sizing.org/cosmic/usage/

Common Software Measurement International Consortium & International Function Point User Group. (2015). *Glossary of terms for Non-Functional Requirements and Project Requirements used in software project performance measurement, benchmarking and estimating.* Montréal, Canada: Author.

Dekkers, C. (2014). *Function Points and Agile Development... Considerations and Opportunities.* Retrieved May 20, 2015, from https://www.linkedin.com/grp/post/2758144-5904564005854285828

Galorath, D. D., & Evans, M. W. (2006). *Software Sizing, Estimation, and Risk Management.* Boca Raton, FL: Auerbach Publications. doi:10.1201/9781420013122

IBM Research. (2014). *SaS hub non-functional requirements.* Retrieved May 20, 2015, from https://www.research.ibm.com/haifa/projects/software/nfr/index.html

Institute of Electrical and Electronics Engineers Computer Society. (2014). *Guide to the Software Engineering Body of Knowledge (version 3.0).* Washington, DC: IEEE.

International Organization for Standardization. (2007). *Information Technology – Software Measurement – Functional Size Measurement. International Standard ISO/IEC 14143:2007.* Geneva, Switzerland: ISO.

International Organization for Standardization. (2011). *Software Engineering – COSMIC – A Functional Size Measurement Method. International Standard ISO/IEC 19761:2011.* Geneva, Switzerland: ISO.

International Software Benchmarking and Standards Group. (2012). *The Performance of Real-time, Business and Component Software Projects – An analysis of COSMIC measured projects in the ISBSG database*. Balaclava, Australia: ISBSG.

Janssen, C. (2014). *Three-Tier Architecture*. Retrieved May 20, 2015, from http://www.techopedia.com/definition/24649/three-tier-architecture

Jensen, R. W., Putnam, L. H. Sr, & Roetzheim, W. (2006). Software estimating models: Three viewpoints. *Crosstalk*, *2*, 23–29.

Jones, C. (2013). *A short history of the Lines of Codes (LoC) metric*. Retrieved May 20, 2015, from http://namcookanalytics.com/a-short-history-of-the-lines-of-code-loc-metric

Kamala Ramasubramani, J., & Abran, A. (2013). A survey of Software Test Estimation Techniques. *Journal of Software Engineering and Applications*, *6*(10), 47–52. doi:10.4236/jsea.2013.610A006

Lind, K., & Heldal, R. (2011). A model-based and automated approach to size estimation of embedded software components. In *Proceedings of the 14th international conference on Model Driven Engineering Languages and Systems (MODELS)*. Wellington, New Zealand: Springer Verlag. doi:10.1007/978-3-642-24485-8_24

National Institute of Standards and Technology. (2011). *The NIST Definition of CloudComputing*. Retrieved May 20, 2015 from http://csrc.nist.gov/publications/nistpubs/800-145/SP800-145.pdf

Oriou, A., Bronca, E., Bouzid, B., Guetta, O., & Guillard, K. (2014). Manage the automotive embedded software development cost & productivity with the automation of a functional size measurement method (COSMIC). In *Proceedings of the Joint Conference of the 24th International Workshop on Software Measurement (IWSM) and the 9th International Conference on Software Process and Product Measurement (Mensura)*. Rotterdam, The Netherlands: IEEE Computer Society Conference Publishing Services.

Parkinson, C. N. (1957). Parkinson's law, or the pursuit of progress. Cutchogue, NY: Buccaneer Books.

Putnam, L. H., & Myers, W. (2003). *Five Core Metrics: The intelligence behind successful software management*. New York, NY: Dorset House Publishing.

Ross, M. A. (2005). *Parametric project monitoring and control: performance-based progress assessment and prediction*. Retrieved May 20, 2015, from http://www.dtic.mil/ndia/2005cmmi/wednesday/ross3.pdf

Schmietendorf, A., Fiegler, A., Neumann, R., Wille, C., & Dumke, R. R. (2013). COSMIC Functional Size Measurement of Cloud Systems. In *Proceedings of the Joint Conference of the 23rd International Workshop on Software Measurement (IWSM) and the 8th International Conference on Software Process and Product Measurement (Mensura)*. Ankara, Turkey: IEEE Computer Society Conference Publishing Services. doi:10.1109/IWSM-Mensura.2013.15

Stern, S., & Guetta, O. (2010). Manage the automotive embedded software development cost by using a Functional Size Measurement Method (COSMIC).In *Proceedings of the 4thEmbedded Real Time Software and Systems conference*. Toulouse, France: ERTS2.

van Heeringen, H. S. (2011). Estimate faster, cheaper... and better! In *Proceedings of the 8th Software Measurement European Forum*. Rome, Italy.

van Heeringen, H. S., & van Gorp, E. W. M. (2014). Measure the functional size of a mobile app using the COSMIC functional size measurement method. In *Proceedings of the Joint Conference of the 24*th *International Workshop on Software Measurement (IWSM) and the 9*th *International Conference on Software Process and Product Measurement (Mensura)*. Rotterdam, The Netherlands: IEEE Computer Society Conference Publishing Services. doi:10.1109/IWSM.Mensura.2014.8

Vogelezang, F. W. (2013a). *The first generation of Functional Size Measurement*. Retrieved May 20, 2015, from http://thePriceofIT.blogspot.nl/2013/01/the-first-generation-FSM.html

Vogelezang, F. W. (2013b). *What is a second generation FSM method*. Retrieved May 20, 2015 from http://thepriceofit.blogspot.nl/2013/02/second-generation-FSM.html

Vogelezang, F. W., & Lesterhuis, A. (2003). Applicability of COSMIC in an administrative environment - Experiences of an early adopter. In *Proceedings of the 13*th *International Workshop on Software Measurement*. Montréal, Canada: Shaker Verlag.

ADDITIONAL READING

Abran, A. (2015). *Software Project Estimating: The fundamentals for providing high quality information to decision makers*. Hoboken, NJ: John Wiley & Sons.

Dumke, R. R., & Abran, A. (2011). *COSMIC function points: theory and advanced practices*. Boca Raton, FL: Auerbach Publications.

Dumke, R. R., Schmietendorf, A., Seufert, M., & Wille, C. (2014). *Handbuch der Software Umfangsmessung und Aufwandschätzung*. Berlin, Germany: Logos Verlag.

Symons, C. R., & Lesterhuis, A. (2014). *Introduction to the COSMIC method of measuring software*. Montréal, Canada: COSMIC.

KEY TERMS AND DEFINITIONS

Data Movement: A base functional component which moves a single data group type. There are four types of data movement: Entry, Exit, Read and Write (COSMIC, 2015a).

Entry: An Entry is a data movement that moves a data group from a functional user across the boundary into the functional process where it is required. An Entry is considered to include certain associated data manipulations.

Exit: An Exit is a data movement that moves a data group from a functional process across the boundary to the functional user that requires it. An Exit is considered to include certain associated data manipulations.

Functional Process: A set of data movements representing an elementary part of the Functional User Requirements for the software being measured, that is unique within that Functional User Requirements and that can be defined independently of any other functional process in that Functional User Requirements. A functional process may have only one triggering Entry. Each functional process starts processing on receipt of a data group moved by the triggering Entry data movement of the functional process. The set of all data movements of a functional process is the set that is needed to meet its Functional User Requirements for all the possible responses to its triggering Entry (COSMIC 2015a).

Functional User Requirements: A sub-set of the user requirements. Requirements that describe what the software shall do, in terms of tasks and services. Functional User Requirements relate to but are not limited to: data transfer (for example Input customer data; Send control signal) data transformation (for example Calculate bank interest; Derive average temperature) data storage (for example Store customer order; Record ambient temperature over time) data retrieval (for example List current employees; Retrieve latest aircraft position) Examples of user requirements that are not Functional User Requirements include but are not limited to: quality constraints (for example usability, reliability, efficiency and portability), organizational constraints (for example target hardware and compliance to standards), environmental constraints (for example interoperability, security, privacy and safety), implementation constraints (for example development language, delivery schedule).

Layer: A functional partition of software system architecture. Software in one layer provides a set of services that is cohesive according to some defined criterion, and that software in other layers can utilize without knowing how those services are implemented. The relationship between software in any two layers is defined by a 'correspondence rule' which may be either, 'hierarchical', i.e. software in layer A is allowed to use the services provided by software in layer B but not vice versa (where the hierarchical relationship may be up, down or sideways), or 'bi-directional', i.e. software in layer A is allowed to use software in layer B, and vice versa. Software in one layer exchanges data groups with software in another layer via their respective functional processes. Software in one layer does not necessarily use all the functional services supplied by software in another layer. One layer may be partitioned into other layers according to different defined software architecture (COSMIC, 2015a).

Non-Functional Requirements: Any requirement for or constraint on a hardware/software system or software product, or on a project to develop or maintain such a system or product, except a functional user requirement for software. Note that system or software requirements that are initially expressed as non-functional often evolve as a project progresses wholly or partly into Functional User Requirements for software (COSMIC, 2015a).

Persistent Storage: Storage which enables a functional process to store a data group beyond the life of the functional process and/or from which a functional process can retrieve a data group stored by another functional process, or stored by an earlier occurrence of the same functional process, or stored by some other process (COSMIC, 2015a).

Read: A Read is a data movement that moves a data group from persistent storage into the functional process which requires it. A Read is considered to include certain associated data manipulation.

Triggering Event: An event, recognized in the Functional User Requirements of the software being measured, that causes one or more functional users of the software to generate one or more data groups, each of which will subsequently be moved by a triggering Entry. A triggering event cannot be sub-divided and has either happened or not happened. Note that clock and timing events can be triggering events (COSMIC, 2015a).

User (Functional User): A (type of) user that is a sender and/or an intended recipient of data in the Functional User Requirements of a piece of software. The functional users of a piece of software to be measured shall be derived from the purpose of the measurement. When the purpose of a measurement of a piece of software is related to the effort to develop or modify the piece of software, then the functional users should be all the senders and/or intended recipients of data to/from the new or modified functionality, as required by its Functional User Requirements (COSMIC, 2015a).

Write: A Write is a data movement that moves a data group lying inside a functional process to persistent storage. A Write is considered to include certain associated data manipulation.

Section 2
Mobile Cloud Computing

This section focuses on important issues to consider when designing and developing applications for the web and the cloud. The first chapter discusses the need to test the cloud, and what to test, in order to assure the services in the cloud are appropriately delivered. The second chapter refers to the use of various programming languages, known as polyglot programming, in the context of web applications creation. The third chapter presents an approach to allow multiple stakeholders to work in a collaborative environment for domain-specific modelling.

Chapter 5
Test Cloud before Cloud Test

Sheikh Umar Farooq
University of Kashmir, India

S. M. K. Quadri
University of Kashmir, India

ABSTRACT

Cloud computing is rapidly gaining significant attention in our day-to-day life. Cloud computing and software testing is one of the hot research areas for both industry and research. While one aspect of this merger, i.e. cloud testing (STaaS), is on real high and is receiving significant research attention, there is a lack of research addressing the other side, i.e. 'testing the cloud'. This chapter tries to differentiate between 'cloud testing' and 'testing the cloud' and explains why 'testing the cloud' is so crucial. In addition, it also explains what tests should be done in order to mitigate the challenges and risks of migrating our businesses to the cloud. This chapter provides a comprehensive tutorial to discuss the testing of cloud and also explains the need, objectives, requirements and challenges in 'testing the cloud'.

INTRODUCTION

Cloud computing has been the talk of the town for the past few years. Be it a computer professional or a naive smartphone user, everybody uses the services offered by the cloud in one way or the other. Cloud has gained a significant amount of attention by providing many significant services remotely in a very cost effective and flexible manner whenever and wherever needed. It involves large scale controlled sharing and contemporized utilization of multiple resources. The presence of cloud is obvious, and it is here to stay, having already proved to be more than just hype. Nicholas Carr, author of IT Doesn't Matter and The Big Switch, strengthens the cloud position and its contribution to the history of technology, and even believes cloud computing, or utility computing, will eventually replace the IT department (Testing the Cloud, 2013).

Cloud computing, not only changes the way of obtaining computing resources, but also changes the way of managing and delivering computing services, technologies, and solutions (Priyadharshini & Malathi, 2014). The features and services provided by the cloud are attracting many organizations to move their businesses or some services to a cloud platform. *Software testing* has been one of the best practice

DOI: 10.4018/978-1-4666-9916-8.ch005

Copyright © 2016, IGI Global. Copying or distributing in print or electronic forms without written permission of IGI Global is prohibited.

areas for migrating to cloud environment (Incki, Ari & Sozer, 2012). Cloud computing is opening up new vistas of opportunity for testing, giving rise to a new phenomenon known as Software Testing as a Service (*STaaS*). It leverages the cloud-based hardware infrastructure and computing resources to perform traditional testing like performance, load, stress, security and compatibility testing for regular, on premises applications (Ananth, n.d.). Testing has traditionally been viewed as a necessary evil because it required a huge, dedicated infrastructure and resources that were used occasionally (Mylavarapu & Inamdar, 2011). Cloud testing utilizes the power of cloud computing, reducing the unit cost of computing, while increasing testing effectiveness. Many companies are using cloud-computing services in testing area more than in any other field. Software testing in the cloud (*cloud testing*) has the capacity to change the way software testing is performed. The impact of the cloud on testing practices has grown with the cloud's growing presence in the IT space.

As cloud continues to stay stronger in current times and is most likely to be there for years to come, and with most of organizations shifting their business to the cloud. Computer scientists need to introspect whether we can really fully rely on the cloud. How do cloud vendors guarantee cloud-related quality of cloud services to the users? To successfully provide cloud services, there needs to be some kind of testing for cloud itself and its services. We need to test the cloud before it can be used to test other applications or for providing any other services. There remains a major misunderstanding concerning the difference between the two terms "*cloud testing and testing the cloud*".

One common misinterpretation is that many seem to use both terms for using the cloud to run or manage the tests themselves. However, the cloud itself poses many issues related to security, compatibility, performance, scalability, functionality, third party dependencies and many more, which need to be tested. The nature of a cloud system implies non-determinism in its behavior due to its distributed and adhoc usage nature, which makes testing a cloud a hard and repetitive but nevertheless a crucial task. Testing cloud infrastructure and applications has its own peculiarities that demand for novel/tailored testing methods and tools. It causes new issues, challenges and needs in software testing. According to *Edan Evantal*, VP research and development at the test automation pioneer QualiSystems, the era of cloud computing has brought new challenges to testing in the network sphere (Testing the Cloud, 2013). As the use of cloud for testing has been growing rapidly in recent times, making us more dependable on cloud, a need for testing the cloud itself has also emerged significantly. Although much work is being done to model and build cloud applications and services, there is significantly less research devoted to testing them (Rimal, Choi & Lumb, 2009).

The primary contribution of this work is to provide a comprehensive knowledge base about '*testing the cloud'*. In this Chapter, besides giving the overview of cloud computing and its services especially *STaaS*, the authors thoroughly discuss the difference between *cloud testing* and *testing a cloud*. The main focus is on discussing '*testing a cloud'* including the need, objectives, requirements and issues. This chapter thoroughly explains the types of testing required for ensuring the quality of the cloud offerings besides explaining its testing lifecycle.

CLOUD COMPUTING AND ITS CHARACTERISTICS

Cloud computing has surfaced as a new and powerful computing paradigm. It continues to stay stronger in current times due to a number of advantages it possesses. This is evident from the fact that "65% of the US companies shifted to cloud in 2011" or "90% of Microsoft's 2011 R&D budget was spent on cloud computing strategy and products" or "80% of the companies have experienced immense progress just within half year i.e. just six months after moving to cloud" (Johnson, 2013). Industry estimates that within the next five years, the annual global market for cloud computing will surge to $100-150 billion or more. Everyone seems to be agreeing on the fact that cloud presence is obvious and is not just hype. The only problem is that not everyone agrees on what it is (i.e. a common definition). The definition seems to be varying among different professionals, which is largely influenced by the way they interact or use the cloud. The details are still evolving, but for most enterprises the cloud is a set of services, data, resources, and networks located "elsewhere". This contrast with the historical centralized data center model – where enterprises purchased, configured, deployed, and maintained their own servers, storage, networks, and infrastructures (Testing the Cloud: DRS, 2011). Both industry and academic circles have been struggling to procure a universally accepted definition of the cloud. In order to truly understand how the cloud can be of value to an organization, it is first important to understand what the cloud really is and what its different components are. So, the big question remains: *What exactly is cloud computing?*

A standard definition by National Institute of Standards and Technology (NIST) defines it as "a model for enabling ubiquitous, convenient, on-demand network access to a shared pool of configurable computing resources (e.g., networks, servers, storage, applications, and services) that can be rapidly provisioned and released with minimal management effort or service provider interaction" (Mell & Grance, 2009).

This cloud model is composed of *five* essential characteristics, *three* service models, and *four* deployment Models. The main essential characteristics of the cloud computing are On-demand self-service, Broad network access, Resource pooling (location transparent), Rapid elasticity and Measured service. The ISO adds multi-tenancy, and scalability to the list.

The concept of cloud as per the NIST revolves around three things, which includes Software, Platform and Infrastructure and accordingly provides the services in the following ways:

1.   Software as a service (SaaS).
2.   Platform as a Service (PaaS).
3.   Infrastructure as a Service (IaaS).

Cloud computing is an environment that encompasses services from *Infrastructure as a Service* at the base, through *Platform as a Service* as a development tool to *Software as a Service* replacing on-premises applications (Rackspace, 2013). The user should be well aware of his requirements before selecting a proper service model. A thorough analysis will help users in choosing where, when, and how they use Cloud Computing. These three service models differ in the amount of control that users have, and conversely, how much they can expect their provider to do (Huth & Cebula, 2011). As we go down the list from *SaaS* to *IaaS*, there is lesser level of abstraction and the subscriber gains more control over what they can do within the space of the cloud. The customer has more control in an *IaaS* system than with a *SaaS* agreement. Similarly, in *PaaS*, we have no direct control over the underlying infrastructure but we can access the created or deployed applications. The three service models and their possible users and usage are shown in figure 1. A part of figure 1 has been adapted from (PCI DSS: CCG, 2013)[1].

The ISO extends NIST's definition by adding network and data storage; and subsequently the following services:

4.   Network as a service (NaaS);
5.   Data storage as a service (DSaaS).

Figure 1. Cloud Service Models and Responsibilities (Partially adapted from (PCI DSS: CCG, 2013)).

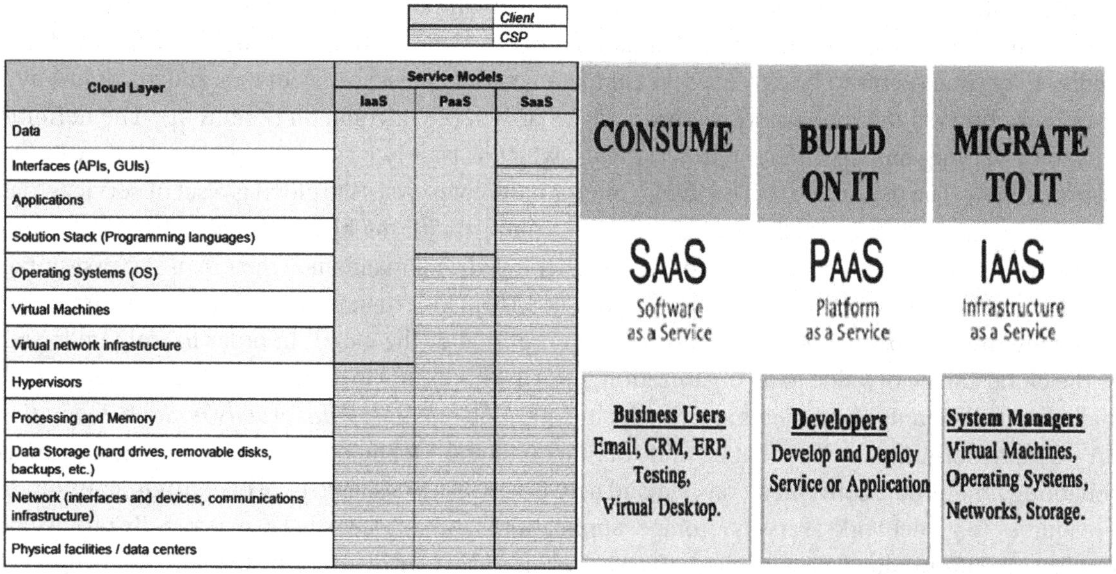

However, we are of the opinion that they should not be incorporated as two separate service models as they fall under the ambit of Infrastructure. The cloud can be deployed in different ways depending on requirements and services you want to offer. Each model has specific characteristics that support the needs of the services and users of the clouds in particular ways. The National Institute of Standards and Technology (NIST) have recommended the followings types of cloud model:

1. Public Cloud.
2. Private Cloud.
3. Hybrid Cloud.

While in public cloud services are available to everyone, in private cloud they are, however, available only to the users within a particular organization. A Hybrid cloud is a combination of public and private. ISO expands on NIST's 2011 definition on cloud deployment models, adding *community cloud* to public, private and hybrid cloud models. Cloud services can be deployed in different ways, depending on the organizational structure, the provisioning location, security requirements, managing and customization capabilities. Since the Cloud is a broad collection of services, organizations can choose where, when, and how they use Cloud Computing. Figure 2 shows various cloud deployment options.

BACKGROUND

Software testing traditionally requires huge infrastructure and resources that were then only used sporadically in an organization.

Cloud computing brings new business opportunities, and causes some major impacts on software testing. Software testing is an important process that organizations have moved to the cloud platform

Figure 2. Cloud Deployment Models.
Source: (Ames, 2012).

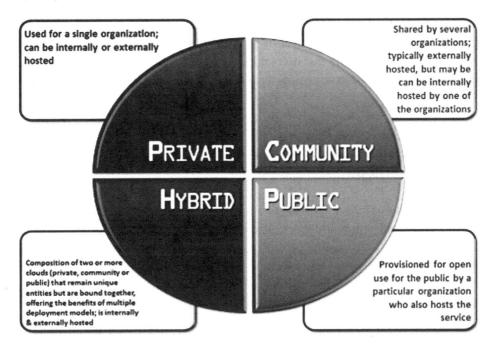

giving rise to a new concept known as Software Testing as a Service (STaaS) which has significantly changed the way testing is performed. The major problems associated with conventional way of testing, listed below, actually became major causes for the embracement of cloud for testing (Mahmood and Saeed, 2013):

1. Testing is a periodic activity and requires new environments to be set up for each project.
2. Testing is considered an important but non-business-critical activity. Moving testing to the cloud is seen as a safe bet because it doesn't include sensitive corporate data and has minimal impact on the organization's business-as-usual activities.
3. Applications are increasingly becoming dynamic, complex, distributed and component-based, creating a multiplicity of new challenges for test teams.

Therefore, these organizations generally opt to migrate to the cloud for testing their applications, especially since it enables them to focus on their core activities, instead of worrying about maintaining their own IT infrastructure for testing (Ananth, n.d.).

With the arrival of cloud computing, the testing activity has enjoyed many benefits like cost reduction, extensive and effective testing and in fact the flexibility, simplicity, geographic transparency, traceability and potential for collaboration have increased, when compared to maintaining an in-house test environment. The benefits provided by the cloud are became a major motivating factor for many organizations to move testing to a cloud platform, giving rise to a new phenomenon known as Software Testing as a Service (STaaS). *STaaS* is an on demand service delivery model, in which testing activities are delivered as a service by using the cloud resources, as and when required. Software testing as a service (*STaaS*) is a faster, better and smarter way of testing applications which besides enhancing effectiveness and efficiency also gives more variety, flexibility and proximity as compared to traditional way of in-house testing. While potential of Cloud based *STaaS* is huge, we really need to introspect whether the cloud is really living up to the expectations of the user by providing the required functionality and at the same time not violating/disturbing anything that users does not want to; like breaching privacy, compatibility etc. The ultimate way to check all this requires us to test the cloud and its offering thoroughly.

TESTING THE CLOUD

Need for Testing the Cloud

Cloud testing has come into sight as a spanking new approach to testing where cloud computing environments are leveraged to imitate real-world user congestion by considerably minimizing costs (Gao, Bai & Tsai, 2011). Cloud-based software testing pertains to testing and evaluating activities on a cloud-based environment and infrastructure by leveraging cloud technologies and solutions. Testing on cloud will yield a number of benefits to an organization in provisions of expenditure and possessions. It is something like "service on demand" or "testing on demand". Software testing like many other processes is shifting to cloud due to the number of factors discussed in above sections. Essentially there are four key factors, which govern the process of taking an existing application requirement to the cloud. These elements provide the appropriate framework for delivering enterprise ready testing on the cloud (Bajpai, 2012):

1. **People:** Subject matter experts with domain knowledge, test experience, management.
2. **Process:** Well developed test process and methodology which would generate more test cases in specific domains.
3. **Governance:** Relationship management, QA Project management office, productivity, demand management, risk mitigation.
4. **Infrastructure:** Public or Private Cloud based test environment, test automation, tools/partners, and test-ware management.

So before moving an application or any process to the cloud environment, besides choosing the right set of people, process, governance and infrastructure, we really need to find out whether we can fully rely on the cloud. There are risks that are inherited when we move to the cloud. For each of the benefits provided by the cloud, we have to identify the particular risks associated with the cloud.

In order to find out whether cloud is really a reliable friend and will not ditch us in any manner, we need to test the cloud and the services offered by it, and only then can we mitigate the risks associated with the benefits provided by the cloud. With more and more providers offering cloud-based services, the technology has suffered from chaotic development, making it almost impossible for companies to ascertain the quality of services offered. Organizations want to lower the cost and time required for the testing but not at the cost of compromising quality of the product. This necessitates testing and ensuring the conformity of cloud that have been snowballing for the recent years. With the increase of the popularity of this paradigm, people started to realize that before expecting too much from the cloud, it should prove itself so that we can find them reliable enough to move our businesses on to the cloud and the importance of *testing the cloud* started to emerge. Testing a Cloud is still new subject in software testing community. Therefore, test engineers and quality assurance managers encounter many challenges in testing software, clouds and cloud-based applications (Mohsenzadeh, 2013). Even today, we do not have a standard approach for testing the cloud; organizations always should undertake a thorough assessment of cloud environment and the services offered by it. This assessment will help organizations not to regret the decision of moving their business to the cloud later on and guarantee quality of service. Testing the cloud will allow the users to mitigate the risks associated with moving the business to the cloud.

The era of cloud computing has brought new challenges to testing. When it comes to testing the cloud, it is clear that there are many aspects to consider. We need to test it for security, privacy, acceptability, availability, load, stress, performance and integrity in the cloud. Testing cloud applications that are hosted and deployed in a cloud environment, or assessing the cloud infrastructure itself (*Sometimes referred to by many as Testing inside Cloud*) is seeing a considerable demand today (Narula & Beniwal, 2013). It requires a dedicated planning and rigorous testing effort of any cloud offering to satisfy the business need of the end user up to great extent. There are already many other issues associated with cloud testing (Mehrotra, 2011) (Gao, Bai & Tsai, 2011):

1. On-demand test environments.
2. Scalability
3. Performance.
4. Security
5. Lack of Standards.
6. Integration and Regression issues.

These issues make testing the cloud more important, because after mitigating these issues, we can make cloud testing in particular and other cloud services in general more effective quality wise.

WHAT TO TEST

So now it is proven beyond doubt that we need to test the cloud that refers to the "verification and validation of applications, environments and infrastructure available on the cloud". This ensures that applications, environments and infrastructure conform to the expectations of the cloud computing business model in both functional and non-functional aspects. *Testing a Cloud* mainly includes functional testing, availability testing, security testing, performance testing (load and stress test), compatibility testing, interoperability testing, disaster recovery testing, and multi-tenancy testing. It is evident that a *'one-size-fits-all'* approach would not work in such a scenario, and may indeed prove to be a recipe for disaster (Ananth, n.d.). Rather, comprehensive cloud testing acquires prime importance that cannot be understated.

Now that testing the offerings of the cloud is compulsory; specific techniques, methods, and tools will need to be applied. The conventional testing tools and techniques were not designed to test this complex and dynamic computing environment. An adaption of old techniques and tools needs to be performed in order to make these methods fit this different type of computing environment. At some point, new tools and methods should be introduced to test some specific offering of the cloud (Falah, Ayadi & Atif, 2013).

Cloud enablement of applications or hosting applications on the cloud is all at one end, but companies also need to understand the risks associated with it and adopt proper mitigation plans, the core of which is testing. The cloud usually differs in terms of services offered; in addition, the clouds also differ in terms of the deployment model. Different kinds of clouds need different types of testing. Organizations need to have a better understanding of the way different types of cloud work, how they impact business and which testing approaches should be used for them. They need to adopt an end-to-end testing approach, starting from requirements to deployment, because each stage has different testing requirements (Ananth, n.d.). The type of testing required to test the cloud depends on a number of general and specific requirements. Usually, testing the cloud includes the following tests:

1. **Functional Test:** This type of testing is carried out to evaluate whether the services offered by the cloud deliver their intended business or process functions. Functional cloud testing is the testing of all the features and functions of a system which includes hardware and software. Besides software, hardware is also tested to evaluate whether it meets the functional and non- functional requirements or not.

2. **Integration Cloud Test:** allows the business to verify the cloud solution will work within the current infrastructure and environments, which ultimately proves that the implementation of a cloud solution does not detrimentally impact any existing systems. Finally, the business requirements must be verified and validated to prove that the end result of the cloud solution will meet the documented needs of the business (Batra & Sharma, 2014).

3. **Performance Test:** This type of testing is carried out to evaluate the general and specific performance objectives of the cloud, which includes properties like response times and throughput rates under certain workload and configuration conditions. Performance testing is most crucial in public cloud due to the usage by large numbers of users. Performance testing is usually done using:
   a. **Load Test:** Load testing evaluates the cloud performance when cloud and/or its services are subjected to the heavy volumes of workload e.g. increasing transactions or data sets on an ad-hoc time basis or filling the operating system's job queue to the capacity etc. The load testing obviously requires significant resources, in terms of physical and operational infrastructure; we usually cannot do beyond certain limits. However, the cloud should be subjected to certain level of load testing.
   b. **Stress Test:** Stress testing evaluates the performance of cloud and its services in extreme conditions with a time constraint (stress test involves element of *time*). E.g. putting different applications on a Virtual Machine (VM), which is already running an application or running, a specific cloud application on VM with a smaller size. Stress testing should not be confused with load testing; a heavy stress is a peak volume of data, or activity, encountered *over a short span of time*. An analogy would be evaluating a typist. A load test would determine whether the typist could cope with a draft of a large report; a stress test would determine whether the typist could type at a rate of 50 words per minute (Myers, Sandler & Badgett, 2011).

4. **Security Test:** This type of testing is perhaps most crucial to the cloud computing and must be performed with great rigor because security is perhaps the most increasing concern of the society with respect to use of the cloud. Security testing is used to evaluate the cloud for general and specific security objectives. To provide better security testing, service providers formalize industry standards that will help them to define the acceptability criteria for cloud offerings in terms of security. Studying the security problems in similar existing systems can derive the general security objectives for the cloud. Web-based applications often need a higher level of security testing than do most applications. Privacy is one of the key areas to be considered in security testing of a cloud;

it's important to safeguard the privacy of the application users and associated information when maintained in cloud. We need to convince our customer base that their data or/and application is safe, else we risk losing customers at very fast rate. We need a privacy-protected testing methodology that ensures private data of users is not exposed to anybody else other than authorized persons only. Security assurance needs to identify the problems and approaches in terms of Loss of control, Lack of trust and Multi-tenancy problems.

5. **Compatibility and Interoperability Test:** A cloud must be able to work and provide services across multiple environments and platforms which are different in terms of hardware, OS, DBMS, browser etc. Compatibility & Interoperability Testing is aimed at verifying whether the application under test interacts and functions as expected with other software and hardware combinations. The compatibility testing evaluates the cloud to ensure that cloud works on multiple environments like different hardware, OS, browsers, hypervisor platforms, databases etc. This is one of the key factors for deciding the success and coverage of the cloud vendor.

6. **Recovery Test:** This testing is carried to ensure data and state recovery in case of hardware/software failure. This testing is more significant especially in case of public cloud. There are always chances of a failure due to system failures; extreme load etc., so the system should be tested for recovery and it should be ensured that service is restored with minimum adverse effect on client and within minimum possible time.

7. **Cloud Scalability Test:** Cloud computing solutions always promise to be scalable. Cloud has to be elastic in nature as elasticity enables cloud infrastructure to scale up and down depending on the need. Scalability testing for cloud services usually calculates the measurements for defining the scalability thresholds and makes sure that offering has the capability to provide scale up or scale down facilities as per the need. An adequate amount of testing is needed to ensure that cloud's promised scalability meets the user requirements.

8. **Cloud Availability Test:** Cloud services must be available at all times as there could be many mission critical activities going on. Regardless of how good the cloud application is, it is of little use if unavailable to users. There should be a kind of assurance that there will be no abrupt downtime such that the business of the client is not adversely affected (Prakash & Gopalakrishanan, 2012). The cloud consumer or application owner can use the cloud to deploy the application at multiple sites that can be *isolated* to prevent any failure at one site from affecting the other sites. But, this introduces the technical problem of synchronizing the application's state and the user's state across the cloud.

9. **User Acceptance Test:** This type of testing is also known as '*beta testing*' is used when the intended users test cloud services in real world environment. User Acceptance testing (UAT) ensures that the application supports the intended business process. UAT is one of the final and critical activities that must be carried out before services are deployed for the final user.

The kind of testing required to evaluate cloud largely depends upon the type of services being offered. The testing should access the quality attributes of the service (both implicit and explicit) for both functional as well as for non-functional requirements. The testing process should aim at finding failures in the cloud before it is deployed in order to avoid future problems. Table 1 adapted from (Mark, 2013) below lists some of the tests that could be used by users, *IaaS*, *PaaS* and *SaaS* providers, and the measurements that they take.

Table 1. Typical Test Required in each Service Model (adapted from (Mark, 2013)).

Layer	Service	Test and Measurements
Carrier	Ethernet L2 EVC	Ethernet OAM Test: Circuit Availability, Loss, Delay, Variation EtherSAM Test (Y.1564): Throughput, Loss, Delay, Jitter (at load)
	IP Connectivity	Ethernet OAM Test: Circuit Availability, Loss, Delay, Variation EtherSAM Test (Y.1564): Throughput, Loss, Delay, Jitter (at load)
IaaS	DNS	DNS Resolution Test: DNS Availability, Response Time, Accuracy
	Switched LAN	Ping Test: Reachability, Loss, Latency.
	Operating System	UDP ECHO Test: Availability, Loss, Latency.
	VPN	VPN Connection Test: VPN Availability TWAMP: Reachability, Loss, Delay, Variation.
	Firewalls	UDP and TCP Port Test: Port Availability, TCP Connection Delay.
	Application Servers	TCP Port Test: Port Availability, TCP Connection Delay.
	Web Server	Web URL Download Test: Web Server Availability, Response Time, Download Time, Throughput.
	Web Load Balancers	Web URL Download Test: Web Server Availability, Response Time, Download Time, Throughput
PaaS	Website Development	Web Page Download Test: Website Availability, Response Time, Download Time, Throughput (for all page content).
	App Development	Web Request Test: Availability, Response Time, Download Time, Throughput.
	Cloud Storage	Cloud Storage Test: Availability, Response Time, Upload and Download Time, Throughput Cloud Replication Test: Replication Time.
SaaS	Web Application	Scripted Web Test: Availability, Success Failure of script, Total Script Time, Each Step Time.
	Cloud E-mail	Email Tests for SMTP, POP3 and IMAP: Email Availability, Response Time Email Delivery Test: Message Delivery Time.
	Hosted PBX	VoIP Call Tests: Availability, MOS, Post Dial Delay, Loss, Latency, Jitter, Buffer Overflow (and Underflow).
	Over-the-Top Video	Video Download Test: Availability, Download Time, Re-buffering, Video Quality.

'Testing the Cloud' Life Cycle

The testing described in above section must be performed throughout the lifecycle of the cloud service whether it is software, platform or infrastructure, as shown in figure 3.

The testing should be conducted in the development environment (popularly known as *alpha* testing) for both functional and non-functional (both implicit and explicit) requirements. Finally when the service is deployed and made available to the cloud user, we must ensure that the service is actually running and delivering as per the user requirement in real environment. After that, we need to go for assurance testing which mostly checks the availability and performance to ensure that SLAs (Service Licensing Agreements) are actually met round the clock. When there is any failure, it is reported to the trouble-shooting staff to rectify the fault. The process continues in a cycle because the services are continuously refined, upgraded with changing and new requirements, which of course includes both functional and non-functional requirements. Therefore, we should always include testing as a part of development cycle

Figure 3. Testing Life Cycle of a service.
Source: (Mark, 2013).

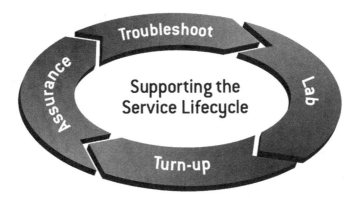

at every stage to ensure that quality expectations of users are met all the time. Customers may utilize the cloud services with the objective of saving their resources, but if the service fails to meet their quality expectations they will switch to another provider or take the application back in-house. The best way to confirm whether the service is really working is to test it. Cloud vendors want to perform tests as close as possible to the customer, which means conducting tests from within the carrier's network by testing the cloud and cloud datacenters where the application is running.

CONCLUSION

The services provided by cloud computing are rapidly influencing IT service providers to migrate their businesses to the cloud. The migration of the business to the cloud has its own set of challenges and risks. If the quality expectations of the cloud users are not fulfilled, they will find some alternate solution or move their business back in-house. The best way to confirm if the service is really delivering up to par and to mitigate any risks involved with migration to the cloud is to thoroughly test the services offered by the cloud. The growth of cloud computing is clear, but it requires rigorous and standardized testing to enable stakeholders to assess risks and ensure proper quality levels and provide users with satisfactory services. However, the traditional testing methods may not fully fit for testing the cloud. The testing should incorporate new or tailored testing methods for fully mitigating the issues and risks associated with cloud computing model. There is still a long way to go to develop a standard and formal testing methodology for *testing a cloud*. The field is in its infancy, but if cloud is to survive and prosper, it has to be done, as the benefits will be enormous as it matures.

REFERENCES

Ames. (2012). *Types of Cloud Computing: Private, Public and Hybrid Clouds*. Retrieved 21 Dec 2014 from http://blog.appcore.com/blog/bid/167543/Types-of-Cloud-Computing-Private-Public-and-Hybrid-Clouds

Ananth, B. (n.d.). *Testing Cloud and Testing using Cloud*. Sonata Software Limited Whitepaper. Retrieved on 25 Dec 2014 from http://www.sonata-software.com/sites/default/files/resources/Cloud_Testing.pdf

Bajpai. (2012). Testing as a Service on Cloud. *Igate*. Retrieved on 27 Dec 2014 from http://www.igate.com/iblog/index.php/testing-as-a-service-on-cloud/

Batra & Sharma. (2014). Cloud Testing: A Review Article. *International Journal of Computer Science and Mobile Computing, 3*(6), 314-319.

Falah, Ayadi, & Atif. (2013). Roadmap to Testing the Cloud Techniques, Methodology, and Tools. *IJCSET, 3*(3), 84-89.

Gao, Bai, & Tsai. (2011). Cloud testing-issues, challenges, needs and practice. *Software Engineering: An International Journal, 1*(1), 9-23.

Huth & Cebula. (2011). The basics of cloud computing. *United States Computer.*

Incki, K., Ari, I., & Sozer, H. (2012, June). A survey of software testing in the cloud. In *Software Security and Reliability Companion (SERE-C), 2012 IEEE Sixth International Conference on* (pp. 18-23). IEEE.

Johnson, L. (2013). *Cloud Computing: Fast Facts*. Retrieved on 10 Dec 2014 from http://www.business-2community.com/tech-gadgets/cloud-computing-fast-facts-0386816

Mahmood & Saeed. (2013). Software engineering frameworks for the cloud computing paradigm. Springer.

Mark. (2013). *Testing the Cloud*. White Paper. Retrieved on 19 Jan 2014 from www.lightwaveonline.com/content/lw/en/whitepapers/2013/01/testing-the-cloud.whitepaperpdf.render.pdf

Mehrotra. (2011). Cloud-Testing vs. Testing a cloud. *Infosys Viewpoint*. Retrieved on 14 Jan 2014 from http://www.infosys.com/engineering-services/white-papers/documents/cloud-testing-vs-testing-cloud.pdf

Mell & Grance. (2009). The NIST definition of cloud computing. *National Institute of Standards and Technology, 53*(6), 50.

Mohsenzadeh. (2013). Cloud Computing Testing Evaluation. *International Journal of Computational Engineering & Management, 16*(6).

Myers, Sandler, & Badgett. (2011). *The art of software testing*. John Wiley & Sons.

Mylavarapu & Inamdar. (2011). Taking Testing to the Cloud, Future of Work. *Cognizant*. Retrieved on 25 Dec 2014 from http://www.cognizant.com/SiteDocuments/ITIS-Cloud-Based-Testing.pdf

Narula & Beniwal. (2013). Cloud Testing-Types, Service Platforms and Advantages. *International Journal of Computers and Applications, 72*(20).

PCI Data Security Standard (PCI DSS) Cloud Computing Guidelines. (2013). Cloud Special Interest Group PCI Security Standards Council. Retrieved on 13 Jan 2015 from https://www.pcisecuritystandards.org/pdfs/PCI_DSS_v2_Cloud_Guidelines.pdf

Prakash & Gopalkrishanan. (2012). Cloud computing solution-Benefits and testing challenges. *Journal of Theoretical and Applied Information Technology*, *39*(2), 114–118.

Priyadharshini & Malathi. (2014). Survey on software testing techniques in cloud computing. *CoRR*.

Rackspace. (2013). *Understanding the Cloud Computing Stack: SaaS, PaaS, IaaS*. Retrieved on 16 Dec 2014 from http://www.rackspace.com/knowledge_center/whitepaper/understanding-the-cloud-computing-stack-saas-paas-iaas

Rimal, Choi, & Lumb. (2009). A taxonomy and survey of cloud computing systems. In *Proceedings of INC, IMS and IDC, 2009. NCM'09. Fifth International Joint Conference on* (pp. 44-51). IEEE.

Testing the Cloud. (2011). *Testing the Cloud: Definitions, Requirements, and Solutions*. Ixia Whitepaper. Retrieved on 14 Dec 2014 from http://www.ixiacom.com/sites/default/files/resources/whitepaper/cloud_testing_white_paper_0.pdf

Testing the Cloud. (2013). *CBR Testing Automation, Special Report*. Retrieved on 10 January 2015 from http://qualisystems.com/wp-content/uploads/2013/08/Testing-the-Cloud1.pdf

ENDNOTE

[1]   Technology layers and their corresponding lines of responsibility may be different for each Cloud Service Provider, even if they use the same terminology to describe their service, and the individual service offerings may or may not align with the responsibly assignments indicated.

Chapter 6
On Polyglot Programming in the Web

Juhana Harmanen
Ada Drive Ltd., Finland

Tommi Mikkonen
Tampere University of Technology, Finland

ABSTRACT

Different programming languages have been designed to solve problems efficiently in different domains. The goal of polyglot programming, a technique where several languages are used in the creation of a single application, is to combine and utilize the best solutions from different programming languages and paradigms in a seamless fashion. In this paper, the authors examine polyglot programming in the context of web applications, where it has been commonly used to create compelling applications, but where there is still considerable potential to improve development in various ways.

INTRODUCTION

Different programming languages have been designed to solve problems efficiently in different domains. For instance, SQL is commonly associated with databases, scripting languages are often used as glue that integrates different programs, and C is used for low-level code. When various programming languages are used in the creation of a single program, the term polyglot programming is used. The goal of polyglot programming is to combine the best solutions from different languages and paradigms in a seamless fashion.

A polyglot system has two essential aspects; the platform used for the integration and the programming languages that are supported by the platform. For instance, when using Java, the Java Virtual Machine (JVM) enables using other languages that build on the same runtime environment. Such languages include Scala and Groovy, which offer different programming paradigms than plain Java.

In this chapter, we examine polyglot programming in the context of web applications. While the approach is in extensive use in today's web development, for example, embedded HTML and SQL or JavaScript with Cascading Style Sheets (CSS) and HTML, only limited research has been conducted on this topic.

DOI: 10.4018/978-1-4666-9916-8.ch006

Copyright © 2016, IGI Global. Copying or distributing in print or electronic forms without written permission of IGI Global is prohibited.

BACKGROUND

The forced separation of languages in writing can be considered somewhat unnatural in this multilingual world. Authors of novels, for instance, sometimes break this separation because it is too restrictive, and journalists and historians combine philosophic prose with statistical facts (Beardsmore, 1978). The Russian author Leo Tolstoy, in his novel War and Peace written in Russian language, frequently borrowed words and phrases from French and German to be as expressive and effective in language as possible. Rare and inventive authors like J.R.R. Tolkien have even made up their own languages.

To some extent, programming languages share properties with natural languages. Each programming language has its own nuances that make it distinct from others. This can be seen as a justification for mixing languages to create a combination of characteristics needed for solving a particular problem that no single language can address elegantly.

Polyglot Programming

The term polyglot programming was first introduced in software development context in 2002 as a hypothesis to use several programming languages within one environment. Later authors tend to use slightly different approaches, for example, "programming in more than one language within the same context", which delegates the definition to what the context is.

From the development perspective, the context is partly constituted by the number of teams and the fashion the resulting software is integrated. Polyglot programming takes place even if one of the teams uses a different programming language than others, and the integration between the parts developed using different languages is tight. However, when the teams need no information on languages other teams are using, polyglot programming no longer takes place. Instead, individual components constitute distinct entities – consider, for example, a service-to-service application in which only well-defined interfaces are needed.

Associated advantages. The definition of productivity is a much-debated aspect of programming languages. Common metrics include lines of code (LOC) and function points per unit time (Delorey et al., 2007; Maxwell et al., 1996; Sebesta, 2009). While it has been claimed that productivity does not depend on programming language (Brooks, 1995), Delorey et al. (2007) presents contradicting view – due to the nature of the problems within the scope of the productivity measurement, any findings from case studies are hard to generalize. Problems include human factors like motivation, skill and experience, and environmental factors like integrated development environment (IDE) and library support, and also factors related to geographical distribution of projects (Cataldo et al., 2008; Cataldo et al. 2007; De Souza, 2005; Sullivan et al. 2001).

Polyglot programming aims to combine and integrate the best solutions from different languages. Therefore, simpler solutions to the problems at hand become available (Fjeldberg, 2008). A suitable language for solving a particular problem will result in shorter solution in terms of LOC because of the built-in primitives and idioms. Following the assumption that developers produce the same amount of code lines regardless of language, polyglot programming allows them solve more problems – and be more productive (Brooks, 1995). In addition to reduced LOC, the thought process of a developer can be simplified as solutions emerge naturally in the appropriate languages. For example, taking advantage of static polymorphic type-checking in functional programming, a large class of errors on race conditions and deadlocks in communication between processes can be caught at compile time (Pareto, 2000;

Flanagan and Abadi, 1999). The use of interpreted languages can also increase productivity, as no code-compile-crash cycles are needed.

A general realization in web development is that developers are more expensive than hardware, and that the importance of a developer's productivity exceeds that of runtime performance (Fjeldberg, 2008). However, the development phase of an application is only a part of the life cycle, and increased productivity from using an appropriate language becomes even more important in the maintenance phase (Vinoski, 2008). An application written with less lines of code has fewer lines to maintain, as well as fewer instructions to follow. Moreover, the number of faults per LOC increases with the total LOC in the application (Ostrand et al., 2005).

Associated disadvantages. Knowledge of different programming languages is essential to benefit from polyglot and poly-paradigm programming (Fjeldberg, 2008). Although it is suggested that developers should learn at least one new programming language per year to evolve (Hunt and Thomas, 1999), in many cases this is not realistic, and also learning a new language and associated idioms, frameworks and patterns may take more than a year. The effort in learning becomes even more challenging when developers are familiar only with a single language and the infrastructure and tools built around it. Programming with a single language often means thinking inside the frame of reference of that particular language – typically programmers are satisfied with whatever programming language they happen to use, because it dictates the way they think about programs. In fact, Graham (2008) presented a conceptual hierarchy with more expressive languages at the top. The so-called blub paradox after a hypothetical language of average complexity called "Blub" states that anyone using a particular programming language knows that it is more powerful than some, but not that it is less powerful than others.

Maintenance phase requires a sufficient knowledge of the languages used. With a large application with a long life cycle, maintenance will be done by different developers or even by a different company than the one that originally developed the application. Every time a new programming language is added, the pool of developers with enough knowledge to maintain the application is reduced. In addition, using a new paradigm parallel to previously used ones will make following the application code even harder. Moreover, the overhead caused by using different programming languages will increase if the tools do not offer interoperability. Support for a new language will therefore only be added when it has gained enough traction and popularity.

Polyglot Pyramid

A polyglot environment has two key aspects, the platform used for the integration and the different programming languages supported by the platform. The possibility to create a new infrastructure without rewriting legacy code has proven to be essential (Feathers, 2004). The so-called polyglot pyramid introduced by Bini (2008) is used to describe and categorize the programming and specification languages used in a polyglot system (Bini, 2008; Evans and Verburg, 2012). Polyglot pyramid presents three layers for different languages (Figure 1).

Statically typed, powerful programming languages tend to gravitate towards the needs of the stable layer. The less powerful general-purpose technologies tend to ascend to the top layer. The dynamic layer in the middle consist of a rich variety of languages with the most flexibility, and in many cases this layer overlaps with other layers. In addition, the three layers of the pyramid represent polyglot programming as a form of separation of concerns (Table 1).

Figure 1. Polyglot pyramid (Bini, 2008; Evans and Verburg, 2012)

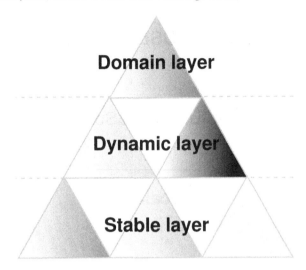

Table 1. Polyglot pyramid layers (Bini, 2008, Evans and Verburg, 2012)

Layer	Description	Examples
Domain specific	Domain-specific language; tightly coupled to a specific part of the application domain	HTML, CSS, Web templating, SQL
Dynamic	Rapid, Productive, Flexible development of functionality	Groovy, Clojure, Jython, JRuby, JavaScript
Stable	Core functionality, stable, well-tested, high performance	Java, Scala

The layers presented in the polyglot pyramid are organized with the stable layer as a wide base (Bini, 2008; Evans and Verburg, 2012). In contrast, a web application typically comprises multiple specification and programming languages located in the domain-specific layer, and the dynamic layer quite often includes more than one programming language. Thus the polyglot programming pyramid can be inverted to present the polyglot system more conveniently. This allows the dynamic layer in the middle to be divided into smaller parts, for example, based on programming language or functionality. Also the different domain-specific languages (DSLs) are now represented as smaller pyramids standing upside down. This strategy is named as a bounded fractal representation of a polyglot system presented by Bini (2008). The bounded fractal representation forms the polyglot system, which consists of these smaller pyramids. The pyramids have no restrictions, and they can all be the same programming language and system, or multiple different ones. The organization of the smaller pyramids depends on the application being designed. Figure 2 represents a polyglot system with a combination of Clojure, Scala, and JavaScript. Any imaginable combination can be used, although it is important to keep in mind that the combination should be best suited for the problem at hand.

The domain layer defines the actual domain rules, which in general means using one or more domain-specific languages. The layer must be adaptive enough, so that it is possible to change rules in production and that domain experts can maintain it. Languages in the domain layer include HTML and SQL, but it is also possible to use general-purpose languages like Groovy, Ruby or Python, which support building

Figure 2. A sample set of compatible elements in the polyglot pyramid (Bini, 2008)

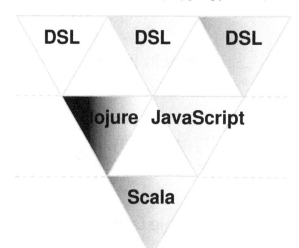

internal DSLs (Fjeldberg, 2008). Technologies of the domain layer are usually utilized by the other two layers to provide domain specific solutions – web pages are written in HTML, CSS are used to simplify content presentation, and SQL is used for data access, usually with powerful object-relational mapping frameworks.

The dynamic layer reflects the essence and dynamic nature of programming languages (Ford, 2006). The goal is to avoid the compilation ceremony (Bini, 2008) that slows down the deployment of new features. Therefore, the dynamic layer includes programming languages like Clojure, Groovy, Ruby, Python, and JavaScript.

The Stable layer forms the hard kernel – or sometimes only a thin foundation – that the system is developed upon. It thrives for performance with static type checking and other properties of programming languages that help in the creation of high-performance software. The stable layer provides the resources and services for dynamic layer to utilize and defines external application programming interfaces (APIs), so that developers can take advantage of static type information for APIs while retaining full flexibility in implementation. The stable layer includes programming languages such as Java and Scala.

DESIGNING POLYGLOT PROGRAMS

Fjeldberg (2008) proposed a degree for polyglotism – usage of multiple programming languages – to differentiate the type of use of polyglot programming. The proposed levels of polyglotism by Fjeldberg (2008) are integration, organization of code, the process that runs the programming languages, and the data being manipulated. Integration is either networked or non-networked, the organization of code separates the code written inside same or different files. Both the same or separate processes are used to run the different programming languages, and the programming languages manipulate either the same object or the same data. Table 2 describes the levels of polyglot programming for different architectures. HTML in conjunction with CSS, JavaScript and a server-side language is referred as HTML++ for abbreviation.

Table 2. Levels of polyglot programming in different systems (Fjeldberg, 2008)

Architecture	Integration	Organization	Process	Data/Object
SOA	Networked	Different files	Different	Same data
Managed runtime	Not networked	Different files	Same	Same object
HTML++ server	Not networked	Different files	Different	Same data
HTML++ client	Not networked	Same files	Same	Same object
CI system	Not networked	Different files	Different	Same data

Guidelines for Architecting Polyglot Programs

After deciding to use multiple languages, a project must be assessed against the layers of the polyglot programming pyramid. The following list highlights project areas suited for these three layers in a project.

- **Domain Specific:** Build, Continuous Integration, Continuous Deployment, DevOps, Enterprise Integration, Pattern modeling, Business rules modeling.
- **Dynamic:** Rapid web development, Prototyping, Interactive administrative and user consoles, Scripting, Tests (such as for test- and behavior-driven development).
- **Stable:** Concurrent code, Application containers, Core business functionality.

Identifying the scenario that could be resolved with an alternative language is just the beginning. It is important to evaluate whether utilization of an alternative language is feasible. Evans and Verburg (2012) proposed five items to consider: 1) Risk exposure of the project area should be revised, and 2) the ease of interoperability with Java considered. 3) Tool support for an alternative language should be examined. 4) The learning curve for a new language should be evaluated, and 5) the ease of hiring experienced developers for the alternative language considered.

Consider a Java implementation of a stable piece of a payment processing system that handles millions of transactions per day. The code has plenty of dark corners with insufficient test coverage. This reveals definitely a high-risk area for a new programming language to be added, especially due to the lack of test coverage and a pool of developers who understand the software in detail. However, when considering the complete system, there is more into it than just the core processing. This situation can be salvaged with better tests and test coverage, which in contrast is a low-risk action (Ford, 2008). Scala, with its sophisticated ScalaTest framework, can remove boilerplate generated with Java's JUnit testing framework, while still enabling the production of familiar JUnit like tests. Improved developer productivity and test coverage would be achieved after the initial learning curve. Comprehensive testing then provides support when the core needs refactoring (Evans and Verburg, 2012). Another low-risk area for experimenting with a new language would be developing a noncritical web console for monitoring the static data behind the original system. Focusing on a limited pilot in low-risk area would allow ease of termination of the project or switching the technology stack without much disruption (Evans and Verburg, 2012). Selecting a language that runs on the Java Virtual Machine then preserves the value of the existing code base (Evans and Verburg, 2012).

A sophisticated development environment is often taken for granted since Java developers have for years benefited from great tool support. Most developers underestimate the time they save once they get comfortable with today's powerful IDEs and build and test tools. While some of the alternative languages, like Groovy for instance, have had longstanding IDE support for compiling, testing and deployment, some other languages have not reached the same level of maturity or sophistication. Still, for example the supporters of Scala feel that the power and conciseness of the programming language itself more than makes up for the imperfections of the unpolished generation of IDEs. A related issue emerges when alternative languages are supported by powerful tools available only for that particular language, like the powerful build tool Leiningen for Clojure. Consequently, a careful consideration is needed to decompose a project to distinct, interoperable components (Evans and Verburg, 2012).

Finally, similarly to developers, organizations have to be pragmatic. Inside an organization, the developers and development teams change. Thus the programming language selections directly affect the developers working on a project but also the hiring process. When programming language enjoys a well-established social and technical infrastructure this is not problematic, since there will be lots of developers with enough knowledge. In contrast, using an in-house tool or an exotic language can lead to recruitment problems.

Poly-Paradigm Programming

Sebesta (2009) classified programming languages according to programming paradigms. Different programming paradigms have distinct strengths and weaknesses and domain areas where the programming paradigm is best suited. Next, we will briefly address some commonly used paradigms and their effect to polyglot architecting.

Following the fundamental computer architecture of the von Neumann-Eckert model where a defined sequence of commands are executed in order of appearance (Tucker and Noonan, 2007), the imperative programming paradigm provides a good performance, because it offers little abstraction. At the same time, the lack of abstraction is a limitation of the paradigm, because without reasonable abstractions the effort to manage and organize a large software system becomes complicated.

The object-oriented programming paradigm focuses on object-oriented decomposition instead of data abstraction and functional decomposition. Objects are represented using a class concept, which encapsulates constants, variables and functions, also supporting inheritance, visibility and information hiding (Tucker and Noonan, 2007). The higher abstraction provides a more natural organization of related aspects, which is especially beneficial in large software systems, although at the cost of performance.

The functional programming paradigm adopts mathematical thinking, and shifts the focus from how something should be computed to what should be computed. Recent interest in functional programming is caused by the introduction of multicore processors, where concurrency becomes an essential factor. Functional programming does not involve any use of variables, but considers everything as a function with an input and a result. Functions interact with one another through functional composition, conditionals, and recursion (Tucker and Noonan, 2007). In addition to concurrency, other important characteristics of functional programming include lazy evaluation and higher-order functions. Lazy evaluation ensures that functions are called and values evaluated only when necessary, therefore infinite expressions can be created and evaluated using only the values needed. Higher-order functions provide the basis for functional programming by allowing functions to be passed on, in addition to values, to other functions (Hughes, 1989). The major problem with functional programming is that it introduces a steep learning curve for developers accustomed to object-oriented programming languages, because a completely different mindset is needed.

Concurrent, parallel, and reactive programming paradigms are increasingly important paradigms. Asynchronous message-passing can be used to implement elegant communication in a client-server application or to parallelize computation. Functional nature of programming languages facilitates the writing of concurrent, parallel, and reactive programs. (Syme et al., 2011; Petricek and Syme, 2011)

The logical programming paradigm adopts declarative thinking, and shifts the focus from declaring how something should be accomplished to what should be accomplished. Logical programming often gives a collection of assertions, or rules about the constraints and outcomes, thus it is also called rule-based programming. Logical programming has two distinct properties which are nondeterminism and backtracking. Nondeterminism allows multiple solutions to a problem, and backtracking is a concept of a partial candidate solution to determine relatively quickly if a solution candidate can possibly be completed to a valid solution (Tucker and Noonan, 2007). The ability to specify what should happen enables the machine to decide how to accomplish the task, and optimize the performance. The disadvantage of logical programming is that the paradigm is very specialized and somewhat limited to the field of artificial intelligence and database information retrieval (Tucker and Noonan, 2007).

A programming language can be either statically or dynamically typed independently of its paradigm. A language that is statically typed requires that types of all variables are statically defined before compilation, while dynamically typed languages allow the declaration of types at runtime and the types can change. An exception is typecasting, which is checked at runtime in many programming languages (Tucker and Noonan, 2007). Statically typed programming languages usually provide better performance because the compiler can make optimizations based on the known types. Dynamically typed programming languages are often interpreted, and thus they allow new features to be implemented and tested without laborious compilation. Because of the type of the variable is implicit in dynamically typed programming languages, the implementations require less LOC in contrast to statically typed languages.

Software development and domain engineering use DSLs which are a type of programming and specification languages dedicated to particular problem domains and representation and solution techniques. DSLs are in extensive use in web development. Examples include CSS, regular expressions and Ant scripts. DSLs are also essential in language-oriented programming (Ward, 1994), and apparent in the polyglot programming pyramid representation. Since DSLs are designed specifically for the problem domain, they increase productivity. However, a considerable effort must be invested in creation of a new DSL, which should be compensated by increased productivity in the long run.

Scripting languages support the writing of scripts, or programs that automate the execution of tasks which could alternatively be executed by a human operator (Loui, 2008). Scripts are used to automate build and compilation process of software applications, web page interactions within web browsers, and in several general-purpose and domain-specific programming languages. Scripting languages offer ease of use through relatively simple syntax and semantics, and a good operating system facilities with built-in interfaces. The source code is interpreted to provide fast turnaround from script to execution. The spectrum of scripting languages varies from general-purpose languages to compact, highly domain-specific ones.

POLYGLOT PYRAMID(S) FOR THE WEB

The polyglot pyramid illustrates the languages used in different domains of a polyglot system. The previously described representation has been criticized to represent only a layered structure of a polyglot software system instead of a fractal structure, where a self-similarity pattern is repeated (Bini, 2008).

Fractals look the same from near as from far (Mandelbrot, 1983), but exclude trivial self-similarity and include the idea of detailed pattern repeating itself (Gouyet and Mandelbrot, 1996). Thus representing different programming languages in a layered manner with the polyglot pyramid requires refinement.

A programming environment is constituted by the programming language and frameworks, libraries and tools, whose role has been increasing. Excellent frameworks and libraries are the main reason for using polyglot programming in web development. The fractal representation can thus be improved by introducing frameworks and libraries, and more so by assessing their contents. Some principles of separation between the layers have to be overlooked, however.

Consider an example web development project shown in Figure 3. In the figure, the stable layer provides a well-tested Java Hibernate database interaction as its core functionality. The dynamic layer is used for rapid web development, and therefore the front-end of the application is implemented using Groovy and its high-productivity web framework Grails. In addition, JavaScript and the powerful jQuery library are used to provide enhanced, dynamic web content. The domain layer is used to identify specific needs of the application, including concatenated HTML markup, CSS presentation semantics, and SQL when communicating with Hibernate.

Polyglot programming pyramid clearly lacks information when aiming at the documentation of the complete polyglot system, because only programming languages are represented. Important decisions like using Hibernate in conjunction with SQL for object-relational mapping and database interaction, or Grails framework for rapid web development are not documented. In addition, the domain layer gives only a vague abstraction with none or little value by specifying DSLs like HTML and CSS. Therefore, by including frameworks and libraries, and by opening them up when necessary as shown in Figure 4, one can represent much more detailed information regarding the polyglot system and its structure. In addition, the separation of concerns is utilized in a deeper manner, since also techniques used in solving the different concerns are expressed separately.

Web software systems – like most other software systems as well – are prone to change requests, whether updating the look and feel or extending the functionality of an application. Even upgrading to a new release of underlying frameworks can imply changes to the source code of an application. Building

Figure 3. Polyglot pyramid of a sample web application

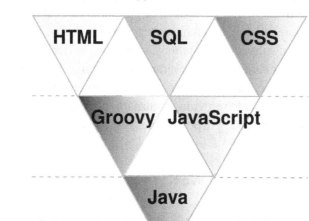

Figure 4. Improving polyglot programming pyramid fractal representation with frameworks

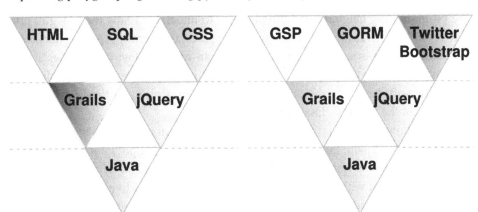

a software system with the required flexibility may prove to be ineffective and laborious when using a single programming language. The selected languages will dictate the paradigms and idioms, but also overrule some others.

Web development allows using different programming and specification languages when addressing different problem domains. Front-end code standards commonly separate the presentation, content and behavior. In addition, web applications usually follow the three-tier client-server architecture where the user interface, business logic, data access are developed and maintained as independent modules. When developing such system, changes to the different layers of the polyglot pyramid should be easy and they should not interact with other layers. Therefore, the polyglot pyramid(s) becomes an important piece of architectural documentation.

A SAMPLE REAL-LIFE SYSTEM

The recent introduction of non-Java programming languages running on the Java Virtual Machine has led to cross-fertilization between Java and other programming languages constructed on top of the JVM. The emergence of polyglot programming in projects involving languages such as Groovy, Scala and Clojure has become a major factor in the evolution of the current Java platform. Java's nature makes it a prominent choice for implementing functionality in the stable layer. A mature general-purpose, statically typed and compiled language has many advantages.

However, these advantages may become a burden in the upper layers. For instance recompilation is laborious, and deployment is a time consuming process. Static typing can lead to long refactoring times due to its inflexibility, and Java's syntax is not naturally well-suited for producing domain-specific languages. The fact that the recompilation and rebuild time of a Java project quickly reaches the 90 seconds to 2 minutes mark will definitely break the developer's flow (Feathers, 2004). In addition, it is a bad practice for developing code that may live only for a few weeks in the production. A pragmatic solution is to take use of Java's rich application programming interface and library support in the stable layer. Similarly, if a particular feature such as a superior concurrency support is required, a pragmatic choice would be to choose another stable layer language with such vantage like Scala. However, working stable layer code should not be rewritten in a different stable layer language (Graham, 2004). The distinction between the programming language and the platform is a critical concept to comprehend. It is essential to separate the programming language and the platform to understand how the polyglot programming on the JVM is feasible. The Java programming language is a general-purpose, concurrent, strongly typed and class-based object-oriented language. The human-readable Java source files are compiled by the javac Java compiler into bytecode class files, which are not human-readable. The Java platform, on the other hand, is the software that provides a runtime environment, in particular the JVM to link and execute the bytecode in the form of class files.

Next, we describe how polyglot programming was applied in four projects where a simple web application was created (Harmanen, 2013). The goal was to experiment polyglot programming in a real-world context. The project was implemented both using solely Java and in conjunction with Groovy. An additional Groovy project with Java domain model was constructed to explore interoperability with legacy code. As for the client side, Vert.x and AngularJS frameworks, both building on JavaScript, were used to enable direct comparison of several polyglot systems. The Vert.x project provided a different approach with its JavaScript client-side application.

A simple web application is often split into four layers: domain model, data access, business logic and web layer for binding other layers to the web environment. The application consists of a small domain model with only simple business logic to add, remove, and list departments and employees. The simplicity of the application limits its ability to demonstrate all cases where different languages and paradigms might be useful, but the design validates that the concept has potential in web development.

Tools used for managing the project(s) are the following. The Java project used Maven for managing the project and its dependencies. Groovy projects benefit from the convention over configuration provided by the Grails framework by using the built-in Grails dependency resolution DSL. Vert.x project is also managed with Maven, and its own module repository is used to fetch required modules. All of the example projects utilize jQuery JavaScript library to simplify the client-side scripting of HTML and to produce more dynamic web content. Another common element is the sleek and intuitive Twitter Bootstrap front-end framework that is used to ease and speed up the content presentation and web development in general.

The architecture of the Java project in Figure 5 follows the four-layer architecture of a simple web application. Domain model represents the real-world problem, repository provides the data access abstraction and service implements the business logic, whereas web module binds the whole application to the web environment. Java provides the basis for the polyglot system in this example, as it is located in the stable layer of the polyglot programming pyramid. Spring, an efficient and versatile web application framework, contributes to the dynamic layer. It, together with related technologies, plays a key part in the design by contributing to all layers.

Similarly, the architecture of the Groovy project in Figure 6 follows the principles of the four-layer architecture, although the repository layer is omitted due to data access is encapsulated in the domain model objects. Domain model represents the real-world problem, service implements the business logic and utilizes the domain model data access abstraction, whereas web module binds the whole application to the web environment. Groovy is the programming language in the stable layer. Grails framework provides fully fledged agile web development environment built upon existing technologies like Spring Framework and Hibernate. Grails follows the principle of convention over configuration and thus strives for quick and simple development providing common features out of the box. Grails is an essential framework, and it contributes to all the layers.

Figure 5. Architecture and Polyglot Pyramid of the Java project

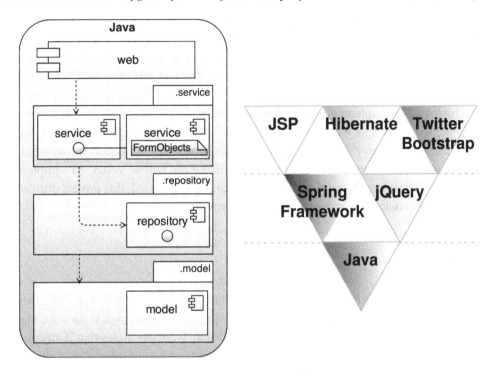

Figure 6. Architecture and Polyglot Pyramid of the Groovy project

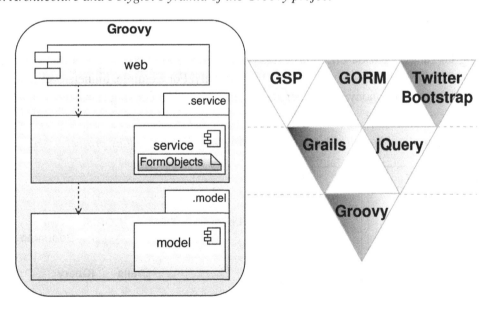

The architecture of the Groovy project with a Java legacy domain model is shown in Figure 7. This project was utilized to research programming language interoperability on the JVM and to provide a proof of concept on how to use Java domain model from a legacy project in a Groovy on Grails web application project. The architecture and the polyglot pyramid are combinations of the architectures and pyramids from previously described Java and Groovy projects.

The Vert.x project differs from the architectural point of view by following the principles of a thin server architecture used to implement a single-page application (SPA), as shown in Figure 8. An application implemented as a single web page with a goal of providing more fluid user experience similar to a desktop application. Groovy was used to provide the server-side functionality whereas Javascript was used to implement the client-side. Both of them utilized the native Vert.x API implementations. Contrary to other projects where a traditional relational database was used, this project utilized a NoSQL document database with data access over an event bus provided by Vert.x.

DISCUSSION

An emerging pattern is visible in the results (Fjeldberg, 2008; Harmanen, 2013). Selecting an appropriate programming language for the task at hand denotes better productivity, though it does not imply that the appropriate or a new programming language should be chosen. It simply states that if any programming language is more appropriate for the task at hand, it should at least be considered regardless of the possible increase in required knowledge or the decrease of developers with enough knowledge in hiring or maintenance.

Amount of Code

Programming languages provide different levels of verbosity and expressiveness that can reduce the amount of code required to implement the same functionality. For example, higher-level functions with more convenient syntax for anonymous inner classes and functional language structures can remove the

Figure 7. Architecture and Polyglot Pyramid of the Java and Groovy legacy project

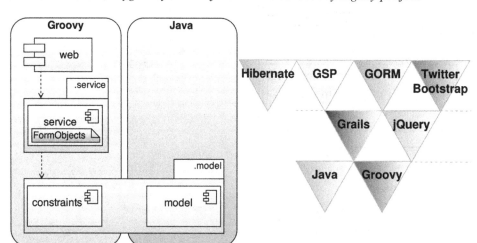

Figure 8. Architecture and Polyglot Pyramid of the Vert.x project

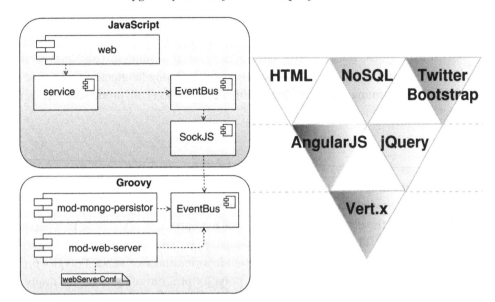

excess use of loop structures in imperative programming languages. Similarly, dynamic languages offer higher level of abstraction and in general reduce repetition.

Programming languages that follow convention over configuration and do not repeat yourself principles can reduce a significant amount of configuration and boilerplate code. In addition, separation of concerns is a powerful tool when packaging applications or reusable resources as modules. Out-of-the-box modules and applications can provide powerful functionalities in just few lines of code.

Lean programming practices can be used to eliminate waste effort and boilerplate code by favoring "pull" design over "push" design. Since implementations are built only to satisfy the needs of business requirements the necessary code is usually shorter. For example, repository pattern can be used to abstract the data access layer and shield the rest of the application implementation from having to know how the persistence works.

In order to make a bigger impact, the chosen programming language has to be applied at a more advanced level. A smaller code base can be achieved by revisiting the whole architecture of the application to correspond with the best practices of the chosen programming languages and frameworks.

Code Quality

Code quality does not directly imply anything about the amount of defects in an application. Architectural patterns and design principles are important factors that reflect on the code quality. These represent guidelines when creating, changing or extending an application, or when introducing new developers.

Different programming languages and paradigms present syntactic advantages that can improve code quality by making the implementations more clear and intuitive. This has the potential to reduce errors by making the code more readable. Furthermore, different frameworks provide syntactic advantages, which can improve the code quality. The increased expressiveness and reduced amount of supportive code reduces the possibility of erroneous code.

Implementations that are more compact and have less boilerplate and irrelevant code enable developers to focus on the relevant sections, thus making the actual business logic more visible. In addition, stronger typing, functional paradigm and clean syntax can help to reduce programming errors like null pointer or class cast exceptions. Immutability and stateless programming are also powerful tools that remove errors in many common places where imperative programming languages might pose errors. For example, functional programming removes loops, which tend to be error-prone sections in imperative programming languages

Productivity

Developers tend to divide roughly into two categories. The language centric developers concentrate their effort on gathering knowledge on new programming languages and features, whereas tool centric developers familiarize with the development tools to enhance productivity. These two perspectives, or more so traits, are competitive. Therefore, the more invested in learning programming language features, the bigger is the benefit, although to the exclusion of tool features and vice versa. Polyglot programmers are though as language centric developers, although polyglot programming does not imply the use of new and unsupported programming languages and features.

Advanced syntax in several programming languages increases developer productivity, since it allows developers to write the intent without the necessary loops and temporary variables. However this requires a comprehensive knowledge of the programming language and frameworks used as well as a good IDE support, which in turn can require additional investment to learning the required skills.

When choosing programming languages and frameworks for web development, the decisions should always be made based on the complexity of the web application and by following the assumption of increased productivity. Tools should make the development experience as enjoyable and productive as possible, which obviously also has an effect on developers' attitudes towards polyglot programming. Architectural approaches such as thin server architecture and single-page application in client-side web application development are becoming de facto standard.

Recommendations

Polyglot programming has the potential to improve web development in various areas. Perceived advantages are increased productivity, reduced amount of code and improved code quality that together promote better maintainability. Perceived disadvantages are the additional effort required in learning, which has an effect on required knowledge, maintainability, and tool support. Although increase in the amount of required knowledge is also perceived as a challenge to improve oneself as a developer rather than an obligation to barely overcome.

Polyglot programming divides the different programming languages roughly into three layers. The particular layers are fit for different problem domains and programming challenges. The stable layer consists of programming languages like Java and Scala to do the heavy lifting, whereas programming languages like Groovy and Clojure are more suitable for tasks in the dynamic layer providing rapid web development. The domain layer consists mainly on domain-specific languages targeting specific problem domains.

The core business functionality of existing production software is almost never the correct place to introduce a new programming language. The core requires a high-grade support with comprehensive test coverage in addition to the proven stability of the programming language. A low-risk area should be chosen for the first deployment of an alternative programming language.

Finally, there are no universal right answers, only guidelines. The unique characteristics of each team and project will impact on the decision of which programming language to choose. The nature of the projects and teams should always be assessed by the managers and senior developers when considering the introduction of a new programming language.

CONCLUSION

In this paper, we have provided a comprehensive research on polyglot programming at a general level, and more particularly in web development and on the Java platform. The work enhances the polyglot programming pyramid to act as an architectural pattern to solve and document problem domains suitable for polyglot programming.

REFERENCES

Beardsmore, H. (1978). Polyglot literature and linguistic fiction. *International Journal of the Sociology of Language, 15*(1), 91–102. doi:10.1515/ijsl.1978.15.91

Bini, O. (2008). *Fractal programming*. Retrieved January 10, 2015, from https://olabini.com/blog/

Brooks, F. (1995). *Calling the Shots. In The Mythical Man-Month: Essays on Software Engineering*. Addison-Wesley.

Cataldo, M., Bass, M., Herbsleb, J., & Bass, L. (2007). On coordination mechanisms in global software development. In *Proceedings of the Second IEEE International Conference on Global Software Engineering*. (pp. 71-80). Munich, Germany: IEEE. doi:10.1109/ICGSE.2007.33

Cataldo, M., Herbsleb, J., & Carley, K. (2008). Socio-technical congruence: a framework for assessing the impact of technical and work dependencies on software development productivity. In *Proceedings of the Second ACM-IEEE International Symposium on Empirical Software Engineering and Measurement*. (pp. 2-11). Kaiserslautern, Germany: IEEE. doi:10.1145/1414004.1414008

De Souza, C. (2005). *On the relationship between software dependencies and coordination: field studies and tool support*. (Doctoral dissertation). University of California, Irvine, CA.

Delorey, D., Knutson, C., & Chun, S. (2007). Do programming languages affect productivity? A case study using data from open source projects. In *Proceedings of the First International Workshop on Emerging Trends in FLOSS Research and Development* (pp. 8-8). Minneapolis, MN. doi:10.1109/FLOSS.2007.5

Evans, B., & Verburg, M. (2012). *The Well-Grounded Java Developer: Vital techniques of Java 7 and polyglot programming*. Manning Publications Co.

Feathers, M. (2004). *Working effectively with legacy code*. Prentice Hall. doi:10.1007/978-3-540-27777-4_42

Fjeldberg, H. (2008). *Polyglot Programming: A business perspective.* (Master's thesis). Norwegian University of Science and Technology, Trondheim, Norway.

Flanagan, C., & Abadi, M. (1999). *Types for safe locking. In Programming Languages and Systems* (LNCS), (pp. 91–108). Springer Berlin Heidelberg. doi:10.1007/3-540-49099-X_7

Ford, N. (2006). *Polyglot Programming.* Retrieved January 10, 2015, from http://memeagora.blogspot.fi/

Ford, N. (2008). *Polyglot Programming. In ThoughtWorks Anthology. Essays on Software Technology and Innovation* (pp. 60–69). ThoughWorks, Inc.

Gouyet, J.-F., & Mandelbrot, B. (1996). *Physics and fractal structures.* Masson.

Graham, P. (2004). *Hackers & painters: big ideas from the computer age.* O'Reilly Media, Inc.

Harmanen, J. (2013). *Polyglot Programming in Web Development.* (Master's thesis). Tampere University of Technology, Tampere, Finland.

Hughes, J. (1989). Why Functional Programming Matters. *The Computer Journal, 32*(2), 98–107. doi:10.1093/comjnl/32.2.98

Hunt, A., & Thomas, D. (1999). *The Pragmatic Programmer: From Journeyman to Master.* Addison-Wesley.

Loui, R. (2008). In praise of scripting: Real programming pragmatism. *Computer, IEEE, 41*(7), 22–26. doi:10.1109/MC.2008.228

Mandelbrot, B. (1983). *The fractal geometry of nature.* W. H. Freeman and Company.

Maxwell, K., Van Wassenhove, L., & Dutta, S. (1996). Software development productivity of European space, military, and industrial applications. *Transactions on Software Engineering, IEEE, 22*(10), 706–718. doi:10.1109/32.544349

Ostrand, T., Weyuker, E., & Bell, R. (2005). Predicting the location and number of faults in large software systems. *Transactions on Software Engineering, IEEE, 31*(4), 340–355. doi:10.1109/TSE.2005.49

Pareto, L. (2000). *Types for Crash Prevention.* (Doctoral dissertation). Chalmers University of Technology, Göteborg, Sweden.

Petricek, T., & Syme, D. (2011). *Joinads: a retargetable control-flow construct for reactive, parallel and concurrent programming. In Practical Aspects of Declarative Languages* (pp. 205–219). Springer Berlin Heidelberg.

Sebesta, R. W. (2009). *Concepts of Programming Languages.* Addison-Wesley.

Sullivan, K., Griswold, W., Cai, Y., & Hallen, B. (2001). The structure and value of modularity in software design. *Software Engineering Notes, ACM SIGSOFT, 26*(5), 99–108. doi:10.1145/503271.503224

Syme, D., Petricek, T., & Lomov, D. (2011). *The F# Asynchronous Programming Model. In Practical Aspects of Declarative Languages* (pp. 175–189). Springer Berlin Heidelberg. doi:10.1007/978-3-642-18378-2_15

Tucker, A., & Noonan, R. (2007). *Programming languages: principles and paradigms* (2nd ed.). Tata McGraw-Hill Education.

Vinoski, S. (2008). Multilanguage Programming. *IEEE Internet Computing*, *12*(3), 83–85. doi:10.1109/MIC.2008.58

Ward, M. (1994). Language-oriented programming. *Software Concepts and Tools*, *15*(4), 147–161.

KEY TERMS AND DEFINITIONS

Multilanguage Application: Application software implemented using several programming languages.

Polyglot Programming: A technique to combine and utilize the best solutions from different programming languages and paradigms in a seamless fashion in creation of application software.

Programming Paradigm: A set of programming concepts and patterns that serve as a way of implementing the structure and elements of application software.

Chapter 7
Cloud–Based Multi–View Modeling Environments

Jonathan Corley
University of Alabama, USA

Huseyin Ergin
University of Alabama, USA

Eugene Syriani
University of Montreal, Canada

Simon Van Mierlo
University of Antwerp, Belgium

ABSTRACT

Complex systems typically involve many stakeholder groups working in a coordinated manner on different aspects of a system. In Model-Driven Engineering (MDE), stakeholders work on models in order to design, transform, simulate, and analyze the system. Therefore, there is a growing need for collaborative platforms for modelers to work together. A cloud-based system allows them to concurrently work together. This chapter presents the challenges for building such environments. It also presents the architecture of a cloud-based multi-view modeling environment based on AToMPM.

INTRODUCTION

Complex systems engineering typically involves many stakeholder groups working in a coordinated manner on different aspects of a system. Each aspect addresses a specific set of system concerns and is associated with a domain space consisting of problem or solution concepts described using specialized terminology. Therefore engineers express their models in different domain-specific languages (DSL) to work with abstractions expressed in domain-specific terms (Combemale, Deantoni, Baudry, France, Jézéquel, & Gray, 2014).

Model-Driven Engineering (MDE) (Stahl, Voelter, & Czarnecki, 2006) is considered a well-established software development approach that uses abstraction to bridge the gap between the problem domain and the software implementation. MDE uses models to specify, simulate, test, verify, and generate code for applications. A model represents an abstraction of a real system, capturing some of its essential properties, to reduce accidental complexity present in the technical space. A model conforms to a metamodel (Kühne, 2006), which defines the abstract syntax of a DSL. The metamodel specifies the permissible concepts, relations and properties that models conforming to the metamodel can have. Models are rep-

DOI: 10.4018/978-1-4666-9916-8.ch007

Copyright © 2016, IGI Global. Copying or distributing in print or electronic forms without written permission of IGI Global is prohibited.

resented with a concrete syntax (graphical or textual) which defines the notations used to represent each model element. MDE activities typically include the development of modeling languages, the design of models, the implementation of model transformations, the run-time execution of models, and the analysis of models. Several modeling tools exist today, such as AToMPM (Syriani, Vangheluwe, Mannadiar, Hansen, Van Mierlo, & Ergin, 2013), EMF (Steinberg, Budinsky, Paternostro, & Merks, 2008), GME (Ledeczi, et al., 2001), and MetaEdit+ (Kelly, Lyytinen, & Rossi, 1996).

Recently, there has been a growing trend toward collaborative environments especially those utilizing browser-based interfaces. Common tools include Google Docs (Google Inc., 2015), Trello (Trello Inc., 2015), Asana (Asana, 2015), and more. Additionally, this trend can be seen in software development tools including WebGME, a web-based collaborative modeling version of GME (Maróti, et al., 2014) and Eclipse webIDE (The Eclipse Foundation, 2015). These tools bring together developers, including geographically distributed teams, in a collaborative development environment to work on a shared set of software artifacts. However, the introduction of these collaborative environments bring new concerns.

In this chapter, we address the need to provide a collaborative environment for domain-specific modeling. Furthermore, in order to ensure consistency and synchronization among the artifacts produced by each stakeholder, we favor a cloud-based environment. Although there is a growing need for such environments, few modeling tools allow multiple stakeholders to work on their modeled system concurrently. In this chapter, we first define the requirement and challenges for a collaborative modeling environment where we enumerate the possible collaboration scenarios. We then present our tool AToMPM, which was designed for collaborative modeling in the cloud, and describe the detailed architecture of how AToMPM solves the challenges of the collaboration scenarios. Additionally, we present competing approaches to ensure consistency and synchronization among shared artifacts with discussion of how the competing approaches differ from the approach applied in AToMPM.

BACKGROUND

Online collaboration tools are very popular with the rise of new HTML5 technologies. Offerings such as Google Docs (Google Inc., 2015), Trello (Trello Inc., 2015), Asana (Asana, 2015) and many others take advantage of sophisticated features of new web technologies. They enable users to accomplish tasks without the need for a native client. Modern modeling tools are primarily native desktop applications, e.g., EMF (Steinberg, Budinsky, Paternostro, & Merks, 2008) and MetaEdit+ (Kelly, Lyytinen, & Rossi, 1996). AToMPM is the first web-based collaboration tool for model-driven engineering. It takes advantage of the ever increasing capabilities of web technologies to provide a purely in-browser interface for multi-paradigm modeling activities. Nevertheless, Clooca (Hiya, Hisazumi, Fukuda, & Nakanishi, 2013) is a web-based modeling environment that lets the user creates domain-specific modeling languages and code generators. However, it does not provide any collaboration support.

Recently, Maroti et al. proposed WebGME, a web-based collaborative modeling version of GME (Maróti, et al., 2014). WebGME offers a collaboration where each user can share the same model and work on it. It has a Mongo database server as a backend for model repository. In contrast to the modelverse, which is a specialized modeling-optimized repository, WebGME uses a simple branching scheme with a generic document-based NoSQL database to manage the actions of different users on the same model. A user may request a branch update after manipulating the model. If other users do not submit branch update requests or do not modify the model in any submitted branch updates (i.e., the model is not changed), then the branch update of the current user is applied and the changes are broadcasted to other users of the same model. When a branch update fails (meaning the model has already been modified in the database) the client can either 1) reject the local change and present the new changes in the server to the user, 2) automatically create another branch from the changes made in the local model, or 3) perform a merge of the local changes with the changes in the server. After completing one of the three options, the user retries a branch update. This simple versioning functions similar to the GIT version control system (GitHub, 2015). Using this version control system, WebGME makes the user work with local copies of models and updates the models in the database only after the user requested a branch update. Even though, it supports multi-user single-view and multi-view single-model scenarios, basing a real-time update on user requests prevents WebGME from having a pure collaborative environment as in AToMPM. The MVC structure from AToMPM provides a view-based system, where each user subscribes to changes in that specific view. Therefore, the user does not need to get all updates of the model from the server and only the elements represented in that view. Furthermore, MVC is a live solution where conflicting updates scenarios are limited and operations will either immediately succeed or fail as appropriate.

The GEMOC Initiative (Combemale, Deantoni, Baudry, France, Jézéquel, & Gray, 2014) has produced GEMOC Studio (GEMOC Initiative, 2015), a modeling system handles a multi-view multi-model scenario. The intent of GEMOC Studio is to provide facilities for DSL developers to define composite DSLs combining multiple DSLs relevant to a project into a cohesive system with well-defined interaction of the various models (Combemale, et al., 2013). GEMOC Studio is contained within the Eclipse ecosystem and therefore a single-user desktop application. The solution provided for the multi-view multi-model is similar to the solution provided by MVC, but does not have the added complexity of handling multiple concurrent users. GEMOC Studio provides an alternative solution for the single-view multi-model scenario, by defining interactions of heterogeneous models. It requires the user to define the relations between models in advance. Thus, the solution is also the refactored single-view multi-model. The authors are not aware of a solution which handles the complexity of representing diverse models with arbitrary intent and notation within a single view that does not require user intervention to define the intersection of the models. The problem is likely unsolvable without some refinement of the domain and relations of the various models.

Eclipse webIDE (The Eclipse Foundation, 2015) is a new project aspiring to provide an in-browser interface for the Eclipse development environment. The project would, thus, present another option for in-browser modeling activities through the available Eclipse modeling tools (e.g., EMF and Epsilon). At the time of writing, the project is still under development, and therefore further discussion of the multi-view modeling capabilities is not possible.

The distributed databases community has also dealt with some of the issues of collaborative environments (Özsu & Valduriez, 2011). However, the primitives of modeling and distributed databases are not the same. Databases are concerned with a restricted set of low level data representations, and collaborative modeling systems utilize higher level abstractions that commonly include domain-specific concerns. However, similar to our view system, distributed databases must handle multiple database instances as external views, either co-located or located separately. Furthermore, distributed databases consider multiple users accessing concurrently, but the database systems lack the complexity of modeling systems.

REQUIREMENTS FOR A COLLABORATIVE MODELING ENVIRONMENT

In the following we first discuss the various collaboration situations that may occur in a collaborative development environment and then focus on how these apply to a domain-specific modeling environment.

General Collaboration Situations

In practice, teams of stakeholders work together in order to produce a coherent and complete system. For example, in the design of an automotive system, stakeholders are partitioned into teams based on their expertise: electrical engineers, mechanical engineers, control engineers, ergonomists, parts assemblers, etc. There are typically three situations when individuals within a team or across teams collaborate in order to produce the overall system:

1. *Stakeholders are working on the exact same artifact.* This is equivalent to having both of them share the same screen. In this case, all changes made by one stakeholder are directly reflected and perceived by the other stakeholders, such as in Google Docs. This situation is useful when, for example, two stakeholders are manually inspecting a model together, if one stakeholder is training the other, or in a development process favoring pair development (like in extreme programming) (Beck, 1999).
2. *Stakeholders are working on different parts of the same artifact.* This situation is useful when artifacts are designed incrementally. This is possible when the language, in which the artifact is described, offers a modularity mechanism that allows one to split its instances into different parts, such as partial classes in C# (Corporation, 2001) and aliases in UML diagrams (Object Management Group, 2012).
3. *Stakeholders with differing expertise are working on distinct artifacts that, together, compose the overall system.* In this case, each artifact represents a concern of the overall system, e.g., the electrical, software, and the security concerns of an automotive. This is useful when a system is designed by separating its concerns, such as in aspect-oriented programming (Kiczales & Hilsdale, 2001).

Collaboration Scenarios in Multi-View Modeling

Modeling tools, frameworks, and language workbenches, such as AToMPM, EMF, and GME, typically consider all developed artifacts as models. In the context of a collaborative effort among individuals, such tools must separate views from models. A view is a projection of the model, showing only a part of the model in its own concrete syntax representation. Models are stored in a cloud-based repository and can only be accessed via their views. Therefore, it is necessary to have at least one view for a model to exist.

In order for tools to support collaborative modeling activities, we refine the previous collaboration situations into four possible collaboration scenarios for multi-view modeling. These are illustrated in Figure 1. For simplicity, we restrict our discussion to two users/views/models, although generalizable to an arbitrary number of each component. For each scenario, we briefly discuss what conflicts can occur when users are connected live to the cloud and an idea on how to resolve them. Note that, in practice, any combination of these scenarios is possible, but we will treat each one separately.

Figure 1. Scenarios in multi-view modeling

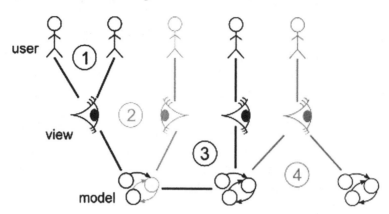

Multi-User Single-View: (① in Figure 1) Two users are working on the same view of the model. They both see the exact same data in the same concrete syntax. Changes made by one user are reflected automatically to the other. In the case of simultaneous conflicting changes (e.g., one user is deleting an element that the other user is updating), the conflict is resolved in a first come, first served fashion.

Multi-View Single-Model: (② in Figure 1) Two users are each working on a different view of the model. The two views may be presenting the same elements in the same or different concrete syntax. They may also share only some or no elements between them. In any case, the views represent a part of the same model and therefore the models in the views conform to the same modeling language. In the non-intersecting views cases, changes in one view are not reflected in the other view. Otherwise, if an element is present in both views, changes in its abstract syntax (e.g., value of the DC voltage in the electrical diagram model) in one view are reflected in the other view. However, changes that only affect the concrete syntax of the element (e.g., length of a wire) are not reflected in the other view. Note that some changes in the abstract syntax of an element may change its concrete representation (e.g., turning a switch on). In the case of simultaneous conflicting changes on a shared element, a conflict management strategy must be put in place to solve the conflict and maintain the two views consistent with each other.

Multi-View Multi-Model: (③ in Figure 1) Two users are each working on a different view and each view is a projection of a different model. The models define together the overall system. This means that elements in each view are part of models conforming to different modeling languages. However, the two models are subject to global consistency constraints (e.g., a method call to an object in a UML sequence diagram can only be established if the UML class diagram has defined that method on the target class of the object). Furthermore, an element in one model may explicitly rely on elements in the other model, by having a reference to it. Only if that reference is part of the view of the second model, then changes to the referenced element in the first model may be reflected in that view. In particular, if the referenced element is deleted in the original model, then a decision must be made for whether the deletion should cascade to the reference or not. Simultaneous conflicting changes to that element are not existent between the two views, since one view passively references the element.

Single-View Multi-Model: (④ in Figure 1) This is a particular case of the previous scenario where one user is working on a view that projects two models, while another user is working on a view of one of these models. In this case, it is the view that makes the link between elements of the two models as opposed to the previous case where that link is defined in the model. Typically, the view represents an abstraction of elements of the two models (e.g., a correspondence relation between the resistors of the electrical circuit and the heat sensor of the engine). This view is generally the one that defines the consistency relation between elements of the models. A change that occurs on the abstract syntax of an element in one of the models may therefore affect the view. This scenario is outside the scope of this chapter.

MULTI-VIEW, MULTI-USER MODELING IN ATOMPM

In this section, we describe how we enhanced the architecture of the modeling environment AToMPM to support multiple users and multiple views to collaboratively perform MDE activities on the cloud. Figure 2 illustrates the different components of this architecture. There are three primary components: client systems, Modelverse Kernel (MvK), and a set of controllers coordinating the other two components. The design is similar to the well-known Model-View-Controller pattern, in which the client is the *view*, the MvK is the *model*, and the controllers are the *controller*. The system is designed to be client agnostic and therefore supports a wide variety of clients. The MvK handles processing all modeling actions, such as primitive requests and execution, directly on models that are stored in a repository. The controllers ensure consistency among clients, views, and models. We therefore denote this latter part of the architecture MVC.

Modelverse Kernel

The Modelverse (Van Mierlo, Barroca, Vangheluwe, Syriani, & Kühne, 2014) is a repository, or database, of models. The Modelverse stores any modeling artefact, including, but not limited to, metamodels, concrete syntax, models, operations, and rule-based model transformations. It is accessible through an interface, consisting of basic CRUD operations. As the Modelverse is unaware of the (semantically)

Figure 2. Overview of Model-View Controllers Architecture

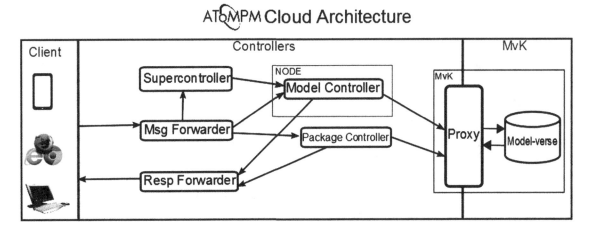

allowed operations, a kernel is necessary to coordinate all operations, and ensure consistency and conformance. This kernel is called the Modelverse Kernel (MvK).

The MvK exposes a public interface consisting of model management operations that allow users to interact with their models while ensuring a consistent data store. It consists of the following operations:

- **Create, Read, Update, Delete (CRUD):** Operations allow the user to manipulate and query logical elements.
- **Conformance Checks:** Allow to check whether one model conforms to another model. In particular, a user can check whether a model conforms to a metamodel. This metamodel defines a set of domain concepts (*classes* with *attributes*) that can be connected with each other (*associations*). It can optionally specify a minimum and maximum bound on these connections, called *multiplicities*. Furthermore, arbitrary constraints can be expressed in a constraint language. The check ensures that the model does not violate any constraint, i.e., it instantiates the correct types, and correctly combines them.
- **Executing:** Models, in particular models of computation. The Modelverse has a built-in, explicitly modeled (minimal) action language whose models can be executed. This allows the user to define operations and execute them.

Figure 3. shows the architecture of the Modelverse as a standalone model repository which is accessible through the MvK. In the figure, the central entity is a model *M*. It conforms linguistically to a linguistic type model, or metamodel, *LTM*. In the physical dimension, one type model is defined. It defines the concepts the Modelverse needs to know about in order to function: classes, attributes, associations, primitive data types, action language, and so forth. It acts both as a type model (to which all models in the Modelverse conform), and an interface definition for the implementation, which defines the representation on a physical medium, of those structures. Although the Modelverse can be seen as a database of models, the representation of those models on physical media, such as a relational database or in-memory objects, is not known to the user. This knowledge is not necessary because of the uniform

Figure 3. Modelverse

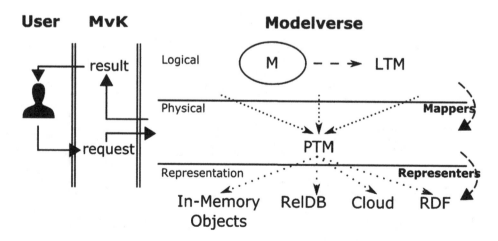

access through the MvK, as model management operations are performed on instances of the physical type model. A user only interacts with models on this conceptual level and will never need to query the actual physical representation. The representation of physical type model elements onto physical media is catered for by *representers*, one for each physical medium. For example, the default representer maps physical type model elements onto in-memory Python objects. Alternative representers would do the same for relational databases, RDF triple stores, and others. With this level of indirection, we make sure that this representation only has to be defined once: we know how to represent physical type model elements, which means we can represent any linguistic concept in the Modelverse, as all elements by construction conform to the physical type model. To ensure this conformance relation is maintained at all times, physical mappers map linguistic elements onto physical elements. In these mappers, it is possible for a language engineer to encode custom instantiation policies. For the built-in formalisms, such as Class Diagrams formalism, these policies are predefined and languages created using those formalisms automatically get assigned a mapper with the expected instantiation semantics.

Any element in the logical dimension can take the role of the model M – indeed, everything in the Modelverse is a model, and all models have a type model.

A user interacts with the Modelverse through the API exposed by the MvK. This user needs not be a human interacting through code: it can be a front-end, allowing a more user-friendly use of the Modelverse. A few examples of front-ends include a visual front-end, a human-usable textual notation, or any (formalism-specific) simulator, that interacts with the Modelverse to simulate the model.

A user request is handled by the MvK as follows. A user, or front-end, sends a request to the MvK. The MvK then redirects this request, after checking whether it is a valid operation, to the Modelverse, where the appropriate modifications and/or queries are performed. The result is returned in the form of a log, which either lists the changes performed as a result of the operation, or, in the case of a non-modifying operation, returns the result of the operation. In the case of an error, the log specifies an error code and message, which the user can inspect to decide on the best course of action.

Controllers

Messages in MVC are processed by a series of controllers that ensure consistency among clients and between view(s) and the model related to the view(s). All operations are sent in the form of a client changelog. Listing 1 shows a sample client changelog that requests to create a new place in a Petri nets model. A user can take actions such as create, read, update, or delete elements in a model (CRUD operations); load a model; add or remove elements from a view; save or execute a model or set of models; and more. These requests are sent into the system through a message forwarder that routes messages to the proper controller for processing. Similarly, responses return to the clients via a response forwarder. Forwarders make use of a simple publish-subscribe pattern to enable clients (and controllers) to subscribe to messages of interest. For example, a client would subscribe to receive updates for a specific view of interest. A client can be subscribed to many views and would receive all updates for each view to which they subscribe.

Listing 1. Sample Create Client Changelog

In the following, we describe how models are represented in the MVC and present the four controller types.

```
{
  "operation_name":"create",
  "location":"hergin.views.petrinet1.view",
  "am_location":"hergin.models.petrinet1",
  "element":"P5",
  "type":"hergin.formalisms.PetriNet.Metamodel.Place",
  "cs_attributes":{
    "position": [ 111,222],
    "scale": [1,1],
    "rotation":0
  },
  "attributes":{
    "token":5,
    "name":"P5"
  }
}
```

Models and Views in MVC

MVC separates models into two categories: abstract models and views. An abstract model represents the abstract syntax of the model of a system. It conforms to the metamodel of a given DSL. A view is a model that conforms to the view metamodel, presented in Figure 4. It references an abstract model and contains a set of elements from the abstract model that are included in the view.

The view also maintains a list of tools that are other models necessary to using the specific view. The most common example of a model to be found in the tools list is a concrete syntax model. By varying the concrete syntax between views, different users may view the same model using varying visualizations (e.g., textual or graphical). Other models included in the tools list could be custom executable models used for simulation or models defining transformation semantics relevant to the model. The tools list is controlled by the user. Models may be added or removed from this list as deemed necessary

Figure 4. The view metamodel

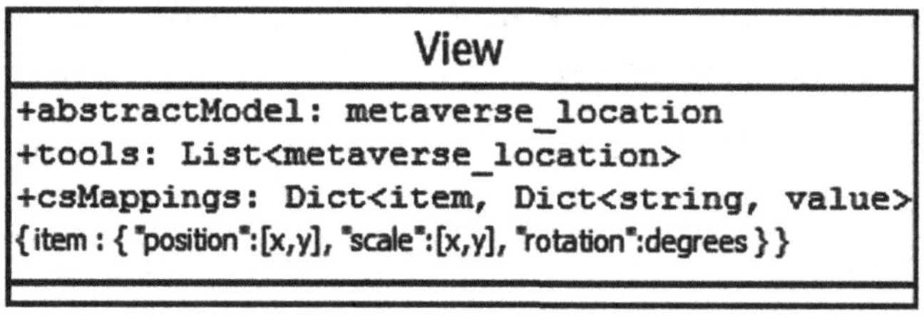

View
+abstractModel: metaverse_location
+tools: List<metaverse_location>
+csMappings: Dict<item, Dict<string, value>
{ item : { "position":[x,y], "scale":[x,y], "rotation":degrees } }

by the user. Finally, concrete syntax information of the model is stored in the view, since it is specific to a representation of the model and, therefore, does not belong to the abstract model. The csMappings dictionary defines the assignment of concrete syntax values to every element from the abstract model that is included in the view. In a graphical view, these values indicate, for example, the absolute position, rotation angle, and size scaling of the element.

This distinction between views and abstract models allows modelers to work with portions of a model and in their own representation, arrangement, and sizing for the elements of their view. The internal consistency can be ensured when elements are updated since all views reference the original elements from the model, but when an element is created or deleted it is possible to lose consistency. Furthermore, internal consistency is not sufficient for a multi-user context. It is also necessary to ensure consistency across many concurrent users.

Model Controller

A model controller manages a given model and all views of that model. Consistency of a model and the associated view(s) is maintained by the model controller. A model controller receives and processes all messages for a specific abstract model and its view(s). The model controller uses the publish-subscribe pattern of the message forwarder to accomplish this goal. Available model operations include CRUD operations on elements and loading a model. Available view operations include adding or removing elements and tools. Whenever a model operation alters a portion of the abstract model, the resulting changelog is sent to users using any view that references the updated portion of the model. The view operations are guaranteed to have no side effect on the model and thus do not need to update users of other views. Users may also send batch changelogs. The batch client changelog must contain only client changelogs intended for a single model controller or the package controller (discussed later). A batch client changelog is merely a convenience for sending large sequences of client changelogs together and is treated as a sequence of operations.

Incoming client changelogs are queued to be processed in the order they are received. The message queue is a FIFO queue. Thus, operations which originate from a later client changelog may fail based on the results of a previous message. To enable automatic resolution of conflicting messages, a message must "win" and a message must fail. By allowing the earlier message to win, the system does not need to process any rollback operations due to conflicting messages. The scenario is mitigated by the publishing of relevant update messages ensuring users each possess a consistent and current copy of the model. Thus, while it is possible that a set of users could send conflicting messages simultaneously, the users would be notified of the resolution for both messages in real time. Furthermore, users are notified of updates generated by other users in real time which reduces the likelihood of conflicting messages being generated.

The execution of operations is not performed at the model controller directly. Rather, the model controller coordinates the processing of operations within the MvK which directly processes all modeling operations. The MvK provides a more restrictive API designed. The MvK provides a pure modeling system where all entities are modeled and every entity is treated as a model. The model controller provides a layer of abstraction on top of the MvK for multi-user, multi-view modeling. The MvK is a simple system designed to process a sequence of basic model operations. The model controller ensures that the sequence of messages is valid and separates models and views which are treated uniformly within the MvK.

Supercontroller and Node Controllers

Model controllers manage all model and view related operations. For each model there is a single model controller. However, the system may have an untold number of models which would need to each have a model controller. If the system maintained these model controllers at all times, a significant amount of resources would be wasted on model controllers that are not in use. To mitigate this issue, we spawn model controllers on an as needed basis. Controlling which model controllers are active and assigning the model controllers to resources is the primary responsibility of the supercontroller.

The supercontroller monitors all client changelogs entering the system. When a client changelog is encountered, which requires a model controller that does not exist, the supercontroller queues the changelog. Any client changelog intended for an active model controller is ignored by the supercontroller. The supercontroller has an associated message processor that handles queued changelogs. The first message encountered for a model controller causes the message processor to generate a temporary backlog for further changelogs and the process of creating a new model controller begins.

The model controller is assigned to a node controller. Node controllers are abstract representations of available hardware computing resources (e.g., nodes in a cluster, CPUs, cores). Node controllers keep track of their assigned model controllers and can generate a load value based on the number of model controllers and other criteria as needed. The load value is used to determine to which node controller a model controller is assigned. Currently, the load value is based on the number of active model controllers, but in the future this value could also take into account frequency of incoming messages or number of users receiving updates for the node's active model controllers.

The supercontroller is responsible for spawning model controllers and maintaining the balance of nodes within the system. The supercontroller ensures there is only ever a single model controller for a given abstract model and its related view(s). The supercontroller also has privileged access to model controllers and may reassign model controllers to new nodes in order to maintain balance in the system. Model controllers could be reassigned based on the appearance of new node controllers (which may be added dynamically) or significant change in the load for a given model controller.

Package Controller

The package controller handles requests not associated with a specific model. In particular, it handles saving, executing and listing models. The latter operation returns a list of available models given certain criteria (e.g., all those conforming to a metamodel or all views of an abstract model). The package controller is a singleton entity meant to serve all active users. To accomplish this goal, the package controller uses a worker pattern. It fairly distributes all client changelogs to a pool of workers that handle the changelog and return a response through the response forwarding service. The execute operation may generate changes to multiple models. In this scenario, the package controller workers can send requests to the model controller through backend communication to ensure consistency is maintained, for example when executing model transformations. Similar to model controllers, the package controller does not directly process operations. Rather, it coordinates operations in the MvK to complete the requested operations.

Client

In this section, we describe a client for the MVC architecture that supports a user interface for collaborative and multi-view modeling. Clients discussed here are mainly graphical user interfaces (GUI); however, textual as well as command-line based clients are also supported.

AToMPM

AToMPM provides an in-browser GUI client for the user. Therefore, there is no installation required to perform modeling tasks. In the back-end, a node.js web server that hosts the pages. The main features of the web-based GUI are:

- Creating DSLs.
  - Creating metamodels.
  - Designing and assigning concrete syntax to metamodel elements.
- Manipulating models through an HTML5 canvas.
  - Creating, updating and deleting elements.
  - Undoing, redoing changes.
  - Copying and pasting elements.
- Executing and debugging model transformations.
- Collaborating with other users in real time.

Statechart-Driven Architecture

Both the back-end and front-end of the GUI client rely on Statecharts for the execution of various features. Basically, when the back-end server starts, it parses the server Statechart and performs the actions encoded in the states. Figure 5 depicts an excerpt of the server Statechart. The main advantage of using a Statecharts-driven architecture is separating the behavior from the structure and layout of the features.

There are two ways in which models are received from MVC: open the model to be edited, or load the model as a tool. From the point of view of MVC, they are both load model requests. However, on the client side, these two requests have a different behavior. The former means that the client renders the elements of that model on the canvas to modify the model. The latter means that the model is to be executed as a tool. Tool execution is performed by executing a required Statecharts model attached to the requested model. As a result of the execution, a toolbar consisting of buttons appears on the canvas. Since the behavior is encoded in the Statechart of the tool, there can be various kinds of actions attached to each button (e.g., creating model elements, executing a model transformation, modifying the appearance, restyling elements). These actions are not limited to the model itself, but can also let AToMPM communicate with external systems, such as an analysis tool that computes the coverability of Petri nets. Figure 6 illustrates a tool that has a toolbar with three buttons, where the first two create Petri net places and transitions, and the third one the model currently loaded on the canvas.

Tools and other models connected to them (e.g., toolbars, Statecharts, buttons) are also models. Thus, AToMPM can read them in edit mode and let the user do the necessary customizations.

Figure 5. Server statechart

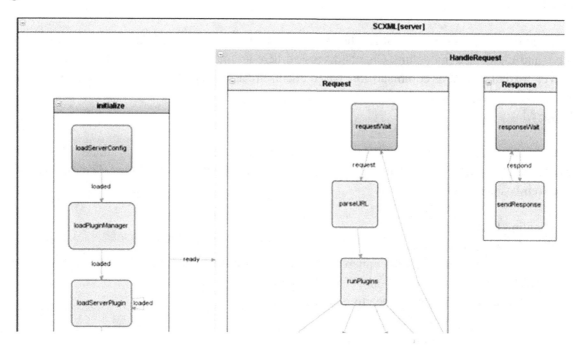

Figure 6. Petri nets Tool

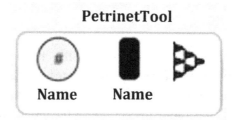

Collaboration Scenarios Supported by AToMPM

AToMPM provides a flexible environment to implement the collaboration scenarios mentioned earlier. Clients do not operate on abstract models directly, but on views. Therefore, in order to create a model, the user must create a view. However, the model itself does not need a view to exist. In order for a user to get updates from a view (i.e. reading a model), he subscribes to that specific view of the model. Many users can subscribe to the same view at the same time, which implements the multi-user single-view scenario. Users can create multiple views for a model by either adding elements from the model to the view or by creating new elements. This implements the multi-view single-model scenario. Users can also subscribe to more than one view, which is required for both multi-view multi-model and single-view multi-model scenarios. As long as a user subscribes to a view, he gets the updates from that view, regardless of how many models that view projects.

Conflicts are inevitable while working with multiple users in a system. AToMPM solves these conflicts in a live online fashion, where all operations either fail or succeed immediately. Additionally,

AToMPM also provides a lightweight chat system between users in case of a manual conflict resolving mechanism, where users can communicate with each other in case of a conflict. The following section discusses how conflicts are handled for each collaboration scenario by the MVC.

SOLUTION AND RECCOMENDATIONS FOR CONFLICTS RESOLUTION IN MULTI-VIEW MODELING

Thus far, this chapter has discussed several challenges related to implementing multi-view modeling especially in a multi-user context. The chapter has also introduced the details of the AToMPM architecture, in particular MVC: a multi-user, multi-view modeling system. However, the details of one sample system do not cover the full breadth of the challenges for multi-view modeling. This section discusses the solutions as present in MVC and contrasting options for addressing these challenges.

Multi-User Single-View

The most basic scenario to consider is a model with a single view used concurrently by multiple users (i.e., multi-user single-view). Here the users are sharing a resource. In this situation, the most straightforward solution is to provide all users with access to a centrally controlled resource where consistency is maintained. This is the approach taken by MVC where the model controllers provide this single central resource that ensures consistency. However, this solution is limited to *always-online* systems. MVC is such an always-online system where access to the central resource is expected. However, some contexts may not favor an always-online solution and prefer periodic updates. In these scenarios, solutions that have been introduced for distributed database systems can be used. The system may maintain local copies and update with the central repository periodically.

To ensure consistency among distributed local copies it becomes necessary to maintain logs of operations and define a commit scheme which handles rollbacks in the case of conflicting operations causing an operation that succeeded locally to fail during commit. In these scenarios, users may lose portions of previously completed work due to the inability to guarantee conflict free scenarios. Always-online systems such as MVC may experience similar scenarios due to latency. Consider the case where a user sends a delete operation while, at the same time, another user sends an update operation for the same element. If the update is received first, both operations will succeed; but if the delete is received first, the update will fail. However, the user's action is not considered complete until the model controller has sent a confirmation of success. Therefore, in practice the system will display the element deleted and then inform the user that the update failed. Thus, the user is aware of the scenario immediately and may take the necessary steps. In an offline model with only occasional update, the user might follow a series of operation which are no longer valid and have to retrace back to the point of conflict.

Here the challenge is ensuring a consistent view of the model for all users. We propose an always-online solution where a central source maintains consistency. The central source might be a distributed or replicated process that uses a strategy to coordinate many nodes, but the operation is only deemed successful when verified by this central source. The advantage is an immediate response to operations and eliminating the need for rollback systems.

Multi-View Single-Model

The second scenario expands the system to enable users viewing distinct segments of model or even distinct notations. Each segment and notation defines a unique view of the model, but users are still editing the same underlying model. In multi-view single-model, edits may be propagated from one view to another. MVC chooses to maintain all views of a given model in the same controller that manages the underlying model, specifically in the model controller. Model controllers are designed to notify users of any view which is affected by an updated element. In this way, the views maintain consistency by all editing the single, centrally located version of the abstract model and updates are published to users of any view that is impacted by the change. This solution follows directly from the MVC solution to multi-user single-view and employs a single central resource to ensure consistency. The MVC follows a two-tier solution (see Figure 7), but this could be expanded to a three-tier solution (see Figure 8). In these figures, boxes represent model controllers. In the three-tier variant, the views each have separate controlling resources. The model treats views as users, and end-users interacting with the views as wrappers of the model. The three-tier variant would reduce computation at the model controlling resource, but at the expense of additional layers of message passing when the model must be updated. MVC is designed with the expectation that the majority operations require execution at the model-controller resource. Therefore, MVC combines these layers to eliminate the network overhead of the additional message passing.

As with multi-user single-view, the MVC solution requires a live connection, but an offline solution as discussed for multi-user single-view would also be viable here. A two-tier solution would provide the same difficulties mentioned previously, but a three-tier solution would exacerbate the complications. Consider a three-tier system where a user might update a view successfully and then later the same

Figure 7. User, Model Controller Two-tier Solution for Scenario 2

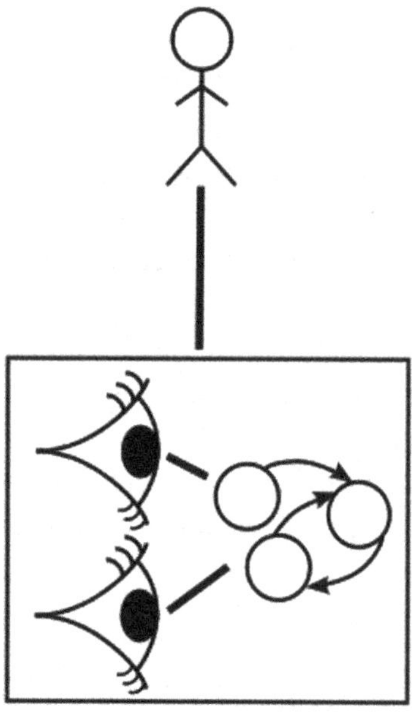

Figure 8. User, View, Model

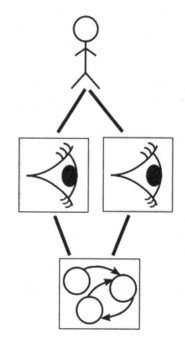

changes might fail when trying to update the model. Here the view would immediately fail and rollback, but then the failure and rollbacks must be propagated to users which may have processed further operations. The complications become increasingly complex to maintain a functional offline solution with only periodic update. Thus, a live approach is preferable when possible. Further scenarios will only discuss a live approach to maintaining consistency. Though the complexity of conflicting scenarios increases further in subsequent scenarios, an offline solution remains feasible with user intervention required to maintain consistency without forcing roll back to a prior consistent state.

Multi-View Multi-Model

The third scenario introduces the added complexity of interrelated models. In many situations, a system contains many varied types of models. In these heterogeneous modeling systems, often models must rely upon each other. To fully support this scenario, facilities must exist to update models automatically when a related model is altered. However, the update process has several variations: live-link, full-copy, and shallow-copy.

A live-link solution maintains the actual model elements in only one locality; i.e., instances of linked elements are references to the original element rather than true model elements. A live-link system would enable models to reference elements from other models and use those elements as though they were defined locally. The Modelverse implements a live-link behavior for model elements. However, the MVC does not provide full support for updating users in this scenario. A user would need to separately subscribe to updates from the model of interest as well as any models related to the model of interest (see Figure 9). An ideal solution would update the user without need to manually subscribe to secondary (or potentially even further removed tertiary models). A planned solution, for future iterations of MVC, enables the model controllers to notify one another of updates through a separate publish-subscribe relationship. The solution would add further complexity to the messaging system of MVC and would likely impact performance when dealing with propagating these updates. In a full solution, the model controllers become both publishers of updates and subscribers of updates. Thus, operations may create cascading messages within the system depending on the complexity of interrelated models present. The current MVC solution enables only direct update to users, but consistency of a user's view of a model, including elements linked from secondary models, can be managed with the user subscribing to the additional models. Thus, a live-link solution to the multi-view multi-model scenario can be managed within MVC, but the current solution requires additional subscriptions by users to receive all necessary updates.

A full-copy system does not have live relations between models (see Figure 10). The link made at the time an element is added to the current model from a secondary model treats the secondary model as a static-unchanging entity. The system can create a full copy of the element (and any required elements) locally to ensure that updates in the related model do not impact the static elements. In a full-copy system, consistency can be maintained as in multi-user single view or multi-view single-model, because the system does not ever need to update the current model based on changes in other models.

A shallow-copy solution would provide means to accomplish the static relation of a full-copy system without strictly requiring a full copy of those elements. Thus, the system can reduce redundancy at the cost of requiring a live-link consistency management scheme. Here, the model elements can be represented by references until a change is made. Once either the original elements are altered in the secondary model or the reference elements are altered in the current model, the system must either maintain multiple versions of the model or perform a full copy and remove the live links. When the secondary model is

Figure 9. Live-link related models   *Figure 10. Full-copy related models*

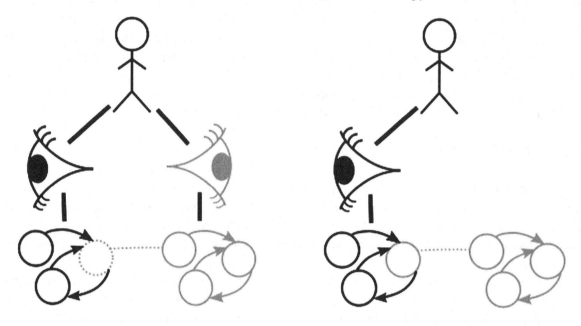

highly unlikely or not allowed to be updated, the shallow-copy solution presents some advantages over the other two solutions. However, in practice, disallowing a secondary model from being updated may not be possible, and the system must be able to handle elements in related models changing regardless of the likelihood of the elements changing.

Single-View Multi-Model

The final scenario for multi-view modeling can be refactored to a special case of multi-view multi-model (see Figure 11). Single-view multi-model covers visualizing elements from many models with potentially diverse notations within a single view. Thus where multi-view multi-model had a current model that might be related to other secondary models, this scenario treats all of the interrelated models as the current model. If we refactor the scenario by adding a single model that incorporates the many models as secondary models (thus adding a level of indirection), the consistency can be maintained using any of the strategies from multi-view multi-model as appropriate, but the system must provide additional facilities to represent these models together. A naïve approach would be to provide separate panels for each notation required, but this approach lacks the ability to represent the logical links between these separate notations. MVC handles the refactored version of single-view multi-model. The disparate models must each be included in a single model using live-links. The unifying model is defined with a notation that unifies the disparate models. The unifying model may also include additional elements which are locally maintained. MVC, thus, can reuse the live-link solution from multi-view multi-model with the many models becoming secondary models. The refactoring requires intentional development in advance to integrate the models.

Figure 11. Refactored Single-View Multi-Model

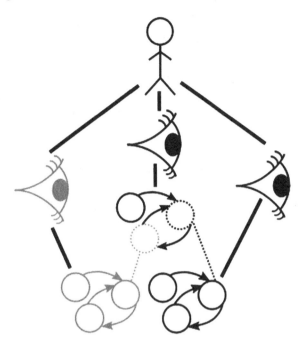

FUTURE RESEARCH DIRECTIONS

AToMPM represents the first effort in providing a cloud-based architecture to support collaborative modeling. Future works include exploring a more complete solution to fulfill all multi-view multi-model scenarios. For that, the MVC needs to be extended to provide facilities for model controllers to publish updates internally to other model controllers. It is nevertheless of paramount importance to provide a scalable solution that does not overly impact the performance from a user's perspective.

Another possible venue for future research is to explore the combination of online and offline solution. WebGME relies on a document-based NoSQL database to maintain the models within the backend system. This system employs a commit strategy where clients may work offline and commit work at a later point. However, the current system does not explore the collaborative modeling scenarios and relies on user intervention to manage conflicting updates. Future research should explore including more automated conflict resolution within such a system.

CONCLUSION

In this chapter, we have discussed the growing trend toward collaborative environments that fit today's needs when teams of domain experts work in a coordinated manner to construct a system. We identified four distinct collaboration scenarios found in practice, combining multiple users, multiple views, and multiple models of the system under study. We argue that a cloud-based multi-view modeling environment addresses that need, and introduce the architecture of our prototype AToMPM, which is a cloud-based environment for collaborative modeling. AToMPM represents a first step toward supporting the need for collaborative modeling through cloud technologies. Its core component, MVC, ensures consistency and synchronization among the artifacts produced by each stakeholder.

Furthermore, the chapter discusses the approach to addressing consistency and synchronization needs implemented in AToMPM. The discussion addresses each of the four collaboration scenarios. We also introduce competing approaches and compare to the approach implemented in AToMPM. AToMPM presents an *always-online* approach where users must have a live connection to the system at all times. This approach provides both synchronization and consistency. However, offline approaches are also possible such as that implemented by WebGME which must resolve sets of changes using a commit process. The offline approaches do not guarantee synchronization and must resolve (potentially complex) conflicting series of operations taken by users. Finally, we discuss some of the many challenges that remain to be solved including improved support for the fourth collaboration scenario and automation of conflict resolution in collaborative modeling systems to enable users to work both online and offline.

REFERENCES

Asana. (2015). *Asana*. Retrieved from https://www.asana.com/

Beck, K. (1999). Embracing change with extreme programming. *Computer*, *32*(10), 70–77. doi:10.1109/2.796139

Combemale, B., De Antoni, J., Larsen, M., Mallet, F., Barais, O., & Baudry, B. (2013). Reifying Concurrency for Executable Metamodeling. In *Software Language Engineering* (Vol. 8225, pp. 365–384). Springer. doi:10.1007/978-3-319-02654-1_20

Combemale, B., Deantoni, J., Baudry, B., France, R., Jézéquel, J.-M., & Gray, J. (2014). Globalizing Modeling Languages. *Computer*, *47*(6), 68–71. doi:10.1109/MC.2014.147

Corporation, M. (2001). *Microsoft C# Language Specifications*. Microsoft Press.

GEMOC Initiative. (2015). *GEMOC Studio*. Retrieved from http://gemoc.org/studio/

GitHub. (2015). *git*. Retrieved from http://git-scm.com/

Google Inc. (2015). Retrieved from Google Docs: http://docs.google.com

Hiya, S., Hisazumi, K., Fukuda, A., & Nakanishi, T. (2013). clooca: Web based tool for Domain Specific Modeling. *MODELS'13 Invited Talks, Demos, Posters, and ACM SRC.*, *1115*, 31–35.

Kelly, S., Lyytinen, K., & Rossi, M. (1996, may). MetaEdit+ A fully configurable multi-user and multi-tool CASE and CAME environment. *Conference on Advanced Information Systems Engineering*. Springer. doi:10.1007/3-540-61292-0_1

Kiczales, G., & Hilsdale, E. (2001). Aspect-oriented programming. *Software Engineering Notes*, *26*(5), 313. doi:10.1145/503271.503260

Kühne, T. (2006). Matters of (Meta-)Modeling. *Software & Systems Modeling*, *5*(4), 369–385. doi:10.1007/s10270-006-0017-9

Ledeczi, A., Maroti, M., Bakay, A., Karsai, G., Garrett, J., & Thomason, C. (2001). The generic modeling environment. *Workshop on Intelligent Signal Processing*.

Maróti, M., Kecskés, T., Kereskényi, R., Broll, B., Völgyesi, P., & Jurácz, L. (2014, October). Next Generation (Meta)Modeling: Web- and Cloud-based Collaborative Tool Infrastructure. *Multi-Paradigm Modeling, 1237*, 41–60.

Object Management Group. (2012, Apr.). *Information technology - Object Management Group Unified Modeling Language, Superstructure*. ISO/IEC 19505-2.

Özsu, T., & Valduriez, P. (2011). *Principles of distributed database systems*. Springer Science & Business Media.

Stahl, T., Voelter, M., & Czarnecki, K. (2006). *Model-Driven Software Development -- Technology, Engineering, Management*. John Wiley & Sons.

Steinberg, D., Budinsky, F., Paternostro, M., & Merks, E. (2008). *EMF: Eclipse Modeling Framework* (2nd ed.). Addison Wesley Professional.

Syriani, E., Vangheluwe, H., Mannadiar, R., Hansen, C., Van Mierlo, S., & Ergin, H. (2013). AToMPM: A Web-based Modeling Environment. *MODELS'13: Invited Talks, Demos, Posters, and ACM SRC. 1115*. CEUR-WS.org.

The Eclipse Foundation. (2015). *Orion*. Retrieved from http://eclipse.org/orion/

Trello Inc. (2015). *Trello*. Retrieved from http://www.trello.com

Van Mierlo, S., Barroca, B., Vangheluwe, H., Syriani, E., & Kühne, T. (2014, oct). Multi-Level Modelling in the Modelverse. In *Proceedings of the Workshop on Multi-Level Modelling*. CEUR-WS.org.

KEY TERMS AND DEFINITIONS

Abstract Model: The abstract syntax of a model representing its essence: entities, relations, and properties that conform to a metamodel.

Always-Online: A system where users are connected to the cloud all the time, as opposed to offline.

Domain-Specific Language: A modeling language that is adapted to a particular application domain, where models are described using a notation fit exactly to the domain.

Metamodel: A model that defines the abstract syntax of a modeling language.

Multi-View Modeling: Modeling activities that users can perform through one or more views.

Node: A computation resource, such as a computer machine, a CPU, or a process.

View: A projection of an abstract model, showing parts or all elements of the model in a specific concrete syntax representation.

Section 3
Mobile Design and Applications

This section covers essential aspects of mobile design and development, namely testing, refactoring, modeling and finished prototypes. The first chapter identifies and discusses relevant quality attributes for mobile applications development. The second chapter present results on how refactoring some anti-patterns can have impact on battery consumption. The third chapter presents a methodology to conduct usability tests in android based web applications. Finally, the fourth chapter in this section introduces a generic mobile solution to provide tracking and localization in any indoor environment.

Chapter 8
Quality Attributes for Mobile Applications

João M. Fernandes
Universidade do Minho, Portugal

André L. Ferreira
Universidade do Minho, Portugal

ABSTRACT

A mobile application is a type of software application developed to run on a mobile device. The chapter discusses the main characteristics of mobile devices, since they have a great impact on mobile applications. It also presents the classification of mobile applications according to two main types: native and web-based applications. Finally, this chapter identifies the most relevant types of quality attributes for mobile applications. It shows that the relevant quality attributes for mobile applications are usually framed in the Usability, Performance, and Maintainability and Support categories.

INTRODUCTION

A mobile application (or just mobile app) is a type of software application developed to run on a mobile device. Mobile applications are a recent type of software application that emerged due to the appearance of many handheld devices, like smartphones, which are considered to be the personal computer of the future (Duffy, 2012), or tablet computers. Mobile devices are expected to be easily carried, held, and used in the hands; hence, mobile devices are characterized by being relatively small devices when compared to desktop computers. For this reason, mobile devices are naturally restricted in several dimensions that strongly affect the operating characteristics of an application that executes on this type of devices. In many cases, the challenges for the software or systems engineer when developing a mobile application are similar to the ones to develop other types of embedded applications (Wasserman, 2010). Common issues include integration with hardware, security, performance, reliability, and storage limitations.

DOI: 10.4018/978-1-4666-9916-8.ch008

Copyright © 2016, IGI Global. Copying or distributing in print or electronic forms without written permission of IGI Global is prohibited.

BACKGROUND

Until recently, mobile devices were characterized for having small display sizes, low processing power, poor connectivity, and limited interaction methods. The range of mobile applications available for these devices was relatively small. Mobile devices have evolved considerably in recent years as result of improvements in mobile technology, mobile networking and mobile computing. Examples are increased processing power of mobile devices, novel forms of user interaction, for example the introduction of the touch feature to operate mobile devices, and new protocols of connectivity. These improvements in the hardware motivated the increase in the range and availability of mobile applications.

Mobile applications are software systems that have specific characteristics when compared with normal desktop applications. Mobile applications differ from desktop applications by having to deal with limitations on specific hardware resources, like display size, processing power and memory to name a few. Probably the most significant difference is that mobile applications run on mobile devices with energy consumption limitations. Increase battery lifetime is a significant concern for both mobile applications developers and hardware manufacturers, namely in what concerns multimedia applications running on mobile devices.

Mobile applications can now take advantage of new hardware capabilities, meaning that they can provide a wider set of functions or use, which inevitably results in more complex software solutions. Development of mobile applications is now closer than before to the development of desktop applications in terms of complexity (examples are *Android OS*, *Apple iOS* and *Windows Phone* mobile operating systems); however the hardware is still a relevant differentiator. These differences motivate the need to understand clearly how the hardware constraints impact the software design decisions. For that purpose, one must understand which quality attributes are more relevant for mobile applications, providing an inevitable link to constraints imposed by the hardware itself. Understanding the possible impact of the hardware of mobile devices in software design decision motivates the discussion of this chapter.

MOBILE DEVICES CHARACTERISTICS

Mobile devices have a set of characteristics that have a great impact on how mobile applications are designed or created (Juárez-Ramírez et al., 2012). These characteristics establish the constraints that influence most technical and non-technical decisions on software applications development for mobile devices. A list of these characteristics is presented in this section.

Small Display Size: Mobile devices have relatively small displays when compared to desktop computers or laptops. Small mobile devices, in particular small smartphones, have display sizes of 4 to 4.5 inches but these can go down to 2.45 inches. Typical smartphones have display sizes between 4.5 to 6 inches and tablets range from 5 up to 13 inches. Mobile applications must be designed to successfully provide the desired functionality in a limited screen size. These conditions contrast greatly with normal applications that are designed to use larger screens. Small screen sizes pose great constraints to usability of mobile apps.

Small Memory Size: Normally, mobile devices have less memory available than desktop computers. Mobile devices, as any computing device, have both ROM (Read-Only Memory) and RAM (Random-Access Memory). ROM, which technically is EEPROM, i.e., Electrically-Erasable Programmable ROM, and so is both readable and writeable by the end user, does not require power to maintain its (non-volatile) data and is basically used by a mobile device to store the operating system, mobile applications, media (photos and video) and files. ROM memory sizes go up to 128 GB (Gigabytes), but typical sizes are around 8 to 16 GB. However, some mobiles devices allow the ROM size to be increased, by using non-volatile memory cards, e.g., SD (Secure Digital) memory cards. Due to memory size restrictions, most mobile applications are relatively small, when compared with desktop applications (e.g., Microsoft Word).

RAM memory is used to store active processes when the mobile device is functioning. RAM memory usage can greatly impact performance of mobile applications running on a mobile device. Mobile devices hold up around 1 or 2GB of internal RAM, while desktop computers typically have 4 to 8GB of RAM. Mobile applications are loaded into RAM to be executed and memory can rapidly become constrained if mobile applications do not make an efficient use of volatile memory. The result is a smaller number of applications loaded and ready to be executed at a given time. Additionally, there is a penalty in performance when RAM needs to be made available to load new applications when no sufficient memory is available. Thus, mobile apps are expected to make a moderate use of RAM memory, which results in faster loading times and increases the number of applications ready to execute.

Small Battery Capacity: Batteries provide the necessary power for mobile devices to work. While hardware manufactures struggle to increase the capacity of the batteries, mobile application developers struggle to make a more efficient use of them. Recent advancements in software technology revolutionized the way mobile devices are used. Multi-purpose mobile devices (smartphones or tablets) that allow access to email, browse the Internet, watch videos, and play games replaced basic mobile phones. Typical smartphones use batteries that can range from 1,570 to 3,400 mAh for smartphones and around 7,000 mAh for high-end tablets. Energy consumption impacts greatly mobile users. Mobile applications must strive for efficiency in terms of energy consumption in order to maximize battery life. This scenario can be achieved, e.g., by improving the algorithms for saving computation cycles.

Network Bandwidth Limitations: Mobile applications often rely on updated content or data to provide value to end users. Therefore, mobile devices must be capable of accessing content or data over a network. Most mobile devices provide more than one form of connectivity by using different network technologies. Wi-Fi technology (usually seen as a synonym of IEEE 802.11) enables mobile devices access to the Internet and private networks, while 3G is commonly used to access the internet. Other protocols, like Bluetooth or NFC (Near-Field Communication), allow direct connections between mobile devices to share data. The most significant difference of mobile devices when compared with desktop computers is that bandwidth provided by existing technologies is relatively smaller when compared with cable connectivity, especially when compared with optical fiber. Mobile applications must use bandwidth knowing that the throughput is limited by available technologies. Nonetheless, wireless technology is evolving rapidly and new Wi-Fi protocols and recent broadband standards, like Mobile WiMAX and Long Term Evolutions (LTE), are closing the gap between wireless and cable bandwidth technologies (Ethernet), thus allowing mobile applications a wider range of applicability, e.g., streaming video.

Multiple Accessories: Mobile devices are often built with different types of sensors, like GPS, accelerometer, gyroscope, barometer, light sensor and digital cameras. Interactions with the sensors occur frequently and imply that a mobile application needs to comply with the operating characteristics of the sensors, namely the operating range, the sensitivity, the accuracy, or the minimum-polling interval. Accessories are used to provide, complement, and enhance mobile devices functionality, being memory cards a good example. Some mobile devices allow built-in ROM memory to be extended by using a flash memory data device that provides additional storage. Mobile applications must consider the different types of accessories available for mobile devices to fully enhance user experience.

Multiple Network Protocols: As mentioned before, mobile devices provide one or more forms of connectivity. Different technologies can be used to provide network connectivity whether for voice or data. Examples are Wi-Fi and 3G or 4G technologies that allow mobile devices to access to data over a network and are broadly used to provide data access for most mobile applications. Other technologies, like Bluetooth or NFC allow short or very-short distance data transitions and are independent of a service provider to interact with other mobile devices. Typically, using Bluetooth or NFC mobile devices interact directly with other capable mobile devices for data transfer. Mobile applications can take advantage of these technologies by choosing the most convenient for their desired functionality. As an example, Bluetooth is very popular for hand-free devices, like headsets and NFC is expectable to be used to implement contactless payments.

Real-World Interaction: Mobile applications provide real-world interaction by interfacing with context information, like user location, time of day, neighboring users and devices. Mobile devices are capable of acquiring and using context information by using built-in sensors, like GPS and accelerometers, and complementing this information with data acquired from the network. Context awareness in mobile computing is an extensive research field and is emerging as a new computing paradigm, where infrastructure and services are seamlessly available anywhere, anytime and in any format (Hong et al., 2009). Mobile applications are now capable of taking advantage of context information that a few years back was not possible.

Always On: Mobile applications are expected to be promptly, quickly and easily available to end users. Opening or loading a mobile application is expected to be possible in a few seconds. This capability stresses resource utilization, namely processor and memory, resulting in high energy consumption that reduces battery life considerably. Mobile devices are evolving to be capable of being readily available to end users and meet very strict power consumption requirements. Always on devices have their hardware designed with dedicated processors for sensor processing tasks, typically control tasks and signal processing that allow the mobile device to enter 'sleep' mode when the device is not being used and 'wake-up' when a stimulus (signal) is given by the user. Mobile applications must be designed to take advantage of these hardware capabilities that are built into mobile devices to enhance functionality and extend battery life.

Individual and Personal Use: According to Salmre (2005), the major difference between mobile and desktop applications is the way in which people use them. Those who use both desktop and mobile applications tend to use the two in different ways. When using a mobile application, the activities of the user tend to be short. As Salmre puts it: "The user is either responding to being interrupted or using the application to make an immediate request of some other person or process." Thus, user interface takes a great importance for mobile applications, as their users are often seeking to quickly complete a simple task, and cannot take advantage of the full range of functionality provided by a traditional desktop application. Contrarily, users of desktop computers tend to have long sessions.

TYPES OF MOBILE APPLICATIONS

Mobile applications can be classified according to two main types: native applications and web-based applications (table 1) (Charland and Leroux, 2011). Native applications are constructed to be used on a specific platform, like iOS and Android, or mobile device. Mobile web applications consist of web pages specifically developed for taking into account the characteristics of mobile devices.

Table 1. Summary of main characteristics of the three types of mobile applications discussed.

Mobile Web	Hybrid	Native
Runs in mobile web browser Built with HTML5+JS+CSS Served by web server No app store needed Can look like native May be responsive or target specific screen sizes	Runs as locally installed app Built with HTML5+JS+CSS Installed on device In embedded web browser Fed by APIs App stores needed Built for specific devices May be responsive	Runs as locally installed app Built with Objective-C (or Java) Installed on device Fed by APIs App stores needed Built for specific devices

Native apps are designed and coded for a specific kind of device. For instance, iPhone apps are written in Objective-C and Android apps in Java. Native apps can usually be found in an app store, such as Google Play, and require the store's approval. They are downloaded from the store and installed on that mobile device. They run exclusively on that type of mobile device and interact with and take advantage of the features of the operating system and other software that is usually installed on that platform. A native application cannot be used for a different platform without major modifications. For example, an app developed for the iOS runs only on Apple devices.

A native apps tends to be faster and more responsive. Because its code is stored on the phone, there is no delay waiting for static content (such as images and text) to be downloaded from the web. While dynamic content still needs to be accessed from the Internet, it is an improvement over the web-based model in which everything needs to be downloaded each time. In some cases, a native app, like a game, when installed, can work with no Internet connectivity requirements.

Native apps offer better user interface features and perform faster, because they are developed to take advantage of the device's built-in features. They can use, for example, the camera, GPS, accelerometer, compass, list of contacts, etc. Native apps are less prone to security issues when compared to web-based applications as a result of decreased need for network access.

Mobile web apps are developed using technologies that one uses to build websites, such as HTML, CSS, and Javascript. A mobile web application is simply accessed by its URL in a web browser (that runs on the mobile device). In most cases, a web app can be seen as a website that mimics a native app. A major characteristic that distinguishes a mobile web application from a standard website is the fact that it is designed to be accessible in a small display, most of the cases with touch-screen interface capabilities. Hence, operations that in websites are operated with mouse clicks are operated using fingers in a mobile web app.

A major benefit related to mobile web applications is that they operate across different devices and operating systems, as long as a web browser is available. Web-based apps do not require users to install new software or manually search for updates. However, full access to features and resources available on mobile devices is not straightforward, since they are platform agnostic and have no direct access to resources of a mobile device as a native app. These limitations are being addressed, for example, by cloud phone platforms (Taivalsaari and Systä, 2012) that provide solutions for web-based apps to work seamlessly on mobile devices.

A third variation of mobile application can also be considered: *a hybrid application*. A hybrid mobile application takes an HTML-based mobile application and inserts it inside a native wrapper. The core of the application uses HTML, JavaScript and CSS, similar to web applications, but the outside is a native shell. Hence, the app runs within a native app framework rather than a browser. The hybrid application are also downloaded and installed on a device. Most users cannot distinguish native from hybrid applications.

Hybrid apps are popular since they allow cross-platform development, an approach that reduces development costs. HTML code components can be reused on different mobile platforms.

QUALITY ATTRIBUTES

The successful development of a software application is tightly linked to the ability of managing software requirements. Development of a mobile application is no different; in particular, it is of primal relevance the elicitation and documentation of quality attributes. A quality attribute (also designated quality requirement or non-functional requirement) corresponds to a set of restrictions imposed to the system under development, establishing, for instance, how usable, attractive, fast or reliable it is (Fernandes & Machado, 2015). Examples of this type of quality attributes are security, modifiability, performance, or portability. Quality attributes of mobile applications are highly constrained by the hardware where the software executes. Hardware characteristics establish constraints to mobile applications and quality attributes must be carefully identified and documented to address these constrains, which assume central relevance in architectural design decisions.

Quality attributes should be contrasted with functional requirements that define the behavior of the software system. Quality attributes and functionality are orthogonal, in the sense that many software designs can achieve the same functionality with distinct levels of quality built in. Therefore, software architects focus more on quality attributes rather than on functionality (Fairbanks, 2010, p. 142). In the majority of the cases, a quality attribute is an emergent property, which implies that it is not possible to locate one place in the source code of the software system with the responsibility for ensuring the accomplishment of that attribute.

There are several frameworks to categorize quality attributes of software systems and products. The ISO/IEC 9126 standard is focused on quality, proposing quality attributes, divided in six main characteristics, for evaluating software products: functionality, reliability, usability, efficiency, maintainability, and portability.

The classification scheme suggested by Sommerville (2011, p. 88) differentiates in a first level the non-functional requirements into three categories:

- **Product Requirements** characterize aspects of the behavior of the system itself, including, for example, (i) reliability, (ii) performance, (iii) efficiency, (iv) portability, (iv) usability, (vi) testability, and (vii) readability.
- **Organizational Requirements** come from strategies and procedures established in the context of the manufacturing process of the system or the client organization, being examples (i) process standards that must be followed, (ii) implementation requirements, like the programming language to be adopted.
- **External Requirements** have origin in external factors to the system and the development process, being examples (i) interoperability requirements that define how the systems interact with other systems, (ii) legal requirements to guarantee that the system is compliant with the laws, and (iii) ethical requirements to make sure that the society in general will accept the system.

There are many other proposals for classifying quality attributes suggested by several authors, for example, Boehm et al. (1978), Roman (1985), Grady and Caswell (1987, p. 159), Jureta et al. (2006), and Meyer (2013, p. 703). All these proposals demonstrate the lack of a consensus in the software engineering community with respect to classification of quality attributes. In this chapter, we adopt the eight categories for quality attributes proposed by Robertson & Robertson (2006) for discussing quality attributes in the scope of mobile applications:

- **Look and Feel:** The visual aspect and the aesthetics of the system, namely the graphical interface.
- **Usability and Humanity:** The easiness of utilization of the system and everything that permits a friendlier user experience.
- **Performance:** Aspects of speed, real-time, storage capacity, and execution correction.
- **Operational:** Characteristics about what the system must do to work correctly in the environment where it is inserted.
- **Maintainability and Support:** Attributes that allow the system to be repaired or improved and new functionalities to be anticipated.
- **Security:** Issues related to access, confidentiality, protection, and integrity of the data.
- **Cultural and Political:** Factors related to the stakeholders culture and habits.
- **Legal:** Laws, rules, and standards that apply to the system so that it can operate.

Generically, all categories need to be considered for a given mobile application, as it is a form of a software system. However, mobile devices characteristics imply that some quality attributes become more critical to the success of a mobile application than others. We discuss these topics in the next section.

RELEVANT QUALITY ATTRIBUTES FOR MOBILE APPLICATIONS

This section identifies and discusses the most relevant types of quality attributes for mobile applications and argues that relevant quality attributes for mobile applications are usually framed in Usability, Performance, and Maintainability and Support categories.

As mentioned in the previous section, all quality attributes are relevant and the relevance of these three types does not imply that the other five types of quality attributes are not important or should be discarded when developing mobile applications. In fact, all types of quality attributes have their relative importance, highly depending on the scope or context that motivates the need and use for a mobile application. For instance, security is a transversal aspect for all types of software applications, mobile ones included. Running third-party applications within a mobile device (that stores private information related to its owner) raises privacy and security risks (Leontiadis et al., 2012). Legal requirements are also important, since any system, regardless of the technology, has obviously to respect the established laws. The choice for highlighting Usability, Performance, and Maintainability and Support categories is that these are almost pervasive in what concerns mobile application development and if discarded or considered not relevant, the perception of quality may be deeply affected.

Usability

Usability is a crucial quality for all types of software products. Usability covers many aspects, like ease of use, personalization, ease of learning, and accessibility. According to ISO, usability is related to the extent to which a given product can be used to achieve specified goals with effectiveness, efficiency, and satisfaction in a specified context of use. A usable system means to the user increased productivity, quality of work, and user satisfaction. Usability also implies reductions in support and training costs. An interesting book on usability, edited by Spiliotopoulos et al., (2010), provides a set of methods and approaches that enable and facilitate the development of usable web systems.

Ease of use is related to the efficiency of utilizing a given system and with the mechanisms that exist to reduce the errors made by the users (for example, an automatic spell checker). Here one should take into account the GIGO (garbage in, garbage out) principle, which indicates that software programs that receive incorrect input data, after processing them, generate undesired output data. The best way to avoid garbage in the output is preventing garbage in the input. For example, when a telephone number must be introduced, it is important to ensure that only digits are typed in and that the number of digits is correct (for instance, in Portugal all phone numbers have 9 digits) and that all possible access codes are available to be chosen (avoiding thus typing in them). If these mechanisms are made available, the chances of introducing an incorrect phone number greatly decrease.

Personalization is associated with the capacity of adapting the system to the tastes and needs of the users, including the choice of the language, currency, time zone and other configuration options (colors, backgrounds, icons). Mobile devices are usually tied to a given person, which wishes to introduce his personal data (phone number, email, contacts, passwords, bookmarks, etc) in the device to configure and personalize it.

Ease of learning is concerned with the way users are trained to use the application. Based on requirements of this type, the development team can prepare training and help procedures for the users. Associated with the ease of learning is comprehensibility that determines if the users intuitively capture the functionalities of the application and how to operate it. In many cases, mobile applications are expected to be so easy to use that no external help is required. Some applications must indeed have very high comprehension levels; if this is not the case, the users resort to other alternatives, i.e., mobile applications provided by the competitors, to satisfy their needs.

Accessibility indicates how easy it is to use the system, for people who are somehow physically or mentally disabled. The disabilities can be related with physical, visual, auditory, or cognitive aspects.

Usability is very likely to be the most crucial aspect of mobile applications, since they are used in many different contexts and environments. The user shall be able to use the mobile application in crowded and noisy environments, which imply that restrictions on the inputs and outputs may apply. In many cases, the device is supposed to be handled with just one hand, while in others two hands may be necessary. This means that mobile applications must be developed with the possibility of being effectively used with either one or two hands.

Responsive design is an increasingly important concern for mobile applications. The main challenge is building applications that ensure the same level of user experience, regardless of screen size and orientation of mobile devices. This can imply show, hide or re-arrange graphical elements like number of text columns, adapting font size, resizing or hiding images to maintain the same level of user experience as mobile applications are used in devices with different screen sizes.

Performance

Performance refers to the capacity of a system to respond to its stimulus, that is, the time necessary to deliver a response to an event or the number of events processed in a specific time unit. It is the degree to which a system can accomplish its functionalities within a given set of constraints. The performance of a system is related to the processing time of a task, response time of an operation, accuracy of the result, reliability, availability, fault-tolerance, storage capacity, and scalability.

In addition to the intended functionality, the behavior of a real-time system must respect a set of timing requirements externally defined. The correction of an answer of the system includes also the instant when it is produced. A late answer is incorrect and constitutes a non-conformity, according to the stipulated behavior for the system. For example, the time limit to fire an alarm in the case of a dangerous situation must be scrupulously met; otherwise, it may not be possible to save the persons and the goods that are being monitored.

Accuracy of the results is related to the precision of a calculation computed by the system, how they are stored and delivered. These factors are relevant for values related, for example, with hours, GPS coordinates, money (rounding of bank interests), scientific calculations, and percentages.

Availability quantifies the percentage of time during which a given system is operational and working correctly. It is a measure of the likelihood that a system will be operating when called upon. It is a very important aspect that has ramifications to other issues: confidence of the users in the products that they use, value of the information, efficiency of the processes, and productivity of the organizations. Availability is normally measured by two indicators: MTBF (Mean Time Between Failures) and MTTR (Mean Time To Repair). MTBF represents the predicted elapsed time between inherent failures of a system during operation, while MTTR is the speed with which the system is able to be available again, after the occurrence of a failure. Availability is expressed by the following formula (Stapelberg, 2009, pp. 417).

Availability = MTBF / (MTBF+MTTR)

Availability is of great importance for providing the desired functionality; only when available the system may provide value to its users. For critical systems it assumes a vital role in design as loss of functionality may imply severe losses, whether in terms of money or human life. This characteristic is not however enough, since the system must also be reliable, since a single error may represent severe damages or even the loss of human lives in more extreme situations. Reliability is the capacity of a system to deliver the correct output over time and is measured by the probability of a system producing correct results in a given period of time. Nowadays, there are various businesses that depend totally on software-based systems that support their operation (for instance, airline, bank, insurance, e-commerce, industry), and the expectation is that these systems are "always" available (i.e., that they have short periods of unavailability) and reliable. Reliability is normally measured by the mean time between failures.

Fault tolerance indicates the capacity of the system in keeping an acceptable level of operation, even in undesirable circumstances. The higher the fault tolerance, the bigger the capacity of the system to continue working, even if some of its components fails. Software engineers must be able to build applications that will acknowledge the presence of faults and to include techniques to tolerate these faults, so that the system still delivers an acceptable quality of service (Koren & Krishna, 2010, pp. 1-2).

Data storage capacity specifies the amount of data that the system should be able to process and store. While the function of storing data is a functional requirement, the respective capacity should be seen as a non-functional requirement.

Scalability is the ability of a system to continue to show high quality of service, even when subjected to a greater number of requests. Scalability can be related with the ability to serve more users simultaneously, treat a higher volume of information, or respond to more requests. In any case, it is assumed that this load increase does not imply significant changes to the system response in order for it to maintain the performance levels. Scalability of software systems often needs to be evaluated taking into account the hardware resources, because it is only possible to determine factors such as response time or number of users that can be served simultaneously, if both the hardware and the software are analyzed as a set.

Maintainability and Support

System maintenance, in general, is divided into four main types: preventive, corrective, perfective, and adaptive. The strategy for maintaining systems is limited by several factors (organization, context, technology, laws, business), which determines how the different types of maintenance efforts are developed over the time to make sure that the system remains useful and updated. Thus, in systems in which maintenance is paramount, it is convenient to consider maintenance requirements during the analysis phase.

Modifiability is an attribute strongly related to maintenance and is dependent on how easy it is to locate the system components that must be changed. In principle, it is preferable that the change has impact on a reduced number of components, since it is more costly and difficult to make modifications in the context of many components.

Portability is also an important characteristic to take into account when developing mobile applications. A mobile application is said to be portable if it is relatively easy and straightforward to move it from one mobile device to another. As noted by Silakov and Khoroshilov (2011), the cost of porting an application to different platforms is smaller as developers consider it the sooner during the development. This characteristic is of paramount importance, as today the market has many platforms, being dominated by Google Android, Apple iOS, and Microsoft Windows Phone.

In terms of support, it is important to know, for example, what kind of support and training the users are expected to receive. It may be necessary to provide technical support services or to include personal or passive assistance, e.g., using tutorials built in the software product that explain how to operate it. Today, it is also common to use videos that explain how to use a given product.

Issues, Controversies, Problems

This section discusses what we believe are the most relevant issues currently in mobile applications development. One of the challenges in mobile application development is the one of portability. As discussed in the previous sections, there are several platforms for which one can develop mobile applications. The ability to have a mobile application available for each platform is a decision that directly impacts the cost associated with development and maintenance of mobile applications.

Achieving desired portability can greatly impact the business decision of developing mobile applications. If portability is desired, one may opt to have a mobile application based on the use of web technologies, but development of the graphical user interface may be the biggest limitation of such approach (Heitkötter et al., 2013) when compared to native language based mobile applications. Also lack of stability in web-based applications seems to be a limitation (Zibula & Majchrzak, 2013). There are now several platforms that support development for hybrid applications and which platforms best satisfy the developers' needs is also a topic (Palmieri et al., 2012).

An increasing relevant issue on mobile application development is efficiency of computation. Although battery efficiency as evolved significantly, it was outpaced by the demand imposed by the software. Mobile applications demand greatly on computing power to provide the desired functionally and this impacts negatively on the use of energy, which decreases the availability of mobile devices. In this topic, developers need to explore how to be more efficient in terms of computation. Energy efficiency might be improved without any changes to hardware by using software solutions that reduce overheads and improve processor utilization (Silven and Jyrkk, 2007).

Mobile applications maintenance and modifiability is an issue as mobile applications have typically a fast update cycle. The need to adjust to customer needs requires frequent updates and evolution in the software. This problem increases when multiple platforms need to be supported and maintainability and modifiability become even more relevant attributes, as cost is multiplied by the number of supported platforms. Design of mobile application must consider upfront the issue of maintenance and modifiability.

SOLUTIONS AND RECOMMENDATIONS

To achieve portability, current solutions focus on using cross-platform frameworks, but with this approach developers need to be aware of its limitations. Mainly, these limitations are related to the quality of the end result in terms of user interface. However, cross-platform frameworks may lower the barrier for developing mobile applications by allowing the use of Web technologies like HTML, CSS and JavaScript, along with the widespread of Web development paradigms. These technologies allow a greater number of developers to easily start developing mobile application without having the effort required to learn native, specific, platform languages, which imply a significant effort to learn (Heitkötter et al., 2013).

Native based mobile applications are probably the best option for developing rich end user interfaces. Native languages seem to provide more flexibility and ease of development when creating the user interface. Also, when designing user interfaces several guiding principles need to be considered to captivate users. Examples of relevant principles to consider are (1) users' limited attention, (2) minimization of keystrokes to completely perform a given functionality, and (3) task-orientation with a minimum set of functions.

In the scope of the mobile devices efficiency issue, developers need to design and develop their software with the mindset of saving computation power, but ensure, at the same time, the same level of functionality. The path to take may involve designing more efficient algorithms to save computation resources and thus as result extend battery life for the same level of functionality. The wide spread of multimedia mobile applications in mobile devices today is an example where improvements on software can help decrease battery consumption by improving the software. Current algorithms for processing media were not designed with the resource limitations in mind and can make a difference (Marius et al., 2010).

FUTURE RESEARCH DIRECTIONS

Our belief is that portability, usability and energy efficiency will drive research of mobile application development. Usability is probably one of the most relevant quality attributes when designing mobile applications. Mobile developers shall try to innovate or differentiate in user experience by researching and developing new user interaction models. These new models will make a significant impact if successful and will allow additional levels of functionality. An example of a possible evolution in new interaction models is augmented reality that certainly will disrupt the range of applicability of mobile applications. An example is augmented reality applied in the automotive industry by allowing a new dimension of driving assistance systems (Gabbard et al., 2014).

Improving energy efficiency on mobile devices will be based in developing approaches to extend battery life. With the increase in the range of functionality made possible by mobiles devices, developers need to be aware that a mobile application is now part of a resource-limited environment. Examples of future research in this topic may consider the Green Software Engineering project that believes software can play an important role in reducing the power used by mobile applications (Rott, 2011).

CONCLUSION

A mobile application is a type of software application, developed to run on a mobile device. The chapter discusses the main characteristics of mobile devices, since they have a great impact on mobile applications. Among those characteristics, one can find for example: small display size, small battery capacity, network bandwidth limitations, and multiple network protocols, always on, and personal use. It also presents the classification of mobile applications according to two main types: native and web-based applications. A third type, hybrid, can also be considered. Building on the information presented, the chapter identifies the most relevant types of quality attributes for mobile applications followed by a discussion on the most relevant issues to be found on mobile application development. Current solutions for the issues presented are discussed and future research directions are identified.

This chapter identifies and discusses relevant quality attributes for mobile applications. It argues that usability, portability, performance and maintainability and support categories are among the most relevant quality attributes for mobile application development. Mobile application development evolved significantly in recent years with technological improvements in mobile devices. These improvements changed the range of applicability of mobile devices and mobile software developers are now taking advantage of these new features and mobile software development will face new challenges and opportunities.

REFERENCES

Boehm, B. W. (1978). *Characteristics of software quality*. North Holland.

Charland, A., & Leroux, B. (2011). Mobile application development: Web vs. native. *Communications of the ACM, 54*(5), 49–53. doi:10.1145/1941487.1941504

Duffy, T. (2012). *Programming with mobile applications: Android™, iOS, and Windows Phone 7*. Boston, MA: Cengage Learning.

Fairbanks, G. (2010). *Just-enough software architecture: A risk-driven approach.* Boulder, CO: Marshall & Brainerd.

Fernandes, J. M., & Machado, R. J. (2015). Requirements in engineering projects. Springer. doi:10.1007/978-3-319-18597-2

Gabbard, J. L., Fitch, G. M., & Hyungil, K. (2014). Behind the glass: Driver challenges and opportunities for AR automotive applications. *Proceedings of the IEEE, 102*(2), 124–136. doi:10.1109/JPROC.2013.2294642

Grady, R., & Caswell, D. (1987). *Software metrics: Establishing a company-wide program.* Upper Saddle River, NJ: Prentice Hall.

Heitkötter, H., Hanschke, S., & Majchrzak, T. A. (2013). Evaluating cross-platform development approaches for mobile applications. *8th International Conference on Web Information Systems and Technologies* (LNBIP), (vol. 140, pp. 120–138). Springer. doi:10.1007/978-3-642-36608-6_8

Hong, J., Suh, E., & Kim, S. J. (2009). Context-aware systems: A literature review and classification. *Expert Systems with Applications, 36*(4), 8509–8522. doi:10.1016/j.eswa.2008.10.071

Juárez-Ramírez, R., Licea, G., Barriba, I., Izquierdo, V., & Angeles, A. (2012). Orchestrating mobile applications: A software engineering view. In R. Aquino-Santos & A. E. Block (Eds.), *Embedded systems and wireless technology: Theory and practical applications* (pp. 41–72). Boca Raton, FL: CRC Press. doi:10.1201/b12298-3

Jureta, I. J., Faulkner, S., & Schobbens, P. Y. (2006). A more expressive softgoal conceptualization for quality requirements analysis. Lecture Notes in Computer Science, 4215, 281–295. doi:10.1007/11901181_22

Koren, I., & Krishna, C. M. (2010). *Fault-tolerant systems.* San Francisco, CA: Morgan Kaufmann.

Leontiasis, I., Efstratiou, C., Picone, M., & Mascolo, C. (2012). Don't kill my ads!: Balancing privacy in an ad-supported mobile application market. *12th Workshop on Mobile Computing Systems & Applications.* ACM. doi:10.1145/2162081.2162084

Marcu, M., Tudor, D., & Fuicu, S. (2010). A view on power efficiency of multimedia mobile applications. In K. Elleithy (Ed.), *Advanced Techniques in Computing Sciences and Software Engineering* (pp. 407–412). Springer; doi:10.1007/978-90-481-3660-5_70

Meyer, B. (2019). *Touch of class: Learning to program well with objects and contracts.* Berlin: Springer.

Robertson, S., & Robertson, J. C. (2006). *Mastering the requirements process* (2nd ed.). Boston, MA: Addison-Wesley.

Roman, G. (1985). A taxonomy of current issues in requirements engineering. *IEEE Computer, 18*(4), 14–23. doi:10.1109/MC.1985.1662861

Rott, J. (2011). *Developing green software.* Retrieved from https://software.intel.com/sites/default/files/developing_green_software.pdf

Salmre, I. (2005). *Writing mobile code: Essential software engineering for building mobile applications.* Boston, MA: Addison-Wesley.

Silakov, D. V. & Khoroshilov, A.V. (2011). Ensuring portability of software. *Programming and Computing Software, 37*(1), 41–47. Springer. doi 10.1134/S0361768811010051

Silven, O. & Jyrkk, K. (2007). Observations on power-efficiency trends in mobile communication devices. *EURASIP Journal on Embedded Systems.* doi 10.1155/2007/56976

Spielberg, R. F. (2009). *Handbook of reliability, availability, maintainability and safety in engineering design.* London: Springer.

Spiliotopoulos, T., Papadopoulou, P., Martakos, D., & Kouroupetroglou, G. (2010). *Integrating usability engineering for designing the Web experience: Methodologies and principles.* Hershey, PA: IGI Global. doi:10.4018/978-1-60566-896-3

Spriestersbach, A., & Springer, T. (2004). Quality attributes in mobile web application development. Lecture Notes in Computer Science, 3009, 120–130. doi:10.1007/978-3-540-24659-6_9

Taivalsaari, A., & Systä, K. (2012). Cloudberry: An HTML5 cloud phone platform for mobile devices. *IEEE Software, 29*(4), 40–45. doi:10.1109/MS.2012.51

Wasserman, A. I. (2010). Software engineering issues for mobile application development. *FSE/SDP Workshop on Future of Software Engineering Research*, (pp. 397–400). doi:10.1145/1882362.1882443

Zibula, A., & Majchrzak, T. (2013). Cross-platform development using HTML5, jQuery Mobile, and PhoneGap: Realizing a smart meter application. *Lecture Notes in Business Information Processing, 140*, 16–33. doi:10.1007/978-3-642-36608-6_2

KEY TERMS AND DEFINITIONS

Mobile Application: A type of software application developed to run on a mobile device. Also named mobile app.

Mobile Device: A computing device that is made for portability, and is thus both compact and lightweight. Smartphones and tablet computers are examples of mobile devices. Recent technological advances have allowed these small devices to be able to perform nearly anything that had previously been accomplished with personal computers. Also named handheld computer.

Quality Attribute: A set of restrictions imposed to the system under development, establishing, for instance, how usable, attractive, fast or reliable it is. Examples of this type of quality attributes are security, modifiability, performance, or portability. Quality attributes of a mobile application are highly constrained by the hardware where the app executes. Also designated quality requirement or non-functional requirement.

Chapter 9
An Analysis of the Effects of Bad Smell-Driven Refactorings in Mobile Applications on Battery Usage

Ana Victoria Rodríguez
ISISTAN, Argentina

Alejandro Zunino
ISISTAN, Argentina

Cristian Mateos
ISISTAN, Argentina

Mathias Longo
UNICEN, Argentina

ABSTRACT

Mobile devices are the most popular kind of computational device in the world. These devices have more limited resources than personal computers and battery consumption is always under user's eye since mobile devices rely on their battery as energy supply. On the other hand, nowadays most applications are developed using object-oriented paradigm, which has some inherent features, like object creation, that consume important amounts of energy in the context of mobile development. These features are responsible for offering maintainability and flexibility, among other software quality-related advantages. Then, this chapter aims to present an analysis to evaluate the trade-off between object-oriented design purity and battery consumption. As a result, developers can design mobile applications taking into account these two issues, giving priority to object design quality and/or energy efficiency as needed.

INTRODUCTION

Smartphones and tablets represent a very attractive market to develop applications, mostly because they are the commonest form of computational devices in the world (Rodríguez et al., 2012). Despite their ever-growing capabilities, these devices have limited resources compared to personal computers. In particular, devices rely on batteries as their energy supply and, while their computational capacity has increased rapidly, battery life-time has increased slowly (Paradiso & Starner, 2005) (Flipsen et al., 2012). Then, even when today's devices have more capabilities, their batteries have shorter duration because more powerful hardware needs more energy to run. In this context, it is important for mobile computing

DOI: 10.4018/978-1-4666-9916-8.ch009

Copyright © 2016, IGI Global. Copying or distributing in print or electronic forms without written permission of IGI Global is prohibited.

research to reduce energy consumption on these devices, especially when a resource intensive application is running. Moreover, there are different levels to do this, in principle operating system level and application level. This chapter chooses to work at the application level taking into account previous works which are focused on certain good object-oriented programming practices for desktop applications, but the environment and battery limitation claim application building should be rethought in the context of energy-efficient application development. Particularly, this chapter focuses on well-known anti-patterns known as Bad smells. There are several works whose main goal is to demonstrate how the refactoring of these Bad smells improves the object-oriented application design and maintenance (Lanza et al., 2006) (Fowler, 1999),but after doing so class designs are much more complex, which might negatively impact on energy consumption (Perez-Castillo & Piattini, 2014) and hence battery usage.

Even though battery consumption is an aspect that affects all mobile devices, they are the most popular computational device and, as a consequence, there is a variety of these devices and their operating systems to operate these devices. Then, this work is limited to a specific kind of device, i.e., running a particular operating system, and on the other hand we target a particular high-level programming language. First, in regard to the targeted mobile operating system, we focus on Android-powered devices because of the widespread nature of the Android platform, which is present in millions of smartphones, tablets, and other devices. Specifically, Android smartphones units were first in the list of best selling operating systems in the United States in the last years, having at the same time an exponential growth. Particularly, their worldwide market share was 48% during the third quarter of 2011, 69% during the second quarter of 2012 and 79% during the second quarter of 2013, more than twice as much as iOS, the second most popular operating system (IDC, 2014).

After selecting the operating system, the second step is to analyze the programming language options to make the experiments because the approach focuses on improving battery consumption at the application level. In this way, there are two options to analyze: Java and Android native code which are the commonest languages used for Android applications. Then, Java is the language selected to use in this chapter because of its popularity and its interesting features, i.e., it has been recognized as being a useful language to develop and execute both computationally intensive code (Mateos et al., 2010) (Mateos et al., 2011) (Taboada et al., 2011) and user-centered applications (PyPL, 2013). Also, Java provides portability, security and robustness (Mateos et al., 2012). In fact, Java provides and supports object-oriented programming, multi-threading and distributed computing implemented at the language level, platform independence, automatic memory management and exception handling, which make it interesting for general purpose applications.

As a result, the main goal of this chapter is advancing towards measuring the energy impact of refactoring Java source code for removing certain Bad smells. This means that the battery consumption of different applications will be evaluated. For each application several versions are produced, an *original* with Bad smell and *refactored* versions without these smells, with different level of refactorings depending on developer preferences. After this, the impact of the refactorings on both battery consumption and class design quality will be evaluated to provide developers a guide about refactorings and their impact on battery consumption and application design. In the same area a previous work (Rodríguez et al., 2012) demonstrates that object creation implies more battery consumption, which allows to predict the behavior of some of our refactorings. For example, *God class* refactorings improve application design at the cost of an increased application's energy consumption because a trivial refactoring for this anti-pattern is to split a God class in two or more classes, which implies more object creation at runtime. This means that trade-offs are needed between energy efficiency on one hand and application design quality and maintainability on the other hand. Specifically, (Rodríguez et al., 2012) demonstrate that battery consumption is mainly affected by object creation, method invocation and Java exceptions usage, this last including numerous object creations and method invocations.

Finally, according to the suggested methodology, it is necessary to use a specialized device to measure energy consumption accurately. Specifically, we used Power Monitor (Monitor, 2014), a tool capable of measuring the power of any device that employs a lithium battery at a frequency of 5 KHz (5,000 times per second). This tool comes along with a software application that shows Voltage and Amperage measurements, and allows users to export this information in different formats (e.g., CSV). Using this tool, the measurement of the impact of different refactorings in a popular smartphone, Samsung Galaxy SIII, was performed.

The rest of the chapter is organized as follows. Section Background presents further details of the problem and related works. Section Bad Smells describes the variety of Bad smells and their associated refactorings. Section Experiments describes in detail the experiments that are analyzed in Section Results. Finally, Section Conclusion presents a summary and the conclusions that are important for mobile application developers.

BACKGROUND

In the last few years there have been different efforts to minimize battery consumption. In this sense, the first step was *offloading*. Offloading is a technique that moves parts of an application from a device with limited resources to servers with more computational power (Kumar & Lu, 2010). For CPU-intensive applications, particularly, this technique gives the illusion of intensive processing on the device along with minimal battery footprint. This way, executing intensive code in mobile devices is now viable (Rodriguez et al., 2011). Then, the traditional conception of mobile devices as being phones or agendas has evolved, and nowadays mobile devices are being integrated to intensive computing infrastructures (Murray et al., 2010) (Rodriguez et al., 2011) to reduce the battery consumption.

Offloading

The popularity of mobile devices led users to expect the same performance from mobile devices as from other devices such as personal computers but mobile devices have limited resources. Then, a solution widely used in this context is to delegate the execution of parts of an application to other non-mobile devices (Sharifi et al., 2011). This technique is used to reduce the energy consumption in mobile devices through delegating the application execution to environments such as Clouds. While the use of Cloud computing has been presented as an option to delegate the execution of pieces of code or *jobs*, this solution presents a variety of problems (Christensen et al., 2003): consumers usually have to pay for the use of the Cloud services and mobile devices should be connected to Internet via Wi-Fi or 3G. Basically, this model is based on sending a job to some surrogates. A surrogate is a computational entity that is connected through a network and takes over some job from another device.

Additionally, it is necessary to analyze in which situations using offloading are reasonable. This can be evaluated, for example, through the execution time of a job. For this evaluation it is necessary to take into account the execution time (TE), the amount of code to transmit (DT), the number of bytes used to receive the result (DR), the transmission bandwidth (BW) and the bandwidth of the reception network

(BR). Then, $T_{offloading} = DT/BW + DR/BR + TE$ shows that offloading is convenient when the estimated execution time on the mobile device is higher than $T_{offloading}$ (Sharifi et al., 2011). Next paragraphs present a variety of related works, which show different proposals to implement this technique.

Spectra (Flinn et al., 2002) is one of the first proposal for offloading centered in the reduction of latency and energy consumption. Spectra uses a function that estimates the resources necessary to execute an application. This function is based on application tracing, using a linear regression model. The power consumption of each job is measured via battery monitors. Additionally, commands used for communication between Spectra and the application have to be introduced manually in the application code.

Furthermore, Chroma (Balan et al., 2007) (Balan et al., 2002) tries to improve Spectra by reducing developer's work. In Chroma, the user defines an utility function for each job describing the weight of each factor (CPU speed for example). Additionally, Chroma comes with a fixed utility function based on network parameters.

Goyal and Carter (Goyal & Carter, 2004) present a system based on virtual machines technology to increase performance and reduce power consumption. Using virtual machines increases the flexibility of the system, and surrogates do not need to be prepared in advance. However, the overhead of initializing a compatible virtual machine is high. Particularly, the mobile device requests a specific virtual surrogate to execute the job. To complete the job, the mobile device ships to the surrogate the URL of the program and a shell script, which handles the job execution.

Slingshot (Su & Flinn, 2005) is also a system based on virtual machines. A main server and all of its substitutes receive all the jobs delegated to execute them. Then, the first response obtained is used, checking its reliability in the home server. Finally, both systems (Slingshot, and Goyal and Carter's system) have no control about which tasks should be delegated and when.

Another offloading technique is MAUI (Cuervo et al., 2010). MAUI performs fine-grained offloading for object-oriented programs. MAUI divides the methods to execute present in the program graph into two types: local and remote. Each method execution represents a job. MAUI uses a linear model to calculate energy consumption and a history-based approach to predict the job execution time.

(Kristensen, 2010) presents Scavenger, a system focused on increasing the CPU power and decreasing the latency time of applications. Scavenger includes an adaptive double profiler based on an estimation of the execution time according to the input size and the application architecture. To make this estimation, every surrogate sends its processing power periodically. However, the execution times of different jobs on each architecture are different and the processing power of surrogates must be calculated according to the jobs, and is not considered.

AIOLOS (Verbelen et al., 2012) is a middleware for Android that takes into account server resources and network state to decide at runtime if a job should be performed on a mobile device. Delegating a job to a surrogate server is convenient when the remote execution time is smaller than the local execution time. A history-based profile is maintained to estimate the local execution time. Additionally, AIOLOS takes into account energy usage. Then, a job should be offloaded if energy is saved by using remote execution ($E_{saved} > 0$). However, (Verbelen et al., 2012) is focused on optimizing the execution time because these parameters are difficult to measure using software tools while the time parameters are estimated trough a history profiler.

Lastly, (Zhang et al., 2010) describes DPartner, a tool that semi-automatically offloads Android applications. Offloading consists of four steps. First, with the help of Java code annotations, it detects which jobs are *movables* classifying as *anchored* jobs those jobs which use some special resources available only on the mobile device. In the second refactoring step the movable jobs are transformed to be able to offload. Third, which jobs should be offloaded are detected. To determine which movable jobs should be offloaded there are numerous rules and algorithms. DPartner employs a per-process based on class clustering to advance the runtime decision. Finally, the last step consists in packaging the modified application. In this work, the energy necessary in a mobile device to offload a job is calculated by using the mapping algorithm between bytecode instructions and energy consumption proposed in (Binder, 2006). When evaluating this offloader, the authors obtained an improvement of up to 98% of performance and obtained up to 84% less energy consumption across test applications.

Benchmarking on Android Devices

This Subsection details works related to benchmarking in Java applications in the context of Android mobile application programming. As mentioned in Section Introduction, Java has been successful for developing intensive code in general (Taboada et al., 2011) and user applications. Besides, it is the high-level programming language of the Android platform.

First, (Bartel et al., 2012) presents a software package called Dexpler that translates Dalvik bytecode to Jimple, an intermediate representation of Java bytecode. Jimple is designed as an alternative to Java bytecode for static analysis of Android applications.

In (Cheng-Min et al., 2011), Java code is compared with Android native code. In the paper, 12 popular benchmarks divided in 8 categories were used to evaluate the performance on Android smartphones. As a result, native code is faster than Java code by 34.2% in average, taking values between 99.98% and -158.39%. While in some particular cases Java code was better, in most cases the native code improves performance. Particularly, Java improves performance in Hash (-158.39%), Heapsort (-26.61%) and Random (-47.72%) benchmarks.

In another similar study, (Sangchul & Wook, 2010) evaluates the performance of Android native code and Java. That work is divided into five areas: communication delay, integer operations, floating-point operations, memory access and heap allocation. In conclusion, although the native code was more efficient, the work recommend native C libraries when the application requires frequent accesses to memory or performs complex calculations.

Another recent work presents an analysis of the performance of Google's coding best practices for Android applications (AndroidDeveloper). These practices are proposed by Google to improve mobile application performance. Specifically, (Tonini et al., 2012) evaluates the improvement of avoiding the use of *getter* and *setter* methods, and using appropriate syntax of *for* cycle (according to Google, the use of *for-each* in collections is three times faster than the use of the traditional *for*). The results showed that avoiding the use of *getter* and *setter* methods is 2.93 faster than using them, and using the appropriate *for* syntax is 1.25 times faster than not using it.

Along a similar line, (Gottschalk et al., 2012) proposes detecting and removing energy-wasteful code using software reengineering. (Gottschalk et al., 2012) analyzes the mobile code structure to find energy wasting patterns called *code smells*. The term *code smell* has been presented and used for performance previously, then, a *code smell* catalog has been exhaustively studied. Finally, (Gottschalk et al., 2012) uses the same term because reuses some studied patterns. (Gottschalk et al., 2012) concludes that detecting *code smells* is viable in practice to remove energy-wasteful coding practices.

In the same way, in (Thiagarajan et al., 2012) an analysis of battery consumption produced by Web surfing is presented. The paper evaluates the energy used by a mobile browser to load Web pages using popular pages such as Amazon or Facebook. Then, (Thiagarajan et al., 2012) studies in detail the battery consumption of each element loaded in a Web page. Additionally, the work analyzes the benefits of using offloading to render Web pages on mobile devices.

Finally, a recent work (Perez-Castillo & Piattini, 2014) analyzes the effect of *God Class* refactoring on power consumption. In this work the authors demonstrate that the refactorings for some well-known antipatterns implies excessive message traffic, which produce more energy consumption. The work evaluates different applications using several tools and plug-in to detect the antipatterns and solve them. As such, it represents an important cornerstone for this chapter since it is tightly related with this chapter and its goal.

BAD SMELLS, REFACTORINGS AND THEIR IMPLICATIONS ON ENERGY USAGE

This Section presents and explains the Bad smell concept and the different categories of Bad smells that are taken into account in this chapter. Additionally, this Section mentions the variety of refactorings proposed to solve each Bad smell. It is also important to mention that, as there are more than twenty bad smell categories recognized by the community, this chapter only addresses the most frequent ones.

Bad Smell

Designing and developing an application with good object-oriented design practices is a complex task. Then, when a team is working on a project it is common to finish the object-oriented design with some imperfections remaining, and this may result in negative consequences for the application features. These code imperfections, which are code sections that have not taken into account good design practices and object-oriented design patterns, are known as 'Code smells' or 'Bad smells'. For example, a well-known Bad smell is Duplicated code which occurs when developers and designers make errors in the data abstraction and repeat the same code in different sections of the application. Since Bad smell concept was introduced by Fowler (Fowler, 1999) in 1999, the community has identified more than twenty Bad smells, some of them are Duplicated code, God Class, Brain Method and Data Class (Lanza et al., 2006), among others. For this chapter, the experiments are centered only on some of them, which are the most frequent. Additionally, the Bad smells chosen are those whose associated refactorings impact directly in the number of objects created and the number of messages sent between objects. This is because this chapter aims to measure the impact of these refactorings on battery consumption. The next paragraphs explain in detail these Bad smells:

- **God Class:** Also called *Long Class* (Fowler, 1999). This Bad smell refers to the classes centralizing most of the application functionality. It means that a Good Class is a class that does a great amount of work alone, delegating only low complex tasks. As a consequence, there are numerous classes that only contain data (*Data Class*), without functionality. Additionally, this Bad smell usually contains duplicate code and long methods (*Brain Methods*). As a result, *God Classes* have a great impact on system design because they affect negatively all quality attributes characteristic of an object-oriented design (reusability, extensibility, etc.), mainly because it is a typical case in which the system is based on a monolithic class.

- **Brain Method:** *Brain methods* are long methods which contain several variables and great complexity. As a consequence, these are methods that are not easy to reuse, understand and test because they have not a defined and particular functionality.

- **No Encapsulated Field:** This Bad smell relates to one of the most important properties of object-oriented programming: information hiding. This bad practice allows external entities to access directly to class attributes.

- **No Self-Encapsulated Field:** Even in the same class, it is advisable to access the attributes by methods. That allows more flexibility, because if it is necessary to change some attribute, it is possible to change only the access method. Then, accessing to attributes directly is considering a bad practice in object oriented programming.

Refactorings

The problems that arise from having bad practices in programming call for techniques to fix them in source code. To remove Bad smells, developers must modify the problematic code portions. This code modification in a finished project is called refactoring. There are several refactoring actions (or refactorings) to solve many Bad smells. In fact, Martin Fowler proposes a catalog with 80 different refactorings to solve these problems.

Before introducing the experiments it is necessary to explain why making refactorings is not a trivial task. For instance, if developers want to refactor a given method, they need to have a precise knowledge about it: they need know what it does, how it does, why it does, which are its parameters and internal variables, and in which context it is used.

However, refactorings are usually performed by experts who are external to the project and do not have this knowledge. Then, the correct use of the tools and good programming practices is essential to allow experts to make refactoring. In the next paragraph these good practices are presented.

The first element to consider is naming. One of the best practices that developers can use when developing an object-oriented system is to use representative names when defining variables, parameters, methods and classes. If the class design has good nomenclature, a name better reflects class responsibility. For example, if the name of a particular method is "ExecuteCommand", then it is extremely easy to determine which method is responsible for executing a command. Method implementation is also important. Let us assume that the body of the example method contains select statements (sentence case). This type of sentences often makes methods difficult to understand and makes it difficult to extend and reuse. As a consequence, a class hierarchy is necessary to remove these kinds of sentences, making methods simpler and object oriented. The next list explains the refactorings that solve the Bad smells presented above in Section Bad Smells.

- **Extract Method:** This refactoring proposes removing portions of a long method, and extract them into new smaller ones. Martin Fowler states that when developers need to insert a comment into a method, it is because there is a possible extraction method which corresponds with the semantics of the comment. That is, it is always better to have short and well appointed methods, so that any class has a good semantics and it is simple to understand.

Figure 1. Replace variable by a query

```
double basePrice = _quantity * _itemPrice;        if (basePrice() > 1000)
if (basePrice > 1000)                                 return basePrice() * 0.95;
   return basePrice * 0.95;                        else
else                                                  return basePrice() * 0.98;
   return basePrice * 0.98;                        ...
                                                   double basePrice() {
                                                      return _quantity * _itemPrice;
                                                   }
```

The main problem that arises when applying this modification is the use of temporary variables that are shared by several code sections. This is mainly because when extracting methods is performed, references to such variables are lost. To solve this problem there are three techniques:

1. Pass the value of the temporary variables as a parameter to the new method. This solution is not the best option because it generates invocations with a long list of parameters.
2. Shorten the field or empty the set of temporary variables. That is, the various portions of code that can be extracted do not share temporary variables. This solution is a good alternative, but it cannot be applied in all cases.
3. Replace temporary variables by a query. When the variable stores an expression the solution is to extract that expression into a new method. Figure 1 shows an example of this situation.

In spite of the variable problems, this refactoring is an efficient refactoring to attack *Brain Methods* since a *Brain Method* is a long and complex method. Thus, if it is divided into several short and simple methods the length and complexity decreases.

- **Input Object as a Parameter:** In general, a long list of parameters in the definition of a method reveals a design problem because the method is probably difficult to understand and modify. Then, if a developer choses the first option to solve the problem presented in the previous refactoring, he/she would have a new design problem. Thus, when there are several methods which take advantage of the same set of parameters, these parameters will be in a special class. Probably, these parameters are highly relevant to other parameters, which accounts for them often being together. Furthermore, the methods that use these parameters have a lot of functionality that can be drawn in this new class. That is, this refactoring is very useful because not only solves the problem of having a long list of parameters, but also can generate a good distribution of functionality. This refactoring is important because it is useful after applying another set of refactorings such as Extract Method. Many times, when the latter refactoring is applied, temporary variables have to be dealt with, and they are often passed as parameters to all the new methods, resulting in this situation.
- **Replace Method by an Object:** Another refactoring to solve Brain Methods is the refactoring called Replace method by an object. This refactoring consists on extracting the *Brain methods* in a new class and then apply the refactoring Extract Method in that class. It is important to mention that applying this technique is more aggressive and complex than only applying Extract Method.
- **Replace Conditional with Polymorphism:** While extracting methods is one of the ways to solve the problem of *Brain Method*, sometimes Extract method or Replace method by an object are not enough because *Brain methods* usually have several conditionals (*if-then-else* or *switch* statements) that prevent making a good separation and add a lot of complexity. Therefore, it is nec-

essary to find a way to remove such conditional maintaining the semantic of the operation. The refactoring Replace Conditional with Polymorphism proposes removing these selections using one of the most important features that object-oriented programming provides, i.e., polymorphism. That mechanism is simple, when a *switch* or a *if-then-else* statement, which asks for the type of an element and then perform an action, is detected the solution is to make a hierarchy of classes that implements this method. Finally, Figure 2 shows a simple example of this refactoring.

- **Move Method:** Sometimes there are methods that are used only for a few external classes. In those cases the functionality of each class is not well defined. One possible solution for this bad practice is to move the method to the class which uses it the most, as shown in Figure 3. However, sometimes the section of code that is used by the external class is only a portion of the method, in that situation the developer must remove only that portion of code, and then apply Move method. This refactoring can be used to solve *Brain methods*.

- **Extract Class:** When there are one or more *God classes* the best solution is to divide the functionality of those classes in more than one class. This refactoring is known as Extract Class and

Figure 2. Replace Conditional with Polymorphism

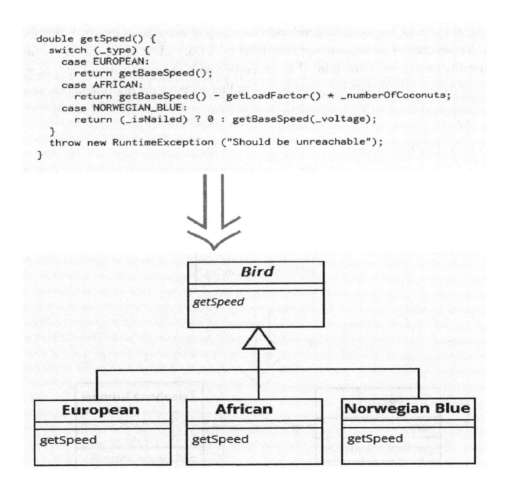

Figure 3. Move method mechanism

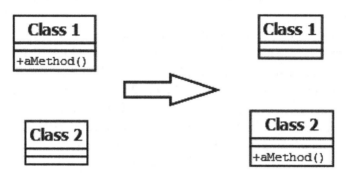

it allows the developer extracting a portion of functionality from a larger class into two or more classes. An example of this type of modification is shown in Figure 4. With this refactoring, developers decrease the effects of *God Class* but often it is not enough. To solve this bad smell it is often necessary to apply several modifications: first, developers have to apply Extract Method of the longest methods that this class contains, then, they can apply Move method and, finally, they have to apply Extract class based on the remaining functionality.

- **Inline Class:** As mentioned before, usually, having God classes commonly leads to Data classes, and as a consequence, developers need a refactoring to solve this Bad smell too. This is the opposite case of Extract Class because developers have to join two classes into one. When developers are in the presence of a class without functionality, a Data Class, there are two options: to add functionality or remove it and join all its properties with another existing class. In general, the class to which all information is moved is the one that accesses the information the most.

Figure 4. Extract class refactoring

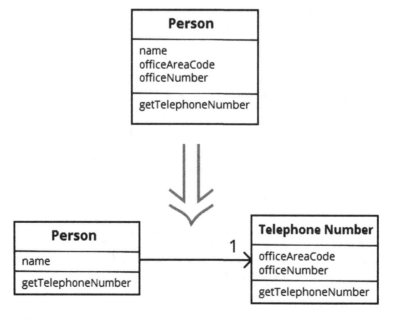

- **Attribute Access:** Fowler defines two refactorings to solve the problem of direct access to attributes:

  1. **Encapsulate Field:** an attribute that is public becomes private and methods that allow access to that attribute (getter and setter) are defined.
  2. **Self-Encapsulate Field:** This refactoring proposes to remove the shortcut to an attribute within the class in which it is defined, and change it by its accessor methods.

Both refactorings help the developer to use Move Method refactoring, since the use of attributes is decoupled from the rest of the class.

- **Refactorings and Battery Consumption:** Although they help developers improving code quality, these refactoring imply some actions that affect negatively the battery. Particularly, these refactorings add new object creations and new method calls. To better understand the impact of these actions, Table 1 is presented. This table is based in a previous work in (Rodríguez et al., 2012) where the individual micro-benchmarks were evaluated. In this table developers can observe that avoiding object creation can save up to 87.43% of energy and avoiding method call can save up to 89.03% of energy. It is noticeable that this values are high values, then, this small modifications in a code have an important impact in the battery consumption of an application. As a consequence, developing a good mobile application is not a trivial task.

EXPERIMENTS

The main goal of these experiments is to evaluate the impact of the proposed refactorings on battery consumption. This Section evaluates the trade-off of applying good object-oriented practices versus practices that consume less battery. For this, a specific process is used for selecting the applications with Bad smells which are evaluated. After choosing the applications, proper refactorings were applied and, then, the measurements were performed to compare the different versions of the same application w.r.t. battery usage.

Table 1. Micro-benchmark evaluation

Benchmark	Number of executions	Gain	Energy saved (%)	Deviation (%)	Execution Time	Time saved
Object Field Access						
Getter-based Access	115,459,467,000	-	2.97	1.97E-4		
Direct Access	919,194,540,000	7.96	87.43	2.13	3.22E-5	83.71
Object Creation						
On-demand Object Creation	1,691,926,500	-	2.70	1.84E-2		
Object Reuse	15,433,805,000	9.12	89.03	2.81	1.74E-3	90.52

The next sections are dedicated to describe the experiments, and to this end these sections present the applications that were used during the experiments, the mechanism used for taking measures and experimental scenarios, and the obtained results.

Test Applications

One of the main goals of this chapter is to evaluate the impact of a set of refactorings on battery consumption in real mobile applications. Then, a set of applications that cover all the Bad smells and refactorings presented in Section Refactorings was chosen. Once the set of applications was chosen, a new version of these applications was developed by applying the applicable refactoring(s). Finally, using a special tool, the battery consumption of each version was measured for comparison purposes. This methodology allows us to objectively analyze the improvements that can be made on an application.

To determine which applications to use, a survey of existing applications in the Android Market was made taking into account which are open-source and could be modified. To cover different types of applications with different features, games and scientific applications were chosen. The applications resulting from the survey were three: Fivestones, Sorter and Apps. The first two are games while the latter is a scientific application used in (Rodríguez et al., 2012). Each of these applications was analyzed to observe the amount of Bad smells present in the code, taking into account only the Bad smells mentioned in the previous Section, i.e. *God Class, Brain Method, No Encapsulated Fields* and *No Self-Encapsulated Fields*. Bad smell counting was performed using JDeodorant. Table 2 shows the study of each application, indicating the amount of Bad smells. Some applications are presented twice in the table because there are two independent algorithms implemented within the same application. The symbol ∞ denotes that there is no attribute browsing through access methods within the class where they are defined, i.e. all accesses present the Bad smell No Self-Encapsulated Field. The following sections give a more detailed explanation of the characteristics of each application.

- **FiveStones:** Fivestones is an implementation of the classic game 'five in line'. The game is a board game in which two players take turns to participate. The game goal is to place cards in turns, trying to obtain a line of 5 consecutive cards (vertical, horizontal or diagonal). Regarding the code, the application has 64 classes, 290 methods and 4700 lines of code. Table 2 shows that 15 *God Class* and 33 *Brain Methods* were detected in this application, in addition to the 362 attributes which are accessed directly.

Table 2. Test applications. Bad smells

Application	God Class	Brain Method	No Encapsulated Fields	No Self-Encapsulated Fields
FiveStones	15	33	15	362
Sorter	1	8	0	30
Apps - Knapsack	2	3	4	∞
Apps - Matrix Multiplication	2	3	4	∞

- **Sorter:** Sorter is a didactic game which graphically illustrates step by step different array sorting algorithms. Within the implemented algorithms are insertion sort, selection sort, bubble, quick-sort and merge-sort. The application displays a set of lines of different sizes disordered and, when the algorithms are executed, the user can see how the ordering proceeds. This code has 12 classes, 65 methods and 565 lines of code, i.e., it is a small application. Then, when the application was analyzed, only one God and 8 Brain Methods were detected. However, the percentage of code affected is high because it is a small application. Similar to FiveStones, this application has 30 attributes accessed directly.

- **Apps:** This is an application that contains three high performance mobile computing applications to solve three well-known scientific problems. The three algorithms implemented are: matrix multiplication, the knapsack problem and Fast-Fourier-Transform (FFT). In spite of the fact that this application implements three algorithms, two of them were evaluated. Specifically, matrix multiplication algorithms and knapsack problem were chosen because they have the largest amount of Bad smells and the greatest use of CPU time.

In regards to the code, the application has 31 classes, 158 methods and around 1636 lines of code. On the other hand, this application has evidence of 5 God Class, 55 Brain Methods and 10 Features Envy. In addition to the attributes which are accessed directly, the Bad smell No Self-Encapsulated Field is present. In summary, the project has many opportunities for refactoring.

Preferences Analysis

Before applying the refactorings it is important to evaluate not only the quantity of Bad smells but also the accumulated time and number of times that the methods containing Bad smells are executed. This is because a refactoring applied in a Bad smell which is executed 99% of the total time has more impact than numerous refactorings applied in Bad smell that are executed only 1% of the total time. For this, two automatic and specialized tools were necessary: first, *JDeodorant* was used to detect the Bad smell and the methods that contain them; second, an ad-hoc application (*Tracer*) was used to measure the time execution and the number of invocations of each method. After data collection it was necessary to evaluate which methods will be refactored taking into account the effort necessary and the trade-off between object-oriented design and battery consumption.

Data Collection

Table 3. and Table 4 show an example of the report obtained for the application Sorter. The first Table shows the report obtained via JDeodorant of each of the code smells detected and the affected entity. In this table, the ranking corresponds with the impact of modifying a certain bad smell in the system design. That means that this ranking gives to developers a guide to decide in which Bad smells they should attack first. In the second Table, all information relevant to the message flow of the application at runtime obtained via the Tracer is shown. In this case, the reader can see that the *makeShader* method is the most invoked one, with more than 50% as depicted in the "Total Invocations (%)" column.

Table 3. Bad smell report for the Sorter application

Code Smell	Entity	Ranking
God Class	eu.danielwhite.sorter.components.SortView	1
BrainMethod	eu.danielwhite.sorter.SortCompare.randomlyPermute(java.lang.Integer[])::void	1
BrainMethod	eu.danielwhite.sorter.algos.SelectionSorter.run()::void	2
BrainMethod	eu.danielwhite.sorter.SortCompare.initStartingState()::void	3
BrainMethod	eu.danielwhite.sorter.SortCompare.onCreate(android.os.Bundle)::void	4
BrainMethod	eu.danielwhite.sorter.components.SortView.onDraw(android.graphics.Canvas)::void	5
BrainMethod	eu.danielwhite.sorter.algos.QuickSorter private.qSort(int, int)::void	6
BrainMethod	eu.danielwhite.sorter.algos.MergeSorter.mergeSubArray(int, int, int, int)::void	7
BrainMethod	eu.danielwhite.sorter.algos.BubbleSorter.run()::void	8
No Self-Encapsulated Field	eu.danielwhite.sorter.algos.Sorter.mFinished	1
No Self-Encapsulated Field	eu.danielwhite.sorter.algos.Sorter.mData	2
...	...	...

Table 4. Message flow report for the Sorter application

Method	Total invocation time (ms)	Number of invocations (%)	Total invocations (%)
...	...	...	...
Sorter.fireSorterDataChange(void):void	705	1,1628	4,5885
EventListener. sorterDataChange(SorterEvent<Integer>):void	705	1,1628	5,7513
SortCompare.run(void):void	711	1,1727	6,9240
SortCompare.refreshList(SortView, Sorter<Integer>):void	721	1,1892	8,1131
SortView.setSorter(Sorter<Integer>):void	721	1,1892	9,3023
Sorter.setDataVal(int, T, boolean):void	1357	2,2382	11,5405
Sorter.getData(void):T[]	1405	2,3173	13,8578
SortView.onDraw(Canvas):void	1405	2,3173	16,1752
Sorter.compareData(T, T):int	1580	2,6060	18,7811
Sorter.doSleepDelay(long):void	3074	5,0701	23,8512
Sorter.getDataVal(int):T	4019	6,6287	30,4800
SortView.makeShader(int, float):Shader	42150	69,5200	100,0000

Method Selection

Once the report with all relevant information to the different applications was obtained, developers had to apply a filter in each of them to determine which of the Bad smells spotted should be refactored. Indeed, in practice, under a scenario where a balance between battery consumption and object-oriented design is desired, developers would refactor code selectively. Moreover, to consider different scenarios, three different broad scenarios with different strategies and preferences were defined:

- **Object Oriented Scenario:** The first considered scenario is the one in which the quality of the object-oriented design is prioritized, eliminating most important Bad smells. Then, specific preferences are defined in Table 5. In this Table developers can see that all *God classes* and *Brain methods* that appear in more than the 90% of invoked methods should be removed. This is because it is considered that these are the Bad smells that influence more the implementation of methods and generate a direct, negative impact on the design. Regarding attributes, nothing is specified about No Self-Encapsulated Field neither about No Encapsulated Field, so these smells were not considered important.
- **Encapsulation oriented scenario:** This second scenario focuses on refactoring the Bad smells considered in the previous case and the Bad smells No Self-Encapsulated Field and No Encapsulated Field. In the preferences, we considered that all the attributes that are part of the 50% most invoked methods would be accessed by accessors methods. These preferences can be see numerically in Table 6.
- **Battery Consumption Oriented Scenario:** The third case is the opposite scenario, in which a developer tries to reduce battery consumption of the application as much as possible. Since battery consumption is influenced directly by the message flow, the specific preferences specifies a situation where the developer removes all access methods that are in the method that represent the 90% of invoked methods. In this case a Table is not presented because there is not a Bad smell to solve.

Table 5. Object-oriented scenario preferences

Code smell	Preference	Percentage of importance	
		Min	Max
God Class	More than 10 methods	10	100
Brain Method	More than 15 lines of code	10	100
No Encapsulated Field	-	-	-
No Self-Encapsulated Field	-	-	-

Table 6. Encapsulation oriented scenario preferences

Code smell	Preference	Percentage of importance	
		Min	Max
God Class	More than 10 methods	10	100
Brain Method	More than 15 lines of code	10	100
No Encapsulated Field	-	50	100
No Self-Encapsulated Field	-	50	100

Figure 5. Example of refactoring proposed by an automatic tool

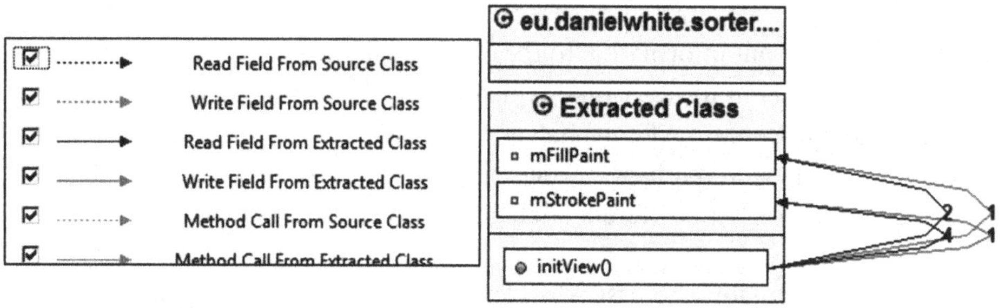

Refactoring Considerations

The first step to apply refactorings is to analyze the list obtained from the previous step (method selection) and verify the Bad smells involved. The main reason for this is that some Bad smells detected are not really Bad smells, e.g. the tool can consider two distinct types or methods just because they have little relationship but in fact they have just enough functionality to be moved to a new entity. Once such cases are identified, developers have to analyze each of the new entities to create, and finally they have to apply refactorings to the project.

Considering a particular case of the Sorter application, and considering Table 3, different refactorings could be considered. First, it has a case of God Class, for which JDeodorant proposes a class extraction that is presented in Figure 5. This extraction has only two attributes and only one method, so the extracted class has not associated functionality, which generates the code smell Data Class. This is one case in which the refactoring should not be applied by developers.

RESULTS

Using an external tool called Robotium to define different test cases, numerical and exact results were obtained. Robotium is an Android test automation framework that allows developers to write and execute tests for Android applications. With Robotium the experiments were executed several times to demonstrate the results. These results allow us to evaluate the effort and trade-off of applying refactorings in the applications. Table 7 shows the consumption measured by the Power Monitor tool for each application. The first column of the table specifies the name application, the second shows its version (considering the different scenarios presented in Section Method Selection), the third shows the execution time, the fourth column presents the Power consumed in average per unit of time (where unit of time is seconds), the fifth column shows the average of power consumption by unit of time, the sixth column shows the standard deviation of each case, and, finally, the last column represents the energy gain of the different versions of the same application w.r.t. the original version. The experiments were performed on a Samsung Galaxy SIII, with the following characteristics: Quad-core 1.4 GHz Cortex-A9 CPU, 2 GB RAM, internal 16GB of storage and lithium ion battery of 2,100 mAh.

To analyze the results it is important to mention that the total battery consumption is calculated with the following formula: consumption = time*power, where *time* refers to the execution time of the test case and *power* refers to the average of watts sampled per unit of time during the execution. It is worth

Table 7. Battery consumption results

Application	Version	Time	Power	Consumption (J)	Standard deviation (%)	Energy consumption (%)
FiveStones	Battery consumption oriented	26.246	1.326	34.224	2.532	-5.505
	Original	26.246	1.375	36.108	3.005	N/A
	Object-oriented	31.143	1.324	40.169	4.659	12.436
	Encapsulation oriented	32.598	1.326	42.442	3.691	16.502
Sorter	Battery consumption oriented	104.111	0.709	73.832	3.055	-1.102
	Original	102.347	0.717	74.646	5.347	N/A
	Object-oriented	104.593	0.738	77.212	4.116	3.322
	Encapsulation oriented	104.593	0.738	77.212	4.116	N/A
Apps – Knapsack	Battery consumption oriented	1.680	1.178	1.968	3.727	N/A
	Original	1.680	1.178	1.968	3.727	N/A
	Object-oriented	4.860	1.176	5.707	1.615	65.515
	Encapsulation oriented	4.860	1.176	5.707	1.615	N/A
Apps - Matrix Multiplication	Battery consumption oriented	1.588	1.592	2.528	2.47	N/A
	Original	1.588	1.592	2.528	2.47	N/A
	Object-oriented	5.003	1.648	8.24	1.11	69.351
	Encapsulation oriented	5.003	1.648	8.24	1.11	N/A

noting that a sample frequency of 5Khz. Taking into account these values, developers have to know that an application can reduce its battery consumption either by reducing its execution time or its energy consumption per unit of time.

Now, analyzing the results, these support the hypothesis presented at the beginning of this chapter. First, for the efficient version of FiveStones, in which some access methods are removed, the battery consumption was reduced in a 5,505%. In Sorter this percentage was lower, i.e. around 1.102%. Moreover, the applications Knapsack and Matrix Multiplication were not significantly modified, so these applications did not show improvement for this scenario. All reductions are relative to the performance of the original versions of the applications.

In the object-oriented and encapsulation oriented scenarios the battery consumption increases because there are more objects and interaction between objects. The results of the Sorter application are the same for these two scenarios because there are not attributes to be used directly within 50% of the refactored methods. On the other hand, the results of FiveStones have an important difference since consumption is increased by 12,436% in the object-oriented scenario and 16.502% in the encapsulation scenario. In the case of the scientific applications the percentage increases up to 69.351%, although two scenarios were not made separately since these were not different, as is the case of Sorter. One of the main reasons for this difference in the percentages between graphical and scientific applications is that the graphical interface is an important component that consumes large amount of battery power (Carroll & Heiser, 2010).

In summary, although not generalizable, the results support the original hypothesis. That is, an object-oriented design tends to carry more battery consumption than a design with less objects and messages between them. Then, when developers try to achieve a better object-oriented design, this may generate a significant impact on battery consumption, and viceversa.

CONCLUSION

This chapter analyzed the trade-off between having a high-quality object-oriented application and having an application that is more energy-efficient. The results presented by different works show that developing a good mobile application is not a trivial task since it is important to evaluate the object-oriented advantages to achieve a good balance with the battery consumption. Basically, this is an important topic since object-oriented programming is one of the most used paradigms in application development, which includes practices that significantly improve the level of modificability, understandability, maintainability, among other attributes of the code. However, a correct use of the paradigm requires the presence of many classes and methods to have a good distribution of functionality, but these features impact negatively on the level of battery consumption of the application, as shown in (Rodríguez et al., 2012). The main reason of this evaluation is that battery life is an important feature for mobile users, then, if they install an application that consumes a lot of battery probably they will not be comfortable with it.

Particularly, the results show that assuring important features of object-oriented design, such as maintainability and flexibility, through removing Bad smells increase battery consumption. As a consequence, developers should evaluate which features can be relaxed to prioritize battery consumption. Even though this chapter does not present a methodology to deal with this trade-off, the steps used to demonstrate how some refactorings have an important impact on battery consumption can be repeated and used by developers to design and develop their own applications while considering these issues. The aim of these steps is to give basic hints to the developer to balance the number of classes and methods that applications have to implement to not consume a lot of battery. In detail, the process behind such steps is divided into several stages, each with a very specific function. In the first stage an analysis of the applications detects the different Bad smells. As explained, these Bad smells are practices that are opposite to the good practices for object-oriented programming. After that, developers have to decide their preferences to allow a "good" balance –according to their needs– between object-oriented design quality and battery consumption. Thirdly, the classes and methods to be changed have to be determined. The last stage is to perform the refactorings. Finally, taking into account the experiments presented, developers can quantify the effort and gains of applying some refactorings in their applications.

ACKNOWLEDGMENT

We acknowledge the financial support by ANPCyT through research grants PICT-2012-0045 and PICT-2013-0464. The first and fourth authors acknowledge their Ph.D. fellowships granted by the National Scientific and Technological Research Council (CONICET).

REFERENCES

AndroidDeveloper. (n.d.). Available at http://developer.android.com/training/articles/perf-tips.html

Balan, R. K., Flinn, J., Satyanarayanan, M., Sinnamohideen, S., & Yang, H. (2002). The case for cybef foraging. *10th Workshop on ACM SIGOPS European Workshop: beyond the PC*, (pp. 87-92). ACM.

Balan, R. K., Gergle, D., Satyanarayanan, M., & Herbsleb, J. (2007). Simplifying cyber foraging for mobile devices. *5th USENIX International Conference on Mobile Systems, Applications and Services (MobiSys)*, (pp. 272-285). USENIX.

Bartel, A., Klein, J., Traon, Y. L., & Monperrus, M. (2012). Dexpler: Converting Android Dalvik Bytecode to Jimple for Static Analysis with Soot. *SOAP, 2012*, 27–38. doi:10.1145/2259051.2259056

Binder, W. (2006). Using bytecode instruction counting as portable CPU consumption metric. *Electronic Notes in Theoretical Computer Science*, 57-77.

Carroll, A., & Heiser, G. (2010). An Analysis of Power Consumption in a Smartphone. *USENIX annual technical conference*, (pp. 271-285). USENIX.

Cheng-Min, L., Jyh-Horng, L., Chyi-Ren, D., & Chang-Ming, W. (2011). Benchmark Dalvik and Native Code for Android System. *Second International Conference on Innovations in Bio-inspired Computing and Applications*, (pp. 320-323).

Christensen, A. S., Moller, A., & Schwartzbach, M. I. (2003). Precise Analysis of String Expressions. *10th International Static Analysis Symposium (SAS), 2694*, 1-18.

Cuervo, E., Balasubramanian, A. K., Cho, D., Wolman, A., Saroiu, S., Chandra, R., & Bahl, P. (2010). *MAUI: Making smartphones last longer with code offload*. 8th international conference on Mobile systems, applications, and services (ACM MobiSys 10).

Flinn, J., Park, S., & Satyanarayanan, M. (2002). Balancing performance, energy, and quality in pervasive computing. *22nd International Conference on Distributed Computing Systems*. doi:10.1109/ICDCS.2002.1022259

Flipsen, B., Geraedts, J., Reinders, A., Bakker, C., Dafnomilis, I., & Gudadhe, A. (2012). Environmental sizing of smartphone batteries. *Electronics Goes Green, 2012*, 1–9.

Fowler, M. (1999). *Refactoring: Improving the Design of Existing Code*. Academic Press.

Gottschalk, M., Josefiok, M., Jelschen, J., & Winter, A. (2012). Removing Energy Code Smells with Reengineering Services. Lecture Notes in Informatics, 441-455.

Goyal, S., & Carter, J. (2004). A lightweight secure cyber foraging infrastructure for resource-constrained devices. *6th IEEE Workshop on Mobile Computing Systems and Applications*, (pp. 186-195). doi:10.1109/MCSA.2004.2

IDC. (2014). Retrieved from: http://www.idc.com/getdoc.jsp?containerId=prUS24257413

Kristensen, M. D. (2010). Scavenger: Transparent development of efficient cyber foraging applications. *EEE International Conference on Pervasive Computing and Communications (PerCom)*. doi:10.1109/PERCOM.2010.5466972

Kumar, K., & Lu, Y.-H. (2010). Cloud Computing for Mobile Users: Can Offloading Computation Save Energy? *Computer, 43*(4), 51–56. doi:10.1109/MC.2010.98

Lanza, M., Marinescu, R., & Ducasse, S. (2006). *Object-oriented metrics in practice*. Springer.

Mateos, C., Zunino, A., & Campo, M. (2010). m-JGRIM: A Novel Middleware for Gridifying Java Applications into Mobile Grid Services. *Software, Practice & Experience, 40*(4), 331–362.

Mateos, C., Zunino, A., Hirsch, M., & Fernandez, M. (2012). Enhancing the BYG gridification tool with state-of-the-art Grid scheduling mechanisms and explicit tuning support. *Advances in Engineering Software, 43*(1), 27–43. doi:10.1016/j.advengsoft.2011.08.006

Mateos, C., Zunino, A., Trachsel, R., & Campo, M. (2011). A Novel Mechanism for Gridification of Compiled Java Applications. *Computing and Informatics, 30*(6), 1259-1285. Available at http://www.cai.sk/ojs/index.php/cai/issue/view/CAI-30-2011-6

Monitor. (2014). *PowerMonitor*. Available at https://www.msoon.com/LabEquipment/PowerMonitor/

Murray, D., Yoneki, E., Crowcroft, J., & Hand, S. (2010). The case for crowd computing. In *2nd. ACM SIGCOMM Workshop on Networking, Systems, and Applications on Mobile Hand-helds*, (pp. 39-44). doi:10.1145/1851322.1851334

Paradiso, J. A., & Starner, T. (2005). Energy scavenging for mobile and wireless electronics. *IEEE Pervasive Computing / IEEE Computer Society [and] IEEE Communications Society, 4*(1), 18–27. doi:10.1109/MPRV.2005.9

Perez-Castillo, R., & Piattini, M. (2014). Analyzing the Harmful Effect of God Class Refactoring on Power Consumption. *Software, IEEE, 31*(3), 48-54.

PyPL. (2013). Available at https://sites.google.com/site/pydatalog/pypl/PyPL-PpopularitY-of-Programming-Language

Rodríguez, A. V., Mateos, C., & Zunino, A. (2012). Mobile Devices-aware Refactorings for Scientific Computational Kernels. 41 JAIIO - AST 2012, (pp. 61-72).

Rodriguez, J. M., Mateos, C., & Zunino, A. (2011). Are Smartphones Really Useful for Scientific Computing? Advances in New Technologies, Interactive Interfaces and Communicability (pp. 35-44). Springer.

Sangchul, L., & Wook, J. J. (2010). Evaluating Performance of Android Platform Using Native C for Embedded Systems. *International Conference on Control, Automation and Systems*, (pp. 1160-1163).

Sharifi, M., Kafaie, S., & Kashefi, O. (2011). A Survey and Taxonomy of Cyber Foraging of Mobile Devices. IEEE, 14, 1232-1243.

Su, Y. Y., & Flinn, J. (2005). Slingshot: Deploying stateful services in wireless hotspots. *3rd International Conference on Mobile Systems, Applications, and Services*, (pp. 79-92). doi:10.1145/1067170.1067180

Taboada, G. L., Ramos, S., Exposito, R. R., Tourino, J., & Doallo, R. (2011). Java in the High Performance Computing arena: Research, practice and experience. *Science of Computer Programming*, v.

Thiagarajan, N., Aggarwal, G., Nicoara, A., Boneh, D., & Singh, J. P. (2012). Who Killed My Battery: Analyzing Mobile Browser Energy Consumption. *WWW, 2012*, 41–50.

Tonini, A. R., Beckmann, M., de Mattos, J. C., & de Brisolara, L. B. (2012). *Evaluating Android best practices for performance*. Academic Press.

Verbelen, T., Simoens, P., Turck, F. D., & Dhoedt, B. (2012). AIOLOS: Middleware for improving mobile application performance through cyber foraging. *Journal of Systems and Software*, *85*(11), 2629–2639. doi:10.1016/j.jss.2012.06.011

Zhang, L., Tiwana, B., Dick, R., Qian, Z., Mao, Z. a., & Yang, L. (2010). Accurate online power estimation and automatic battery behavior based power model generation for smartphones. *International Conference on Hardware/Software Codesign and System Synthesis*, (pp. 105-114). doi:10.1145/1878961.1878982

KEY TERMS AND DEFINITIONS

Android: Is a Linux based operating system for mobile devices.

Bad Smell: Is a surface indication (code snippet) that usually corresponds to a deeper problem in the system.

Brain Method: Is a long method which contains several variables and great complexity.

Energy Efficiency: Is the use of the least amount of energy to execute mobile applications as possible.

God Class: Is a class that centralizes most of an application's functionality.

No Encapsulated Field: Is a bad practice that allows external entities to access directly to class attributes.

No Self-Encapsulated Field: Is a bad practice that allows accessing directly to the class attributes.

Offloading: Is a technique that moves parts of an application from a device with limited resources to servers with more computational power.

Refactoring: Is a restructuring in a finished source code without changing its external behavior.

176

Chapter 10
Usability Software Engineering Testing Experimentation for Android–Based Web Applications:
Usability Engineering Testing for Online Learning Management System

Hina Saeeda
National University of Sciences and Technology, Pakistan

Fahim Arif
National University of Sciences and Technology, Pakistan

Nasir Mehmood Minhas
Pir Mehr Ali Shah Arid Agriculture University, Pakistan

ABSTRACT

For success of android applications working in cloud environments usability testing is vital as the user usability satisfaction is the leading point in market. Authors are testing usability of the learning management system of (National university of science and Technology Pakistan)ten usability factors system content visibility, system learn ability, accessibility, operability, consistency, feedback, error message production, error prevention, and ease to remember system operations are chosen on the basis of these key factors proper experimentation on users who access LMS by their smart phones using android applications in cloud environments is conducted .Pre-test was conducted for measuring the initial requirements of experimentation process after that the detailed experimentation was performed to measure the usability factors presence in android based web applications operated in cloud environment. The results are statistically summarized against.

DOI: 10.4018/978-1-4666-9916-8.ch010

Copyright © 2016, IGI Global. Copying or distributing in print or electronic forms without written permission of IGI Global is prohibited.

INTRODUCTION

The success of a web application has its roots deep into the usability analysis and testing. Access to a web application from Android devices is another key issue of usability. Android web applications are providing ease to users. On the other hand they are also creating difficulties for users in a usability sense, as a new user cannot easily pick and understand the interface of Android apps and web apps, and their way of operating. If the Android apps, and specifically web apps accessed through Android devices, are tested for usability prior to launching to the market, and even after the launching, many of the conflicts regarding usability issues of these apps can get resolved beautifully.

Android devices are providing the ultimate way of accessing web applications from cell phones using cloud environments. Users of Android applications and smart phones are increasing, as people are more attracted toward mobile computing devices use, due to the benefits these devices are providing, such as mobility, ubiquity, etc.

In current market scenarios where the technology enhancement and innovation is on peak and competition is really tough, the success of any software application depends a lot on its usability factors as the usability factors may be used to confirm that the user is feeling that it is easy to operate the application, the user is feeling that the steps of the application operability are easy to remember, in short that the user or customer is satisfied with the ease of operate that application is providing to user during operation in all senses . Usability factors not only help ensuring that the user is mentally comfortable while operating the application, but also that, physically, the user is not in any trouble while operating the application. For success of Android applications and web applications in Android devices, the surety of usability is vital and not ignorable as the customers' or end users' usability satisfaction is the leading point in market business.

So it is not only recommended to test the Android web applications for usability before launching them to the market but also after launching, for gaining valuable feedback from market and end users .

In this chapter, the authors are covering some important usability testing techniques for Android based web applications while working in cloud environments.

Usability engineering is a branch of software engineering. Usability is about the human and computer relations and friendly interactions.

Usability enhances task accomplishing power of users by providing user friendly interfaces. Usability engineering is applicable mostly everywhere in the software and computer science (Blandford, Keith, Connell, & Edwards, 2004).

Web applications are a vastly growing area in software and computer sciences. Success criteria of web based applications depend on satisfaction of the end user.

The end user rates a web application as satisfactory if he feels that it is easy to understand, learn remember and to operate (Amalfitano, D., Fasolino, A., & Tramontana, P, 2011). All these properties are available in a web application if its usability is tested verified and validated. Nowadays, usability is considered very important for the web interfaces.

The concept of usability emerged at the end of 1970s. In the documents of ISO 9241-11 specification, this term is defined officially as following (Andreasen, M. S., Nielsen, H., Schrøder, S., & Stage, J, 2007): "extent to which a product can be used by specified users to achieve specified goals with effectiveness, efficiency and satisfaction in a specified context of use". In this definition, effectiveness stands for correct and complete degree of user accomplishing certain tasks and achieving a specific goal, efficiency means the ratio between the degree of accomplishment and the resources costs (such as time), and satisfaction is the extent of users satisfaction and acceptance in the use of products.

In 1993, Nielsen made a thorough explanation about usability in his book Usability Engineering following (Andreasen, M. S., Nielsen, H., Schrøder, S., & Stage, J,2007):

1. Learnability: the system should be easy to learn;
2. Efficiency: the use of the system should be high efficiency;
3. Ease of remembrance: the system should be easy to memory;
4. Error: the system should have lower error rates, and can prevent the disastrous mistakes;
5. Satisfaction: the system should be used with comfort.

Other researchers' work shows that enhancing the usability of web applications showed a great increase in the number of users (Moritz & Meinel, 2010). The current age is offering mobile based web applications which allow users to directly access web apps from their cell phones using different software. The latest technology in that field is Android operating system for smart phones to access web base applications and run them. Android has been launched by Google as an open-source Mobile phone operating system; it is a Linux-based Platform; its major parts are the operating system, Middleware, user interface and application Software (Andreasen, Nielsen, Schrøder, & Stage, 2007).

Mobile devices and applications offer important benefits to their users, in terms of portability, location awareness, and accessibility.

A number of studies have examined usability challenges in the mobile context, and offered meanings of mobile application usability and methods to evaluate it (Nayebi, Desharnais, & Abran, 2012).

Complex computer systems are finding their way into everyday life, and with a much broader customer base. This has made usability more critical. As a result, companies are seeing the benefits of designing and developing their products with user oriented methods instead of technology oriented methods, and are endeavoring to understand both user and product, by investigating the interactions between them (Nayebi, Desharnais, & Abran, 2012).

The increasing mobile application market demands that the developers develop fine quality applications for surviving in the market (Blandford, A., Keith, S., Connell, I., & Edwards, H, 2004). The quality prospect of the apps contains good design, learn ability, access but the most important property is usability testing.

All well reputed universities are providing online learning management systems to their students, and most of the students access these web bases learning systems by their cell phones, especially by Android based devices, accessing their data spaces in the cloud. Thus, the usability testing is vital for these applications. In this paper the usability of the Learning management system of NUST-NATIONAL UNIVERSITY OF SCIENCE AND TECNOLOGY PAKISTAN is tested experimentally, different approaches in use are covered for usability measurements and a mix of these discussed approaches are applied for testing the usability of the university LMS (learning management system).

The results gathered are statistically analyzed and, on the bases of these results, solutions to the problems are suggested and concluded.

Figure 1. Usability Testing Techniques (Amalfitano, Fasolino, & Tramontana, A GUI Crawling-Based Technique for Android Mobile Application Testing, 2011)

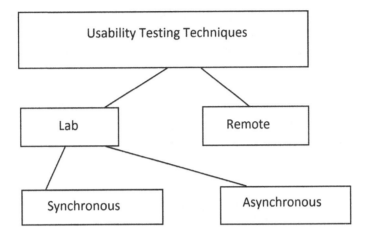

Background

Usability Testing in Literature Review

Since the 1990s, usability testing is done by using different techniques, like cognitive modeling, expert heuristics, pluralistic usability walkthrough, etc. (Andreasen, Nielsen, Schröder, & Stage, 2007).

There are two popular techniques to test usability. The first one is lab testing and the other is field study. Traditionally, usability testing is done using lab testing because in lab it is easy to collect data and all equipments are available. In the second technique usability testing is done in the environment where the technology is going to be in used because it is related to the real world (Amalfitano, Fasolino, & Tramontana, A GUI Crawling-Based Technique for Android Mobile Application Testing, 2011). This is also called remote usability testing (figure 1).

The lab study or experimentation is again divided into synchronous and asynchronous testing.

The synchronous test is performed in real time and the test monitor is separated spatially from the test subject, while in asynchronous mode the test monitor and the test subject are separated both spatially and temporally (Andreasen, Nielsen, Schröder, & Stage, 2007). According to some authors, the synchronous method is equivalent to traditional method (Belli, Budnik, & White, 2006).

Remote testing technique is based on client sever concept where the observer can be an ordinary computer connected with a network connection. Here the server is connected with the client and gets all the data from the client. The problems can be found by analyzing data. The camera captures shots only when there is a change on the screen. The reason is that during mobile operation the time taken by each operation is usually long. The images are then collected from the client, then are converted to PNG for smaller size, saved and named according to their timestamps, in order to transfer them to the server via WI-FI. These images show all the operations performed by the user and the time spent on each operation, and also the sequence of operations. Here, the server displays pictures synchronously. After that, a test player is used to play screen shots (Andreasen, Nielsen, Schröder, & Stage, 2007) in one of the following ways:

Play Frame by Frame: In this technique we set the number for how much frames to play per second.

Play in Time: In this technique images are played in real time one by one according to their timestamp (Andreasen, Nielsen, Schrøder, & Stage, 2007), (Belli, Budnik, & White, 2006). Timestamp shows two things one is time spent on each operation and second is what operation is done. It helps the analyzer to analyze the data after the experiment.

The next step is a questionnaire, which consists of two parts: subjective part and objective part. The objective part contains questions about the background of the user and their interaction in experiment. It usually has odd option category scale. The subjective part contains the user's feeling, opinion, advice and so on (Andreasen, Nielsen, Schrøder, & Stage, 2007).

As Android application behavior is event-driven, many techniques are there for testing Android applications using EDS (Event Driven System) testing. However, it is important to understand how this approach can be used to obtain a cost-effective testing technique. Many EDS(Event Driven System) testing approaches require suitable models of the system or sub-system to perform tests, such as Event-Flow Graphs, Event-Interaction-Graphs, or Finite State Machines (Amalfitano, Fasolino, & Tremonton, 2010), (Marchetto, Tonella, & Ricca, 2008), (Thompson & Torabi, 2007), (Mesbah & Van Deursen, 2009), discover the analysis of user session traces for conducting test cases (Memon, Banerjee, & Nagarajan, 2003), or are based on GUI rippers (Mesbah & Van Deursen, 2009) or Web 253 (an Internet bot that systematically browses the World Wide Web) application crawlers (Sakuraashe, Sasindranasivapalan, & Warren, 2009) that decrease possible flow of events that can be transformed into test cases. While using these approaches to perform Android testing, the first requirement is the selection of the considered models to get event types and the sources used for Android application.

As a result, new reverse engineering and GUI Ripping approaches (Amalfitano, Fasolino, & Tremonton, 2010) need to get the important models, platforms and tools (Marchetto, Tonella, & Ricca, 2008). When an automatic testing technique is used to test Android applications, which is based on crawler, it produces a model named as GUI tree. It consists of nodes and edges. Here the nodes show the interface of Android application and edges show event based transitions between nodes. To get this model the crawler fires an event on the user interface. It captures two things: one is information about the interface, and another is the event which is used to decide whether further events will be fired or not. Here the interfaces are used to form GUI where their connection is established by using transition relationship. Each interface is distinguished by activity instance and is formed by a set of widgets (a visual item of the interface is named as widget). It performs its operation by an instance of view class, a dialog class or menu class item. Each widget is distinguished by some properties having related values, meaning that each widget is differentiated by their size, color, position, and caption (Amalfitano, Fasolino, & Tremonton, 2010). In some cases the widget has a property for the user to provide input at run time. When an event occurs this means that a transition is performed between interfaces. In Android application there are two types of events. The crawler algorithm is used to produce a GUI tree that is able to run two testing techniques. Automatic crash test (Zhifangliu, Liu, & Openggao, 2009) main features are that it is used to show applications faults. To perform crash test the test cases which are used show the sequence of events connected with each other using paths of GUI tree to connect root node to the leaf node. Regression testing is performing after changes have been made. In this test, previous test cases are first run, firstly to check whether the behavior of the application has changed or not, and also to see

Table 1. Frameworks for measuring usability of mobile applications (Yumei w u & zhifang liu, 2009)

Framework Proposed by	Framework name	Stands for	Test Application	Detail	Test Cases Detail
Sakura et al.	Hermes	-	Hermes tool for J2me.	It is a framework to write test and for running it has distributed run time environment and also produce outcome of test	Its test cases are device independent and based on XML scripts and test can only perform on physical devices
Zhifang liu	SOA	-	It only validate test instance of simple local phone software and perform operation on the complex adaptive mobile application	As it is a mobile test frame work which is based on SOA architecture.	It gives client test framework for mobile application and use COM component division, design and also component interface design as a base.
Zhifang Liu	ART	Adoptive random testing	For mobile application	This test case generation technique only consider static context variable	-
Domenico Amalfitano et al.	Crawler	-	Android application	It automatically build a model for GUI	Through this technique the test case which are obtain can perform rapid crash testing and regression testing
Yumei Wu et al.	OCR	Optical character recognition	Mobile devices	It is new technique of GUI modeling for mobile devices and is responsible for image processing to extract character information.	-

what the new emerging problems are. In both testing techniques it is recommended to use the same test cases and find suitable solutions to check differences in the application behavior. This is usually done by comparing user interface sequence in both tests. In literature review there is evidence of frameworks for the testing of usability for mobile applications. Each framework is giving some specific solution for the usability problem (see Table 1).

EXPERIMENTATION FOR THE USABILITY TESTING OF ANDROID BASED WEB APPLICATIONS

In experimentation we followed a mix of techniques and the idea is taken from (Qing Li, Tao Wang, Jing Wang & Yun Li, 2011) with some modifications. All the students that participated in the experimentation belong to NUST-NATIONAL UNIVERSITY OF SCIENCE AND TECNOLOGY PAKISTAN. The experimentation method was divided into two major steps:

1. Field Study (Pre-test)
2. Lab Study

Field Study (Pre-Test Phase) of Experimentation

Prior to the original experimentation we conducted a pre-test for the users who were using Android based devices to access the LMS (Learning Management System) of NUST-NATIONAL UNIVERSITY OF SCIENCE AND TECNOLOGY PAKISTAN. The purpose of this pre-test is to assess the users, by eliciting the previous knowledge about the system and skills with the operation of the system. For this purpose, a questionnaire of 11 questions was prepared. In this questionnaire, very basic questions regarding the use of Android based applications are covered; questions about the accessing of online courses information and learning of the system are included. The pre-test questions cover all the basic usability concerns of users in detail. The results are gathered by a field study and the gathered results are statistically measured. For each of the questions asked in the pre-test during the field survey, the answers' results are given in Table 2. We can say that the pre-test is evaluating the users' current knowledge and it also helps in judging the skills level of each user, meaning to what extent the user has command on the system operability, to what extent the user is using the system in daily life, how important the system is for the user daily life? Is the system adding something beneficial to the user life? If yes than what is the effect of individual elements of the system on the users' performance, such as the design, font size, text style either effect the learning of the user or not? If these things are affecting the learning of the user, than what about the system response time; how efficient it is? How much cognitive load it puts on the user? If the user is used to use the system in daily routine for learning purpose than how much is he familiar with the technology used in the application development?

No hardware or software is used in the pre-test as compared to the Lab test. This pre-test questionnaire covers all the emotional factors of a user, such as what the user thinks about the structure of LMS? General and oral know how of the user about the system. What does the user think about the modules of the LMS? Is it easy to work with the system? All these basic questions are covered by the pre-test questionnaire, which provides us very helpful material prior to conducting the actual experiment. We get the percentage of users using the system comfortably and, on the basis of this result we further narrow down the measurements of key factors of usability about the system to statistically measure and analyze. Pre-test helped us in conducting a pilot study before the actual experimentation; this pre-test is providing a base line for the Lab pre-test capturing. This pre-Test is judgment based Test or study which gives the surety that members going to take part in the actual experimentation are well known to the domain of the problem for which the study is going to be conducted. The pre –Test is an example of field study in true sense. In Pre-test the authors are gathering information from the users of the technology and assessing their level of understanding towards the problem. Pre-Test is beautifully connecting the people involved in the experimentation from mental involvement in experimentation (filling the questionnaires) to the physical involvement in the experimentation, as the pre-test is providing a bridge between the user and the actual experimentation phase. Meanwhile the Pre –test is also catching the basic level of insight of the actual users about the problem domain and usage of related technology devices.

Results of Field Study (Pre-Test) Phase of Experimentation

Table 3. shows the results of the field study (pre-test phase of experimentation), and figures 2 to 7 show the corresponding pie charts of the pre-test questionnaire results.

Table 2. Pre-Test Questions.

1. Are you skilled in installing and using most software on your phone? A. skilled B. can operate C. not skilled
2. Did you know about mobile apps? A. know very much B. know some C. don't know
3. Did you know about Android mobile apps? A. know very much B. know some C. don't know
4. Do you know about mobile learning? A. know very much B. know some C. don't know
5. Have you ever learned by online course? A. have learned B. have heard about C. don't know
6. Did text style and font size in the course effect on your learning? A. it is good B. the font is too small C. the color is not comfortable D. no effect
7. Can you find the items very quickly according to the task? A. very quickly B. needs to find carefully C. not easy to find
8. Is it easy to find out your current course in LMS? A. it has an obvious title B. needs to identify title carefully C. difficult to know
9. Did the name of module in LMS describe its content well? A. quite well B. not so accurate C. inaccurate
10. Do you think the structure of the LMS is reasonable? A. reasonable B. needs small revision C. too bad, can't understand it
11. How is the access speed of this website A. Quick B. Ordinary C. Slow

Table 3. Field study results.

S:No	Questions	Options	Percentage
1	Installing and using	Skilled	66.67
		Can operate	16.67
		Not skilled	16.67
2	Knowledge about mobile apps	Know very much	33.33
		Know some	66.66
		Don't know	0
3	Knowledge about Android mobile apps	Know very much	58.33
		Know some	41.66
		Don't know	0
4	Knowledge about mobile learning	know very much	50.00
		Know some	25.00
		Don't know	25.00
5	Have you ever learned by online course?	Have learned	66.66
		Have heard about	33.33
		Don't know	0
6	Did text style and font size in the course effect on your learning?	It is good	91.66
		The font is too small	8.33
		The color is not comfortable	0
		No effect	0
7	Can you find the items very quickly according to the task?	Very quickly	50.00
		Needs to find carefully	33.33
		Not easy to find	16.66
8	Is it easy to find out your current course in LMS?	It has an obvious title	33.33
		Needs to identify title carefully	33.33
		Difficult to know	33.33
9	Did the name of module in LMS describe its content well	Quite well	75.00
		Not so accurate	16.66
		Inaccurate	8.33
10	Do you think the structure of the LMS is reasonable?	Reasonable	41.66
		Needs small revision	41.66
		Too bad, can't understand it	16.66
11	How is the access speed of this website?	Quick	41.66
		Ordinary	58.33
		Slow	0

Figure 2. Pie charts for the answers to questions 1 and 2 of the pre-test questionnaire

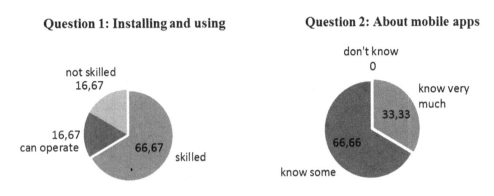

Figure 3. Pie charts for the answers to questions 3 and 4 of the pre-test questionnaire

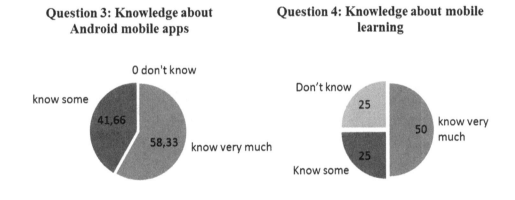

Figure 4. Pie charts for the answers to questions 5 and 6 of the pre-test questionnaire

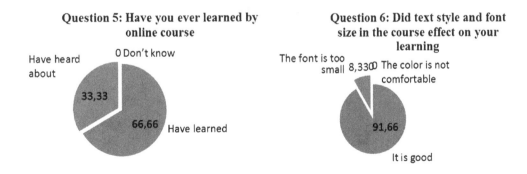

Figure 5. Pie charts for the answers to questions 7 and 8 of the pre-test questionnaire

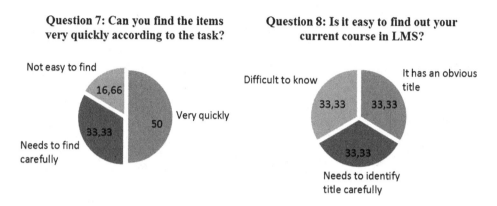

Figure 6. Pie charts for the answers to questions 9 and 10 of the pre-test questionnaire

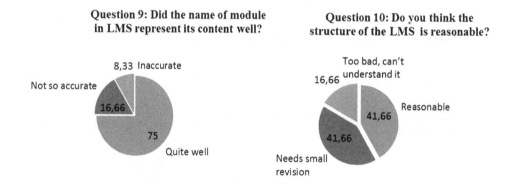

Figure 7. Pie chart for the answers to question 11 of the pre-test questionnaire

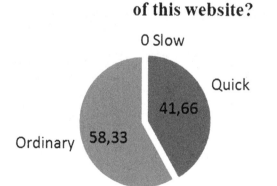

Lab Study Phase of Experimentation

After the completion of the first phase of experimentation, which was the pre-test phase, the second part of experimentation has been conducted. The second part of experimentation included a lab study. In the lab study, students accessed their LMS (Learning Management system), using their own Android cell phones, and they rated the ten usability factors related to the LMS (Learning Management system). As these students were asked to access their LMS accounts from their personal cell phones, the size, type, and memory aspects of these devices were different for each student. Accordingly, these ten questions were rated by a sample of different 40 students belonging to different courses.

These ten usability factors are:

1. System content visibility
2. System learnability
3. Accessibility
4. Operability
5. Consistency
6. Feedback
7. Efficiency/Response time
8. Error message production
9. Error prevention
10. Ease of memorization of system operations

Each individual student during experimentation was observed carefully and his / her comments regarding the questions and related answers were recorded carefully.

Table 4., below, is showing the questionnaire used for assessment of these key factors of usability of a system.

Table 4. Labs –Test Questionnaire.

11. The system content is visible clearly? A. strongly disagree   B. disagree   C. neutral   D. agree   E. strongly agree
12. It was very easy to learn how to use the LMS? A. strongly disagree   B. disagree   C. neutral   D. agree   E. strongly agree
13. It is really difficult to access the LMS by the Android based cell phone? A. strongly disagree   B. disagree   C. neutral   D. agree   E. strongly agree
14. It was a great to operate the LMS by Android based cell phones? A. strongly disagree   B. disagree   C. neutral   D. agree   E. strongly agree
15. Design is consistent and follow same pattern on whole system? A. strongly disagree   B. disagree   C. neutral   D. agree   E. strongly agree
16. System is providing adequate feedback to users about their actions. A. strongly disagree   B. disagree   C. neutral   D. agree   E. strongly agree
17. Can you find the items very quickly according to the task and system response time is good? A. strongly disagree   B. disagree   C. neutral   D. agree   E. strongly agree
18. The system is moderate at error message providing? A. strongly disagree   B. disagree   C. neutral   D. agree   E. strongly agree
19. System is well designed and prevents errors? A. strongly disagree   B. disagree   C. neutral   D. agree   E. strongly agree
20. Once the tasks performed, are these easy to remember? A. strongly disagree   B. disagree   C. neutral   D. agree   E. strongly agree

The questionnaire is built on Likert skill technique.

After conducting the lab study, the data has been analyzed against each question asked, and then the percentage has been found out against each option. By this study the LMS is analyzed and each key factor is evaluated statistically.

Using this data, the authors caught different shortcomings in usability factors of the LMS, by communicating to the participant we got their views on how to change the factors. The results and pi-charts will clearly represent these factors in detail. The Lab study was conducted with the following parts:

1. Participants accessing LMS by using Android based cell phones applications.
2. Participants' operations on the LMS
3. Communication with participants
4. Filling of questionnaire by participants
5. Evaluating the results statistically

The questionnaire used for this purpose is containing ten questions; each question is representing one usability key factor. The questions are: the system content is visible clearly? It was very easy to learn how to use the LMS? It is really difficult to access the LMS by the Android based cell phone? It was great to operate the LMS by Android base cell phones? Design is consistent and follow same pattern on whole system? System is providing adequate feedback to users about their actions? Can you find the items very quickly according to the task and system response time is good? The system is moderate at error message providing? System is well designed and prevents errors? Once the tasks performed, are these easy to remember? The Lab-test questionnaire can be found in table 4.

Results of Lab Study Second Phase of Experimentation

Table 5. shows the results of the Lab study phase of experimentation, and figures 8 to 12 show the corresponding pie charts of the lab-study questionnaire results.

Table 5. Lab study results.

Key factors	Strongly Disagree	Disagree	Neutral	Agree	Strongly Agree
System content visibility	0	7.5	12.5	40	20
System learn ability	2.5	5	7.5	32.5	27.5
Access ability	5	10	35	25	25
Operability	0	17.5	40	17.5	0
Consistency	2.5	5	20	47.5	25
Feedback	0	17.5	20	37.5	25
Response	0	10	17.5	32.5	40
Error message providing	2.5	0	30	40	27.5
Error prevention	2.5	5	22.5	40	30
Easy to remember	40	5	10	15	30

Figure 8. Pie charts for the answers to questions 1 and 2 of the Lab-study questionnaire

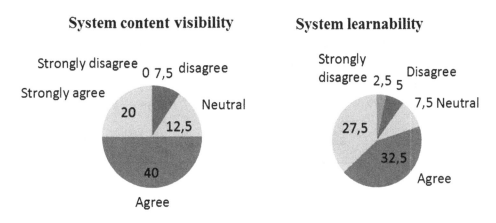

Figure 9. Pie charts for the answers to questions 3 and 4 of the Lab-study questionnaire

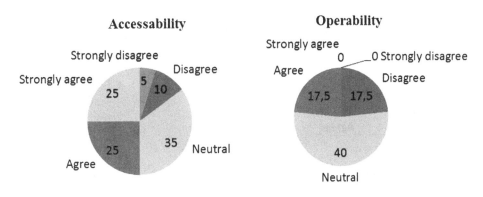

Figure 10. Pie charts for the answers to questions 5 and 6 of the Lab-study questionnaire

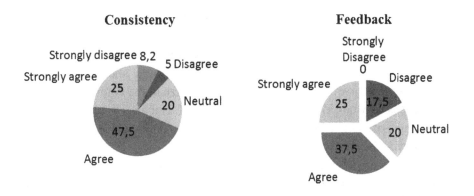

Figure 11. Pie charts for the answers to questions 7 and 8 of the Lab-study questionnaire

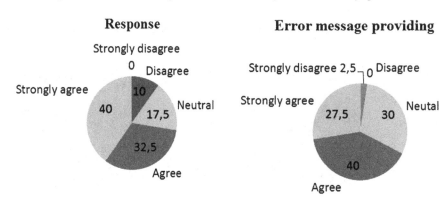

Figure 12. Pie charts for the answers to questions 9 and 10 of the Lab-study questionnaire

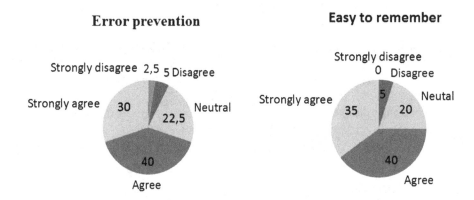

RESULTS OF USABILITY FACTORS AND IDENTIFIED PROBLEMS

After the detailed analysis of experimentation results it is found that most of the users faced problems during the communication process with their devices.

Authors divided these problems in two levels; one is the pre Test- level and second is the Experimentation level. In Pre-Test initial level of problems faced by Android users were judged and in Experimentation the detailed problems regarding usability factors of the Android web application were analyzed. In pre Test, 11 questions were asked to the participants. The questions were:

1. Are you skilled in installing and using most software on your phone? 2. Did you know about mobile apps? 3. Did you know about Android mobile apps? 4. Do you know about mobile learning? 5. Have you ever learned by online course? 6. Did text style and font size in the course effect on your learning? 7. Can you find the items very quickly according to the task? 8. Is it easy to find out your current course in LMS? 9. Did the name of module in LMS its content well? 10. Do you think the structure of the LMS is reasonable? 11. How is the access speed of this website?

In statistical analysis, 66.67 percent of people were enough skilled to install and work on Android applications, 16.67 percent just were able to operate the systems and the problem faced was that 16.67 percent of the people were not properly skilled to operate the system. In the second question, the people ratio about knowing very much about detailed mobile apps was 33.33 percent, the people who were having some knowledge of mobile apps were 66.66 percent and 0.0 percent of the people answered to the worse point saying that they were not aware of mobile apps at all.

According to the survey 50 percent of people were familiar with mobile learning, 25 percent were having some information about mobile learning and 25 percent at whole were even not familiar with mobile learning. In the survey, while asked the question to participants have you ever learned by mobile learning, 66.66 percent replied yes we have learned by mobile learning, 33.33 percent replied we heard about it but did not use mobile learning, while 0.0 percent answered that did not know about mobile learning which was in fact a good result.

In the question "did text style and font size in the course effect on your learning?" the answers were 91.66 percent people said it is good, 8.33 percent replied the font is too small, 0.0 percent replied the color is not comfortable, 0.0 percent of the people answered that it had no effect on them. In question "can you find the items very quickly according to the task?" Very quickly was replied by 50 percent, Needs to find carefully was replied by 33.33 percent people, while 16.66 percent people replied it is not easy to find the content.

Is it easy to find out your current course on LMS? It has an obvious title 33.33 percent people replied, Needs to identify title carefully 33.33 percent replied, while 33.33 percent replied that it was Difficult to know.

The system measured statistics for usability factors shows that system learn ability, access ability, error tolerance, error prevention message and feedback are key factors of usability engineering that are less in percentage. The solution that is recommended is to enhance the usability testing of the mobile applications prior to the launching to the market and improvement of usability factors on the basis of users' feedback, while they are launched to the market so continuous improvement will take place.

In question "did the name of module in LMS match its content well?" the answers given were, quite well 75 percent, not so accurate 16.66 percent and Inaccurate 8.33 percent replied. In question "do you think the structure of the LMS is reasonable?" the answers gathered were Reasonable, 41.66 percent replied, Needs small revision, 41.66 percent replied, Too bad/can't understand it, 16.66 percent replied. In question "how the access speed of this website is?" the answers were Quick, 41.66 percent replied, Ordinary, 58.33 percent replied, and Slow, 0.0 percent replied.

So in Pre –Test the major problems identified were installation and usage of mobile apps, information about mobile learning, finding the related item on LMS according to the task and structure and design issues of build apps for using.

This was all about pre-Test assessment results. Now, moving towards actual experimentation, the 10 questions asked were about 10 basic usability factors:

The system content is visible clearly? It was very easy to learn how to use the LMS? It is really difficult to access the LMS by the Android based cell phone? It was great to operate the LMS by Android based cell phones? Design is consistent and follows the same pattern on the whole system? System is providing adequate feedback to users about their actions? Can you find the items very quickly according to the task and system response time is good? The system is moderate at error message providing? The system is well designed and prevents errors? Once the tasks performed are easy to remember?

Regarding the students' answers, 20 percent strongly agreed, and 40 percent agreed, that the system content was clearly visible; 12.5 percent were neutral, 7.5 percent disagreed and 0.0 percent strongly disagreed.

About system Learnability, 27.5 percent strongly agreed that the system was very easy to learn how to use, 32.5 percent agreed, 7.5 percent were neutral, 5 percent disagreed and 2.5 percent strongly disagreed.

Does the system provide good Access ability? 25 percent strongly agreed, 25 percent agreed, 35 percent were neutral, 10 percent disagreed and 5 percent strongly disagreed.

Does the system provide Operability? 0.0 percent strongly agreed, 17.5 percent agreed, 40 percent were neutral, 17.5 percent disagreed and 0.0 percent strongly disagreed.

Does the system provide Consistency? 25 percent strongly agreed, 47.5 percent agreed, 20 percent were neutral, 5 percent disagreed and 2.5 percent strongly disagreed.

Is the system providing good Feedback mechanisms? 25 percent strongly agreed, 37.5 percent agreed, 20 percent were neutral, 17 percent disagreed and 0.0 percent strongly disagreed.

Is the system response time good? 40 percent strongly agreed, 32.5 percent agreed, 17.5 percent were neutral, 10 percent disagreed and 0.0 percent strongly disagreed.

On failure, the system is providing Error messages? 27.5 percent strongly agreed, 40 percent agreed, 30 percent were neutral, 0.0 percent disagreed and 2.5 percent strongly disagreed.

The system is good in Error prevention? 30 percent strongly agreed, 40 percent agreed, 22.5 percent were neutral, 5 percent disagreed and 2.5 percent strongly disagreed.

The system is Easy to remember? 30 percent strongly agreed, 15 percent agreed, 10 percent were neutral, 5 percent disagreed and 40 percent strongly disagreed.

After these clear statistical results the highlighted problems found are that the system was not easy to remember, error prevention was not up to the desired mark, and the system was averagely easy to operate.

CONCLUSION

Usability engineering plays a vital role in software engineering projects' success.

The customers' satisfaction level measures the success criteria of any project. Usability engineering is providing help in building the customer or end user satisfaction level; it is clear that the more the customer is comfortable with using the product the more market scope and praise the product will gain.

Nowadays, Android web applications, mobile learning and cloud environments are on their peak; people will go towards the apps that are user friendly, easy to use and easy to remember.

Usability engineering is a vast domain. Here the authors are taking just vital usability factors for measuring the usability of an online learning management system when used through an Android based mobile device. Usability factors implementation is a key to success in any web based learning system, especially if they are accessible by users on Android based cell phones.

For measurement of usability different techniques may be used. No unique technique is good or bad; it depends on the scenario of application.

The LMS (Learning management system) offered by NUST-NATIONAL UNIVERSITY OF SCIENCE AND TECNOLOGY PAKISTAN is accessible by thousands of the users for different purposes through their cell phones. It is providing a tremendous service to the user, and with the help of usability testing, and enhancement of its performance, improvements are possible.

Satisfactory usability conditions will help in user satisfaction and high performance. It is also concluded that usability testing of mobile applications are really very important; usability must be measured and tested prior to launching a product to the market and also after the launching so that its continuous improvement can take place.

REFERENCES

Amalfitano, D., Fasolino, A., & Tramontana, P. (2011). A GUI Crawling-Based Technique for Android Mobile Application Testing. *Fourth International Conference on Software Testing, Verification and Validation Workshops* (pp. 252 - 261). IEEE. doi:10.1109/ICSTW.2011.77

Amalfitano, D., Fasolino, A. R., & Tremonton, P. (2010). Rich Internet Application Testing Using Execution Trace Data. *Proc. of Second International Workshop on Testing Techniques & Experimentation Benchmarks for Event-Driven Software* (pp. 274- 283). IEEE. doi:10.1109/ICSTW.2010.34

Andreasen, M. S., Nielsen, H., Schrøder, S., & Stage, J. (2007). What happened to remote usability testing? An empirical study of three methods. *Conference on Human Factors in Computing Systems.* doi:10.1145/1240624.1240838

Belli, F., Budnik, C., & White, L. (2006). Event-based modeling, Analysis and testing of user interactions: approach and case study. Wiley.

Blandford, A., Keith, S., Connell, I., & Edwards, H. (2004). Analytical Usability Evaluation for Digital Libraries: A Case Study. *Joint ACM/IEEE Conference on Digital Libraries* (pp. 27 - 36). IEEE. doi:10.1145/996350.996360

Li, Wang, Wang, & Li. (2011). Case study of usability testing methodology on mobile learning course. *Advanced Intelligence and Awareness Internet (AIAI 2011).*

Marchetto, A., Tonella, P., & Ricca, F. (2008). State-Based Testing of Ajax Web Applications. *Proceedings of 2008 Int. Conf. on Software Testing, Verification and Validation* (pp. 121-130). IEEE CS Press. doi:10.1109/ICST.2008.22

Memon, A., Banerjee, L., & Nagarajan, A. (2003). GUI ripping: reverse engineering of graphical user interfaces for testing. *Proceedings of the 10th Working Conference on Reverse Engineering* (pp. 260-269). IEEE CS Press. doi:10.1109/WCRE.2003.1287256

Mesbah, A., & Van Deursen, A. (2009). Invariant-based automatic testing of AJAX user interfaces. *Proc. of International Conference on Software Engineering* (pp. 210-220). IEEE CS Press. doi:10.1109/ICSE.2009.5070522

Moritz, F., & Meinel, C. (2010). Mobile web usability Evalution –Combining the Modified Think Aloud Method with Testing Emotional, Cognative Aspects of the usage of web Application. *9th International Conference on Computer and Information Science* (pp. 367 - 372). IEEE.

Nayebi, F., Desharnais, J.-M., & Abran, A. (2012). The state of the art of mobile application usability evaluation. *25th IEEE Canadian Conference on Electrical & Computer Engineering* (pp. 1 - 4). IEEE. doi:10.1109/CCECE.2012.6334930

Sakuraashe, S., & Warren, L. (2009). Hermes: A tool for testing mobile devices a application. *Software Engineering Conference.*

Thompson, S., & Torabi, T. (2007). A process Improment Approach to improve Web From Design and Usability. *18th International Workshop on Database and Expert Systems Applications* (pp. 570 - 574). Regensburg: IEEE.

Yumei, W. U., Liu. (2011). A model based testing approach for mobile device. *American Journal of Engineering and Technology Research, 11*(9), 3536-3542.

Zhifangliu, L. B., & Openggao, X. (2009). SOA based mobile application software test framework. *8th international conference on reliability, maintainability and safety* (pp. 765-769). IEEE.

KEY TERMS AND DEFINITIONS

Usability: Measures the capability of a product in allowing a user to achieve his/her goals, i.e. it measures the degree to which a product is fit for purpose. Factors typically used for measuring a software system usability are system status visibility, learnability, accessibility, ease of use and operability, consistency, system feedback, efficiency and response time, helping users recognize errors and solutions, user guidance and error prevention, and ease of memorization of system operations.

Usability Testing: Is a technique to assess the usability of a product by making real users use the product in a controlled environment, obtaining their opinions and sometimes observing them and registering their actions.

Chapter 11
A Domain Independent Pedestrian Dead Reckoning System Solution for Android Smartphones

João Paulo Quintão
Instituto Politécnico de Viana do Castelo, Portugal

Luis Pereira
Instituto Politécnico de Viana do Castelo, Portugal

Sara Paiva
Instituto Politécnico de Viana do Castelo, Portugal

ABSTRACT

In this paper we propose a domain independent Pedestrian Dead Reckoning System that can be applied to any indoor environment. We describe the entire solution and adopted architecture. The user can create new indoor spaces, define reference points in it, positions for future access and also track his current location. In order to track the user's position, we solve several walking detection false positives including a common problem with most pedometers. We present results of conducted tests that show a 98% accuracy of the system. Finally, we present the developed prototype.

INTRODUCTION

Location-based services (LBS) became an emergent area for mobile applications since most smartphones allowed to track the user's location. Outdoor location is currently very accurate using the Global Positioning System (GPS) and one of its most common applications is car or pedestrian navigation systems. However, tracking user´s location is also necessary in indoor environments and the lack of GPS makes this an active research area as providing an accurate indoor location is yet challenging (Vidal & Marron, 2014). One common approach is the use of Access Points (AP) and a map of Received Signal Strength Indication (RSSI) which has as main disadvantage the need to recalculate the entire map when AP´s physi-

DOI: 10.4018/978-1-4666-9916-8.ch011

Copyright © 2016, IGI Global. Copying or distributing in print or electronic forms without written permission of IGI Global is prohibited.

cal location is changed. RFID tags can also be used but this approach demands an innumerous number of tags throughout the building with the correspondent costs associated. Another important aspect to bear in mind when choosing the technology is the control we will have on the indoor space. If a school board decides to provide track and navigation abilities to provide its students with important functionalities such as locating classrooms or teacher´s offices, then the school board has the power to acquire the necessary hardware to implement such a system. However, there are innumerous places we, as end users, would like to have indoor tracking and navigation abilities but we have no access to the system to perform the necessary changes. Examples are supermarkets or libraries where users could benefit from location services to track products or books. In these scenarios, programmers' can´t depend on APs or RFID tags (because they would not have access to them even if they existed) which automatically exclude these options. A suitable alternative is to use smartphone sensors namely the more common ones such as acceleration, gravity or the gyroscope that are present in almost all smartphones. This method is known as Pedestrian Dead Reckoning (PDR) (Kang & Han, 2014), where the current position is obtained based only on a reference position and data from sensors. Current PDR proposals have a detection method that tries to capture the walking swing. This approach is followed by many pedometer applications and the main problem is that a false positive is obtained when the user is standing still and shaking the phone up and down. Another issue with the majority of current proposals is the use of the indoor environment floor plan. While it produces a friendlier interface, it limits the applications of the system as sometimes (as we referred earlier for the cases of supermarkets or libraries) we don´t have access to that information which shouldn´t exclude the possibility to provide location and tracking services in such environments.

In this paper we provide an extension to the previous work we developed (Paiva 2015) where we introduced a domain independent PDR system for indoor tracking and location that assumed no hardware exists in a given indoor environment. The system is able to provide users with the capability to mark a position for future access in the indoor space such as a given product´s location within a supermarket or a book in a library. With the proposed system, each user can create several indoor environments (each one representing a particular indoor space he attends) and mark positions so he can easily find them later. The representation of the indoor environment does not use any floor plan so the system doesn´t become dependent of a specific space/domain. We use the Android Operating System for the application development and its sensors to track user´s location and help him find a previously marked position. In concrete, in this paper we extended the description of the architecture of the solution and detail/improve two modules of the system.

In the next section we present some related work and then we briefly introduce Android sensors, a fundamental component of our proposal. Next we introduce the developed solution, namely the architecture and supporting database as well as each of its modules along with the developed algorithms. We present an evaluation of the conducted tests and achieved results and finish with conclusions and future work.

BACKGROUND

Several PDR systems are continuously being proposed to solve several situations where GPS cannot be used. One such example is proposed in (Constandache et al, 2010) where the users propose CompAcc, a simple and practical method of localization using phone compasses and accelerometers. For the user´s tracking, the authors record a person's walking patterns and match it against possible path signatures generated from a local electronic map. As main challenges to use this approach the authors mention noisy phone sensors and complicated human movements. Achieved results show a location accuracy of less than 12m in regions where today's localization services are unsatisfactory or unavailable. A similar approach of the tracking technique using walking patterns is used in (Vidal & Marron, 2014) where a model is presented to track pedestrians in real-time in indoor environments using exclusively the sensors embedded in current off-the-shelf smartphones. The model includes three modules to collect the raw sensor data, detect motion events and represent the results over the blue print of a building. A series of algorithms and mechanisms are implemented to detect corners and count the number of steps and distance walked by the user. The evaluation of the system shows a combined tracking accuracy of 89.93% analyzed segment by segment and an accumulative error for detecting the final destination fewer than 4.5%. SmartPDR (Kang & Han, 2014) is yet another proposal with inertial sensors which present results with the largest locating error of 1.62 meters. In concrete, SmartPDR is a smartphone-based pedestrian dead reckoning solution that tracks users in anonymous buildings. By exploring the inside of a building with a smartphone, SmartPDR estimates the current location of the user on Google Maps. The two main contributions are: 1) extend the field of pedestrian tracking systems to indoor environments and introduce a method to track users with pervasive mobile devices; 2) design a complete system that runs on the smartphone device and verify its robustness. Shala and Rodriguez present a study (Rodriguez 2011) of sensors to detect user's movement, pace and heading and present results with an accuracy of less than two meters. The project examines the level of accuracy that can be achieved in precision positioning by using built-in sensors in an Android smartphone. The project is focused in estimating the position of the phone inside a building where the GPS signal is bad or unavailable. The approach is sensor-fusion: by using data from the device's different sensors, such as accelerometer, gyroscope and wireless adapter, the position is determined. The results show that the technique is promising for future handheld indoor navigation systems that can be used in malls, museums, large office buildings, hospitals, etc. Other study was conducted by Chandgadkar (Chandgadkar 2013) and focuses on optical markers to guide users in unfamiliar indoor environments. The author proposes a navigation system for smartphones capable of guiding users accurately to their destinations in an unfamiliar indoor environment, without requiring any expensive alterations to the infrastructure or any prior knowledge of the site's layout. Kourogi and Kurata (Kourogi & Kurata, 2014) proposed a method of estimating the moving direction for smartphones based on the patterns of acceleration and angular rate in the frequency domain. Experimental results show that the accuracy of PDR localization is below 2% of walking distance travelled while the smartphone is subject to the change in situation held by user in motion. Another study was performed by Li, Chen and Sun (Li et al, 2013) that propose a collaborative dead reckoning navigation system to reduce the accumulated error of PDR system. The CPDR system takes advantage of the nearby users' newer positioning information and utilizes opportunistic Kalman filter to correct the target user's current position. In (Do-Xuan et al, 2014) the authors present a positioning system that not only can be used in indoor environment but also outdoor environment with smartphone. The system focused on displacement estimation by utilizing the accelerometer sensor and gyroscope sensor built-in a smart-phone which is placed in the hand. Step detection on walking and holding the smart phone process results an average error of 1.946% and average error of rotation angle is 3.52%. Using QR code to read the actual coordinate has reduced error distance from 1.89 meter down to 1 meter. Kakiuchi and Kamijo (Kakiuchi & Kamijo, 2013) proposed a novel model of stride length estimation fitted to the running motion. It allows a PDR system to switch its estimation method according to whether the pedestrian is walking or running. The first experimental results showed that the method estimates the stride length more adaptively and accurately. Another final example is provided in (Khalifa 2013) where the author propose a novel concept of adaptive- PAC, which seeks to reduce activity classification complexity of a PAC-aided PDR system. Adaptive-PAC is based on the observation that at any time, there is only a small subset of facilities in the immediate proximity of the user that she can possibly use in the near future.

The two main drawbacks we found in these proposals is the facility to produce a false positive when using only a walking pattern recognition and the domain dependent system when using floor plans. Besides pure PDR approaches there are also hybrid approaches that combine PDR with other techniques such as WiFi (Fang et al, 2005) (Panyov, 2014) (Ban et al, 2015) (Lin 2013) (Radu & Marina, 2013). These hybrid approaches, while valid in some scenarios, do not suit ours as we cannot rely on WiFi existence nor access to the APs information in unfamiliar indoor environments.

ANDROID SENSORS

As afore mentioned, a pure PDR system uses smartphone sensors. In this section we will refer to Android sensors that we need to use to support the system. Most Android-powered devices have built-in sensors that measure motion, orientation, and several environmental conditions. These sensors are capable of providing raw data with high precision and accuracy, and are useful in several situations such as monitor three-dimensional device movement and/or positioning, or monitor changes in the ambient environment near a device. There are three broad categories of sensors in the Android platform: 1) motion sensors which measure acceleration forces and rotational forces along three axes. This category includes accelerometers, gravity sensors, gyroscopes, and rotational vector sensors; 2) environmental sensors which measure various environmental parameters, such as ambient air temperature and pressure, illumination, and humidity. This category includes barometers, photometers, and thermometers; 3) position sensors which measure the physical position of a device. This category includes orientation sensors and magnetometers. Android sensors can be hardware-based or software-based. A hardware-based sensor means that the obtained data comes directly from a measured property of a physical component built into the mobile device. A software-based sensor is not a physical device as it obtains data from one or more hardware-sensors. The most important sensors for the purpose of this paper are the linear acceleration sensor, the gravity sensor and the gyroscope. The linear acceleration sensor is available since Android 2.3 (API 9). It can be a software or hardware sensor. It measures the acceleration force in m/s2 that is applied to a device on all three physical axes (x, y, and z), excluding the force of gravity. One of its common uses is to monitor the acceleration along a single axis. The gravity sensor is also available since Android 2.3 (API 9) and it can also be a software or hardware sensor. This sensor measures the force of gravity in m/s2 that is applied to a device on the three physical axes (x, y and z). This sensor is usually used to detect shakes or tilts. Finally, the gyroscope sensor is available also since Android 2.3 (API 9) and it is a hardware sensor. It measures a device's rate of rotation in rad/s around each of the three physical axes (x, y, and z). A common use is to detect rotation. The coordinate system used by these sensors is defined relative to the screen of the phone in its default orientation (portrait). The X axis is horizontal and points to the right, the Y axis is vertical and points up and the Z axis points towards the outside of the front face of the screen. Coordinates behind the screen have negative Z values.

Figure 1. Position for the system to assume a walking movement

PDR SOLUTION

Overview

The Pedestrian Dead Reckoning System we propose aims two main objectives, besides the obvious functionality of location and tracking in an indoor environment: 1) minimize the false positives in the walking detection, 2) be domain independent. When first using the application, the user should start by creating a new indoor space or select one he has already created. For newly created spaces, the user should insert at least one reference point such as the entrance. Different floors should be treated as different spaces at this point. When standing in a reference point, the user should start walking so his position is tracked by sensors. In the smartphone screen, the user can see his current position, reference points, previously marked positions and can also mark the current position along with a description for future access. Some applications for this system, being domain independent, are finding products in supermarkets, books in libraries, classrooms in schools, etc. An important aspect we assumed for the entire system´s design is the phone´s position when the user is using the application. If he is in a supermarket or school trying to find a particular position, it is expected that he is looking at his phone. For this reason, the system will consider the user is walking if he is actually moving and holding the phone in his hand as shown in Fig. 1.

Architecture

For the purposes described above, the architecture of the system, shown in Fig. 2, uses three different sensors: linear acceleration, gyroscope and gravity. These sensors feed the three main modules of the system:

- **WDM – The Walking Detection Module:** Uses data from the linear acceleration and the gravity sensors to make the decision if the user is walking or stopped, according to the walking position assumed shown in Fig. 1.
- **DCM – The Distance Calculation Module:** Uses data from the linear acceleration sensor and is also related to the WDM as distance is only calculated when the user is walking.
- **TDM – The Turns Detection Module:** Uses data from the gyroscope to detect 90° and 180° turns in both directions

Figure 2. Architecture of the proposed PDR system

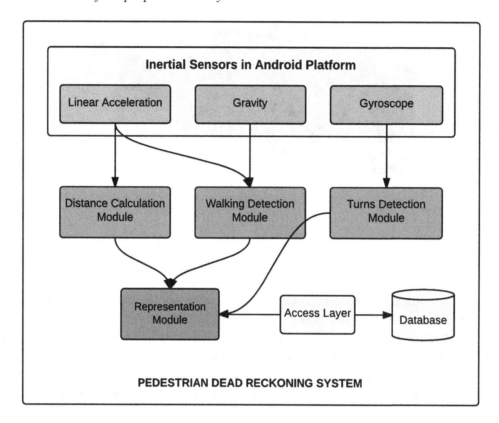

The other components that complete the architecture are:

- **RM – The Representation Module:** Uses data from all the other modules to produce an interface for the user.
- **Database:** Persistent storage for all application information
- **Access Layer:** Layer used to all communications between RM and Database

The database, shown in Fig. 3, stores all application data including user and login information. Each person using the system can create multiple places each one representing a particular indoor space the user usually attends. In each space the user can add products and reference points.

WDM: Walking Detection Module

For an accurate indoor tracking and location system, the method for detecting a walking movement is crucial. In this particular case, where the user needs to look at his smartphone screen to locate a marked position, we will only consider a walking movement if the user is actually walking and holding the phone as shown in Fig. 1. After testing Android´s motion sensors (accelerometer, gyroscope, linear acceleration, gravity and rotation vector) we concluded linear acceleration provides valuable information to be

Figure 3. Database model.

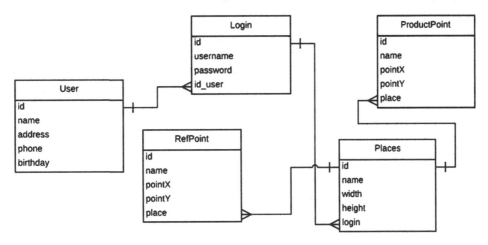

used in a movement detection method. We tested different walking situations and the obtained y-axis values are shown in Fig. 4.

- Graph a) shows a repeating pattern of a user walking in a straight line for 4 seconds and then stopping for other 4 seconds.
- Graph b) shows a repeating pattern of a user walking with turns for 4 seconds and then stopping for other 4 seconds.
- Graph c) shows a repeating pattern of a user walking for 8 seconds and then stopping for 2 seconds.

The graphs curves (a, b and c) show an evident variation in the y-axis in the three situations when the user is walking. After analyzing all set of values we calculated the absolute value of the difference

Figure 4. y-axis and z-axis values of the linear acceleration sensor with several walking movements (a, b and c) and phone up and down shake (d)

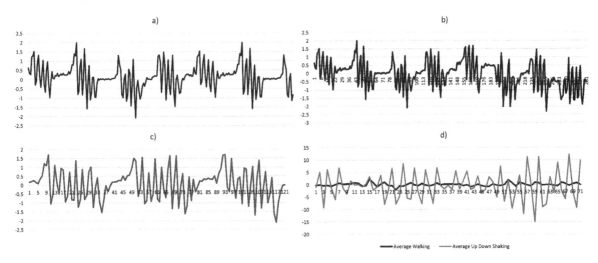

between consecutive readings and determined that at least one in three of those values is higher than 0.8 when the user is walking.

Therefore, the implemented method reads linear acceleration y-axis values and calculates the absolute value of the difference between current value and previous value. After three iterations, a check is performed to see if any of the difference values is greater than 0.8 and in this case we consider a walking movement. At a given sensor reading r, the decision to consider a walking movement is given by Equation (1):

$$\left(abs\left(lavy_r - lavy_{r-1}\right) > threshold\_y\right) \vee$$
$$\left(abs\left(lavy_{r-1} - lavy_{r-2}\right) > threshold\_y\right) \vee$$
$$\left(abs\left(lavy_{r-2} - lavy_{r-3}\right) > threshold\_y\right)$$

(1)

In Equation 1, *lavy* stands for linear acceleration value on the y-axis, r represents the current iteration value received from the sensor, *r-1* represents the sensor value received before r and *r-2* the sensor value received before *r-1*.

Finally, the *threshold_y* represents the value we concluded by the performed tests to be the more appropriate to get the more accurate results. The current threshold value is 0.8.

Eliminating Walking Detection False Positives

A common approach in pedometer applications as well as most PDR proposals is based on walking pattern recognition that fails to distinguish walking from shaking the phone up and down. This happens because the shaking movement "tricks" the walking detection method that thinks the user is walking. This is clearly a false positive that we also solve with sensor values. In concrete, we use the z-axis value of the linear accelerometer sensor. Fig. 4 (d) shows two lines: the blue one and with less variations represents the average values of z-axis in three walking situations (the same ones used to create graphs a, b and c); the orange line with several peaks represents two up and down shakes movements (one faster and another one slower). The results show a clear difference between the two situations which allows us to filter false positives obtained from shaking the phone up and down. The pattern in the z-axis values we found that allows us to distinguish the shake and walking movements is similar to the one previously described for the y-axis. We concluded that the average of the three absolute differences calculated using the current and previous z value is always greater than 4.5 in a shake movement and below that when walking. So, in addition to Equation 1, the walking detection has also the validation shown in Equation 2, at a given sensor reading r.

$$\frac{\sum_{i=0}^{2} abs\left(lavz_{r-i} - lavz_{r-1-i}\right)}{3} < threshold\_z$$

(2)

Another false positive we need to eliminate is the rotation of the screen phone to the right or left from the assumed position shown in Fig. 1. For this purpose, we add another sensor, the gravity sensor that has a 9.5 value when the phone screen is facing up. From this position, if we start turning the phone to the right or to the left this value starts decreasing and presents a value close to 7.5 with a 25° rotation from the initial position. We assumed this position does not interest to our purpose as the user no long can see the screen correctly. So the final validation we add to our walking detection method is the one represented by Equation 3.

$$gvz > threshold\_z2 \tag{3}$$

The complete algorithm for the walking detection is shown in Algorithm 1. This algorithm runs in the method onSensorChanged(), a method defined by the SensorEventListener interface that fires whenever a new value is returned by any of the sensors that were previously registered (in this case two: Linear Acceleration and Gravity).

Algorithm 1. The algorithm performed to detect a walking movement whenever a new value from the linear acceleration sensors and gravity is received

```
1: procedure WALKING_DETECTION (event)
2: sensorType ← event.sensor.getType()
3: if (sensorType == 'gravity) then
4: gravCheck ← true
5: else
6: gravCheck ← false
7: if (sensorType = 'linearacceleration') then
8: if (iteration == 0) then
9: diff1y ← event.values[1] – previousY
10: previousY ← event.values[1]
11: diff1z ← event.values[2] – previousZ
12: previousZ ← event.values[2]
13: {increment iteration}
14: if (iteration == 1) then
15: diff2y ← event.values[1] – previousY
16: previousY ← event.values[1]
16: diff2z ← event.values[2] – previousZ
17: previousZ ← event.values[2]
18: {increment iteration}
19: if (iteration == 2) then
20: diff3y ← event.values[1] – previousY
21: previousY ← event.values[1]
22: diff3z ← event.values[2] – previousZ
23: previousZ ← event.values[2]
24: {reset iteration}
25: laYCheck ← checkY(diff1y,diff2y,diff3y)
26: laZCheck ← checkZ(diff1z,diff2z,diff3z)
27: if (gravCheck & laYCheck & laZCheck) then
28: Show: Walking detected
29: end procedure
```

DCM: Distance Calculation Module

The distance calculation is another system´s module that has a direct relation with the WDM. As expected by the user, the distance is only calculated when a walking movement is detected, so the algorithm for the distance calculation is dependent of the result of the walking algorithm.

To calculate the travelled distance, we use y-axis values of the linear acceleration sensor. We collected data and manually marked whenever the user placed a foot on the floor. Fig. 5 shows the results obtained of a 2.8 meters walk. The figure presents two similar lines that only differ in the manually marked positions. The line with the highest peaks was multiplied by 4 in the marked positions so a clear comparison could be made to the original values. It is evident that the moments a foot is placed on the floor has a direct relation with a y peak (positive or negative). We use this reasoning to calculate distance considering the user´s height (pre-configured information) and a 0.4 multiplication factor to obtain the average step distance. The algorithm used by the distance calculation module is presented in Algorithm 2.

TDM: Turns Detection Module

This module intends to provide the system with the ability to detect user turns in the indoor environment. We tested the x, y and z axis values from the gyroscope holding the phone in our hand and rotating the person along with the phone in the sequence presented in the left side of Fig. 6: S represents the start position, position 1 is reached after turning left 180°, position 2 is reached turning right 90°, position 3 is reached turning left 90°, position 4 is reached turning right 180°, position 5 is reached turning right 90° and finally position 6 is reached turning left 180°.

Figure 5. y-axis values of linear acceleration with step marks and original values

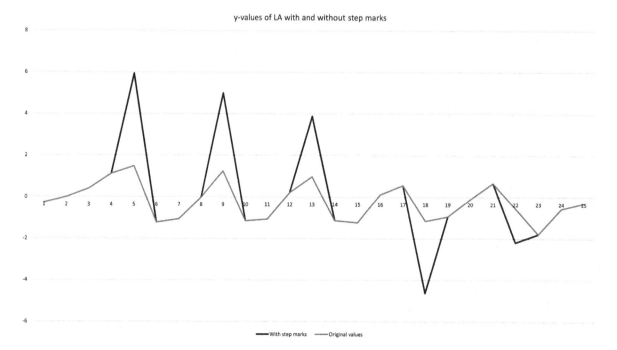

Algorithm 2. The algorithm performed to calculate distance whenever a new value from the linear acceleration is received

```
1: procedure CALCULATE_DISTANCE (event)
2: sensorType ← event.sensor.getType()
3: if (sensorType = 'linearacceleration') then
4: if (walking) then
5: curValue ← event.values[1]
6: if (valuesArray.size() == 0)
7: {add curValue to valuesArray}
8: else
9: if (valuesArray.size() == 1)
10: peakDirection ← "DOWN"
11: if (curValue > valuesArray.get(0)) then
12: peakDirection ← "UP"
13: {add curValue to valuesArray}
14: else
15: if (peakDirection = "UP" &&
16: curValue < valuesArray.get(valuesArray.size()-1)) then
17: meters ← meters + height * 0.4
18: {reset valuesArray}
19: peakDirection ← "DOWN"
20: else
21: if (peakDirection = "DOWN" &&
22: curValue > valuesArray.get(valuesArray.size()-1)) then
23: {reset valuesArray}
24: peakDirection ← "UP"
25: end procedure
```

Figure 6. x,y and z axis values of gyroscope when the user rotates from a initial position S and 6 other positions.

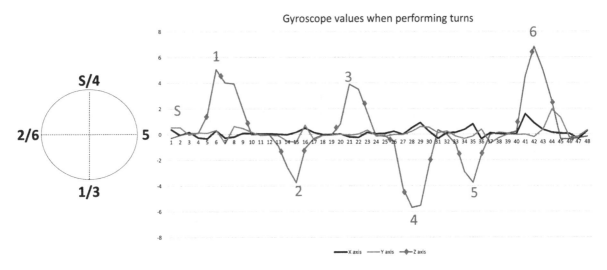

From the analysis of data, it seems evident that in the position shown in Fig. 1 and making rotations, the z axis provides the more accurate results. The x axis also makes detections in almost all cases but not so clearly. The obtained values of the z axis allow us to conclude the following: right turns present negative values and left turns present positive values. The highest value we obtained for 90° turns was of 3.9 (position 3) so we defined the threshold of 4.2, so there is a margin. On another hand, the minimum value we obtained for 180° turns was of 5.05 (position 1) so we defined the threshold of 4.8 to consider a 180° turn.

RM: Representation Module

This module corresponds to the Android Application itself, namely the Activity responsible for showing the indoor space, the user´s position and direction as well as entrance location and other marked spots. Fig. 7 shows how the application is structured. When the user enters it, he can create a new user if he hadn´t done so already or then enter his credentials. After logging in, he can create a new space or view a previously created space, that is stored in the database. When a place is chosen the user can see reference points and products previously created and he can also start moving which will trigger the sensors to track the user´s position. At any time the user can create new points which are stores in the database.

Figure 8. shows the application and its main functionalities. Fig. 8 (a) shows the necessary information to create a new user in the system. Fig. 8 (b) shows the creation of a new space where the user must

Figure 7. Android application structure

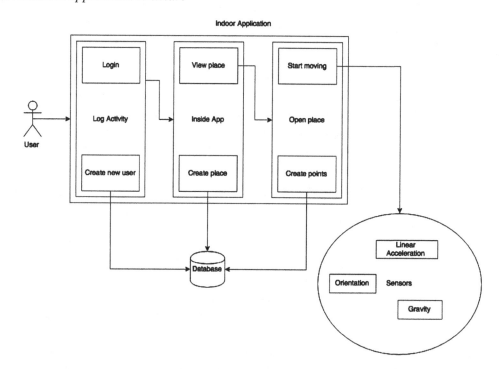

Figure 8. (a) create a new user; (b) create a new place; (c) open an existing place; (d) adding a new point; (e) movement information

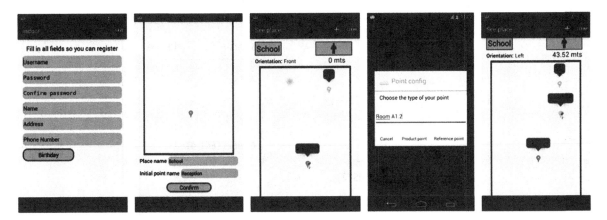

specify the name/description of the space and an initial/reference point such as the entrance. If the user chooses to open an existent space, he will be presented with the information shown in Fig. 8 (c) namely:

- The name of the space (in this case School)
- A symbol in the top right corner showing if the user is standing still or walking (in this case the user is standing still)
- The walked distance so far since the user chose this place
- The current orientation the user is walking - forward, left, right or behind (in this case he is walking forward)
- Reference points marked with a blue symbol (in this case one is created and represents the reception)
- Other points marked with a green symbol (in this one is created and represents the bar)
- The current position marked with a red pin

At any time, the user can insert a new point pressing the green plus icon in the top of the application. He is then presented with the screen showed in Fig. 8 (d) where he specifies the name of the point and its type (if it is a reference point or a product point). Finally, Fig. 8 (e) shows that point already inserted in the place and also some distance walked. In this case, the user walked 43.52m and is currently turning left, near Room A1.2.

EVALUATION

In this section we describe the conducted tests to evaluate the accuracy of the developed algorithms. We used two different devices: a Samsung Galaxy S4 with Android version 5.0.1 and an Alcatel One Touch Idol with Android version 4.1. The indoor environment selected was the Instituto Politécnico de Viana do Castelo, in concrete a 15 meters by 15 meters' space. We defined four routes to encompass various

Figure 9. Routes tested in an indoor environment

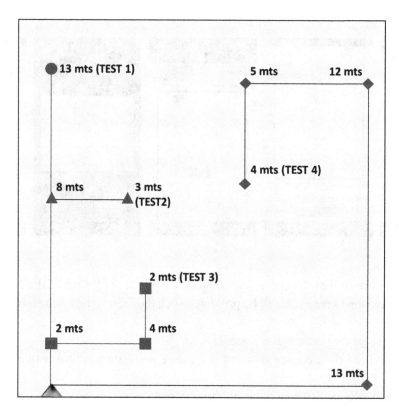

situations, where we could have smaller segments and larger segments, shown in Fig. 9. All routes were travelled continuously in the turns.

The obtained values are represented in Table 1. The minimum deviation was in route 1 with a total meter of 13 and 12.92 were detected with a 0.08 meters' deviation. The maximum deviation was in route 2, with 11 meters in total and 11.46 were calculated. In all four routes we obtained an average deviation of 0.26 meters from the real distance which provides a total accuracy of 98.05%.

Table 1.

	Route 1	Route 2	Route 3	Route 4
Seg1	12,92	8,16	2,04	12,92
Seg2	-	3,3	4,08	12,24
Seg3	-	-	2,04	4,76
Seg4	-	-	-	3,74
Real mts	13	11	8	34
Calc. mts	12,92	11,46	8,16	33,66
Deviation	0,08	0,46	0,16	0,34
Accuracy	99,38	95,82	98	99

FUTURE RESEARCH DIRECTIONS

For future work, we will enhance the system in several ways: further improve the accuracy of the algorithms as we are aware that even with a high rate of accuracy at this moment, random and completely unexpected movements of the phone can still create false positives. We would also like to allow the user to be able to low his arm with the phone if he realizes he has to walk an entire corridor preventing him from holding the phone all the way. Another feature we will add is the support for landscape mode demanding the recalculation of the thresholds currently defined for portrait.

CONCLUSION

In this paper we presented a Pedestrian Dead Reckoning System with two main contributions for the indoor environment research area development: 1) the definition of a walking detection module that eliminates several false positives namely a common one that consists of shaking the phone up and down simulating the typical walking pattern and 2) a domain independent system that can be used in any given space such as a school, supermarket, library, shopping stores, etc. The architecture of the PDR system developed has 4 modules to achieve the final result: a Walking Detection Module, a Distance Travelled Module, a Turn Detection Module and a Representation Module. These modules are fed with data from three sensors: linear acceleration, gravity and gyroscope. We conducted tests that showed an accuracy of 98.05%.

REFERENCES

Ban, R., Kaji, K., Hiroi, K., & Kawaguchi, N. (2015). Indoor positioning method integrating pedestrian Dead Reckoning with magnetic field and WiFi fingerprints. In *Eighth International Conference on Mobile Computing and Ubiquitous Networking* (pp. 167–172). doi:10.1109/ICMU.2015.7061061

Chandgadkar, A. (2013). *An Indoor Navigation System For Smartphones*. Imperial College London.

Constandache, I., Choudhury, R., & Rhee, I. (2010). Compacc: Using mobile phone compasses and accelerometers for localization. In IEEE INFOCOM (pp. 1–9). IEEE.

Dead Reckoning System — The NavMote Experience. (n.d.). *IEEE Transactions on Instrumentation and Measurement*, *54*(6), 2342–2358. doi:10.1109/TIM.2005.858557

Do-Xuan, T., Tran-Quang, V., Bui-Xuan, T., & Vu-Thanh, V. (2014). Smartphone-based pedestrian dead reckoning and orientation as an indoor positioning system. In *International Conference on Advanced Technologies for Communications* (pp. 303–308). doi:10.1109/ATC.2014.7043402

Kakiuchi, N., & Kamijo, S. (2013), Pedestrian dead reckoning for mobile phones through walking and running mode recognition. In *16th International IEEE Conference on Intelligent Transportation Systems* (pp. 261–267). doi:10.1109/ITSC.2013.6728243

Kang, W., & Han, Y. (2014). SmartPDR: Smartphone-Based Pedestrian Dead Reckoning for Indoor Localization. *IEEE Sensors Journal*, *15*(5), 2906–2916. doi:10.1109/JSEN.2014.2382568

Khalifa, S. (2013). Adaptive pedestrian activity classification for indoor dead reckoning systems. In Indoor Positioning and Indoor Navigation (pp. 1–7).

Kourogi, M., & Kurata, T. (2014). A method of pedestrian dead reckoning for smartphones using frequency domain analysis on patterns of acceleration and angular velocity. In *Position, Location and Navigation Symposium* (pp. 164–168).

Li, Y. T., Chen, G., & Sun, M. T. (2013). An Indoor Collaborative Pedestrian Dead Reckoning System. In *42nd International Conference on Parallel Processing* (pp. 923–930) doi:10.1109/ICPP.2013.110

Lin, X. (2013). Apply Pedestrian Dead Reckoning to indoor Wi-Fi positioning based on fingerprinting. In *15th IEEE International Conference on Communication Technology* (pp. 206–210).

Paiva, S. (2015). A domain independent Pedestrian Dead Reckoning System for Tracking and Localization. *IEEE International Conference on Computational Science and Engineering*.

Panyov, A. a., Golovan, A. a., & Smirnov, A. S. (2014). Indoor positioning using Wi-Fi fingerprinting pedestrian dead reckoning and aided INS. In *Int. Symp. Inert. Sensors Systems* (pp. 1–2). doi:10.1109/ISISS.2014.6782540

Radu, V., & Marina, M. (2013). Himloc: Indoor smartphone localization via activity aware pedestrian dead reckoning with selective crowdsourced wifi fingerprinting. In Indoor Positioning and Indoor Navigation (pp. 28–31).

Rodriguez, A. (2011). *Indoor Positioning using Sensor-fusion in Android Devices*. School of Health and Society Sweden.

Vidal, A., & Marron, J. J. (2014). Real-time pedestrian tracking in indoor environments. In *Proceedings of IEEE Latin-America Conf. Commun* (pp. 1–6). IEEE.

KEY TERMS AND DEFINITIONS

Location-Based Services (LBS): Computer services that use location as the main data for its features. A known and common use nowadays for this LBS are social networking applications that make use of location as an additional information for posts and photos. They are also used in indoor location, work, personal life or entertainment. LBS are usually and mostly access via mobile devices through Wi-Fi or 3G/4G.

Indoor Location: Refers to tracking and locate objects inside a given space/building such as airports, museums, schools, shopping malls, hospitals, among other. One of the biggest difficulties is the inability to use the Global Positioning System to obtain the user´s current position. The alternatives currently used involve Wi-Fi, RFID or sensors.

Pedestrian Dead Reckoning (PDR): Process that allows to calculate one´s position based on a previously known position and in step detection, length estimation and heading determination. It usually has a significate margin of error and this is the reason why it was substituted by GPS (Global Positioning System) wherever it is available which doesn´t happen in indoor environments making PDR a good alternative in these situations. Other applications for this process include animal and vehicles navigation.

Smartphone: A cellular phone with some computer features such as an operating system and the ability to run applications as a web browser, calculator, email software, among others. The majority of current smartphones have internet connectivity easily allowing user´s to access the world wide web or use the social networks. Some known operating systems for smartphones are Android by Google or iOS by Apple.

Smartphone Sensors: Most smartphones currently come with a variety of sensors that can be used to improve certain tasks of our daily lives and give useful and important information to the user. The Android platform has three main sensors categories: motion (accelerometers, gravity sensors, gyroscopes, and rotational vector sensors), environmental (ambient air temperature and pressure, illumination, and humidity) and position sensors (orientation sensors and magnetometers).

Section 4
Model–Driven Approaches to Mobile Computing

This section presents model-driven development approaches to mobile applications' development. The first chapter presents a MDD approximation to generating Android native applications from models, and the second discusses producing mobile applications through partial code generation from existing Java desktop applications.

Chapter 12

Model–Driven Development of Data–Centered Mobile Applications:
A Case Study for Android

Jorge Amadeu Alves Pereira da Silva
Instituto Politécnico de Viana do Castelo, Portugal

Sara Paiva
Instituto Politécnico de Viana do Castelo, Portugal

Antonio Miguel Rosado da Cruz
Instituto Politécnico de Viana do Castelo, Portugal

ABSTRACT

Increasing adoption of mobile smart devices demands a growing number of mobile applications (apps). Each of these applications must often be deployed to different mobile platforms, such as Android, iOS or Windows. Many of these applications are data-oriented, enabling the user to manage information, by creating, updating, deleting and retrieving data on his smart mobile device. By using a model-driven development approach, it is possible to generate a platform independent user interface model from a domain model, which represents the information structure of the application domain, and then have different code generators for each different target platform. This chapter presents such an approach together with a case study for Android apps.

INTRODUCTION

The increasing adoption of mobile smart devices, throughout the world, is demanding a growing number of mobile applications (apps). Nowadays, people use a variety of these applications for daily activities such as getting driving directions, finding a pharmacy or checking the weather. Other applications exist that allow the user to create from scratch his personal information such as daily notes, book/cd inventory, and grocery shopping list, amongst others. A common feature of these last applications is the need to

DOI: 10.4018/978-1-4666-9916-8.ch012

Copyright © 2016, IGI Global. Copying or distributing in print or electronic forms without written permission of IGI Global is prohibited.

perform simple operations on data, such as creating, retrieving, updating or deleting data, making them fall under the umbrella of data oriented applications. Through generalization and parameterization of these common features, the development process can be streamlined and automated leading to a less time consuming and less costly apps development process.

There are currently a variety of tools for mobile application development. The decision to use a native or a cross-platform tool must take into account the benefits and disadvantages of both approaches. Native apps provide a more fluid and responsive user interface, a better performance, the ability to use all platform functionalities and a simpler distribution process. Additionally, there are less security issues in native apps, support for developers is more easily found, the design creation is simpler and the performance is better, as it is supported by the operation system itself. On the other hand, the costs are reduced when cross-platform tools are used, since cross-compilation allows the same sources to generate outputs for different platforms avoiding the need to have specialized teams in each platform intended to target. For this reason, cross-platforms' development presents a high rate of code reusability. Finally, it is generally easier to find web developers than mobile devices' native programmers, making native skills usually be more expensive (Madaudo & Scandurra, 2013).

Model driven development (MDD) approaches, like Domain Specific Modeling (DSM) (Kelly & Tolvanen, 2008), or the OMG's Model Driven Architecture (MDA) (Warmer *et al.*, 2003), are based on the successive refinement of models and on the automatic generation of code and other sub-models, allowing the software engineers and developers to focus on platform independent modeling activities rather than programming activities. This allows them to focus on concepts of the problem domain, and the way they shall be modeled in order to produce a software solution, rather than being diverted by technical issues of the solution domain. Within an MDD setting, code can be automatically generated to a great extension, dramatically reducing the most costly and error prone aspects of software development (Frankel, 2003).

In the next section, an overview of MDD techniques and of the characteristics of Android native applications is given. Afterward, an overview of existing approaches to the model-driven development of mobile apps is given.

The main focus of the chapter lies, then, on presenting a model-driven approach for generating Android native applications. Then, a discussion on future and emerging trends and some recommendations on future research directions are made. Finally, some concluding remarks are presented.

BACKGROUND

Model-Driven Development

Introduction

Model-driven development (MDD), as suggested by its name, is a software development paradigm driven by the activity of modeling software (Warmer *et al.*, 2003), in which models are first class citizens, being code pushed to a second plan.

MDD approaches software development by constructing models that may be refined (transformed) through different levels of abstraction, from a platform independent level, or a computation independent level, to a platform specific model that is directly mapped to final code (see figure 1).

Figure 1. Model transformations from more abstract to more concrete models

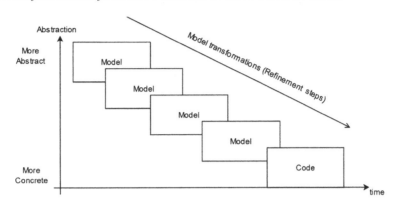

The first models constructed in a MDD process are platform independent models (PIM), meaning that they model a system in a platform independent way. A PIM can be defined in a computation independent way, denoting that besides being platform independent it is also computation independent. A computation independent model (CIM) specifies only what is expected to be made or computed, whereas a PIM may specify how to make those computations, provided the specification is made in a platform independent way. A CIM is typically only dependent of domain or business concerns. This way, a CIM is independent of implementation platforms and describes the problem from the point of view of the business or domain environment. It is a model of the business to which a software system is going to be built (Silva & Videira, 2008).

A model may be composed of several model artifacts, each one modeling a different view of the system. Platform independent models may be the only models made by the modeler's hand. Indeed, MDD recommends the definition of model-to-model (M2M) transformation processes that enable the transformation of PIMs to other PIMs or to platform specific models (PSMs). Typically, when a CIM exists, a default PIM may also be generated by a M2M process.

A PIM may model a software system by modeling its structural, functional, behavioral and presentational aspects. It consists of a system specification in a platform independent way. At any moment, a given aspect or view of the system may be obtained from the others by a M2M transformation process that implements a set of mappings that are defined between the respective metamodels (see Figure 2). When the PIM is satisfactory, the next step is to transform it into a platform specific model (PSM), which is a model of the system lying on assumptions about a given platform specific issues or features. From a PSM, code may be automatically generated by using a model-to-code (M2C) transformation process, that is a code generation process (Cruz, 2010).

At any moment, a model may be subject to model-to-text (M2T) generation for documentation purposes. Acronyms M2C and M2T are typically used interchangeably, as code can be understood as a special case of text (Cruz, 2010).

MDD provides a way of collecting the knowledge about a company's systems, and storing it in the form of models. These models may, then, be adapted and transformed as new business environments take place or technological changes occur (Petrov & Buchmann, 2008).

M2M and M2T processes operate over models. The transformation processes may be defined as functions from one model type to another model type. A model type is defined by a metamodel, which

Figure 2. Model transformation conforms to defined mappings between source and target metamodels
Source: Cruz, 2010

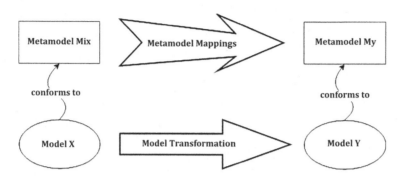

is a model that defines a model. A given model must always conform to a defined metamodel. Figure 3 presents the metamodel levels in OMG's Model-Driven Architecture (MDA), which is OMG's approach to model-driven development.

At the top level (M3), the metametamodel level, there is the Meta-Object Facility (MOF), which is a standard language for defining metamodels. Below the metametamodel level, where MOF is defined, other MOF-based metamodels may be defined. This is the meta-model level (M2), and is where the Unified Modeling Language (UML), and other metamodel-level languages, are defined. The MOF conforms to itself, and it is defined according to its own definition. UML is defined through MOF, and it conforms to the MOF. The model level (M1) is where models are defined by using a metamodel defined in the above level. Each UML model, made for some specific domain, conforms to UML, and is at metamodel level M1. A UML model defines a domain specific language (DSL) for modeling instances of that domain. A specific model instance is at metamodel level M0 (OMG, 2013).

Figure 3. Metamodel levels defined for OMG's MDA
Source: Cruz, 2010

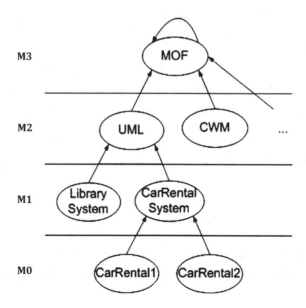

When modeling within a MDD setting, the software modeler must take into account that models are not only for human reasoning about the system being built, but are mainly for enabling the automation of some software process steps or activities. For that purpose, models must be rigorous, complete and unambiguous (Cruz, 2010).

Model Transformations

Model transformation processes, namely model-to-model (M2M) and model-to-text (M2T), have different purposes (Jézéquel, 2005). Model-to-text transformations aim the generation of code or documentation (e.g.: Java, XML, HTML). Model-to-model transformations aim the refinement of models, their refactoring, reverse engineering, application of patterns, generation of new model views (PIM-to-PIM), PIM-to-PSM transformations, or any model engineering activity that can be automated.

M2T techniques can be categorized into (Jézéquel, 2005; Cruz, 2010):

- **Visitor-Based Approaches:** traverse the internal representation of a model (abstract syntax tree) and write code to a text stream.
- **Template-Based Approaches:** are based on the construction of templates, which consist of the target text containing slices of meta-code to access information from the source model.

M2M techniques comprise (Jézéquel, 2005; Cruz, 2010):

- General purpose programming languages (e.g.: Java, C#)
- Generic transformation tools (e.g.: XSLT)
- CASE tools scripting languages (e.g.: Rose)
- Dedicated Model transformation tools (e.g.: ATL & MTL (INRIA), QVTEclipse)
- Meta-modeling tools (e.g.: MetaCase, Kermeta)

Whichever the M2M technique, it provides a declarative or an imperative paradigm and language for specifying model transformations. Declarative languages describe relationships between variables in terms of functions or inference rules, which are then submitted to an algorithm with an inference engine to produce a result. They specify what to do, or what shall be the relations between source and target models. Imperative languages specify explicit manipulation of the model instances, stating how to do the transformation, or how to derive a target model from the source one.

Declarative and imperative paradigms may be combined into a hybrid style that uses a declarative precondition, used to identify elements that may trigger an imperative transformation rule, and finally apply a declarative post-condition to the model elements generated by the application of the rule (Jézéquel, 2005; Cruz, 2010).

Advantages of MDD Approaches

Model-driven development approaches try to solve the following problems (Cruz, 2010; Warmer *et al.*, 2003; Silva & Videira, 2008):

- **The Productivity Problem:** Today software projects productive activities are coding and testing. Because of that, software team members spend little time modeling or documenting systems. This becomes a problem when the team is dismantled and other people need to maintain the software for fixing bugs or enhancing functionality. MDD tries to solve this problem by transferring the productive activities from coding and testing to modeling, and basing the software development process in model-to-model and model-to-text automatic transformations. Models, being at a high abstraction level, are easier for newcomers to understand, lowering the effort and cost of software maintenance.

- **The Portability Problem:** Every year new technologies become popular and, either because they solve real existing problems, or because tool vendors stop supporting old technologies, or even just because customers want to have the latest model of a given technology, systems often need to be ported to new technologies. Consequently, previous investments in the older technologies lose value. MDD, helps maintaining the value of previous investments by basing the production of code in automatic model-to-code transformation processes.

- **The Interoperability Problem:** Organizations have, typically, several software systems that need to interoperate. MDD leverages the notion of component from code level to model level, i.e. models may be component oriented, and code generated from models must be interoperable. With other software systems also being generated from their models, interoperability at model-level may be transported to code-level.

- **The Maintenance and Documentation Problem:** Writing documentation has always been considered by software developers as a waste of time, because they feel their main task is to produce code. Also, when projects get late, what is most likely to be cut off from the project's deliverables is documentation. Lack of, or low quality, documentation increases the difficulty, time and cost of software maintenance activities. Having documentation and code desynchronized also promotes the outdating of documentation when maintaining the code. Solutions to this problem have involved the generation of documentation from code, but this only solves the problem for low-level documentation. Higher level documentation and models are rarely updated during maintenance. MDD tries to solve this by having code and documentation produced automatically from models.

The UML Metamodel

The Unified Modeling Language (UML) aims to provide system architects, software engineers, and software developers with tools for analysis, design, and implementation of software-based systems as well as for modeling business and similar processes (OMG, 2013).

A UML model consists of three major categories of model elements, each of which may be used to make statements about different kinds of things within the system being modeled (OMG, 2013):

- **Classifiers:** A classifier describes a set of objects. Objects have a state (set of structural features called attributes) and relationships to other objects.
- **Events:** An event describes a set of possible occurrences, which is something that happens and has some consequence regarding the system.
- **Behaviors:** A behavior describes a set of possible executions. Executions are performances of sets of actions over some period of time, which may generate and respond to occurrences of events. Possible actions include to access and change the state of an object.

The UML specification (OMG, 2013) presents the abstract syntax and semantics of the UML language through a set of interrelated packages. The top element of the UML hierarchy is *Element*. An *Element* may have multiplicity, order or uniqueness characteristics, in which case it is a *MultiplicityElement*. A *NamedElement* is an *Element* with a name, and a *TypedElement* is an *Element* with a type. A *Namespace* is a named element that can own other named elements. A *Classifier* is a namespace whose members can include features. And, a *Feature* is a *RedefinableElement* that declares a behavioral or structural characteristic of instances of classifiers. A *RedefinableElement* is a named element that can be redefined in the context of a generalization (Cruz, 2010).

A *Class* is a classifier whose features are attributes and operations. Attributes of a class are represented by instances of *Property* that are owned by the class. Some of these attributes may represent the ends of associations. *Property* is a structural feature of a classifier.

From the UML specification (OMG, 2013), after which the above considerations about UML concepts and language constructs were made, it is possible to consolidate relations through UML generalizations and arrive to the compact metamodel depicted in Figure 4, which subsets the UML metamodel for class models.

Figure 4. Consolidated excerpt of the UML Metamodel for Class models

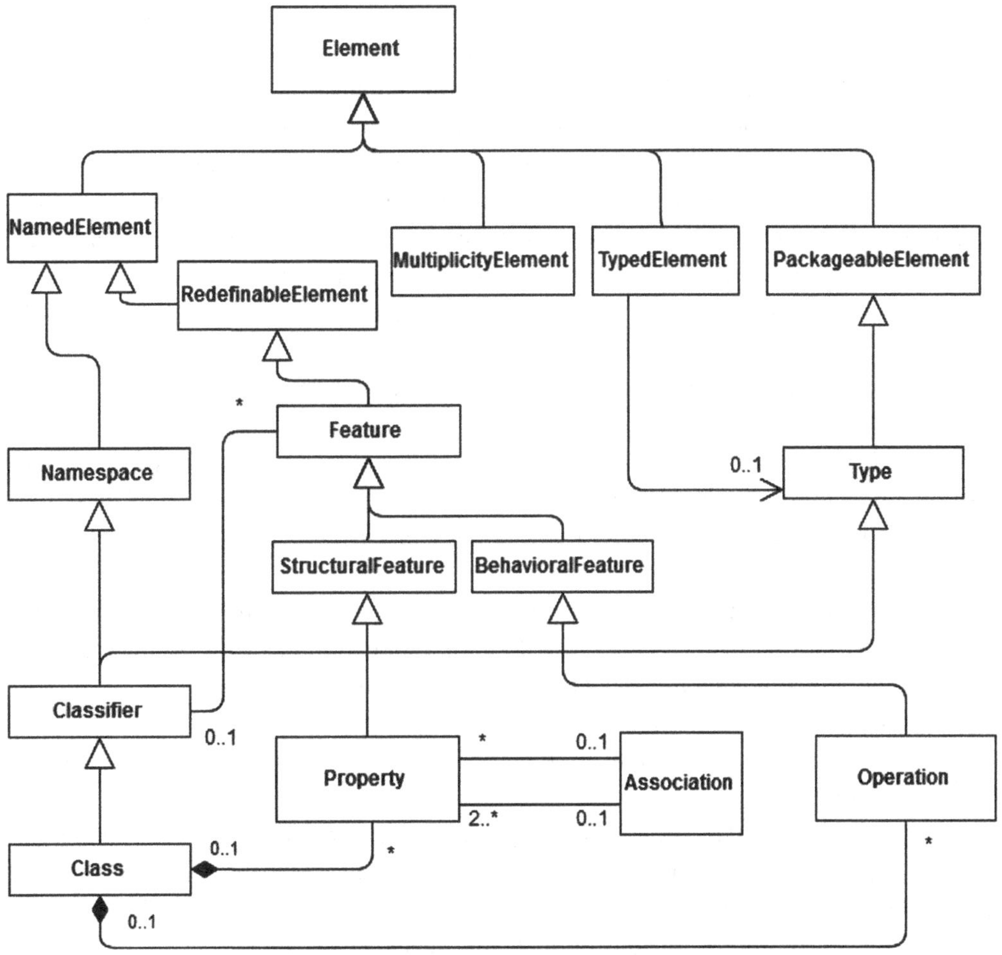

A Class has, then, a set of owned attributes, which are *Properties*. Each attribute has a *Type*. A class may be a subclass of another class, and may have several superclasses (UML has multiple inheritance). Associations link properties, attributes, of classes and by doing so they create a relationship between those two or more classes.

Android Native Applications

Introduction

In this section, the main challenges to mobile apps development are presented along with the most relevant aspects to be taken into account when developing an android application, such as the structure, layouts, navigation, controls and menus.

Challenges to Mobile Development

The growth in the use of mobile phones in general, and Android smartphones in particular, led to a continuous search for more appealing, simple and interactive user experience. In fact, an unintuitive and complex interface can jeopardize the success of an application. Challenges to mobile design are presented at the hardware and software levels (Sá & Carriço, 2011). The most important hardware challenges include:

- **Limited Input Capabilities:** The small size of mobile phones compared with personal computers represents a challenge for text insertion. Even when a keyboard is presented on-screen, the space of each keyboard is small and it is easy to press the wrong key, even with a stylus.
- **Limited Output Capabilities:** The information to present to the user is sometimes extensive and the smartphone screen can be insufficient for a clear visualization of the entire contents.
- **Power Management Unit:** The power management unit of the smartphone influences the ability to execute a given application, which has a direct relation to the performance of the overall system.

On the other hand, software challenges to be considered in mobile development are:

- **Hierarchical Menus:** While this is a common functionality found in desktop applications, its transition and adoption to mobile applications is not so easy. The main goal of these menus is to allow users to find a given task easier but it is not consensual how many entries should exist in each level to achieve a better user experience.
- **Navigating and Browsing:** This challenge is intrinsically related to the size of the mobile devices. The amount of information presented in a desktop application has to be segmented and reorganized when presented in a mobile device, in order to be easily understood.
- **Images and Icons:** The inclusion and need of graphics in mobile applications must be well thought, as it will have a direct implication in the performance of the application especially when large graphic contents are used.
- **Interaction with the Environment:** The type of interaction adopted by the mobile application is strongly influenced by the context in which the application will be used. As an example, an application designed to be used in a car will have different interaction types compared to the same application designed to be used while comfortably seated (Huang, 2009).

Structure of Android Applications

The main component of an Android application is the *Activity*, which provides a screen that allows users to interact with the application to perform a given task. The lifecycle of activities allows programmers to intervene in certain moments of the activity creation, such as when it is, for example, paused, destroyed or resumed, enabling to control the use of resources to save battery and improve system performance. Activities can also include *Fragment*s, which are a reusable portion of the interface with a given behavior. The creation of an activity involves two types of files that are associated with each other: a JAVA file and a XML file. The JAVA file is responsible for implementing the functionality of the activity whereas the XML file defines the user interface layout. Beside activities and layouts, Android applications have resources such as icons, menus or styles to control the UI appearance. An important file that keeps essential information about the application is the AndroidManifest.xml file that has to exist with this exact name in the root of the project. Among other information it defines the package of the application, the several existing activities and the Activity that represents the entry point of the application, permissions needed by the application and the minimum Android API version that is able to run the application.

Layouts

The most common layouts that an activity can use are linear layouts, relative layouts or listviews. These can be combined between themselves. Linear layouts group controls, as the name indicates, in a linear way, horizontally or vertically. In a relative layout, each control is positioned relatively to the parent view or other controls. Some common properties in relative layouts are:

- **alignParentTop:** Aligns the top of the control with the parent control.
- **centerVertical:** Centers the control vertically in the parent.
- **layout_below:** Places the control below another control.
- **toRightOf:** Places the control to the right of other control.

Finally, listviews are typically used to display a list of items, stored in a database or an array and associated to the *Listview* through an *Adapter*. There is a specific activity to handle listviews, called *ListActivity* that simplifies the implementation of some *Listview* related features, such as filling or obtaining a reference for future use. On the other hand, if the application is built using fragments, a *ListFragment* should be inserted in the activity layout.

Navigation

Android has several patters to implement navigation such as tabs, swipe views or a navigation drawer. Tabs are a common navigation control, which that allow the user to explore and switch between different views of the application to access different functionalities or browse specific data. Swipe views, often used with tabs, provide lateral navigation between sibling screens using a horizontal finger gesture. Finally, the navigation drawer provides a panel accessible through the left edge of the screen and presents the main navigation options of the application.

Controls

The creation of the user interface is based on several widgets, text fields, containers, date and time controls and expert controls, according to the current palette categorization in the official Android Studio IDE. Widgets include *Button, RadioButton, CheckBox, Switch, ToggleButton, ImageButton, ImageView, ProgressBar, SeekBar, RatingBar, Spinner* and *WebView*. In the text fields category several pre-configured text controls exist such as password, e-mail, phone, time, date, signed number or decimal number. Regarding containers, the following are available: *RadioGroup* (to group several RadioBut-tons), *ListView, GridView, ExpandableListView, ScroolView, SearchView* and *VideoView*. For date and time data entering and manipulation, there are the *TextClock* and *AnalogClock* controls and also the *Chronometer, Date, TimePicker* and the *CalendarView*. Finally, in the expert category, controls such as *AutoCompleteTextView, NumberPicker, ZoomButton, Surface* or *TextView* are found to allow the user to achieve more advanced functionalities.

Menus

Menus are a common component in most applications and are of particular importance to mobile applications as they help to provide features without taking up space in the interface. Two of the most used menus in Android applications must be highlighted: options menus and context menus.

Options menus are typically located in the Action Bar. The Action Bar is a window feature located on the top of the screen with the application information along with the options menu. The options menu provides general features concerning the interface, such as adding a new record.

The context menu is associated with some controls and only appears when the user performs a long-click. A typical use is to provide a context menu in the listview control to provide actions for each item in the list, such as remove or edit. As with the activities, also menus are defined using XML.

Related Work

Although a recent subject, model-driven development of native mobile applications has already some approaches, which have been proposed in the literature in the last few years. Vaupel et al. (2014) propose an approach that allows developing a flexible mobile app on different abstraction levels: compact modeling of standard app elements, detailed modeling of individual elements, and separate provider models for specific custom needs. The approach proposes a metamodel for specifying behavior.

Kramer et al. (2010) have developed MobDSL, a domain specific language (DSL) for specifying mobile applications in a platform independent way. This approach does not generate native code for the supported mobile platforms. In fact, it generates code for a virtual machine which needs to be deployed for each different platform.

Balagtas-Fernandez *et al.* (2010) developed Mobia modeler and framework, which enables non-technical users, typically some domain experts, to model an application's user interface and functionality through configurable components, in a platform independent way (Mobia PIM). Then, a model mutator transforms the Mobia PIM to a platform specific model, which is then merged with templates for generating code for specific mobile platforms.

Heitkötter & Majchrzak (2013) have created MD², which is a framework for cross-platform model-driven mobile development, consisting of a DSL for describing business applications concisely and of generators that automatically create complete iOS and Android apps from this specification.

Applause (Applause) proposes a DSL to describe mobile applications and a number of code generators based on Eclipse and Xtext that use these descriptions to generate data-centric native applications for the major mobile platforms (iOS, Android, Windows Phone). ModAgile Mobile (ModAgile) also proposes an approach to the model-driven generation of data-centric mobile apps allowing efficient multi-platform development. Both demand a rather fine-grained modeling of the applications' user interface.

Other works have aimed to simplify the work demanded for the modeler to model a mobile application in a MDD setting. Ribeiro & Silva (2014) have extended the XIS approach, which enables the generation of code from platform independent UIM and other non-UI models, so that it may now generate a platform independent UIM from a set of other non-UI models and then derive a default platform specific model and, afterwards, native code for Android or iOS mobile platforms.

MODEL-DRIVEN GENERATION OF ANDROID NATIVE APPLICATIONS

Introduction

Model-driven software development is a process of progressive refinement of models. At the starting point, a set of platform independent interrelated models facilitates the thinking about the system being developed. These set of models may comprise formal, machine understandable, constraints or invariants (such as enabled by OCL).

This section presents a case study, for Android, of our approach to model-driven generation of Mobile data-driven applications.

Architecture of the Approach

In the approach presented herein the set of initial platform independent models is confined to a simple domain entities model, which is subjected to model transformations that lead to a platform independent UIM (see Figure 5), then to an Android specific UIM, and finally to code.

The starting point is a domain model, represented through an XML file produced by the Amalia Project modeling tools (https://sites.google.com/site/amaliaproject). Our tool (a Java application) loads this file and creates an in memory representation of the domain model. Then, an in-memory platform independent user-interface model (UIM or UI model) is generated, based on the Domain Model, using information from every entity class and their interrelationships. The final step is the creation of an Android application, which uses as input the in-memory platform independent UI model and a set of code templates to generate a functional implementation of a user interface. Future work will generate the database and the CRUD logic from the domain model.

The Domain Model conforms to the meta-model depicted in Figure 6, which is compatible with the UML meta-model for class diagrams, and is a simplification of the one presented in (Cruz & Faria, 2010). A domain model is composed of entity classes and class relations. Each entity class owns a set of attributes. Generalization, Composition, Aggregation and Association between domain classes are class relations. All class relations, except generalization, have cardinality at each end. As suggested in

Figure 5. Model transformations, applied as refinement steps, from the domain model until application code

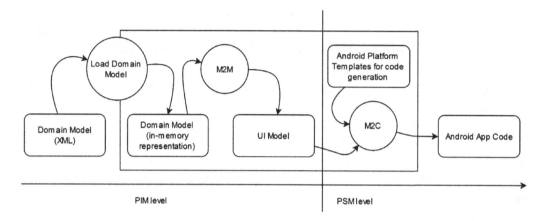

(Cruz & Faria, 2010), and because the generation process is solely based on the domain model, there must exist one and only one class marked as the navigation root (with its *isNavigationRoot* attribute set to True). This class will correspond to the entry point in the generated application.

To better illustrate the approach's transformations process, in the following subsections, we will use a running example based on the domain model in Figure 7. In this model the System class is marked as the navigation root, and thus represents the entry point of the application.

Figure 6. Domain model Metamodel

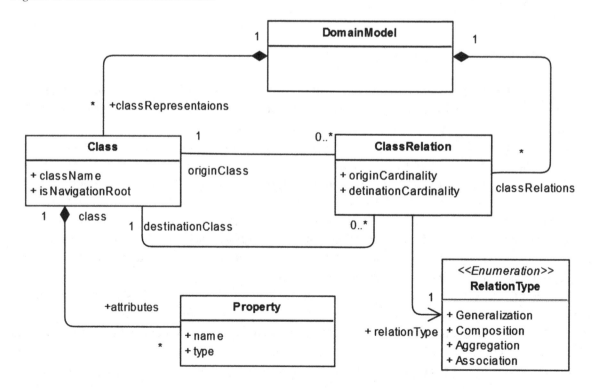

Figure 7. An example of a Domain model to illustrate the transformations that will generate the Android Application

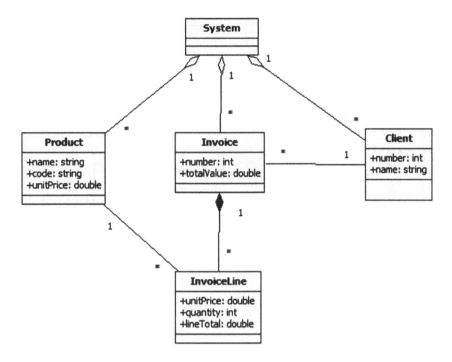

Transforming a Domain Model into a Platform Independent UI Model

The platform independent UI model conforms to the metamodel depicted in Figure 8. This metamodel is based on the UI metamodel proposed in (Cruz & Faria, 2010), although simplified. Nevertheless, it adds to that metamodel a metaclass Navigation that enables representing the navigation path between interaction spaces.

The following model to model (M2M) transformation rules, for generating a platform independent UI model from a domain model were defined in (Cruz, 2010):

- **DM2UIM01:** Transform single base entities and primitive type attributes.
- **DM2UIM02:** Transform enumerated type properties.
- **DM2UIM03:** Transform inherited properties.
- **DM2UIM04:** Transform derived entities and derived attributes.
- **DM2UIM05:** Transform associations, aggregations and compositions.
- **DM2UIM06:** Transform user defined operations.
- **DM2UIM07:** Transform the navigation root.

The M2M transformation process used in this chapter for generating the platform independent UI model is based on the rules DM2UIM01, DM2UIM03, DM2UIM05 and DM2UIM07, referenced above, but it also uses the relations between entities in the domain model to generate a tree of Navigation objects. Table 1 illustrates the domain model features and the associated generated UIM features produced in the M2M transformation process.

Figure 8. UIM Metamodel

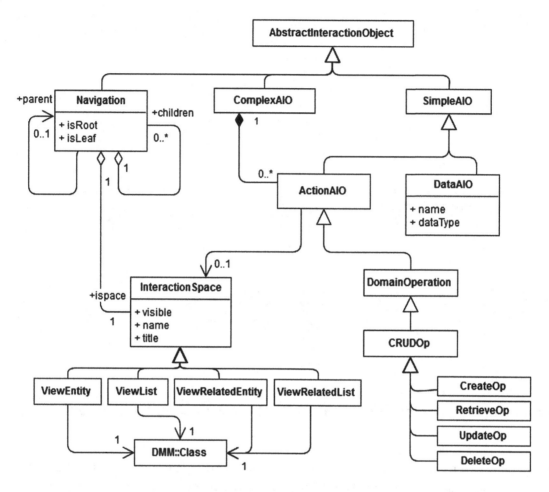

Table 1. Domain model concepts and the associated generated UIM elements

Domain Model Feature	Generated UIM Feature
Domain entity class (*isNavigationRoot =* True)	Root **Navigation** object (*isRoot* = True)
Domain entity class (*isNavigationRoot =* False)	• **Navigation** object, associated to a • **ViewList/ViewEntity** instance, which comprises a collection of • **DataAIOs**
Inheritance	• A **DataAIO** object, for each inherited attribute in the • **InteractionSpace** generated from the specialized class.
To-many association, aggregation or composition	• Select the domain entity classes that will be handled to generate the next level of **Navigation** objects, associated to a **ViewRelatedList** instance. • Each association, aggregation or composition also generates an **ActionAIO** that allows navigating from the current **InteractionSpace** to the one corresponding to the target entity class, or a **ViewList** to select the instances to associate.
To-one association, aggregation or composition	• Select the domain entity classes that will be handled to generate the next level of **Navigation** objects, associated to a **ViewRelatedEntity** instance. • Each association, aggregation or composition also generates an **ActionAIO** that allows navigating from the current **InteractionSpace** to the one corresponding to the target entity class, or a **ViewList** for selecting the instance to associate.

The model to model (M2M) transformation process that generates the platform independent UI model uses the relations between entities in the domain model to generate a tree of Navigation objects (figure 9). In that tree's root is a Navigation object derived from the class marked as the navigation root, in our example this is the System class. The sole purpose of this root Navigation object is to provide access to the interaction spaces generated from the entities aggregated in the navigation root. To do so, each of those entities will be used to generate another Navigation object. In our example, Product, Invoice and Client will serve as input to generate Navigation objects under the one derived from System. This first level of Navigation objects, immediately under the root, will have each Navigation object associated to a ViewList object, which is a type of interaction space. A ViewList object is associated with a domain entity class and represents a way to access all the instances of an entity. These ViewList instances comprise ActionAIOs specialized as the CRUD domain operations (CRUDOp) create, update and delete. This makes possible to create a new instance, and update and delete an existing instance of the domain entity associated to the ViewList from within the ViewList interaction space.

Figure 9. Navigation Tree generated from our running example

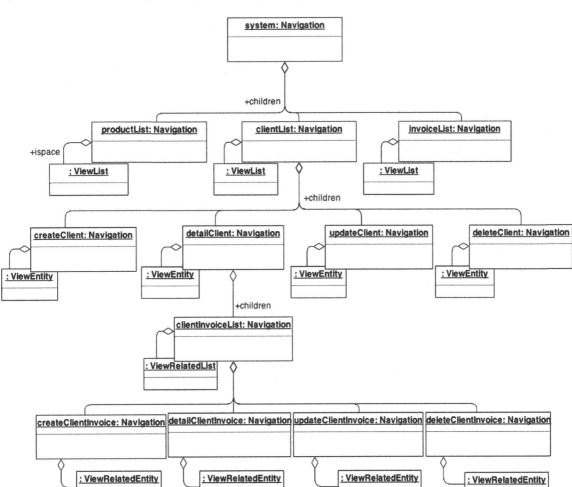

The second level of Navigation objects, under the root Navigation object, will contain ViewEntity objects. These objects represent the possibility to have access to a particular instance of an entity, for visualizing its details or for editing purposes. Each ViewEntity interaction space is also associated with a domain entity class, and is associated with a CRUDOp operation. The ViewEntity will contain as many DataAIOs as its associated domain entity class contains attributes. One DataAIO for each attribute. If the domain model has Generalization relations between classes, the ViewEntity will also contain DataAIOs derived from the attributes of the domain classes on the upper hierarchy of the corresponding domain entity class.

At this level each to-many composition, aggregation or association relations in the domain model will generate Navigation objects, each associated with a ViewRelatedList, having a child Navigation object associated with a ViewRelatedEntity. The purpose of these navigation objects is similar to those associated with ViewList and ViewEntity but restricted by the master entity. For instance, in our running example, this would allow, from within the ViewEntity interaction space associated to the Client domain entity, to access a ViewRelatedList associated with Invoice, listing all the invoices associated to a given client. And, from there, to access a ViewRelatedEntity to see the details of the selected invoice.

Similarly, each to-one association relation in the domain model will generate a Navigation object associated with a ViewRelatedEntity, having a child Navigation object associated with a ViewList. The reason here is to see the details of the associated instance in the ViewRelatedEntity, but be able to create or select another in the ViewList.

Transforming a Platform Independent UI Model into an Android Application

The transformation process, which transforms the platform independent UI model into an Android application, is based on a set of code templates that provide the structure and the look and feel of the application. At the moment there are no configuration options to alter the user interface.

At the entry point, the application implements a *Navigation Drawer*, which will display the main navigation options available to the user. The transformation process reads the Navigation objects, children of the root Navigation object in the UI model, and uses the name of each one to create an item in the *Navigation Drawer*. The code excerpts below present the transformation flow. The final result, for our running example, can be seen in Figure 10.

In a first step the process uses a class named *EntitiesMoverAndTransformer* to change the Entities. java template to generate the *Entities* class:

```
//omitted code
public void makeApp(UserInterfacePIM pim){
entitiesUnderTheRoot = pim.getRootChildrenEntities();
//Make a copy of the Entities.java template, change it and move it to
//the source folder of the Android app
EntitiesMoverAndTransformer etMover = new EntitiesMoverAndTransformer();
etMover.generateEntitiesClassFile(entitiesUnderTheRoot);
//omitted code
```

Figure 10. Generated Navigation Drawer for the proposed domain model

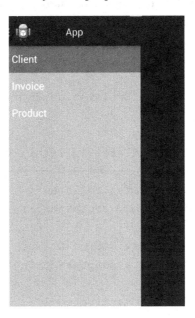

Entities is a simple class with three getter methods, one to return a String array with the names of the Navigation objects directly under the root, other that returns the name of an entity for a given index and the third method returns the index of an entity for a given name. This class is generated by changing only the initialization of a String array (pattern [entities] in the template) that will have the names of the interaction spaces children of the Navigation root. Once generated, it is used to get the list of entity names to put in the Android Navigation Drawer, to set the title every time de *ListFragment* is changed, and to find out the index of the entity when the *New* button on the action bar is pressed.

Excerpt of the Entities.java template:

```java
public class Entities {
 private static final String[] entities = [entities];
 public Entities(){}
public static String[] getEntities(){
 return entities;
 }
 public static int getEntityIndex(String name){
 return Arrays.asList(entities).indexOf(name);
 }
 public static String getEntityName(int index){
 return entities[index];
 }
```

The NavigatonDrawerFragment.java file remains unchanged. The intended behavior is achieved by the use of the *Entities* class as illustrated bellow:

```
public class NavigationDrawerFragment extends Fragment {
// The Array used in the ArrayAdapter
 private final String[] entities = Entities.getEntities();
//omitted code
@Override
 public View onCreateView(LayoutInflater inflater, ViewGroup container,
 Bundle savedInstanceState) {
 mDrawerListView = (ListView) inflater.inflate(
 R.layout.fragment_navigation_drawer, container, false);
//omitted code
//the ArrayAdapter populates the Navigation Drawer
 mDrawerListView.setAdapter(new ArrayAdapter<String>(getActionBar()
  .getThemedContext(),
  android.R.layout.simple_list_item_activated_1,
  android.R.id.text1, entities));
//omitted code
return mDrawerListView;
}
```

This will allow the user to navigate between the Android graphical constructs that will be derived from the interaction spaces in the UIM. In the action bar a single button (button *New* in Figure 11) will provide access to the create operation associated with the selected item.

Figure 11. ListFragment for Product showing the first field of each record and a new button on the action bar to create a new record

As stated before, under the root of the UIM Navigation objects there is a first level of Navigation objects associated to ViewList instances, each associated to an entity class in the domain model. This type of interaction space is transformed into an Android *ListFragment*, shown in Figure 11, with a very simple layout, enabling listing the DataAIO that is derived from the first attribute of the entity associated to the ViewList.

By using the same basic structure for transforming all instances of ViewList, it is possible to have a common *ListFragment* and a set of segregated classes generated from the ViewList instances associated to the first level of Navigation objects in the UI model.

An *EntityModel* template is used to generate a class for each domain entity class. The pattern [entity] will be substituted by the name of each class:

```
public class [entity]Model implements I_Entity{
 //every record will be an EntityInstance
 //this will be used to as on simulations of CRUD operations
 private static ArrayList<EntityInstance> entityList =
 new ArrayList<EntityInstance>();
 public [entity]Model(){
 }
// omitted code
 //CRUD operation simulations
 @Override
 public void addEntityInstance(EntityInstance entity) {
 [entity]Model.entityList.add(entity);
 }
 @Override
 public void deleteEntityInstance(int index) {
 [entity]Model.entityList.remove(index);
 }
 @Override
 public void updateEntityInstance(int index, EntityInstance entity) {
 [entity]Model.entityList.set(index,entity);
 }
 //The list to use in the ListFragment
 @Override
 public List<String> getEntityIdentList() {
 ArrayList<String> ident = new ArrayList<String>();
 for (EntityInstance entity: entityList){
 //the first attribute in the class but implementation can change
 ident.add(entity.getIdentField());
 }
 return ident;
 }
//omitted code
 }
```

From the ViewList instances associated to the Navigation objects at the first level in the UIM's Navigation tree, in our example, the transformation process generates ClientEntityModel, ProductEntityModel, InvoiceEntityModel and EntityModelFactory, as presented in the code below:

```
public void makeApp(UserInterfacePIM pim){
 //entities under the root of the system
 entitiesUnderTheRoot = pim.getRootChildrenEntities();
// omitted code
//Setting up the EntityFactory and EntityModels
 //for the entities under the root
 EntityFactoryMoverAndTransformer eFactory =
 new EntityFactoryMoverAndTransformer();
 EntityModelMaker modelMaker = new EntityModelMaker();
 eFactory.generateEntityFactoryClassFile(entitiesUnderTheRoot);
 modelMaker.generateEntityClassFiles(entitiesUnderTheRoot);
```

The EntityModelFactory is generated from the template EntityModelFactory.java by replacing the pattern [insert entity cases] by the code to create and return the correct type of EntityModel object, as presented below:

```
public class EntityModelFactory {
 public EntityModelFactory(){}
 public I_Entity getEntityModel(int index){
 switch (index){
 [insert entity cases]
```

Depending on the selection on the Navigation Drawer the content of the *ListFragment* changes, rendering the corresponding list by changing the content of the *ArrayAdapter* as illustrated in the code bellow:

```
//omitted code
@Override
public void onActivityCreated (Bundle savedState){
 // finding out the option selected
 int option = getArguments().getInt(ARG_SECTION_NUMBER);
//Get the right model, all models implement the same interface
 I_Entity model = new EntityModelFactory().getEntityModel(option);
// A List with the first attribute of a class
 List<String> items = model.getEntityIdentList();
// setting the adapter to show the items in the items in the ListFragment
 this.adapter = new ArrayAdapter<String>(getActivity(),
 android.R.layout.simple_list_item_1,items);
 setListAdapter(this.adapter);
//omitted code
```

At the end of the transformation process the generated app will react to the user input screens as shown in figure 11.

The creation of a new record or entity instance needs to be presented to the user in the appropriate form. To be able to start the right Activity when the action bar *New* button is pressed, an IntentMaker class is used. At transformation time, this class is generated from a template in order to be able to return the correct *Intent* to start the Activity that supports the appropriate form. The generation of this class is similar to the generation of the EntityModelFactory by changing the pattern [insert intent cases] with the code necessary to create and return the appropriate *Intent*, as shown in the code below:

```
public Intent getIntentForEntityView (Context ctx,int modelIndex){
 switch (modelIndex){
 [insert intent cases]
 //omitted code
```

Once the IntentMaker is in place, the Activity can be called by the following code:

```
//omitted code
if (id == R.id.action_new){
 //Index for the selected entity or model
 int modelIndex = Entities.getEntityIndex(this.mTitle.toString());
//Get the Intent for the selected entity
 //and start the correct Activity
 Intent i = new IntentMaker().getIntentForEntityView(this, modelIndex);
 startActivity(i);
}
//omitted code
```

The layout for each form is generated from the information in the ViewEntity in one of the children Navigation objects under the first level of Navigation Objects. Every DataAIO, in the ViewEntity, is used to produce an Android *EditText* with a Hint and the UIM's CreateOp gives origin to a create button, as shown in the code excerpt bellow:

```
private void makeActivityLayoutSimple(Navigation nav){
 View view = nav.getViewElement();
 // omitted code
 //A new layout XML document
 DocumentBuilderFactory docFactory =
 DocumentBuilderFactory.newInstance();
 DocumentBuilder docBuilder = docFactory.newDocumentBuilder();
// LinearLayout root Element
 Document doc = docBuilder.newDocument();
 Element rootElement = addLinearLayout(doc);
// insert editText
 for (DataElement d: view.getDataElements()){
```

```
addEditText (doc, rootElement, d.getName ());
 }
 //omitted code
for (I_CrudOp crud: view.getCrudOperations()){
//omitted code
addButton (doc, rootElement, crud.getCrudOpName());
 }
 //omitted code
// generate the layout file
 makeXMLFileFromDocGeneral(doc, middleName, layoutNameEnding);
//omitted code
```

When used by the creation Activity produces an interface similar to the one from our example, in Figure 12.

Each form layout is used by a different Activity with similar behavior. To generate those Activities, a BaseActivity.java file is used as template. Inside it the portions of variable code are marked with tags (patterns [class name], [layout name] and [entity name]). At transformation time, those tags are changed and each new file will have a different name, the correct layout and access to the correct EntityModel class.

Figure 12. Activity presenting the creation form to a new Product, using a layout generated by the transformation process

The code bellow shows the substitution points inside BaseActivity.java template:

```
public class [class name] extends Activity {
 //omitted code
 @Override
 protected void onCreate(Bundle savedInstanceState) {
super.onCreate(savedInstanceState);
setContentView(R.layout.[layout name]);
// omitted code
 btnCreate.setOnClickListener(new OnClickListener(){
@Override
 public void onClick(View v) {
 // A Map to collect the input form the user
 Map <String,String>fields = new HashMap<>();
// omitted code
 // editTextList is a List with all the EditText in the layout
 for(EditText et: editTextList){
 fields.put((String) et.getHint(),
 et.getText().toString());
 }
// ActualInstance is a representation of the user data
 //for the new record
 new [entity name]Model().addEntityInstance(
 new ActualInstance (identFieldString, fields));
// omitted code
```

At run time this activity is able to send to the correct EntityModel a Map with a representation of the form. With this representation the EntityModel is able to update the data and the change is reflected in the *ListFragment*, as is seen in Figure 13.

Update and Delete operations are available through a context menu associated with a *LongClick* on the items in the *ListFragment*. The details of a record will be accessible through a *Click*. All these operations use a layout similar to the one used in the creation form showing detail information in Edit-Text objects, for the update form, or TextView objects, for the details or delete form, derived from the DataAIO objects in the UI model. A simple button is also generated using the corresponding CRUDOp (update or delete), and a button to navigate to lists of related instances presented with a similar structure to those under the Navigation Root but with master-detail restrictions.

FUTURE RESEARCH DIRECTIONS

In the present state of development, our approach's transformation process is rather restrictive, providing only one solution and making assumption on the data to be presented in every ListFragment. These are points to improve in the near future. Further work needs to be made to enable choosing between different types of interface and to allow the differentiation of the ListFragments by making possible to choose the

Figure 13. ListFragment for Product updated with the new product

Table 2. UIM concepts and the associated generated Android classes

UIM Metamodel Concepts	Generated Android Classes
Navigation (if *isRoot*) for accessing children	NavigationDrawerFragment
ViewList	ListFragment
ViewEntity	Activity
ViewRelatedList	ListFragment or ListActivity
ViewRelatedEntity	Activity
DataAIO	EditText or TextView
ActionAIO/DomainOperation/CRUDOp	Button

fields, attributes of the domain model entity, to include in each list. As proposed in (Cruz, 2010), this may be done by adding tagged values in the domain model («ident») for tagging the attributes that are useful for the user to identify a given entity instance.

Other point of future improvement is the implementation of the Model classes that will implement persistence logic for storing the entity instances in a database.

In the approach presented herein the initial platform independent model is restricted to a simple domain entities model, which is transformed into a platform independent UIM and then to an Android specific UIM, and finally to code. Another future research direction is to extend the initial platform independent model to a set of integrated domain and use case models, as suggested in (Cruz, 2010; Cruz & Faria, 2010).

A process for generating iOS applications from the same platform independent UI model is also a future development of this research.

CONCLUSION

This chapter proposes an approach to the model-driven development of data-oriented mobile apps. A metamodel for platform independent UI modeling and a transformation process for Android application have been presented. The transformation process, implemented in Java is two-fold. First, a transformation from a UML aligned domain model to a platform independent UI model is completed, and then a transformation from the platform independent UIM to an Android application is made. The former transformation is a visitor-based approach, where the in-memory object graph representing the domain model is traversed, and the transformation rules are applied, originating as output another in-memory object graph, now representing the platform independent UIM according to the presented metamodel. The latter transformation, from the UIM to an Android app, is a template-based approach, as explained before.

The approach demonstrates the feasibility of generating complete native data-oriented applications from a UML aligned domain model. Similar approaches have been overviewed, and future research directions have been sketched.

REFERENCES

Applause. (n.d.). Retrieved from: https://github.com/applause/applause

Balagtas-Fernandez, F., Tafelmayer, M., & Hussmann, H. (2010). Mobia Modeler: Easing the Creation Process of Mobile Applications for Non-Technical Users. In *Proceedings of the 15th international conference on Intelligent user interfaces* (IUI'10), (pp. 269-272). Hong Kong, China. doi:10.1145/1719970.1720008

Cruz, A. M. R. (2010). *Automatic Generation of User Interfaces from Rigorous Domain and Use Case Models*. (PhD Dissertation). University of Porto.

Cruz, A. M. R., & Faria, J. P. (2010). A Metamodel-Based Approach for Automatic User Interface Generation. In *International Conference on Model Driven Engineering Languages and Systems* (MODELS 2010) (LNCS), (vol. 6394, pp. 256-270). Springer Berlin Heidelberg. doi:10.1007/978-3-642-16145-2_18

Frankel, D. S. (2003). *Model Driven Architecture - Applying MDA to Enterprise Computing*. Indianapolis, IN: Wiley Publishing, Inc.

Heitkötter, H., & Majchrzak, T. (2013). Cross-platform Development of Business Apps with MD2. In *International Conference on Design Science Research in Information Systems and Technology* (DESRIST 2013). Springer. doi:10.1007/978-3-642-38827-9_29

Huang, K. (2009). Challenges in Human-Computer Interaction Design for Mobile Devices. In *Proceedings of the World Congress on Engineering and Computer Science*.

Jézéquel, J.-M. (2005). *Model Transformation Techniques*. Retrieved January 13, 2015, from http://people.irisa.fr/Jean-Marc.Jezequel/enseignement/ModelTransfo.pdf

Kelly, S., & Tolvanen, J-P. (2008). *Domain Specific Modeling: Enabling Full Code Generation*. Wiley-IEEE Computer Society Press.

Kramer, D., Clark, T., & Oussena, S. (2010). MobDSL: A Domain Specific Language for multiple mobile platform deployment. In *International Conference on Networked Embedded Systems for Enterprise Applications* (NESEA). IEEE. doi:10.1109/NESEA.2010.5678062

Madaudo, R., & Scandurra, P. (2013). Native versus Cross-platform frameworks for mobile application development. In *Proceedings of Eclipse-IT 2013 – VIII Workshop of the Italian Eclipse Community*.

ModAgile. (n.d.). Retrieved from: http://www.modagile-mobile.de

OMG. (2013). *OMG Unified Modeling Language (OMG UML)*. Version 2.5, September 2013. OMG.

Petrov, I., & Buchmann, A. (2008). Architecture of OMG MOF-based Repository Systems. In G. Kotsis, D. Taniar, E. Pardede, & I. Khalil (Eds.), *Proceedings of the 10th International Conference on Information Integration and Web-based Applications & Services (iiWAS '08)* (pp. 193–200). New York, NY: ACM. http://doi.acm.org/10.1145/1497308.1497346

Ribeiro, A., & Silva, A. R. (2014). XIS-mobile: a DSL for mobile applications. In *Proceedings of the 29th Annual ACM Symposium on Applied Computing (SAC '14)* (pp. 1316–1323). New York, NY: ACM. http://doi.acm.org/10.1145/2554850.2554926

Sá, M., & Carriço, L. (2011). Designing and Evaluating Mobile Interaction: Challenges and Trends. Foundations and Trends in Human–Computer Interaction, 4(3), 175-243.

Silva, A., & Videira, C. (2008). UML, Metodologias e Ferramentas CASE (vol. 2). Centro Atlântico, Lda. (In Portuguese)

Vaupel, S., Taentzer, G., Harries, J., Stroh, R., Gerlach, R., & Guckert, M. (2014). Model-Driven Development of Mobile Applications Allowing Role-Driven Variants. In *Model-Driven Engineering Languages and Systems, Proceedings of 17th International Conference, MODELS 2014* (LNCS), (*vol. 8767*, pp. 1-17). Springer International Publishing. doi:10.1007/978-3-319-11653-2_1

Warmer, J., Bast, W., Pinkley, D., Herrera, M., & Kleppe, A. (2003). *MDA Explained - The Model Driven Architecture: Practice and Promise*. Addison-Wesley Professional.

KEY TERMS AND DEFINITIONS

Android: Operating system developed by Google, designed for mobile devices such as smartphones, tablet computers and smart TVs.

CIM: Computation Independent Model, a model specifying a software system's characteristics in a way independent of the way those characteristics shall be implemented.

iOS: Operating system developed by Apple, designed exclusively for Apple mobile devices such as iPhone, iPad or AppleTV.

Metamodel: A Model defining a language, concepts and constructs for building other models.

Model-Driven-Development: Software development approach that considers model building, instead of coding, as the main development activity. Successive model transformations will ultimately produce the final code.

PIM: Platform Independent Model, a model specifying a software system's characteristics implementations in a way independent of the platform to which it will be deployed.

PSM: Platform Specific Model, a model specifying a software system's characteristics implementations in a way specific for the platform to which it will be deployed.

Chapter 13
Migrating JAVA to Mobile Platforms through HAXE:
An MDD Approach

Pablo Nicolás Díaz Bilotto
Universidad Nacional del Centro de la Provincia de Buenos Aires, Argentina

Liliana Favre
Universidad Nacional del Centro de la Provincia de Buenos Aires, Argentina& Comisión de Investigaciones Científicas de la Provincia de Buenos Aires, Argentina

ABSTRACT

Software developers face several challenges in deploying mobile applications. One of them is the high cost and technical complexity of targeting development to a wide spectrum of platforms. The chapter proposes to combine techniques based on MDA (Model Driven Architecture) with the HaXe language. The outstanding ideas behind MDA are separating the specification of the system functionality from its implementation on specific platforms, managing the software evolution, increasing the degree of automation of model transformations, and achieving interoperability with multiple platforms. On the other hand, HaXe is a very modern high level programming language that allows us to generate mobile applications that target all major mobile platforms. The main contributions of this chapter are the definition of a HaXe metamodel, the specification of a model-to-model transformation between Java and HaXe and, the definition of an MDA migration process from Java to mobile platforms.

INTRODUCTION

Nowadays mobile devices come with their users all the time and everywhere. Among other novel features, mobile devices contain global positioning sensors, wireless connectivity, built-in web browsers and photo/video/voice capabilities that allow providing highly localized, context aware applications. Mobile phones have become as powerful as any desktop computer in terms of applications they can run, however, the software development in mobile computing is still not as mature as it is for desktop computer and the whole potential of mobile devices is wasted (Waserman, 2010).

DOI: 10.4018/978-1-4666-9916-8.ch013

Copyright © 2016, IGI Global. Copying or distributing in print or electronic forms without written permission of IGI Global is prohibited.

Although mobile technologies present new opportunities for services and businesses, they also present development and implementation challenges. Some mobile applications must also determine the user location before offering the service and then track the location to adapt services and information accordingly. Besides, an additional challenge is to achieve the required level of security, reliability and quality of mobile applications. Various authors describe challenges of mobile software development, for example, in (Dehlinger & Dixon, 2011) authors highlight creating user interfaces for different kinds of mobile devices, providing reusable applications across multiple mobile platforms, designing context aware applications and handling their complexity and, specifying requirements uncertainty. Thompson et al. (2011) remark issues related to ensuring that the application provides sufficient performance while maximizing battery life.

A current problem in the engineering community is the rapid proliferation of mobile platforms (Lettner, Tschernuth & Mayrhofer, 2011). The high cost and technical complexity of targeting development to a wide spectrum of platforms, has forced developers to make applications tailored for each type of device. Within mobile development, many companies have different development teams redoubling the software engineering efforts for functionally similar mobile applications. In many cases, developers prefer to implement an application once and deploy it to different platforms with minimal effort. In this direction, an open source multiplatform programming language called HaXe has emerged integrating the native behaviors of the different platforms targeted in development projects (Dasnois, 2011).

To manage a huge diversity of technologies, mobile development needs novel technical frameworks for information integration and tool interoperability. Some works propose to exploit the MDD (Model Driven Development) paradigm to simplify multi-device development (Brambilla, Cabot, & Wimmer. 2012) (Dunkel & Bruns, 2007). A specific realization of MDD proposed by the Object Management Group (OMG) is MDA (Model Driven Architecture) (OMG MDA, 2014).

The outstanding ideas behind MDA are separating the specification of the system functionality from its implementation on specific platforms, managing the software evolution from abstract models to implementations, increasing the degree of automation of model transformations, and achieving interoperability with multiple platforms. Models play a major role in MDA, which distinguishes at least Platform Independent Model (PIM) and Platform Specific Model (PSM). An MDA forward engineering process focuses on the automatic transformation of different models that conform to MOF metamodels. The essence of MDA is the Meta Object Facility Metamodel (MOF) that allows integrating different kinds of software artifacts (MOF, 2008) (MOF, 2011). The MOF 2.0 Query, View, Transformation (QVT) metamodel (QVT, 2012) allows expressing model transformations

The OMG ADM Task Force (ADMTF) has defined a set of metamodels aligned with MOF that allow describing various aspects of the software modernization (ADM, 2015). Metamodels such as Knowledge Discovery Metamodel (KDM) and Abstract Syntax Tree Metamodel (ASTM) aim at improving the process of understanding and evolving software applications and enabling architecture-driven reverse engineering (KDM, 2011) (ASTM, 2011).

CASE tools based on MDA do not support forward engineering processes for HaXe (CASE MDA, 2015). We consider beneficial to integrate HaXe with MDA. The first step in the integration direction is to have a definition of HaXe aligned with the MDA standards, particularly MOF. Then, we defined a MOF metamodel for HaXe, which allows specifying meta-level transformations from transformation languages such as QVT or ATL (Atlas Transformation Language) (Jouault & Kurtev, 2005) (Jouault et al, 2008) (Jouault et al., 2006). Specifically, this chapter will include a description of an MDA migration process from object-oriented code (Java in particular) to different mobile platforms. The main steps of this process are the specification of an ATL-based metamodel transformation between Java and HaXe and, the implementation of cross-platform, multi-device mobile applications.

The proposal was validated in the open source application platform Eclipse considering that some of its tools and runtime environments are aligned with MDA standards. For example, EMF (Eclipse Modeling Framework) provides facilities for metamodeling and an execution engine for models that supports the creation of a Java class model (EMF, 2015) (Steinberg, et al, 2009). EMF has evolved starting from the experience of the Eclipse community to implement a variety of tools and to date is highly related to MDD. Ecore is the core metamodel at the heart of EMF. The subproject M2M supports model transformations that take one or more models as input to produce one or more models as output. Another subproject is Acceleo, which is an implementation of the M2T transformation standard of the OMG for EMF-based models (MOFM2T, 2008) (Acceleo, 2015) Today, the most complete technology that supports ADM is MoDisco which provides a generic and extensible framework to facilitate the development of tools to extract models from legacy systems and use them on use cases of modernization. As an Eclipse component, MoDisco can integrate with plugins or technologies available in the Eclipse environment. (MoDisco, 2012) (Bruneliere et al., 2014)

The chapter includes a use case, the migration of a Java application, "The Set of Mandelbrot". It is simple but it allows us to exemplify in the chapter the different steps of the migration process from Java to HaXe.

BACKGROUND

In this section, we firstly describe existing approaches for the development of mobile applications related to MDD. Finally, we give a general description of our contribution in the context of standards of MDA and HaXe.

Recently, there have been architectures and frameworks that facilitatethe development of mobile applications. In the following, we mention new approaches that align these developments with MDD.

Braun and Eckhaus (2008) propose a new software architecture with the objective of providing the same service as mobile Web service as well as mobile application. The authors report on the feasibility study that they conducted in order to evaluate whether to use model driven software development for developing mobile applications. They argue that the architecture is flexible enough to support mobile Web services and mobile applications at the same time. They have develop a metamodel to describe mobile application and have shown how to generate mobile application from that model.

Dunkel and Bruns (2007) describe the project BAMOS and an architecture designed and implemented for the generic and flexible development of mobile applications. A declarative description of the available services supports the architecture. The authors describe a model driven approach for generating almost the complete source code of mobile services.

Kim (2008) goes through mobile development process and architectural structures and their analysis with empirical mobile application development. The architecture and architecture role on the development has been studied in mobile application and multiplatform service development.

Bowen and Hinze (2011) outline a proposal for supporting mobile application development by using models as inputs to an emulator. The authors describe an MDD-based emulator for using in the design of graphical interfaces and interactions. They propose transform functional behavior and requirement models with design restrictions into emulated applications.

Kramer, Clark and Oussena (2010) describe a DSL (Domain Specific Language), named MobDSL, to generate applications for multiple mobile platforms. They perform the domain analysis on two cases in the Android and iPhone platforms. This analysis allows inferring the basic requirements of the language defined by MobDSL.

The proliferation of mobile devices generated the need to adapt desktop applications to mobile platforms. Améndola and Favre (2013) describe a reengineering process that integrates traditional reverse engineering techniques such as static and dynamic analysis with MDA. The article describes a case study that shows how to move CRM (Customer Relationship Management) applications from desktop to mobile platforms. The proposal was validated in the open source application platform Eclipse, EMF, EMP, ATL and Android platform.

Pérez Castillo, et al. (2013) describe ANDRIU, a reverse engineering tool based on static analysis of source code for transforming user interface tiers from desktop application to Android. ANDRIU was been developed for migrating traditional systems to Android applications although it was designed to be extended for different migrations to others mobile platforms.

Our Contribution

In the existing literature, we did not find an integration of HaXe with MDA. We consider it beneficial and then, this work proposes to integrate the HaXe platform with MDD (MDA in particular) and, to define an MDA migration process from Java code to mobile platforms through HaXe. This process includes automatic analysis of existing code, model transformation to target platform models and code generation.

The main contributions are the definition of an Ecore metamodel of HaXe, the definition of *java-2haxe* metamodel transformation and the ability to compile and run applications on platforms such as Android, iOS or other environments. This approach allows us to define families of transformations, all model instances that conform to a metamodel.

Figure 1 summarizes our approach. The first step is the parsing of the Java code to build a complete model of code. This step is performed by using MoDisco tool that allows extracting a Java model that

Figure 1. MDA Migration Process

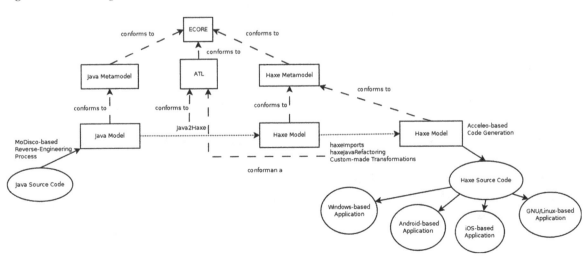

conforms to a Java metamodel. The metamodels Java, ATL and Haxe conform to the Ecore metamodel. The ATL transformation *java2haxe* generates from the Java model a HaXe model. Other transformations such as *JavaHaxeRefactorings* (that eliminates dependencies of Java platforms) or *JavaImports* (that completes information about type imports that Java language consider implicit) transform the model. From a model HaXe, it is possible to generate a source code in HaXe by using Acceleo. HaXe allows writing mobile applications that target all major mobile platforms in a straightforward way.

The underlying process follows model driven development principles: all artifacts involved in the process can be viewed as models that conform a particular metamodel, the process itself can be viewed as a sequence of model-to-model transformations and all the extracted information is represented in a standard way through metamodels.

THE HAXE LANGUAGE

Haxe is an open-source high-level multiplatform programming language and compiler that can produce applications and source code for many different platforms from a single code-base (Dasnois, 2011). Cannasse (2014) summarizes the HaXe principles as follows: "support mainstream platforms", "write once, reuse everywhere", "always native, no wrapper", "generated but readable" and "trust the developer".

The HaXe programming language is a high level programming language that mixes features of object oriented languages and functional ones. It is similar (but not pure) to object-oriented languages. The compiler supports novel features such as type inference, enforcing strict *type safety* at compile time.

In the following, we informally summarizes the main features of the HaXe language described by the developers at (http://haxe.org/documentation/introduction/language-feature.html). In the section "The HaXe metamodel" we partially show the proposed specification of the HaXe language as an Ecore metamodel.

Language Features

- **Abstract Type:** "An abstract type is a compile-time construct which is represented in a different way at runtime. This allows giving a whole new meaning to existing types".
- **Anonymous Structures:** "Data can easily be grouped in anonymous structures, minimizing the necessity of small data classes."
- **Array Comprehension:** "Create and populate arrays quickly using for loops and logic".
- **Classes, Interfaces and Inheritance:** "HaXe allows structuring code in classes, making it an object-oriented language. Common related features known from languages such as Java are supported, including inheritance and interfaces".
- **Conditional Compilation:** "Conditional Compilation allows compiling specific code depending on compilation parameters."
- **Generalized) Algebraic Data Types:** "Structure can be expressed through algebraic data types (ADT), which are known as enums in the HaXe Language".
- **Inlined Calls:** "Functions can be designed as being inline, allowing their code to be inserted at call-site. This can yield significant performance benefits without resorting to code duplication via manual inlining".

- **Iterators:** "Iterating over a set of values, e.g. the elements of an array, is very easy in Haxe courtesy of iterators. Custom classes can quickly implement iterator functionality to allow iteration".

- **Local Functions and Closures:** "Functions in HaXe are not limited to class fields and can be declared in expressions as well, allowing powerful closures".

- **Metadata:** "Add metadata to fields, classes or expressions. This can communicate information to the compiler, macros, or runtime classes".

- **Static Extensions:** "Existing classes and other types can be augmented with additional functionality through using static extensions".

- **String Interpolation:** "Strings declared with single quotes are able to access variables in the current context"

- **Partial Function Application:** "Any function can be applied partially, providing the values of some arguments and leaving the rest to be filled in later."

- **Pattern Matching:** "Complex structures can be matched against patterns, extracting information from an enum or a structure and defining specific operations for specific value combination."

- **Type Parameters, Constraints And Variance:** "Types can be parametrized with type parameters, allowing typed containers and other complex data structures".

HaXe easily adapts the native behaviors of the different platforms targeted in development projects enabling extremely efficient cross-platform development, ultimately saving time and resources. Currently there are nine supported target languages: Javascript, Neko, PHP, Python, C++, Actionscript3, Flash, Java and, C#.

In the context of Mobile App Development, HaXe allows writing mobile apps that target all major mobile platforms and run at native speed. The C++ target allows us to target Android or iOS and OpenFL (www.openfl.org) provides support for creating interfaces using a Flash-like API. OpenFL is a free and open source software framework and platform for the creation of multi-platform applications and video games. OpenFL programs are written in HaXe and may be published to Flash movies, or standalone applications for Microsoft Windows, Mac OS X, Linux, iOS, Android, BlackBerry OS, Firefox OS, HTML5 and Tizen.

THE HAXE METAMODEL

The essence of MDA is MOF that provides the ability to design and integrate semantically different languages such as general-purpose languages, domain specific languages and modeling languages in a unified way. Significant advantages can be made of this unification to construct powerful mobile design environments.

A metamodel describes a family of models whose elements are instances of the metaclasses of the respective metamodel. The kind of entities and relations defines the kind of metamodel. For instance, a metamodel for Java code includes entities (metaclasses) for classes, fields, operations, methods, constructors, parameters and interfaces. Methods and constructors are subtypes of operations. Interfaces are associated with classes. On the other hand, a PSM-Java metamodel distinguishes entities such as Java-metamodel entities and another entities such as associations (Favre, 2010).

The OMG standard for defining metamodels is MOF. Its modeling concepts are "classes, which model MOF meta-objects; associations, which model binary relations between meta-objects; Data Types, which model other data; and Packages, which modularize the models" (MOF, 2006, pp. 2-6). Consistency rules are attached to metamodel components by using OCL (OCL, 2014). MOF provides two metamodels: EMOF (Essential MOF) and CMOF (Complete MOF). EMOF favors simplicity of implementation over expressiveness. CMOF is a metamodel used to specify more sophisticated metamodels (MOF, 2008).

The Eclipse Modeling Framework (EMF) is the core technology in Eclipse for MDD. EMF allows the definition of metamodels on the metamodeling language called Ecore viewed as the official implementation of EMOF.

The HaXe metamodel was defined in Ecore, although a textual representation in OCLinEcore was used. The OCLinEcore Editor overcomes some limitations of the Ecore Editor, for instance, Ecore does not detected syntactic and semantic errors in the OCL (OCLinECore, 2015). Ecore allows embedding OCL using annotations automatically maintained. Another advantage is that OCLinEcore works with text representations instead of using XMI, allowing greater modifiability, readability and better integration with versioning tools such as Git or SVN. Even with these advantages, we observed that the OCLinEcore editor has various limitations such as the omission of comments to keep the metamodel or lack of expressions to represent literal enumerations. Therefore, we decided to use it only as input method to modify the generated XMI, which we used in the remaining steps of the proposed process (XMI, 2011).

The main metaclasses of the HaXe metamodel are those that allow specifying an application using HaXe as language. One of the main metaclasses of the metamodel is *HaxeModel*, that serves as element container used to describe an application and store additional information on it, for example, some options of compilation and different metaclasses for modeling such as modules, classes and packages.

Figure 2 shows a metaclass diagram including the main metaclasses of the model and their interrelations. The metaclasses used directly by *HaxeModel* are *HaxeModule* and *HaxePathReferentiable*. Starting from the relations *haxeModules*, *referenced* and *elements*, the class *HaxeModel* allows storing different information. Relation *haxeModules* allows accessing the different HaXe modules used in the project. Through relation *elements* it is possible to access the different elements of the package tree. Relation *referenced* provides access to elements which are referenced in the project but are not defined completely. In the case of relations and referenced elements, the type used is *HaxePathReferentiable*, which is the parent type of metaclasses such as*HaxeType and HaxePackage.* It is worth considering that the Composite pattern was the suitable structure to use in the design of this diagram (Gamma et al., 1994).

Figure 3 shows a diagram of types of the HaXe metamodel, The Haxe language includes seven kind of types: *class* (the types *class* and *interface*), *function, abstract type, enumeration, anonymous structures, dynamic* and *monomorph*. The last two types were not considered. The type *dynamic* can be expressed as an instance of the metaclass *HaxeClass*. The type *monomorph* is used only for inferring types due to HaXe was designed as a strongly typed language, but with features that allows programmers do not define the types of certain elements.

In addition to the metaclasses for the 5 types of classes, the metaclass *HaxeTypeAccess* was added. It allows specifying references to types abstractly, and then to be specialized by *HaxeClassifierAccess*, which deals only with references to classes, interfaces and enumerations, besides considering the implementation of parameters to types via the relation *parameterMapping*.

Figure 4 shows the diagram of classes and interfaces of the HaXe metamodel. The *HaxeClass* metaclass (that is used in the Class metamodel), allows modeling the various classes and interfaces that appear in a project. This metaclass contains the attribute *isInterface* that indicates whether is an interface or a class, to avoid making two metaclasses with a similar structure. This metaclass is related to several metaclasses such as *HaxeClass, HaxeField, HaxeConstructors, HaxeOperations* and HaxeAttributes.

Figure 2. Main metaclasses of HaXe metamodel

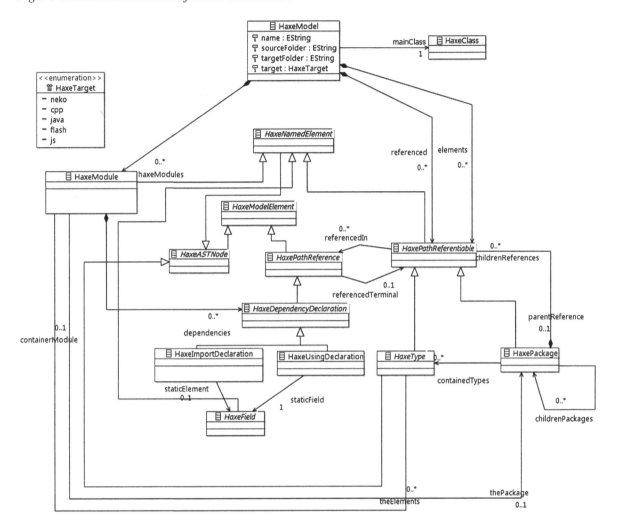

Figure 5 shows the metamodel of classes. *HaxeClass* is related by composition with the *HaxeField* metaclass via the *HaxeFields* relation which is inherited from *HaxeFieldContainer*, containing at once, all the elements that define the structure of the class, such as methods, constructors, attributes and properties. From *HaxeFields,* relationships *Haxe Constructors, Haxe Operations* and *Attribute* are derived, getting of them all constructors, operations and attributes of a particular class or interface. Inheritance relations between classes and interfaces were modeled using the *implementation* and *generalization* relations. HaXe allows classes to be parameterized using a similar mechanism to other programming languages like C ++ or Java.

Figure 3. HaXe metamodel: Metaclass diagram of types

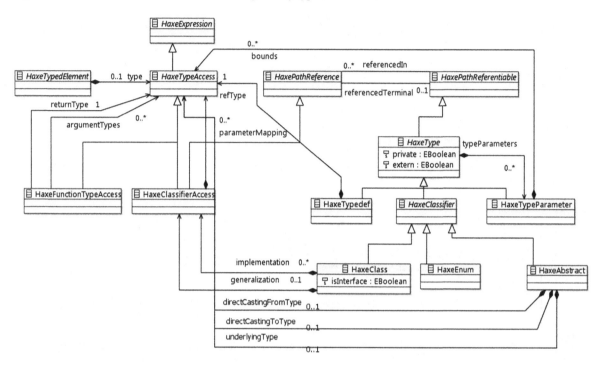

Figure 4. Haxe Metamodel: Classes and Interfaces

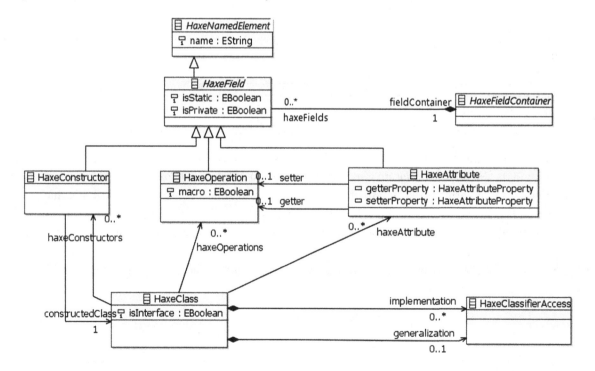

Figure 5. Haxe Metamodel: Class

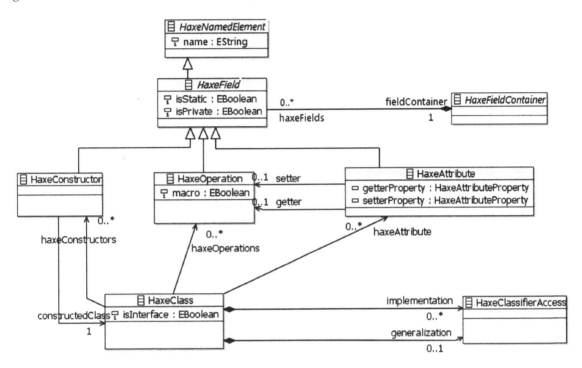

The full Haxe metamodel can be found in (Diaz Bilotto, 2015). Next, we partially show the text of HaXe metamodel in OCLinEcore..

```
package haxe: _'org.eclipse.emf.ecore.haxe' = 'http://haxe.unicen.edu.ar'
{enum HaxeTarget { serializable }
        {               literal neko;
            literal cpp;
            literal java;
            literal flash;
            literal cs;
            literal js;
        }
        class HaxeModel
        {       documentation 'root class for all haxe models';
            attribute name: String[1] { id }
            {
                    documentation 'name of the model';
            }
            attribute sourceFolder: String = 'src'
            {
                    documentation 'folder where haxe sources are stored';
            }
```

```
            attribute targetFolder: String = 'out'
            {
               documentation 'folder name used by haxe to put all the gen-
erated stuff';
            }
            attribute target: HaxeTarget
            {
                    documentation 'compilation target used in this model';
            }
            property mainClass: HaxeClass[1]
            {
                    documentation 'reference to the main class, it must
contain a static                                   main ';
            }
            property elements: HaxePathReferentiable[*] { composes unique
}
            {
                    documentation 'elements contained in the model';
            }
            property referenced: HaxePathReferentiable[*] { composes
unique }
            {
                    documentation 'referenced items in the model, not
generated but                                  used';
            }
            property haxeModules: HaxeModule[*] { composes }
            {
                    documentation 'physical modules relationship';
            }
            invariant sourceFolderNotEmpty: sourceFolder.size() > 0;
            invariant targetFolderNotEmpty: targetFolder.size() > 0;
            invariant mainClassHasMainMethod: not (mainClass.haxeOpera-
tions
                    ->select(x: HaxeOperation | (x.name.matches('main')
and x.isStatic                         and x.formalParameters
                •       ->isEmpty()))
                    ->isEmpty());
            invariant nameNotEmpty: name.size() > 0;
            invariant nameNotNull: name <> null;
        }
        abstract class HaxeModelElement
        {
            documentation 'base class for all models elements';
        }
```

```
abstract class HaxeASTNode extends HaxeModelElement
{
        documentation 'base class for haxe AST elements (haxe Class-
es,                             Expressions, etc.)';
        property comments: HaxeComment[*] { ordered composes }
        {
                documentation 'relationship used to contain comments';
        }
}
abstract class HaxeNamedElement extends HaxeASTNode
{
        documentation 'class used in named elements';
        attribute name: String
        {
                documentation 'element name';
        }
        invariant nameNotEmpty: name.size() > 0;
}...
```

FROM JAVA TO HAXE

Transformations are crucial in MDA and allow the mapping between models. QVT (Query/View/ Transformation) is the OMG standard language to express transformations on MOF models (QVT, 2011). Few CASE tools support QVT or at least, any of the QVT languages such as Relational QVT and Operational QVT. It is worth considering that QVT declarative is in its "incubation" phase and only provides editing capabilities.

The MMT (Model-to-Model Transformation) Eclipse project is a subproject of the top-level Eclipse Modeling Project that provides a framework for model-to-model transformation languages (MMT, 2015). Transformation engines plugged into the Eclipse Modeling infrastructure allow executing transformations. In this context, ATL was defined. It is a model transformation language and a toolkit that provides ways to produce a set of target models from a set of source models. To date, ATL is the most used transformation language due to its maturity degree (van Amstel et al., 2011).

Transformations are defined at metamodel level. In our approach, transformations are performed between the source metamodel (Java) and the target metamodel (HaXe). We express the transformations in the transformation language ATL. We use the native compiler of ATL and the EMF Transformation Virtual Machine (EMFTVM) that is a runtime engine for the ATL (Wagelaar, 2011) (Wagelaar et al, 2011). A detailed description of ATL may be found at (Jouault et al., 2008).

The main transformations are *java2haxe, javaHaxeRefactoring* and *haxeImports*. The *java2haxe* transformation is central and transforms syntactic elements between the Java metamodel and the Haxe metamodel. The *javaHaxeRefactoring* transformation reorganizes and modifies the syntactic elements in such a way to adapt own behavior of the Java language. The *haxeImports* performs changes in the imports of the own packages of the Java framework, which require a specific treatment. In this transformation, import clauses are added for items belonging to the package java.lang which are recognized implicitly by the framework as dependencies in Java but need to be explicit in HaXe classes.

ATL mainly focuses on the model-to-model transformations, which can be specified by means of ATL modules. An ATL module is composed of the following elements:

- A header section that defines the names of the transformation module and the variables of the source and target metamodels.
- An optional import section that enables to import some existing ATL libraries
- A set of helpers that can be used to define variables and functions.
- A set of rules that defines how source model elements are matched and navigated to create and initialize the elements of the target models

In the following, the *java2haxe* transformation is partially shown. A detail description of the ATL transformations may be found at (Diaz Bilotto, 2015)

```
module java2haxe;
create OUT: haxe from IN: java;
helper context java!BodyDeclaration def: isMainMethod(): Boolean =
if (self.modifier -> oclIsUndefined() or self.name -> oclIsUndefined())
then false else self.name -> matches('main') and self.modifier.static endif;
helper context java!Model def: hasMainClass(): Boolean =
java!ClassDeclaration.allInstances() -> select(x | x.isMainClass()) -> isEmp-
ty();
- simple but ... it doesn't support multiple mains ...
helper context java!Model def: chooseMainClass(): java!ClassDeclaration =
java!ClassDeclaration.allInstances() -> select(x | x.isMainClass()) -> first();
helper context java!ClassDeclaration def: isMainClass(): Boolean =
self.bodyDeclarations -> exists(x | x.isMainMethod());
helper context java!BodyDeclaration def: isStaticBody(): Boolean =
if (self.modifier.oclIsUndefined()) then false else self.modifier.static en-
dif;
helper context java!BodyDeclaration def: isAbstract(): Boolean =
if (self.modifier.oclIsUndefined()) then false else self.modifier.inheritance
= #"abstract" endif;
helper context java!AbstractTypeDeclaration def: noConstructor(): Boolean =
if (self.bodyDeclarations -> oclIsUndefined())
then true
else if (self.bodyDeclarations -> isEmpty())
        then true
        else self.bodyDeclarations -> select(x | x.oclIsKindOf(java!Constructo
rDeclaration)) -> isEmpty()
        endif
endif;
helper context java!BodyDeclaration def: sanitizedBodyDeclarations():
```

```
Sequence(java!BodyDeclarations) = self.bodyDeclarations -> reject(x | x.oclIsK
indOf(java!AbstractTypeDeclaration) or
x.oclIsKindOf(java!FieldDeclaration));
helper context java!AbstractTypeDeclaration def: multipleConstructor(): Bool-
ean =
if (self.noConstructor())
then false
else self.bodyDeclarations -> select(x | x.oclIsTypeOf(java!ConstructorDeclara
tion))-> size() > 1
endif;
helper context java!AbstractTypeDeclaration def: isInnerClass(): Boolean =
if (self.abstractTypeDeclaration -> oclIsUndefined()) then false else true en-
dif;
helper context java!ASTNode def: container(): java!AbstractMethodDeclaration =
if (self.refImmediateComposite()->oclIsKindOf(java!AbstractMethodDeclaration))
then self.refImmediateComposite() else self.refImmediateComposite().contain-
er()
endif;
…
rule model {
from javaModel: java!Model
to  haxeModel: haxe!HaxeModel (
name <- javaModel.name,
elements <- javaModel.ownedElements,
referenced <- javaModel.orphanTypes -> select(x | x.usagesInTypeAccess ->
notEmpty() and x.oclIsKindOf(java!Type) and (not x.
oclIsTypeOf(java!ParameterizedType)) and (not x.
oclIsTypeOf(java!WildCardType))) -> collect(x | thisModule.Type(x))-> asSet(),
haxeModules <- javaModel.compilationUnits,mainClass <- javaModel.chooseMain-
Class())
do {thisModule.targetModel <- haxeModel;}}
abstract rule ASTNode {
from  s: java!ASTNode
to t: haxe!HaxeASTNode (comments <- s.comments)}
abstract rule namedElement extends ASTNode{
from s: java!NamedElement
to t: haxe!HaxeNamedElement (
name <- s.name)}
rule packages extends namedElement {
from s: java!Package
to t: haxe!HaxePackage (
parentReference <- s.package,
childrenReferences <- s.ownedPackages)}
abstract rule namedElement extends ASTNode{
```

```
from s: java!NamedElement
to t: haxe!HaxeNamedElement (
name <- s.name)}
rule packages extends namedElement {
from s: java!Package
to t: haxe!HaxePackage (
parentReference <- s.package,
childrenReferences <- s.ownedPackages)}
abstract rule typeDeclaration extends namedElement {
from s: java!AbstractTypeDeclaration
to t: haxe!HaxeType (
commentsAfterDeclaration <- s.commentsAfterBody,
commentsBeforeDeclaration <- s.commentsBeforeBody,
parentReference <- s.package)}
rule enum extends typeDeclaration
{from s: java!EnumDeclaration (s.abstractTypeDeclaration -> oclIsUndefined())
to t: haxe!HaxeEnum (haxeFields <- s.enumConstants)}
...
```

A CASE STUDY

We describe a semi-automated process in which the developer has some interventions due to the following facts:

- The excessive complexity of the *java2haxe* model-to-model transformations;
- The lack of all the functionality available in Java platform in the HaXe platform;
- The difficulty to solve quality attributes requirements problem, such as;
- Performance or usability, in an automated way.

Next, we describe a simple case study, "The set of Mandelbrot" (Sedgewick & Wayne, 2008) that was migrated from Java to HaXe. The migration required modifications to both the original application and the application transformed to achieve compile and run the application in a mobile environment. The migration process includes all steps described in Figure 1.

The original application consists of a main class, called *Mandelbrot* that is responsible for the calculation of "the set of Mandelbrot" and serves as entry point for the application (see Appendix 1). It also includes several classes that collaborate in the realization of the task. The class *Mandelbrot* is responsible for generating the set and displaying it as image. To perform these tasks, the class depends on other two, called *Picture* and *Complex*, the first is used as a data type that supports the manipulating of digital images using AWT and Swing. The second class is a data type used to model complex number with their respective operations. To improve the structure and allow migration, different refactorings must be done (see Appendix 2).

The migration process performs the following tasks:

1. Recover a model from the refactored application
2. Apply the transformations *java2haxe, javaHaxeRefactoring* and *javaImports* on the model generates above.
3. Generate the source files from the code generator
4. Modify the generated code adapting it to mobile platforms.

Although the generated code is syntactically correct, it does not compile due to refers to proprietary technologies of Java such as Swing and AWT. To run on mobile environments, we use OpenFL and HaxeUI (that is an open source, multi-platform application-centric user interface framework designed for HaXe and OpenFL). After completing the implementation of the classes dependent of OpenFL or HaxeUI, the different artifacts involved in the project are built using Lime. Lime is a flexible, lightweight layer for Haxe cross-platform developers that supports native, Flash and HTML5 targets with unified support for Windowing, Input, Events, Audio, Render contexts, Network Access and Assets. The project runs on multiple platforms, generating the corresponding executable using the default options for each of them. Appendix partially depicts the result of the different steps of the process: the Java source code, the refactored Java source code, the transformed source code and the migrated code (in HaXe) (http:// haxe.org).

Discussion

Our work shows the viability of semi-automatic migration processes based on MDD (MDA in particular). Due the fact that the objective of the migration is not only "compile" an application in a mobile platform but also to create a modified version of the application using quality criteria, the process can not be fully automated.

Next, we informally compare the model-driven migration process with brute-force re-development migration.

A crucial limitation of our approach is to require preliminary activities that requires time and cost, for instance we need to define metamodels if they do not exist. It is assumed that using a brute-force redevelopment, developers do not need training to write model transformations, however the programming interfaces of these languages generally restrict the kind of transformation that can be performed. In addition, general-purpose languages do not provide a sufficient level of abstraction to specify them. Changes will be difficult to write and understand and, therefore their maintenance is hard.

On the contrary, model driven transformations are expressed in specialized languages for that purpose. Model transformations allow developers to concentrate on conceptual aspects of the relations between models and then to delegate the production of the transformation rules. We can consider that the generation of models by model transformations in ATL, aims to generate models "Correctness-by-Construction" with respect to metamodel specifications.

Even with these issues, there is still activities done by hand and the migrated application has to be tested. A general limitation on both processes is the cost of testing due to the fact these activities in general are handled manually. In the context of model driven approaches there is a need to reduce the cost of testing by defining semiautomatic process based on metamodels.

Beyond the previous issues, we consider that mobile developers need frequently adapt software components and applications developed in Java or C. Then, model driven migration processes could be reused and the cost of preliminary activities recovered.

CONCLUSION AND FUTURE RESEARCH DIRECTIONS

This chapter proposes an approach for adapting object-oriented software in Java to mobile platforms. A migration process, based on the integration of MDA and the HaXe platform, has been proposed and described. The main contributions of our approach are the definition of a metamodel for HaXe, the specification of a metamodel transformation between a source Java metamodel and a target Haxe metamodel, and a generic and extensible migration process for the implementation of cross-platform, multi-device mobile applications from Java code.

The proposal was validated in the open source application platform Eclipse considering that some of its tools and run-time environments are aligned with MDA standards. We believe that our approach provides benefits with respect to processes based only on traditional migration techniques. The migration from Java to mobile platforms can be performed semi-automatically, within the limits of the tools. It was possible to transform applications into mobile ones without rewriting them completely.

The migration process can be divided in smaller steps focusing in specific activities, and be automated thanks to the chaining of model transformations. All the involved artifacts can be reused, modified for evolution purposes or extended for other purposes.

The metamodel approach enables covering different levels of abstraction and satisfying several degrees of detail depending on the needs of the migration and is the key for interoperability. All artifacts can be actually represented as models so that there is no information loss during the migration process.

Model transformations allow developers to concentrate on the conceptual aspects of the relations between models and delegate the implementation of the transformation.

The definition of an Ecore metamodel for HaXe is the main contribution to the MDA process in general. It allows us to express model-to-model transformations in a transformation language such as ATL. In this chapter we described the transformation between Java and HaXe but the process can be applied to other languages, such as C, C ++ and C#, if the Ecore metamodel for them is defined.

We plan to externalize the HaXe metamodel to facilitate its reuso in other projects (which are not necessarily related to migration process). As future work, we propose to integrate the HaXe metamodel with the MoDisco plugin, specifically as a reverse engineering technology. Another interesting aspect would be to consider metrics by using the metamodel SMM provided by MoDisco to evaluate the quality of the generated application (SMM, 2015).

We plan to continue testing, extending and improving the process in the context of other technological spaces. Our approach has already shown to work on real applications of medium size. More work to improve the performance when tackling large applications can complete our results. We foresee to apply our approach in real industrial projects.

REFERENCES

Acceleo. (2015). *Obeo. Acceleo Generator.* Retrieved April 15, 2015, from http://www.eclipse.org/acceleo/

ADM. (2015). *Architecture-driven modernization task force.* Retrieved April 15, 2015, from http://www.adm.org

Améndola, F., & Favre, L. (2013). Adapting CRM systems for mobile platforms: An MDA perspective. In *Proceedings of the 2013 14th ACIS International Conference on Software Engineering, Articial Intelligence, Networking and Parallel/Distributed Computing* (SNPD´13) (pp. 323-328), Los Alamitos: IEEE Computer Society. doi:10.1109/SNPD.2013.25

ASTM. (2011). *OMG Architecture-driven Modernization: Abstract Syntax Tree Metamodel (ASTM).* Retrieved April 15, 2015, from http://www.omg.org/spec/ASTM

Bowen, J., & Hinze, A. (2011). Supporting mobile application development with model-driven emulation. *Journal of the ECEASST, 45,* 1–5.

Brambilla, M., Cabot, J., & Wimmer, M. (2012). *Model-Driven Software Enginneering in Practice, Synthesis Lectures on Software Engineering.* Morgan & Claypool Publishers.

Braun, P., & Eckhaus, R. (2008). Experiences on model-driven software development for mobile applications. In *Proceedings of Engineering of Computer-Based Systems, IEEE International Conference and Workshop on the Engineering of computer Base Systems* (pp. 490-493), Los Alamitos: IEEE Computer Society. doi:10.1109/ECBS.2008.50

Bruneliere, H., Cabot, J., Dupé, G., & Madiot, F. (2014). MoDisco: A Model Driven Reverse Engineering Framework. *Information and Software Technology, 56*(8), 1012–1032. doi:10.1016/j.infsof.2014.04.007

Cannasse, N. (2014). *HaXe. Too Good to be True?* GameDuell Tech Talk. Retrieved April 15, 2015, from http://www.techtalk-berlin.de/news/read/nicolas-cannasse-introducing-haxe/

CASE MDA. (2015). *Committed companies and their products.* Retrieved April 15, 2015, from www.omg.org/mda/committed-products.htm

Dasnois, B. (2011). *HaXe 2 Beginner's Guide.* Packt Publishing.

Dehlinger, J., & Dixon, J. (2011). Mobile application software engineering: Challenges and research directions. In *Proceedings of the Workshop on Mobile Software Engineering* (pp. 29-32). Berlin: Springer-Verlag.

Diaz Bilotto, P. (2015). *Software development for mobile applications through an integration of MDA an HAXE.* (Undergraduate thesis). Computer Science Department, Universidad Nacional del Centro de la Provincia de Buenos Aires, Argentina.

Dunkel, J., & Bruns, R. (2007). Model-driven architecture for mobile applications. In Business Information Systems (LNCS), (vol. 4439, pp. 464-477). Berlin: Springer-Verlag. doi:10.1007/978-3-540-72035-5_36

EMF. (2015). *Eclipse Modeling Framework (EMF).* Retrieved April 15, 2015 from http://www.eclipse.org/modeling/emf/

Favre, L. (2010). *Model Driven Architecture for Revese Engineering Technologies: Strategic Directions and System Evolution.* Hershey, PA: IGI Global. doi:10.4018/978-1-61520-649-0

Gamma, E., Helm, R., Johnson, R., & Vlissides, J. (1994). *Design Patterns: Elements of Reusable Object-Oriented Software.* Pearson Education.

Jouault, F., Allilaire, F., Bézivin, J., & Kurtev, I (2008). ATL: A model transformation tool. *Science of Computer Programming, 72*(1), 31-39.

Jouault, F., Allilaire, F., Bézivin, J., Kurtev, I., & Valduriez, P. (2006) ATL: a QVT-like transformation language. In *Companion to the 21st ACM SIGPLAN Symposium on Object-oriented programming systems, languages, and applications* OOPSLA '06 (pp. 719-720). New York: ACM Press. doi:10.1145/1176617.1176691

Jouault, F., & Kurtev, I. (2005). Transforming models with ATL. In *Satellite Events at the MoDELS 2005 Conference* (LNCS), (vol. 3844, pp. 128-138). Berlin: Springer Verlag. doi:10.1007/11663430_14

KDM. (2011). *Architecture-Driven Modernization: Knowledge Discovery MetaModel (KDM), versión 1.3.* Retrieved April 15, 2015, from http://www.omg.org/

Kim, H. K. (2008). Frameworks of process improvement for mobile applications. *Engineering Letters, 16*(4), 550-555.

Kramer, D., Clark, T., & Oussena, S. (2010). MobDSL: A domain specific language for multiple mobile platform deployment. In *Networked Embedded Systems for Enterprise Applications (NESEA), 2010 IEEE International Conference* (pp. 1-7), Los Alamitos: IEEE Press. doi:10.1109/NESEA.2010.5678062

Lettner, M., Tschernuth, M., & Mayrhofer, R. (2012). Mobile platform architecture review: Android, Iphone, Qt. In Computer Aided Systems Theory EUROCAST 2011 (LNCS), (vol. 6928, pp. 544-551). Berlin: Springer-Verlag.

MMT. (2015). *Model-to-Model Transformation. Eclipse Modeling Framework.* Retrieved April 15, 2015, from https://www.eclipse.org/mmt/

MoDisco. (2012). *Model discovery.* Retrieved April 15, 2015 from http://www.eclipse.org/MoDisco

MOF. (2006). *OMG Meta Object Facility (MOF) Core specification version 2.0.* OMG Document Number:formal/formal/2006-01-01. Retrieved April 15, 2015 from http://www.omg.org/spec/MOF/2.0

MOF. (2008). *OMG. Meta object facility (MOF) 2.0 Query/View/Transformation Specification.* Retrieved April 15, 2015 from http://www.omg.org/spec/MOF/2.0

MOF. (2011). *OMG Meta Object Facility (MOF) core specification version 2.4.1.* OMG Document Number:formal/2011-08-07. Retrieved April 15, 2015 from http://www.omg.org/spec/MOF/2.4.1

MOFM2T. (2008). *MOF Model to Text Transformation Language, Version 1.0.* Retrieved April 15, 2015, from http://www.omg.org/spec/MOFM2T/1.0/

OCL. (2014). *OMG Object constraint language (OCL), version 2.4.* Retrieved April 15, 2015, from http://www.omg.org/spec/OCL/2.4

OCLinEcore. (2015) *OCLinEcore Editor*. Retrieved April 15, 2015, from http://wiki.eclipse.org/MDT/OCLinEcore

OMG MDA. (2014). *MDA guide version rev. 2.0 OMG Document ormsc/2014-06-01*. Retrieved 15 April, 2015, from http://www.omg.org/cgi-bin/doc?ormsc/14-06-01

Pérez Castillo, R., García Rodriguez, I., Gómez Cornejo, R., Fernández Ropero, M., & Piattini, M. (2013). ANDRIU. A Technique for Migrating Graphical User Interfaces to Android. In *Proceedings of The 25th International Conference on Software Engineering and Knowledge Engineering (SEKE 2013)* (pp. 516-519) Boston: Knowledge Systems Institute.

QVT. (2012). *QVT: MOF 2.0 query, view, transformation:Version 1.1*. OMG Document Number: formal/2011-01-01. Retrieved April 15, 2015 from http://www.omg.org/spec/QVT/1.1/SMM

Sedgewick, R., & Wayne, K. (2008). *Introduction to programming in Java: An interdisciplinary approach*. Boston: Addison Wesley, Pearson.

SMM. (2015). *OMG Software Metrics Meta-model version 1.0*. Retrieved April 15, 2015 from http://www.omg.org/spec/SMM/1.0

Steinberg, D., Budinsky, F., Paternostro, M., & Merks, E. (2009). EMF: Eclipse Modeling Framework (2nd ed.). Addison-Wesley.

Thompson, C., Schmidt, D., Turner, H., & White, J. (2011). Analyzing Mobile Application Software Power Consumption via Model-Driven Engineering. *Proceedings of PECCS, 2011*, 101–113.

Van Amstel, M., Bosems, S., Kurtev, I., & Pires, L. F. (2011). Performance in model transformations: experiments with ATL and QVT. In *Proceedings of the 4th international conference on Theory and practice of model transformations* (ICMT' 11) (LNCS), (vol. 6707, pp. 198-212). Berlin: Springer-Verlag. doi:10.1007/978-3-642-21732-6_14

Wagelaar, D. (2011). A revised semantics for rule inheritance and module superimposit-ion in ATL. In *Proceedings of the 3rd International Workshop on Model Transformation with ATL (MtATL11)* (pp. 62-74).

Wagelaar, D., Tisi, M., Cabot, J., & Jouault, F. (2011). Towards a general composition semantics for rule-based model transformation. In *Proceedings of the 14th International Conference on Model Driven Engineering Languages and Systems, MODELS 2011 Model Driven Engineering Languages and Systems* (LNCS), (vol. 6981, pp. 623-637). Berlin: Springer-Verlag. doi:10.1007/978-3-642-24485-8_46

Wasserman, A. I. (2010). Software engineering issues for mobile application development. In *Proceedings of the FSE/SDP workshop on Future of software engineering research* (FoSER '10), (pp. 397-400). New York, NY: ACM. doi:10.1145/1882362.1882443

XMI. (2011). *OMG MOF 2 XMI mapping SpecificationOMG*. Document Number: formal/ 2011-08-09. Retrieved April 15, 2015 from http://www.omg.org/spec/XMI/2.4.1

KEY TERMS AND DEFINITIONS

Acceleo: A code generator using EMF models in input. It is an implementation of the MOFM2T standard, from OMG for performing model-to-text transformation.

ATL (Atlas Transformation Language): A model transformation language and toolkit developed on top of the Eclipse platform that provides ways to produce target models from source models.

Eclipse Modeling Framework (EMF): An Eclipse-based modeling framework and code generation facility for building tools and other applications based on a structured data model.

Ecore Metamodel: The de facto reference implementation of EMOF (Essential Meta-Object Facility), a subset of MOF. It is the core metamodel of EMF.

HaXe: An open source toolkit based on a modern, high level, strictly typed programming language, a cross-compiler, a complete cross-platform standard library and ways to access each platform's native capabilities.

Metamodeling: The process of generating a "model of models"; the essence of Model Driven Development approaches.

Meta-Object Facility (MOF): A meta-metamodel from the Object Management Group (OMG) that defines a common way for capturing the diversity of modeling standards and interchange constructs involved in MDA.

Mobile Technology: The technology used for cellular communication.

Model Driven Architecture (MDA): An initiative of the Object Management Group (OMG) for the development of software systems based on the separation of business and application logic from underlying platform technologies. It is an evolving conceptual architecture to achieve cohesive model-driven technology specifications.

MoDisco: A generic, extensible and global framework to develop model-driven reverse engineering tools to support use-cases of existing software modernization.

Software Migration: The process of moving from the use of one operating environment to another operating environment that is, in most cases, thought to be a better.

APPENDIX

1. JAVA Source Code

```
/*************************************************************************
 *  Compilation:  javac Mandelbrot.java
 *  Execution:    java Mandelbrot xc yc size
 *  Dependencies: StdDraw.java
 *
 *  Plots the size-by-size region of the Mandelbrot set, centered on (xc, yc)
 *
 *  % java Mandelbrot -.5 0 2
 *
 *************************************************************************/
import java.awt.Color;
public class Mandelbrot {
    // return number of iterations to check if c = a + ib is in Mandelbrot set
    public static int mand(Complex z0, int max) {
        Complex z = z0;
        for (int t = 0; t < max; t++) {
            if (z.abs() > 2.0) return t;
            z = z.times(z).plus(z0);
        }
        return max;
    }
    public static void main(String[] args)  {
        double xc   = Double.parseDouble(args[0]);
        double yc   = Double.parseDouble(args[1]);
        double size = Double.parseDouble(args[2]);
        int N   = 512;   // create N-by-N image
        int max = 255;   // maximum number of iterations
        Picture pic = new Picture(N, N);
        for (int i = 0; i < N; i++) {
            for (int j = 0; j < N; j++) {
                double x0 = xc - size/2 + size*i/N;
                double y0 = yc - size/2 + size*j/N;
                Complex z0 = new Complex(x0, y0);
                int gray = max - mand(z0, max);
                Color color = new Color(gray, gray, gray);
                pic.set(i, N-1-j, color);
            }
        }
        pic.show();
    }
}
```

2. Refactored Java Source Code

```java
package ar.edu.unicen.exa.haxe.mandelbrot;
/*****************************************************************************
 * Compilation: javac Mandelbrot.java Execution: java Mandelbrot xc yc size
 * Dependencies: StdDraw.java
 *
 * Plots the size-by-size region of the Mandelbrot set, centered on (xc, yc)
 *
 * % java Mandelbrot -.5 0 2
 * *************************************************************************/
public class Mandelbrot {
        private  BasePicture pic;
        private  double xc;
        private  double yc;
        private  double size;
        private  int max;
        private  int n;

        public Mandelbrot() {
                this(-.5, 0, 2,255,512);
          }

         public Mandelbrot(double xc,double yc,double size,int max, int n)
{
                this.xc = xc ;
                this.yc = yc;
                this.size = size;
                this.n = n;
                this.max = max;
                pic = new Picture(n, n);
           }

         public Mandelbrot(double xc,double yc,double size,in
t                                 max,BasePicture pic) throws IllegalImag-
eSize {
                if (pic.getHeight() != pic.getWidth()) throw new
IllegalImageSize();

                this.xc = xc ;
                this.yc = yc;
                this.size = size;
```

```
                    this.n = pic.getWidth();
                    this.max = max;
                    this.pic = pic;
            }
            // return number of iterations to check if c = a + ib is in Mandelbrot
set
            public static int mand(Complex z0, int max) {
                    Complex z = z0;
                    for (int t = 0; t < max; t++) {
                            if (z.abs() > 2.0)
                                    return t;
                            z = z.times(z).plus(z0);
                    }
                    return max;
            }
            public static void main(String[] args) {
                    new Mandelbrot(.1015,-.633,0.01,255,1024).calculate();
            }
            public void calculate() {

                    for (int i = 0; i < n; i++) {
                       for (int j = 0; j < n; j++) {
                          double x0 = xc - size / 2 + size * i / n;
                          double y0 = yc - size / 2 + size * j / n;
                          Complex z0 = new Complex(x0, y0);
                          int gray = this.max - mand(z0, max);
                          pic.setRGB(i, this.n - 1 - j, gray, gray, gray);
                             }
                       }
                    pic.show();
            }
    }
```

3. Transformed Source Code

```
package ar.edu.unicen.exa.haxe.mandelbrot;
class Mandelbrot
{
        public static function new_Mandelbrot_7 (): Mandelbrot {
                var tmp: Mandelbrot = new Mandelbrot();
                tmp.ctor_Mandelbrot_7();
                return tmp;
        }
```

```
        public static function new_Mandelbrot_8 (xc: Float, yc: Float, size:
Float,              max: Int, n: Int): Mandelbrot {
            var tmp: Mandelbrot = new Mandelbrot();
            tmp.ctor_Mandelbrot_8(xc, yc, size, max, n);
            return tmp;
        }
        public static function new_Mandelbrot_9 (xc: Float, yc: Float, size:
Float, max: Int,        pic: BasePicture): Mandelbrot {
            var tmp: Mandelbrot = new Mandelbrot();
            tmp.ctor_Mandelbrot_9(xc, yc, size, max, pic);
            return tmp;
        }
        public static function mand (z0: Complex, max: Int): Int {
            var z: Complex = z0;
            {
                var t: Int = 0;
                while (t < max)
                {
                    {
                            if (z.abs() > 2.0)
                            return t;

                            z = z.times(z).plus(z0);
                    }
                    t++;
                }
            };
            return max;
        }
        public static function mainMethod (args: Array<String>): Void {
            Mandelbrot.new_Mandelbrot_8(.1015, -.633, 0.01, 255, 1024).
calculate();
        }
        public function calculate (): Void {
            {
                var i: Int = 0;
                    while (i < n)
                {
                    {
                        {
                                var j: Int = 0;
                                while (j < n)
                                {
```

```
                                                 {
                                      var x0: Float = xc - size /
2 + size * i / n;

                                      var y0: Float = yc - size /
2 + size * j / n;

Complex(x0, y0);                      var z0: Complex = new

mand(z0, max);                        var gray: Int = this.max -

                                      pic.setRGB(i, this.n - 1 -
j, gray, gray, gray);

                                             }
                                             j++;
                                      }
                                 };
                              }
                              i++;
                           }
                  };
                  pic.show();
        }
        function new ()
        {
        }
        function ctor_Mandelbrot_7 () {
        }
        function ctor_Mandelbrot_8 (xc: Float, yc: Float, size: Float, max:
Int, n:         Int) {
                this.xc = xc;
                this.yc = yc;
                this.size = size;
                this.n = n;
                this.max = max;
                pic = Picture.new_Picture_6(n, n);
        }
        function ctor_Mandelbrot_9 (xc: Float, yc: Float, size: Float, max:
Int, pic:         BasePicture) {
                        if (pic.get_height() != pic.get_width())
                        throw new IllegalImageSize() ;

                    this.xc = xc;
                this.yc = yc;
                this.size = size;
```

```
                        this.n = pic.get_width();
                        this.max = max;
                        this.pic = pic;
                }
        public static function main (): Void {
                mainMethod(Sys.args());
        }
        var pic:BasePicture;
        var xc:Float;
        var yc:Float;
        var size:Float;
        var max:Int;
        var n: Int;
}
```

4. Migrated Source Code

Source code of the class Mandelbrot translated into HaXe after being modified to be executed on OpenFL and HaXeU

```
class Mandelbrot
{
   public static function new_Mandelbrot_9 (xc: Float, yc: Float, size: Float,
max: Int,
        pic: BasePicture): Mandelbrot {
                var tmp: Mandelbrot = new Mandelbrot();
                tmp.ctor_Mandelbrot_9(xc, yc, size, max, pic);
                return tmp;
   }
   public static function mand (z0: Complex, max: Int): Int {
        var z: Complex = z0;
        {
           var t: Int = 0;
           while (t < max)
           {
              {
                 if (z.abs() > 2.0)
                 return t;

                 z = z.times(z).plus(z0);
              }
              t++;
           }
        };
```

```
        return max;
    }
    public function calculate (): Void {
        {
            var i: Int = 0;
            while (i < this.n)
            {
                {
                    {
                        var j: Int = 0;
                        while (j < this.n)
                        {
                            {
                                var x0: Float = this.xc - this.size / 2 + this.size *
i / this.n;
                                var y0: Float = this.yc - this.size / 2 + this.size *
j / this.n;
                                var z0: Complex = new Complex(x0, y0);
                                var gray: Int = this.max - mand(z0, this.max);
                                pic.setRGB(i, this.n - 1 - j, gray, gray, gray);
                            }
                            j++;
                        }
                    }
                };
            }
            i++;
        }
    };
    pic.show();
    }
    function new ()
    {
    }
    function ctor_Mandelbrot_9 (xc: Float, yc: Float, size: Float, max: Int,
pic: BasePicture) {
        if (pic.getHeight() != pic.getWidth())
        throw new IllegalImageSize() ;
        this.xc = xc;
        this.yc = yc;
        this.size = size;
        this.n = pic.getWidth();
        this.max = max;
        this.pic = pic;}
```

```
    public function getPic(): BasePicture
    {
        return pic;
    }
    public var pic:BasePicture;
    public var xc:Float;
    public var yc:Float;
    public var size:Float;
    public var max:Int;
    public var n:Int;
}
```

Chapter 14
Android Executable Modeling:
Beyond Android Programming

Olivier Le Goaer
University of Pau, France

Franck Barbier
University of Pau, France

Eric Cariou
University of Pau, France

ABSTRACT

Within the model-driven engineering field, model execution consists in interpreting the model through a dedicated execution engine instead of executing a code based on, or generated from, the model. The class of modeling languages endowed with such executability is called i-DSML (interpreted Domain-Specific Modeling Language). This is an important development shift because a modeling effort seamlessly substitutes to a programming effort. This alternative way for building increasingly complex software is particularly beneficial to the mobile applications market where fast development and agility are recognized as key factors of success. This chapter illustrates how parts of an Android mobApp can be modeled and executed by leveraging a well-known i-DSML, namely UML 2 State Machine Diagrams and the PauWare engine thereof. Beyond this specific case, the proposed installation of PauWare on Android OS sets up the foundation for a whole range of mobApps, provided that they are modeled with the Statecharts formalism.

INTRODUCTION

Among the manifold forms taken by abstraction, modeling has proved its efficiency for handling complexity of software development, contrasting with classical programming all focused on source code. Indeed, models abstract away details to concentrate on particular, high-level, viewpoints on the system to be built. As such, they offer good reasoning supports to designers. Models are so powerful that they have earned their place in the software engineering through a dedicated sub field called Model-Driven

DOI: 10.4018/978-1-4666-9916-8.ch014

Copyright © 2016, IGI Global. Copying or distributing in print or electronic forms without written permission of IGI Global is prohibited.

Engineering (MDE). After having been intensively used as contemplative assets until the mid 2000, models have been turned into productive assets, relying on automated transformation chains ending predominately to source code. It is worthwhile mentioning that this evolution owes much to the OMG's MDA initiative (Miller *et al.*, 2003). A more recent trend is to see a model as an end in itself by directly executing it (Lehmann *et al.*, 2010 and Combemale *et al.*, 2012). The analogy could be now that of an "animated" or "enacted" blueprint; it may serve as a way of simulation of course, but also as a full-fledged executable system so that the implementation stage is totally skipped. This vision shift from static (albeit productive) model to dynamic model tends to abolish the boundaries between modeling and programming; its slogan might be "*What you model is what you get*" (WYMIWYG).

The entirely model-centered and hence fast development allowed by interpretable models is particularly interesting when focusing on tiny devices or on embedded software like Smart-* (Phones, Watches, Glasses, TVs…) equipment. Indeed, these applications are characterized by a high time-to-market pressure and a rapid fluctuation of user's requirements, while they run on top of fast-paced platforms. This situation is going to explode with the future Internet of Things (IoT), and the arrival of a multitude of connected objects. Because a growing number of these systems are running with Android, we choose this operating system to put into practice our ideas.

This chapter is organized as follows: we first provide an overview on what is the recent i-DSML approach. Then, we focus on the Statecharts i-DSML and the PauWare engine and how to take advantage of it when building Android mobApps. Next, we exemplify on a toy mobApp that provides energy-saving assistance, and give all implementation details on a separate section. We also explain how it is possible to cope with changes once the mobApp is deployed. Finally, related works are discussed before we conclude.

i-DSML AT A GLANCE

It is worth recalling that modeling is all about abstraction. Modeling challenges programming in the sense that it requires different skills, neither more nor less valuable, just different. A smart software engineer makes routinely and fluently the round-trip between these two levels of abstraction.

While the models, as outputs of a modeling process, were often considered as contemplative artifacts before the 2000s (intended to be printed and pinned to wall, to be caricatured), the situation has deeply changed since: everyone is nowadays making a productive use of models. This shift has been logically accompanied with a "modeling liberation/emancipation" supported by the concept of domain-specific modeling languages (DSML) (Fowler, 2010): everyone was encouraged to use multiple modeling languages, for each particular aspects of software, not only relying on mainstream, general-purpose modeling languages (GPML). The productive usage of models written with a DSML requires executability, which is thereby no longer the exclusive attribute of programming languages. As noted by Mernik (Mernik *et al.*, 2005), model execution can be achieved in two ways:

- Compiled DSML: DSML constructs are translated to base language constructs and library calls. People are mostly talking about code generation when pointing at this approach;
- Interpreted DSML: DSML constructs are recognized and interpreted using an operational semantics processed by an execution engine. With this approach, no transformation takes place; the model is directly executable.

In fact, reaching executability from a reduced amount of information calls for a trick: In both case, the efforts alleviated through modeling are counterbalanced by the energy that have to be put either in the transformations to be written or in the execution engine to be developed, respectively. But nevertheless (a) these efforts are done only once so that (b) the subsequent required skills are then just a matter of modeling.

With interpreted domain-specific modeling languages (the term i-DSML is coined in Clarke *et al.*, 2013), the ability to run a model prior to its implementation is a time-saving and henceforth cost-saving approach for at least two reasons:

1. It becomes possible to detect and fix problems in the early stages of the software development cycle;
2. Ultimately the implementation stage may be skipped.

There is no universal model execution engine. Each DSML is associated with a dedicated execution engine (a kind of Virtual Machine or VM). Thus, one can find Petri Nets engine, BPMN engine, Statecharts engine and so on. Defining the precise class of models eligible to execution upon a VM is still controversial, but we can say that any DSML embodying an execution flow can be turned into an i-DSML from the moment its execution semantics is clearly defined and implemented into an engine. Every variation in the execution semantics, even minor one, may give rise to a new engine and, to a lesser extent, a new i-DSML version. This is the case for example when talking about Statecharts models, where two major semantics coexist: those from Harel and those from UML (Crane & Dingel, 2007). This simply means that there can be two distinct execution engines for a single i-DSML

BRINGING i-DSML TO ANDROID: THE CASE OF STATECHARTS

Statecharts provide an amply expressiveness making easy to foresee their potential when running directly on mobile devices. This potential is even quite obvious in the areas of ambient intelligence, ubiquitous computing and IoT.

As mentioned before, Statecharts are turned into an i-DSML since it comes with its dedicated execution engine. Here, we use the PauWare engine dedicated to UML 2 State Machine Diagrams and available on www.pauware.com.

Statecharts Formalism

Statecharts were introduced by David Harel in 1987 (Harel, 1987) as a formalism for visually modeling the behavior of reactive systems. With the introduction of UML 2.0 came the Rhapsody semantics (Harel & Kugler, 2004), which are more in tune with modeling software systems.

Statecharts are comprised of a set of states with transitions between them. Transition labels are in the form *e[c]/a*, where *e* is the event name, *[c]* is a guard condition (optional), and *a* is an action. Upon receiving event *e*, if there isa transition from the current state on *e* with *[c]* evaluating to true, then the transition is triggered, executing *a* and moving the Statechart to the target state. States can have *OnEntry* and *OnExit* blocks where more actions reside. The current state is considered a modal property of the Statechart. The semantics additionally allow for sub-states, inner and outer transitions, history states (when returning to a state with sub-states), and orthogonal components.

The event-based formalism of Statecharts is very flexible and hence a natural choice to model a large range of features when building software, whether targeting a mobile platform or not. One can use it to describe the user navigation between the screens, manage multimodal user interfaces, describe control flow of a program, cope with data exchange rules over a network, or even define some artificial intelligence (Dragert *et al.*, 2012). More generally, it serves at representing the successive modes of any relevant entity of the system.

It is interesting to notice that the Android platform itself manages internally its application components' lifecycle according to specific finite state machines. Likewise, a number of internal key services like telephony for example, are typically switching between different states (Dialing, Busy, Time-out, etc.). Power of modeling is also evidenced by the fact that the Android team is using Statecharts visual notation in the official documentation[1] because it knows that communicating with a model prior of showing abrupt code snippets is the most efficient way for training a large community of developers.

PauWare Engine and API

PauWare engine is a lightweight execution engine for state machines coded in Java that hence runs on the top of any Java-like VM (including Dalvik VM or the new Android Runtime). It is released for several platforms, depending on whether reflection capabilities are available like for Java SE APIs and Android APIs (java.lang.reflect) or missing like for Java ME. It can be imported in any Java-based project as a standalone library (JAR file).

PauWare can be viewed as a combination of three ingredients as schematized in *Figure 1*.

1. The regular way to describe a UML state machine in PauWare simply consists in writing raw Java code for instantiating states and to build the structure of the state machine by combining the states and adding between them transitions. Another way consists in inflating the code from serialized formats: either through a standard XMI file produced by your favorite UML modeler or in SCXML (State Chart XML is a W3C standard for defining state machines[2]).. As a consequence, either by handwriting or generating its code from XML formats, a UML state machine is present within the final application code (through the in-memory instances of PauWare dedicated classes representing states and their relationships). This state machine is semantically equivalent to a UML state machine modeled through any UML modeler but has here simply a Java-based representation.

Figure 1. Schematic view of PauWare

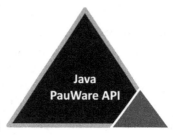

Engine that executes the loaded
model (« run-to-completion »)

Java PauWare API

Code/xml that describes the
statechart model to be loaded

Free implementation of
guards & actions
(called by reflection from the engine)

2. The engine is designed to perform run-to-completion cycles onto a statechart model. The term "run-to-completion" comes from the official UML2 specification and refers to the cycle that processes an event occurrence by triggering the right transitions and calling the required operations until the events source dries up. PauWare engine implements the full UML 2 semantics that deals with sophisticated features like concurrency, shallow/deep history, transition conflict management, etc.

3. The actions and guards are user-defined. They are free implementations of methods located anywhere in the Java program which will be called from the engine thanks to the reflection mechanism provided by the Java language. At this stage, it is very important that the implementation does not contain any control logic; if so, this may interfere with (or even contradict) the specification embodied by the model.

Including the PauWare library in an Android project, this results in increasing solely of 101 KB the APK file plus the memory footprint of the statechart loaded. To give an order of magnitude, we recall that the average size of APK (excluding video games) is 6 MB and that most newer mid end android phones have 512MB Ram a few mid end have 1GB. From an execution point of view, the additional layer introduced by the engine is negligible when considering modern devices running with Android.

Toward Android MobApps Powered by PauWare

As the PauWare API is a core library that works in an agnostic manner, it is not an out-of-the-box product. It is required to define a "connector" whose purpose is to ensure that the model's elements are tied to the context in which they are immersed. Notably, it is important to bind abstract events, guards and actions described at the model-level with their platform-specific counterparts. Thus, the Android connector will catch events that occur and will bring them up to the engine for their processing. In the

Figure 2. Boilerplate Android software architecture powered by PauWare

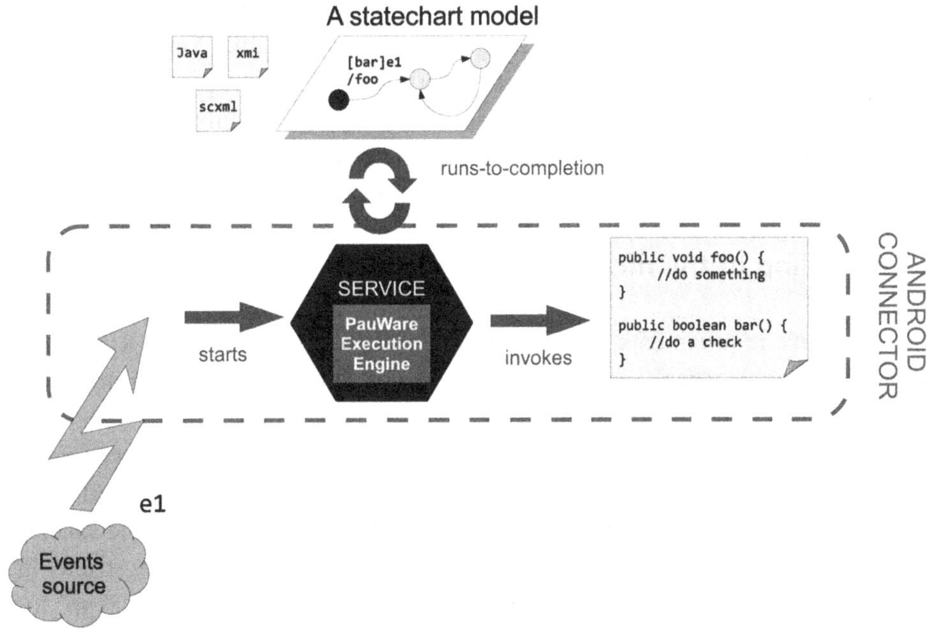

opposite way, the Android connector will ensure that concrete actions are enacted onto the device from the statechart under execution. The proposed common architecture is depicted in the Figure 2 below.

The events source may be of any nature: it can be UI-related events, sensor-related events, system-related events (See the running example of the next Section), GPS-related events, or to a lesser extent, any user-specific events. As an example, an event e1 (saying a onClick() callback from a button on the UI) will start the engine to be processed. Here lies the binding between a program-level event (i.e. an Android callback invoked) and the equivalent model-level event (one can imagine an event named "onClick" or renamed for the occasion). According to the current state of the statechart model under execution, the corresponding action will be launched and whose concrete implementation will be found as an hard-coded Java method with the same name (saying foo() in the Figure). Here lies the reverse binding, between a model-level action and the program-level action.

The work of PauWare is typically a background task and henceforth does not require a plain UI (i.e. screens). That means that PauWare has to be wrapped into a service, which is an Android application component that performs longer-running operations.

Based on this boilerplate architecture, it is now possible to foresee a large panel of mobile applications whose heart is relying on a statechart model.

ANDROID MOBAPPs: AN EXAMPLE

To illustrate the ideas presented so far, let us imagine a tiny mobApp to help end-users to manage the energy of their device, either tablets or smart phones. This kind of free mobApp pullulate on Google Play Store, categorized under the productivity label. The management proposed here does not reside in the battery or CPU consumption of the third-party apps installed but instead on the end-user behavior in different situations. This app, dubbed "Energy Assistant", takes the form of an avatar giving (not too serious) advices to the end-user based on both the battery level and the usage of her/his device.

This very simple mobApp is paradoxically a headache to program. At glance, the program code is going to be polluted by a bunch of controls (nested if or switch-case statements) and variables to remember what happened. Such a code becomes quickly unmaintainable. Yet, a wise developer ought to have the idea of applying a well-known design pattern for this type of problem, namely the "State" pattern from (Gamma *et al.*, 1995). This choice leads to meta-programming because the implicit states of her/his base program are now reified as data, so-called metadata. The Statecharts i-DSML approach presented here is nothing more than that but goes one step further.

Statechart Modeling of the mobApp Behavior

According to the above requirements, any engineer who is accustomed to the UML State Machine Diagrams formalism quickly gets the result showed in *Figure 3*. It is worthwhile to mention that, at this stage, only a superficial knowledge of Android is enough.

The statechart is composed of four states, including a composite state, and seven transitions. This statechart has no final states meaning that the mobApp runs endlessly until it is forced to close or when the device is shut down. This is the expected behavior for this kind of app. For the sake of simplicity, there are no guards (useless here) and the name of the event at the model-level are strictly the same that at the program-level so that the binding is straightforward: they will be passed "as-is" to the engine.

Figure 3. Specification of the behavior of the mobApp by means of an UML 2 State Machine Diagram

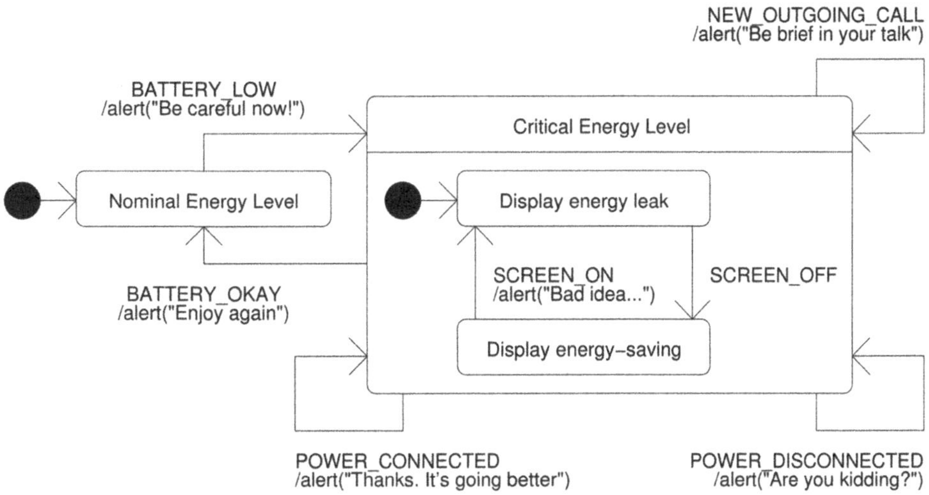

Indeed, we kept seven distinct events coming from the list of native system-related events supported by Android[3] that we judged relevant from an energy viewpoint.

The BATTERY_LOW and BATTERY_OKAY events refer to a variation of the threshold value of the status of charge of the battery. SCREEN_ON and SCREEN_OFF occur when the display surface (OLED basically) is activated or deactivated by the user, by a timer as well. POWER_CONNECTED and POWER_DISCONNECTED mean that the owner intentionally decided to plug or unplug her/his device to an external energy source. Incoming calls are ignored by the assistant insofar they do not result from a desire of the user, but every outgoing call is caught by a new NEW_OUTGOING_CALL event.

The unique kind of action triggered when crossing transitions is to alert the end-user with a comment that aims at providing friendly guidance for the energy management of her/his smart device.

Modeling with the PauWare API

As an illustration we give a preview of raw Java code corresponding to the model depicted in Figure 3, and its equivalent expression in SCXML (Box 1 and Box 2). For recall, both are allowed by PauWare. Either the software engineer writes out all the code or it can be generated by third-party tools.

SOFTWARE ARCHITECTURE IMPLEMENTATION

Once we obtained the statechart model under any PauWare-ready format, we build the mobApp by instantiating the boilerplate architecture presented in Figure 2. Thus, three parts have to be hand-coded to settle the definitive Android connector, as depicted in Figure 4:

- Code for catching the relevant events
- Code for wrapping the execution engine and bridging A and C
- Code for the (single) action

Box 1. PauWare-ready Java code corresponding to the State Machine of Figure 3

```java
import com.PauWare.PauWare_engine.*;
...
//States definition
AbstractStatechart nominal, critical;
nominal = new Statechart("Nominal Energy Level");
critical = new Statechart("Critical Energy Level");
//Sets the initial state
nominal.inputState();
//Combination (mutually exclusive) of the
//states for building the state machine
Statechart_monitor machine = new Statechart_monitor(nominal.xor(critical),
"Energy Assistant Behavior");
//Transitions definition and
//setup of reflective calls to alert() method
machine.fires(Intent.ACTION_BATTERY_LOW, nominal, critical, true, this,
"alert", new Object[] {"Be careful now!"});
machine.fires(Intent.ACTION_BATTERY_OKAY, critical, nominal, true, this,
"alert", new Object[] {"Enjoy again"});
...
```

Box 2. PauWare-ready SCXML code corresponding to the State Machine of Figure 3

```xml
<?xml version="1.0"?>
<scxml xmlns="http://www.w3.org/2005/07/scxml"
    version="1.0"
    name="EnergyAssitantBehavior"
    initial="Nominal Energy Level">
    <state id="Nominal Energy Level">
          <transition event="BATTERY_LOW" target="Critical Energy Level">
                <send event="alert">
                        <param name="string" expr="Be careful now!"/>
                </send>
          </transition>
    </state>
      <state id="Critical Energy Level" initial="Display energy leak">
          <state id="Display energy leak">
                <transition event="SCREEN_OFF" target="Display energy-sav-
ing"/>
          </state>
          ...
    </state>
</scxml>
```

Figure 4. Instantiation of the boilerplate architecture for the Energy Assistant mobApp

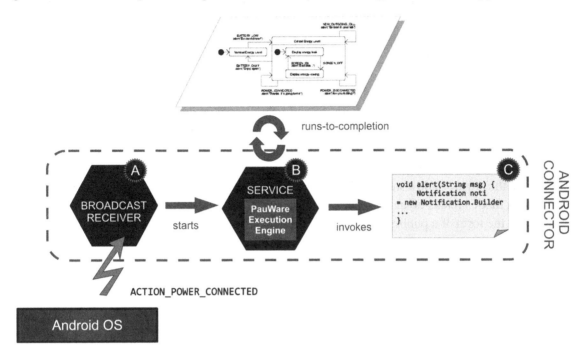

Let us have a closer look at these implementations in the following subsections.

Part A: Event Sniffer

Because the events source is the Android OS itself, we need a special Android component to catch system-related events: a broadcast receiver. Thanks to the identical naming between an event in the statechart model and an event stored in the action[4] part of intents emitted by the system, the receiver just delegates to the engine the event it catches.

```
public class EventSniffer extends BroadcastReceiver {
  @Override
  public void onReceive(Context arg0, Intent arg1) {
    Intent i = new Intent(arg0, WrappedEngine.class);
    i.setAction(arg1.getAction());
    arg0.startService(i);
  }
}
```

The "Broadcast Receiver" component is registered to listen to the seven native events above mentioned. Each of the seven distinct event registrations is done programmatically because some of them do not work when manually declared in the manifest. This fosters the possibility of dynamically configuring the receiver from an arbitrary statechart. This solution only requires a quick analysis phase when the model is loaded to elicit the set of events actually used (among 120 available), and to accordingly register/unregister the receiver.

Part B: Wrapped Engine

Wrapping PauWare engine into a service component ensures a global persistency while the device is running, even outside of any interaction with the end-user. Persistent data include the loaded model and the current execution state of the latter, which is recorded inside the engine.

When the service is first created, it properly installs the "BroadcastReceiver" and loads the statechart model. Then, every time an event is sniffed out, it is processed through the startCommand() method which impels the engine to do a step within the run-to-completion cycle. The service is hence used here in unbounded mode (versus bounded mode). If a transition is eligible, the corresponding action is performed under the form of a public Java method called by reflection from the engine service.

```java
public class WrappedEngine extends Service {
  //reference to the PauWare engine
  private AbstractStatechart_monitor theEngine;
  private void installBroadcast() {
    EventSniffer s = new EventSniffer();
    registerReceiver(s, new IntentFilter(Intent.ACTION_SCREEN_ON));
    registerReceiver(s, new IntentFilter(Intent.ACTION_POWER_DISCONNECTED));
    // The same for the 5 other events
  }

  // Here goes the raw code of the model (see the previous Section)
  private void loadModelFromRawCode() { ... }

  //Here is the public method invoked by reflection (see Part C below)
  public void alert(String msg) { ... }

  @Override
  public void onCreate() {
    installBroadcast();
    loadModelFromRawCode();
  }

  @Override
  public int onStartCommand(Intent intent, int flags, int startId) {
    theEngine.run_to_completion(intent.getAction());
    return Service.START_NOT_STICKY;
  }
}
```

Part C: Message Alert

We simply focus here on the *alert("message")* action that will be mapped to the notification mechanism, which is an important part of Android UI. For recall, notifications are messages displayed to the user in the notification area that appears in the top bar on the device's screen. Other notification modes are supported like sound, LED pulse or vibration. Each new notification replaces the former one in the notification area; they are not stacked.

```
public void alert(String msg) {
    NotificationCompat.BuildermBuilder =
    newNotificationCompat.Builder(this)
    .setSmallIcon(R.drawable.notification_icon).setContentTitle(msg);
    NotificationManagermNotif = (NotificationManager) getSystemService(Context.
NOTIFICATION_SERVICE);
    mNotif.notify(0, mBuilder.build());
}
```

UPDATE MADE EASY

The most interesting side effect of the i-DSML solution is its impact on the ways the mobApp can be modified subsequently. We see at least two techniques:

- Instant update
- Self-adaptation

Instant Update

While the behavior is usually hard-coded into the application we showed that it is here externalized as a model, that is, metadata. Because metadata, as any other data, are serializable and exchangeable over the network (SCXML format is well-suited for that), it becomes possible to load a new model on-demand. Potentially, loading a new model is equivalent to defining a completely new application in its way to behave. The shape of the new statechart loaded can be totally different but, of course, the panel of possible updates is limited by the set of actions and guards already implemented into the application that remains unchanged. We refer to this by "instant update" versus "classical update" which implies a service disruption for the end-user due to the necessity to entirely reinstall the APK. Because the new statechart overrides the old one, the run-to-completion cycle is reset. Nevertheless, when the new statechart is just a variant of the current one, it is much more desirable to seamlessly adapt the on-going run-to-completion cycle. But this requires mapping the current state in the old model to the current state of the new model, buffering incoming events during the replacement time interval and then reintroducing them subsequently. Such state recovery procedure is a non-trivial and error-prone feature that is not yet available in PauWare (figure 5).

Supporting instant update calls for a specific version of the architecture, including a component responsible for the adaptation. A "push" method allows the server to tell the device that fresh metadata

Figure 5. – Update-enabled version of the software architecture powered by PauWare

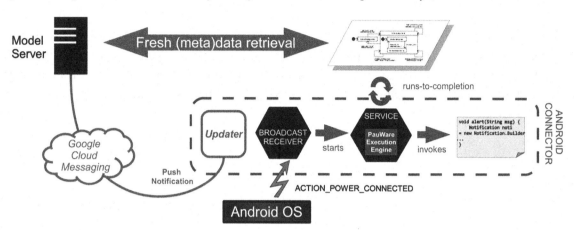

(i.e. a new model) are available. Then the device can download and replace the current model under execution by the engine. A ready-to-use push technology is provided by the Google Cloud Messaging (GCM) service for Android. Another lower-level solution is WebSockets[5], a protocol that allows a bi-directional communication.

It is not obligatorily the mobApp vendor that decides to publish a new update via its servers. Reconsidering the IoT, this technique allows envisioning global applications (e.g. cyber-physical systems) where class of similar objects can exchange their running model in order to mimic each other.

Self-Adaptation

The presented update technique obviously requires an access to outside world and makes the assumption of the existence of third-party software (a model server, mobApps running on other devices, etc.). For those that run in a closed world, the executable model approach pursues a more ambitious goal: self-adaptation. Indeed, i-DSML is a very good candidate because a model under execution is not obligatorily static like in the previous running example but can be modified on-the-fly with CRUD actions (Create-Read-Update-Delete) which then immediately result in an alternative execution path. Reconsidering the energy assistant example, just imagine removing transitions, adding new states or inserting guards, according to some predefined rules. This supposes that these actions are enacted by a decision (learning-based or not) control unit, which is embedded into the mobApp. Interested readers can refer to the works presented in (Cariou *et al.*, 2013).

RELATED WORK

There is a large body of work in the literature dealing with the productive usage of (MDA-compliant or not) models in order to develop software for mobile platforms (Dunkel *et al.*, 2007 and Braun *et al.*, 2008 and Balagtas-Fernandez *et al.*, 2010 and Min *et al.*, 2011 and Kraemer, 2011 and Wang, 2011 and Parada *et al.*, 2012). Most of them are based on UML 2 models, notably Class Diagrams and Activity Diagrams.

This is an unsurprising situation because the static model approach is not related to any technological frame; it evenly works for building desktop applications, mobile applications, Web applications and so on. Instead, the newest approach of dynamic model implies to be closer to the target platform because the model ought to be directly executed on the latter. At this stage, one can find other commercial or open source tools dealing with (among other things) UML State Machine diagrams execution. We can cite Cameo Simulation Toolkit, LieberLieber AM|USE 2.0, IBM Rational Software Architect Simulation Toolkit and IBM Rational Rhapsody, etc. Unfortunately, these execution engines are desktop-oriented because they are integrated into complete CASE workbenches. Consequently, numbers of them use direct execution for simulation purpose only, and then rely on code generators, thus moving away from the original i-DSML idea which aims at skipping the generation phase. Nevertheless, similarly to PauWare which is a lightweight engine written in Java, SCION engine is a lightweight execution engine written in JavaScript but it may have a bug in the SCXML execution semantics[6]. For all these reasons, to our knowledge, there are no feedbacks on i-DSML for smart devices so far.

Related works to ours can also be found indirectly on the side of cross-platform mobile development techniques. Indeed, to deal with the technology independence, some of them like Apache Cordova or Rhodes, require an execution engine running on the target whether embodied by the Web browser for the former or by a specific Ruby VM for the latter. Anyway, the engineer is always expected to think at the program-level and does not rise at the model-level as demonstrated in this chapter.

CONCLUSION

We definitively entered the modeling era: using models is an established practice within a modern software engineering process, from early sketching phases up to testing and deployment. Among the multiple known usages of models, we explained in this chapter how i-DSML can change the software development habits, turning models into directly executable assets through an engine. The i-DSML approach is the shortest path between a model (i.e. an abstract object) and a running software system (i.e. a concrete object), along with the promise to support updates and adaptations more easily than with classical programming.

We exemplified this idea with a mobApp called "Energy Assistant" running on Android, modeled almost entirely with UML 2 State Machine Diagrams DSML and interpreted by PauWare engine. We offered a basis for further Android mobApps thanks to a boilerplate architecture powered by the PauWare technology. We choose Android because it quickly established itself as a leader of the mobile operating systems and because it has the potential to reach a broad panel of smart objects in the near future. Targeting other mobile OS simply means developing new connectors for PauWare.

Even if the work presented here all focused on Statecharts, other classes of automata could be envisioned, like timed automaton or the extended state diagram formalism provided by SysML, and, more generally, anything fairly different from that.

All of the elements developed in this chapter lead us to the reasonable conclusion that the ideal mobApp is hybrid, containing some part programmed in the classical way and some others that are far best resolved with the executable model approach. However, the idea of an exclusively execution model-based application is not so unrealistic; executable UML (a.k.a fUML) was a first attempt from OMG (OMG, 2011) and there is a good chance that new initiatives will arise in the coming years.

REFERENCES

Balagtas-Fernandez, F., Tafelmayer, M., & Hussmann, H. (2010). Mobia modeler: easing the creation process of mobile applications for nontechnical users. In *Proceedings of the 15th international conference on Intelligent user interfaces*, (pp. 269–272). ACM. doi:10.1145/1719970.1720008

Braun, P., & Eckhaus, R. (2008). Experiences on Model-Driven Software Development for Mobile Applications. In *Proceedings of 15th Annual IEEE International Conference and Workshop on the Engineering of Computer Based Systems*, (pp. 490–493). IEEE. doi:10.1109/ECBS.2008.50

Cariou, E., Le Goaer, O., Barbier, F., & Pierre, S. (2013). Characterization of Adaptable Interpreted-DSML. In *European Conference on Modelling Foundations and Applications* (LNCS), (vol. *7949*, pp. 37–53). Springer. doi:10.1007/978-3-642-39013-5_4

Clarke, P. J., Wu, Y., Allen, A. A., Hernandez, F., Allison, M., & France, R. (2013). Towards Dynamic Semantics for Synthesizing Interpreted DSMLs. In *Formal and Practical Aspects of Domain-Specific Languages: Recent Developments*. IGI Global. doi:10.4018/978-1-4666-2092-6.ch009

Combemale, B., Crégut, X., & Pantel, M. (2012). A Design Pattern to Build Executable DSMLs and associated V&V tools. In *Proceedings of the 19th Asia-Pacific Software Engineering Conference (APSEC 2012)*. IEEE.

Crane, M. L., & Dingel, J. (2007). UML vs. classical vs. rhapsody statecharts: Not all models are created equal. *Software & Systems Modeling*, *6*(4), 415–435. doi:10.1007/s10270-006-0042-8

Dragert, C., Kienzle, J., & Verbrugge, C. (2012). Statechart-Based AI in Practice. In *Proceedings of the eighth AAAI conference on artificial intelligence and interactive digital entertainment*. AAAI.

Dunkel, J., & Bruns, R. (2007). Model-driven architecture for mobile applications. In Business Information Systems (LNCS), (vol. 4439, pp. 464–477). Springer Berlin Heidelberg.

Fowler, M. (2010). *Domain Specific Languages* (1st ed.). Addison-Wesley Professional.

Gamma, E., Helm, R., Johnson, R., & Vlissides, J. (1995). *Design Patterns: Elements of Reusable Object-Oriented Software*. Boston, MA: Addison-Wesley Longman Publishing Co., Inc.

Harel, D. (1987). Statecharts: A visual formalism for complex systems. *Science of Computer Programming*, *8*(3), 231–274. doi:10.1016/0167-6423(87)90035-9

Harel, D., & Kugler, H. (2004). The Rhapsody semantics of Statecharts (or, on the executable core of the UML). *Lecture Notes in Computer Science*, *3147*, 325–354. doi:10.1007/978-3-540-27863-4_19

Kraemer, F. A. (2011). Engineering android applications based on uml activities. In *Proceedings of the 14th International Conference on Model Driven Engineering Languages and Systems*, (pp. 183–197). Springer.

Lehmann, G., Blumendorf, M., Trollmann, F., & Albayrak, S. (2010). Meta-Modeling Runtime Models. In Models@run.time Workshop at MoDELS 2010 (LNCS), (vol. 6627). Springer.

Mernik, M., Heering, J., & Sloane, A. M. (2005). When and how to develop domain-specific languages. *ACM Computing Surveys*, *37*(4), 316–344. doi:10.1145/1118890.1118892

Miller, J., & Mukerji, J. (2003). *MDA Guide Version 1.0.1*. Object Management Group (OMG). Retrieved from http://www.omg.org/mda/specs.htm#MDAGuide

Min, B.-K., Ko, M., Seo, Y., Kuk, S., & Kim, H.-S. (2011). A uml metamodel for smart device application modeling based on windows phone 7 platform. In Proceedings of TENCON 2011 - 2011 IEEE Region 10 Conference, (pp. 201–205). IEEE.

Parada, A., & de Brisolara, L. (2012). A model driven approach for android applications development. In *Proceedings of the 2012 Brazilian Symposium on Computing Systems Engineering*, (pp. 192–197).

Semantics Of A Foundational Subset For Executable, U. M. L. Models (FUML). (2011). Version 1.0. Object Management Group (OMG). Retrieved from http://www.omg.org/spec/FUML/1.0

Wang, Z. (2011). The study of smart phone development based on uml. In *Proceedings of the 2011 International Conference on Computer Science and Service System*, (pp. 2791–2794).

ENDNOTES

[1]   https://developer.android.com/guide/

[2]   http://www.w3.org/TR/scxml/

[3]   120 are available. The list can be found at android-sdks\platforms\android-17\data\broadcast_actions.txt.

[4]   It is a little bit confusing but what Android calls "actions" refer to our events in a statechart.

[5]   WebSockets were originally designed to be implemented in Web browsers and Web servers, but they can be used by any client or server application.

[6]   http://www.franckbarbier.com/PauWare/Jacob_Beard_case/

Section 5
Mobile Networks Design

This section discusses mobility management in different heterogeneous networks, and a SIP-PMIP Cross-Layer Mobility Management Scheme for providing seamless mobility support for terminal, personal, network and service mobility is proposed.

Chapter 15
SIP-PMIP Cross-Layer Mobility Management Scheme

Muhammad Laminu
Ramat Polytechnic Maiduguri, Nigeria

Batula AbdulAzeez
Guaranty Trust Bank, Nigeria

Sufian Yousef
Anglia Ruskin University, UK

ABSTRACT

Heterogeneous networks have attracted a lot of interest due to its support provision for a large number of networks at an effective cost. Mobility Management also plays an important role in the heterogeneous network in providing a seamless mobility support for both devices and users, which poses a serious challenge. In this chapter, the researchers propose SIP-PMIP Cross-Layer Mobility Management in order to provide a seamless mobility in heterogeneous wireless networks. In effect, the researchers design a Cross-Layer Mobility Management Scheme, which can handle terminal, network, personal and session mobility. To demonstrate, video conferencing is included in the modeling, simulation and implementation of the module using Riverbed Modeler.

INTRODUCTION

The next generation all-IP network is expected to provide access to all the services required at anytime and anywhere at a data rates of 100Mb/s and 1Gb/s for high and low mobility scenarios. As of now, no single radio access technology can deliver such services in rather different networks in an area providing services (Anderson, K; 2012). In order to benefit from the existing infrastructure, the 4G network architecture will be designed in such a way that it will accommodate all the existing networks. That is, it is a heterogeneous network with increased capacity efficiency in the area. Another important feature of the next generation mobile system is the mobility between the heterogeneous networks consisting of different networks. Mobility management which is a necessity in the 4G system is made up of mobility

DOI: 10.4018/978-1-4666-9916-8.ch015

Copyright © 2016, IGI Global. Copying or distributing in print or electronic forms without written permission of IGI Global is prohibited.

and handover management. "The Session Initiation Protocol (SIP) makes this experience achievable" (Atayero *et al.*, 2012:16). Also, the Proxy Mobile Internet Protocol (PMIP) is a protocol which enables mobility in a heterogeneous network with additional hardware and software (Ruckus wireless, 2013), like middleware. The above mentioned mobility management protocols work at different layers of the protocol stack and thus each layer in the stack contributes to the development of a mobility management in the 4G systems. This entails the need for a cross-layer design which is termed as the violation of the protocol stack.

The Session Initiation Protocol is an application layer signalling protocol designed by IETF between 1996 and 1999 at Columbia University for initiating, modifying, monitoring and terminating internet sessions such as video, messages, online games, etc. It is a negotiating protocol, which uses the Real-time Transport Protocol/ Real-time Transport Control Protocol (RTP/RTCP) for transport/control of media, and Session Description Protocol (SDP) for negotiating media.

SIP defined two major networks elements, namely: User Agent (UA) and Network Server. The user agent contains both the User Agent Client (UAC) and the User Agent Server (UAS) while the network server contains the proxy, location, registration, redirect and universal resource locators (URL). The UAC creates the session by issuing an invitation and the UAS responds by sending a reply message. The SIP request message is made up of the following basic messages: Register, Invite, ACK, Options, Bye and Cancel.

SIP is used in facilitating PSTN- internet interworking and also to control services that are terminal and network independent. It provides some level of session mobility management support in that the location services and SIP re-negotiation features allow a user to remain in contact even if they change terminals during session (Wisely *et al.*, 2002).

The proxy Mobile Internet Protocol (PMIP) is an IP mobility management network protocol introduced by IETF in order to assist in the support of IP mobility in a low latency, high data-rate across a heterogeneous network with various access technologies. It gives mobile terminal access to mobility without involvement in the management of their IP mobility signalling (Sanchez, M. I. et al; 2013) and hence depends on an additional software and hardware implemented on the mobile terminal (Ruckus wireless, 2013).

Mobility management is supported in PMIP by two key elements: the Mobile Access Gateway (MAG) and the Local Mobility Anchor (LMA). The LMA in the mobile core is responsible for maintaining the location of the mobile terminal in the Localized Mobility Domain (LMD) and forwarding the data traffic of the mobile terminal by maintaining an IPv6-in-IPv6 channel with the MAG which is in the core network.

In PMIP, the mobile terminal always maintains its IP address as it moves from one point to another within the LMD managed by an LMA. Similarly, "the operation of PMIPv6 does not require the mobile node (MN) to implement any modification or extra software in its layer-3 stack, although it may require the assistance of some layer-2 mechanisms to work more efficiently. These mechanisms are known as link-layer triggers, and are required to quickly detect a change of layer-2 Point of Attachment (PoA)" (Sanchez *et al.*, 2013).

Thus, the main aim of the chapter is to devise and assess a set of intelligent strategies and workable algorithms for multi-layer mobility management architecture and cross-layer methodologies and mechanisms for a fifth generation heterogeneous mobile network over a real-time test bed applications.

This can be achieved through the following objectives:

- Design a 5G heterogeneous mobile network;
- Design an optimized multi-layer mobility management scheme for the above heterogeneous networks for various mobility scenarios, with the focus on the integration of SIP and PMIPv6 with new cross-layer signalling design;
- Design new mobility management algorithms for terminal, session, personal, service and ad hoc mobility schemes;
- Interface the mobility management architecture and the real-time applications;
- Design analysis and evaluation of the mobility requirements for the application under various types of mobility management schemes.

BACKGROUND

Evolution of the Mobile/Cellular Networks

The mobile telecommunication sector has witnessed a rapid growth in the mobile telecommunication subsection in the past decade. The rising number of both mobile subscribers and providers led to the evolution of the communication systems. The evolution from one generation to the other is characterised by a transition from circuit-switched (CS) to packet-switched (PS) to all-IP and changes in data rates. In the past years, wireless networks have followed many paths towards evolution whose main objective is to bring about high performance and efficiency (Sharma, P., 2013). The next generation mobile network also referred to as 4G is pictured as a host to the various networks in a heterogeneous manner enabling interaction through an all-IP based structure with high mobility and data rates.

Sharma, Pankaj (2013) traced the evolution of the mobile wireless communication networks from first generation to fifth generation (1G-5G) as well as future prospective of next generation communication network. He describes the first generation (1G) as the an analogue system used only for speech transmission, first introduced in 1979; 2G introduced in the late 1980s is a digital system and is generally associated with GSM. The 3G systems provide services at 2Mbps and were first commercially launched in October 2001. In 4G systems, the multimode mobile terminals should be able to select among the various networks that made up the heterogeneous network any time anywhere and terminal mobility is inevitable. Finally, he describes the 5G as a World Wide Wireless Web (WWWW) and denotes a phase beyond the 4G/IMT-Advanced standards and has a bright future because it can handle best technologies and offer cheaper handsets to its clients by promoting super core concept, where all network providers will be connected through a single backbone with one infrastructure regardless of their access technologies with better coverage, high bit rates, less power consumption and cheaper deployment costs.

Anderson, Karl (2012) surveys the most common networks in the revolution of wireless networks. He started the evolution with the GSM which is the most popular and was defined in its first version in 1990 by the European Telecommunication Standards Institute (ETSI). For the 3G systems, Anderson (2012) discusses the UMTS as the successor of GSM and the most popular which is followed by the CDMA systems. In the fourth generation, the LTE, WiMAX and WLAN are the most popular and they are expected to be the Next Generation Wireless Network (NGWN).

Mshvidobadze, Tinatin (2012) provides a high level overview of the evolution of Mobile Wireless Communication Networks from 3G to 4G and described LTE (Long Term Evolution) as the 4G mobile network technology. "LTE is strongly positioned to lead the evolution in the communications industry for several years. It improves spectral efficiency, simplifies deployment of all-IP real time services, facilitates integration with non-wireless networks, and support interworking with legacy wireless technologies. It achieves all of these things through a flat, scalable architecture that is designed to manage and maintain service QoS in a mobile environment with significantly higher data throughput" (Mshvidobadze, 2012).

Yousef, Sufian (2013) traces the evolution of the mobile telephone systems to the first generation (1G).

The Global System of Mobile Communication (GSM)

The second generation mobile network is a digital system and has many advantages over its analogue counterpart. It provides capacity gains by allowing one frequency to be used by many users either through code multiplexing or time division. It also supports text messaging and improves security. Due to the absence of a standard specification governing both first and second generations, about four systems (technologies) were developed for the 2G systems. These are: Digital Advanced Mobile Systems (D-AMPS); Global System for Mobile Communications (GSM); Code Division Multiple Access (CDMA); and Personal Digital Cellular (PDC). Among these, GSM is by far the most successful and widely used 2G systems (Korhonen, 2003) as it provides terminal mobility and user seamless roaming between GSM networks. It uses a Subscriber Identity Module (SIM) card which has the subscriber identity and helps both the network and mobile to identify each other and authenticate conversations. The GSM which is a second generation mobile system uses the TDMA/FDMA multiple access techniques with an FDD duplexing method. It has a spectrum allocation of 850 – 915MHz in the uplink and 935 – 960MHz in the downlink with a bandwidth of 200 KHz for each physical channel. Total number of channel available for each direction is 124 and the number of user per channel is 8 with a data rate of 270.833Kb/s, and a bit period of 3.693µs. The time division multiple access TDMA has a frame size of 4.615ms, the number of slots per frame is 8 and the slot duration is 0.576923ms. For its operation, the GSM uses the 0.3GMSK modulation technique with a speech coding of 13Kb/s Regular Pulse Excitation with Long Term Predictor (RPE-LPT) and interleaver period of 40ms maximum, using two consecutive 20ms blocks of data. The user of GSM has a data transfer capability of short messaging service, circuit-switched data and GPRS for packet data.

The GSM architecture can be grouped into three major parts; the Mobile Station (MS), Base Station Subsystem (BSS) and the Mobile Subscription Centre (MSC).

The mobile station is the mobile user and can be recognised by the BTS through the SIM card used. The MS is connected to the BTS (Base Transceiver Station) which consist of radio transmitter and receivers via an air interface. The BTS is connected to the Base Station Controller (BSC) via an A-Interface. The BSC performs radio control function. The BSC is connected to MSC also via an A-interface. The MSC is the heart of GSM network because it controls call by creating route to and from PSTNs and switching controls during handover. It performs its duties with the help of the VLR, HLR, EIR and OMC.

Third Generation Mobile Networks (3G)

The challenge posed by the International Telecommunication Union (ITU) in the mid-1980s challenging the telecommunication industries to come out with a single system with a universal standard which is capable of providing better quality of service (QoS) and security as compared to 2G gave birth to the third generation (3G) mobile systems. The 3G system, unlike the 2G is all about digital voice and data and is intended to provide high-quality of voice, message, multimedia and web browsing (Tannenbaum & Wetherall, 2011).

Ten years after posing the challenge, ITU in 1997 offered a specification for the 3G called the IMT-2000. The IMT means International Mobile Communications and the 2000 stands for the year of launch, operation frequency and bandwidths. The specifications include high speed, wide range of services, mobility maintenance, security, roaming and mobile payments. Boudriga (2010:204) outlined the following security objectives of 3G: to accomplish the required mobile user authentication; to adopt the challenge and response authentication concept; to ensure message generated by user is adequately protected; to protect mobile users against misuse and theft of mobile systems; to ensure resources and services are protected; and to support emergency services.

There are many technologies that that proposed to the IMT-2000 specifications but only two became the most successful. These are: the WCMDA (Wideband Code Division Multiple Access) and UMTS (Universal Mobile Telecommunication Systems). But with the 3GPP (3G Partnership Project) agreements which consist of most important telecommunications industries and bodies proposed a standard specification for the 3G systems based on the GSM/GPRS extended network and the ETSI's UTRA (Universal Terrestrial Radio Access) radio interface. The radio interface of the 3GPP is promoted by the 3GPP-2 by specifying an interface compatible with the IS-95 systems.

The 3G Network Architecture

The network architecture of 3G consists of three major parts: the user equipment (UE) or mobile station (MS); the radio access also called UMTS Terrestrial Radio Access Network (UTRAN); and the core network (CN).

- **The User Equipment or Mobile Station:** This is the device which gives one access to use a mobile network service. It consists of a Universal Subscriber Identity Module (USIM) which allows the user to use a specific SIM card of his choice. The mobile device uses the UMTS techniques for its operation and operates in Circuit Switching (CS), Packet Switching, or both packet and circuit switching (PS/CS) mode.
- **The Radio Access Network (UTRAN):** The UTRAN which manages the radio access part of the network consist of the Node-B (Base Station) and the Radio Access Controller (RNC).
- **The Core Network:** The core network consists of two domains, namely the Circuit-Switching (CS) and the Packet-Switching (PS) domain. The CS domain consists of the MSC, HLR, VLR, SCP and the AuC; while the PS domain consists of the SGSN and the GGSN. It main function is to provide a connection between the user and its destination on the internet and is also responsible for the storage and management of information. The third generation Universal Mobile Telecommunication System (UMTS) operates in two modes; TDD and FDD. In the FDD mode, it has a spectrum allocation of 1850 – 1910MHz for uplink and 2110 – 2170MHz for downlink and in the TDD mode, it has an allocation of 1900 – 1920MHz and 2010 – 2025MHz and each of these bands for the TDD mode is used for both uplink and downlink transmissions with a separation of134.8 – 245.2MHz (110MHz). The channel spacing is 5 in UMTS with a centre frequency of in the integral multiple of 200 KHz and chip rate of3.84Mc/s. the transmitter power output of the

base station (UE) is21, 24,27, or 33dBm while receiver sensitivity of -121dBm for base station and -117dBm for UE at a bit rate of 10^{-3}.the power control steps are 1,2, or 3dB for UE and 0.5 or 1dB for base station and the maximum possible change in the transmit power level on TPC commands are 26dB for UE and 12dB for base stations with a data rate of 144Kb/s in rural outdoor, 384Kb/s in urban/suburban outdoor; 2Mb/s in indoor or low-range outdoor.

Fourth Generation (4G)

The ITU-R defined the fourth generation in 2007 based on ITU-R M.1645 Recommendation. The fourth generation (4G) also termed IMT- Advanced systems is meant to solve the problems and limitations of the third generation and with the intention of providing high Quality of Service (QoS) and security. This can be achieved by integrating mobile/ cellular networks with wireless networks. That is merging all the networks such as GSM, 3G, GPRS, Wi-Fi, WiMAX, LTE, Femto and TETRA for all-IP networks with high throughput, low latency infrastructure and secure applications (Youssef, 2013). Hence, the network architecture of the 4G system should be the hybrid of all the networks which is one of the major challenges. It is expected to operate at a frequency band of between 2 – 8GHz and a bandwidth of 100MHz or more. The 4G system will deploy such access technologies OFDM, CDMA or TDMA for its radio system with a data rate of 20 – 100Mbps in mobile mode and mobile speed of 200Km/h.

The fourth generation (4G) is expected to play a vital role in people's lives in the wireless world. Apart from the provision seamless mobility between the various networks (providers), it is proposed to ensure a high bit rate, smooth video streaming and an intelligent network that will connect the whole universe by providing a global access and portability across all mobile terminals. The fourth generation according to Rao, K.R.; Bojkovic, Z.S. and Milovanovic (2006) has several issues such as IP-based core network, and a seamless mobility management among others.

Govil, J. & Govil, J (2007) attempt to make an assessment in development, transition, and roadmap for fourth generation mobile communication system which was described as MAGIC (Mobile multimedia, Anytime, anywhere, Global mobility support, integrated solution, and Customized personal service) with a perspective of wireless convergence domain and future research issues. The 4G system is a system which is projected to provide an acceptable global standard through integration and to allow resource sharing among multiple users by supporting IP-based applications. But "there must be a low complexity of implementation and an efficient means of negotiation between the end users and wireless infrastructure" (Govil, J. and Govil, J.; 2007).

Jayanthiladevi *et al.* (2013) describe the 4G systems as the Future Advanced Mobile Universal Systems-FAMOUS providing stable system performance, quality services and will support comprehensive and personalised services. The fourth generation which is a seamless integration of existing wireless technologies will be a global network that will be able to cater for users' needs on a personalised level. But "backward compatibility is the core issue so that the new emerging technology supports the previous infrastructures" and "best hope is to start developing next generation technologies now" (Jayanthiladevi *et al.*, 2013).

Duan, Huang & Walrand (2013) also describe the 4G as a system that provides much higher data rates to address the ever-increasing demands for high-speed multimedia communications. And analyses the existing network operators' timing of upgrading their services by considering a 4G competition market and develops a game theory for studying the interactions of network providers; and shows the impact of the 4G upgrade on the profits of the providers due to increased competition even though service providers select different times for upgrading their systems to avoid severe competition.

All-IP Networks

The 4G is an all-IP based network that provides control of networks and transportation across and within multiple access networks based on Internet Protocol version 6 (IPv6) by providing mobility at high rates with the aim of providing mobile terminals with a seamless experience for all services within and across the various existing networks.

The 4G network according to Rao, Bojkovic & Milovanovic (2006) is capable of supporting: inter-operator information interchange for multiple-operator scenarios; Confidentiality; Personal mobility; terminal mobility; paging; Quality of Service (QoS); and Monitoring and measurement functions.

There are many technologies that are evolving to meet the fourth generation IMT-Advanced standard, but the ones with the expectations of meeting the requirements are WiMAX and LTE.

Local IP Address (LIPA)

Local IP Access (LIPA) is the capability for an all-IP based device(s) to access a consumer's home-based local area network as well as the wider Internet directly using the air interface of a femtocell, or Home NodeB (HNB). The use of LIPA allows for greater performance, innovative services that networked both mobile and home networks, and the off-loading of traffic from the packet core network of the operator which is principally meant for the Internet.

The use of LIPA has some tremendous benefits which include:

- "For mobile operators, the ability to offer LIPA via the HNB would mean higher revenues by way of value added services without having to invest significantly in upgrading network infrastructure to cope with the higher speeds that such applications would demand.
- For subscribers, LIPA would mean faster and more secure on-the-move data transfer since traffic within the home network would not travel outside the subnet. Users could add customized high-speed applications like file transfer, video streaming and device sharing without involving the operator's core network, thus avoiding associated bottlenecks and possibly yielding lower data costs since the operator is not burdened.
- For ISPs, who might or might not be part of the same company as the mobile operator, LIPA would mean the ability to offer specialized high-value services with higher quality of service. Thus, the offering of LIPA for mobile devices via the HNB would present a win-win-win situation for all parties involved" (Siddhartha & Madhur, n.d.).
- Reduction in the number of hops taken by the IP data to reach the destination.
- Another benefit would be the ability to communicate with other devices within the local subnet without having to go through the core network of the mobile operator, hence keeping local traffic truly local.

With the growing rate of devices such as mobiles, laptop data cards, USB dongles, etc. increasing globally, most subscribers are using their mobile devices not just for voice but also for data services and both mobile and internet service providers are trying their best to ensure that customers have the twin benefits of high mobility and high speed data access (Siddhartha & Madhur, n.d.).

Because service providers are trying to meet the ever increasing demand for Internet data access using high-speed mobile network infrastructure which are as a result of the rising content available on-line via email, social networking sites, blogs, RSS feeds, multimedia calls, streaming video and online music coupled with faster and higher capacity equipment driven by personal digital assistants (PDAs), smartphones and netbooks; many operators are faced with the limitations of bandwidth and network capacity thus putting a tremendous stress on the existing network infrastructure. Hence operators are investing significantly to ensure that the existing network capacity on the access network which involves the introduction of HNBs ensures efficient usage of radio spectrum by allowing home users to access the network through the HNB using a local IP backhaul link to the core network; as well as in the core of the network meets the current demand. This in turn puts an increasing quantity of tension nodes of the core network such as SGSN and GGSN since more HNBs connected to the core network means that these nodes have to handle exponentially higher traffic. Since HNBs typically use the ISP's broadband link to provide backhaul connectivity to the core network, it would lessen the stress on core network nodes if IP traffic generated via the HNB were routed through the ISP's Internet access gateway. Providing access to the home network connected devices (i.e., desktop/laptop computers, Internet-enabled gaming systems, media centres and so on) provides a rich canvas for the development of services that leverage both these devices and the mobility/broad connectivity of the wireless network.

The Requirements for Local IP Access (LIPA)

The requirements for LIPA can be broadly categorised into two, namely:

1. LIPA to the home network. Here, the mobile terminals (MTs) should be able to at the same time depending upon the destination exchange information through the core network of the operator and LIPA to the home-based network; and also access other devices on the home network through the HNB. This is decided by the HNB.
2. IP access to the Internet. IP access to the Internet should be possible without the need to traverse the network of the operator (Siddhartha & Madhur, n.d.).

LIPA Scenarios

According to TS 22.220, LIPA breakout is performed in the same residential/enterprise IP network. This breakout is at a Local GW (L-GW) in the residential/enterprise IP network.

Selective IP Traffic Offload (SIPTO)

In line with the need to reduce operational costs for MNOs, 3GPP recommended several mechanisms for optimizing the network for IP traffic which included selective IP traffic offload (SIPTO), with the main objective of introducing mechanisms which will enable operators to move traffic to its destinations at the minimal costs. This internet data offload solution provided either to a local network of a femtocell or at/above an evolved node B (eNB) in the macro network to facilitate offload of both radio access network and core networks if used in the local network or to enable core network offload if used in a macro network environment (Monrad, 2011).

The SIPTO service allows an operator to offload selected traffic also denoted to as SIPTO traffic such as internet or corporate network traffic, towards a defined IP network near to the mobile terminal's (MT) point of attachment to the access network. It is based on an enhanced gateway selection function that has the capability to select a mobile core network gateway close to a RAN node (Sankaran, 2012).

When a mobile terminal demands to access a service that the service providers has defined to be offloaded locally through SIPTO offload, the packet data network (PDN) connection will therefore be established through a local PDN gateway (LPGW) distinct for SIPTO traffic offload.

The key drivers for the adoption of SIPTO which has immense benefits to operators according to Katanekwa & Ventura (2013) are as follows:

- Reduction of core network load
- Reduction of IP backhaul costs
- Support for content distribution networks (CDNs)
- Lower capital expenditure (CAPEX)

SIPTO Scenarios

Two types of breakout architectures are distinguished according to TS 22.101. SIPTO for Macro-Cellular breakout point is close to the User Equipment's point of attachment to the access network, and that it shall be possible to support mobility for offloaded traffic, which means that the breakout point is "at or above RAN". Furthermore, SIPTO for H(e)NodeB Subsystem allows the breakout to be located either in the residential/enterprise network as LIPA, or "above" H(e)NodeB in the hierarchical view of the mobile operator network i.e. in the backhaul or at the H(e)NodeB-GW.

Consequently, two types of breakout architectures are distinguished:

- Architectures with breakout "at or above RAN" (covering macro and some H(e)NodeB SIPTO scenarios);
- Architectures with breakout "in the residential/enterprise IP network" (covering LIPA and some H(e)NodeB SIPTO scenarios).

Similarly, selected IP traffic offload for the Home (e)NodeB Subsystem may support the following three scenarios:

Scenario 1: Home (e)NodeB Subsystem and backhaul are provided by the same operator;
Scenario 2: Home (e)NodeB Subsystem and backhaul are provided by different operators;
Scenario 3: Local Breakout point (L-PGW) for LIPA/SIPTO is located in a private address domain, e.g. behind a NAT gateway.

LIPA-SIPTO Architectures and Solutions

In addition to the requirements of the ability for the UE to request a LIPA PDN using a well-defined APN; or a specific indication independent of the APN; the solutions for local IP access and selected IP traffic offload for Home (e)NodeB Subsystem shall fulfil the service requirements described in TS 22.220.

Similarly, the solutions for selected IP traffic offload for the macro network shall fulfil the service requirements described in TS 22.101 and for macro (3G and LTE) shall fulfil the following architectural requirements:

- It shall be possible to perform traffic offload without user interaction.
- For UTRAN, the traffic offload shall be performed on or above the RNC node.
- The impact on the existing network entities and procedures by introducing traffic offload shall be minimized (3GPP TR 23.829 V10.0.1 (3GPP TR 23.829, 2011).

The H(e)NodeBs supporting LIPA shall be able to provide Intranet type access to the home based network. Also it good to keep in mind that if the home based network provides a route to other private networks or to the public internet, then these networks may be accessible via LIPA.

The H(e)NodeBs supporting LIPA shall be able to provide access to the multicast groups that are active on the home based network:

- A H(e)NodeB supporting LIPA shall allow UEs to join multicast groups active on the home based network.
- It shall be possible for a H(e)NodeB supporting LIPA to forward multicast traffic from the home based network to the UE and from the UE to the home based network.

For LIPA and SIPTO, the following architectural principles are applicable according to 3GPP TR 23.829 V10.0.1 (3GPP TR 23.829, 2011):

1. For traffic going through the mobile operator's Core Network, the SGW/SGSN User Plane functions are located within the Mobile Operator's Core Network;
2. Mobility management signalling between the UE and the network is handled in the Mobile Operator's Core Network;
3. Session management signalling (bearer setup, etc.) for LIPA, SIPTO traffic and traffic going through the mobile operator's Core Network terminates in the Mobile Operator's Core Network;
4. Reselection of a UE's offload point for SIPTO traffic that is geographically/topologically close to the user shall be possible during idle mode mobility procedures.

Solution 1: Local IP Access and Selected IP Traffic Offload solution based on traffic breakout performed within H(e)NodeB using a local PDN connection;
Solution 2: Local IP Access and Selected IP Traffic Offload at H(e)NodeB by NAT;
Solution 3: GGSN allocation to offload point;
Solution 4: Selected IP Traffic Offload at Iu-PS;
Solution 5: Selected IP Traffic Offload solution based on local PDN GW selection;
Solution 6: Local Gateway based Architecture.

The 5G Mobile and Wireless Communication Network

The 5G communication system is like the 4G system is also heterogeneous in nature as it encompasses different technologies and Mobile Terminals interlinking data, things and people in a seamless exchange of information. The way to 5G systems are paved by two major documents, namely: 1) "The IMT Vision" titled "Framework and Overall Objectives of the Future Development of IMT for 2020 and Beyond" with the objective of defining the framework and overall objectives of IMT for 2020 and beyond to drive the future developments for IMT (deadline July, 2014). 2) "IMT Future Technology Trends" (deadline October, 2014) with the objective to provide a view of future IMT Technology aspects 2015 – 2020 and beyond and to provide Information on trends of future IMT technology aspect (Afif, 2013)

The 5G is expected to be an open innovation platform or network that optimizes itself for expanding capability for anywhere, anytime, anyhow connectivity for tens of millions of applications and hundreds of billions of machines that will provide fundamental infrastructure for smart cities (Huawei, 2014) and vehicular connectivity. It is also expected to provide an increased battery life of MTs and capacity in dense urban environment and coverage in remote areas and airplanes (Thibaut, 2014)

In order to achieve the above, the 5G network must be built to provide an amazingly fast experience at a very high data rate of between 1Gb/s to 10Gb/s which will support Ultra-High Definition video, virtual reality and other immersive multimedia applications at a fibre-like user experience that will support mobile cloud services. Thus, providing a great service for a very large crowd of several billions of applications and hundreds of billions of machines (users) by providing best experience at zero latency, response time and reliable connection that is, less than 1millisecond latency to support real time mobile control and vehicle-to-vehicle applications and communications.

Heterogeneous All-IP Networks

The fourth generation of the mobile telecommunication system is an open-based global network which seamlessly interworks the various wireless networks to provide voice, data and multimedia over a single all-IP based core network. The IP-based network has the advantages of compatibility with already existing protocols such as MIP and SIP; and independence from access networks.

Integration of Heterogeneous Networks

Unlike the other generations which are designed to provide users with moderate bandwidths, the next generation mobile system will be design in such a way that it integrates all the already existing networks and new emerging networks, services and terminals (Rao *et al.*, 2006). Designing a heterogeneous wireless and mobile network for all-IP network has gained a lot of attention in the mobile Telecommunication sector. The major challenge is to connect between different technologies such as GSM, 3G, Wi-Fi, WiMAX, LTE, Femto and TETRA to support each other by providing end-to-end communication. The two concepts of wireless and cellular network has different radio access technologies; the cellular system which gave birth to current wireless technologies divides the area into a geographical region called cells and the base station which has an antenna installed at the centre of the cell. Hence, they are called a wide area networks (WANs) which provide high data. The wireless network on the other hand provides a wide range of coverage. This implies that complementing these technologies (networks) through the provision of interactions between the heterogeneous networks will provide a next generation network which will support high mobility at high data rates.

Also the existing wireless network depends on such infrastructure s as base stations, gateways etc. of their services limits the availability of the network in some areas. But because next generation mobile networks are meant to provide services anytime and anywhere, the system allows for the integration of an ad hoc network which is an infrastructure less network into the system.

Many researchers have proffer ways of integrating heterogeneous networks using interworking solutions. Park, H. *et al.* (2012) has proposed gateway service which is provided through message encapsulation with MIH protocol header. Nithyanandan & Parthiban (2012) suggested a heterogeneous network through gateway relocation.

Zhou *et al.* (2013) present a novel miniaturized reconfigurable and switchable feeding network to cover GSM, GPS, 3G and LTE. It was made up of four individually reconfigured conventional Wilkinson power dividers. The dividers are reconfigured using PIN diode switches and by controlling the bias voltage of the PIN diodes, the operating frequency of the feeding network can be converted between four different bands in order to accommodate the above mentioned networks. These are: 600MHz-900MHz to satisfy the application of LTE US which uses 700MHz, LTE UK (800MHz), and GSM which uses 850MHz and 900MHz; 1.2GHz-1.6GHz for GPS L1 (1.575GHz) and GPS L2 (1.227GHz); 1.8GHz-2.2GHz which targets different GSM (1800MHz, 1900MHz) and 3G standards; and 2.4GHz-2.6GHz which is used to cover LTE Europe which uses 2.6GHz and Wi-Fi (2.45GHz).

The design which was implemented on FR4 substrate can be applied to commercial multiband communication systems and hence "forms an important step towards realizing a truly global mobile phone" (Zhou *et al.*, 2013).

Chen *et al.* (2011) proposed the Advanced Vertical Handoff Translation Centre (Advanced VHTC) architecture for Wi-Fi/WiMAX heterogeneous wireless networks with the aim of improving QoS through packet format translation and MIH based mechanism for vertical handover. This in turn minimizes the time for handover and improves quality and persistent connection service.

The framework provides a good integrated network which allows MTs to have a seamless roaming in the heterogeneous wireless networks and exchange data conveniently.

Interworking Devices

The use of interworking devices in the next generation mobile networks system will play an important role hence it is based on the integration of heterogeneous systems. Mobile terminals in order to create a seamless mobility between the various networks tries to access the core network by selecting any available accessible network. This resulted in the need for an interworking device such as middleware, software-defined radio (SDR), etc.

To provide interaction between the various networks, organizations have developed interworking solutions for heterogeneous networks, (Park, H. *et al.*, 2012). For example, IEEE developed Media Independent Handover (MIH) framework to provide vertical handovers between different networks and suggested Access Network Query Protocol (ANQP) to serve as interface protocol to wireless networks (IEEE Standards, n.d.). 3GPP developed Access Network Discovery and Selection Function (ANDSF) for interworking between 3GPP and non-3GPP networks (3GPP, n.d.). WiMAX also provided solutions for interworking with other networks (WiMAX Forum, n.d.).

Middleware

Middleware is a set of standardized applications often used for software that serve as a communication protocol between an operating system and applications. Middleware is used at the application layer on top of the operating systems and communication stacks

Aiftimiei, C. *et al.* (2012) presents the strategies followed by the European Middleware Initiative (EMI) which is a collaboration among the major European middleware providers such as ARC, dCache, gLite and UNICORE with the aim of evolving and consolidating all the existing middleware stacks by facilitating their interoperability and deploying them on a large infrastructure thereby establishing a sustainable model for the future maintenance and evolution of the components comprising the middleware. "Complimenting this commitment is the implementation of ScienceSoft, an EMI initiative to build a network developers and users" (Aiftimiei, C.; et al; 2012).

Albayrak *et al.* (2008) propose a network-aware middleware that will utilize network resources and adapt their configuration to service demands and are capable of addressing future challenges. But the "major next step would be to bring everything together in a systematic fashion" and "this would ensure the availability of a consistent and running middleware that can be simply deployed and used in future networks"(Albayrak *et al.*, 2008).

Hongjun *et al.* (2010) propose a mobile Message Oriented Middleware (MOM) framework that will support data sharing in a mobile computing environment by an XML- coded data which packed in the form of a message and passed through a mobile terminal connected with MOM executed on fixed terminals and then shared among grouped mobile terminals over an ad hoc network using replication and reconciliation. Though it shows a transparent data sharing in a heterogeneous network, there is need for improvement in the algorithm to make small footprint of mobile terminals and make it practical with a power saving schemes.

Bae, Y-S. *et al.* (2010) present an adaptive middleware based on the Universal Middleware Bridge (UMB) that provides adaptive autonomic configuration and autonomous fault for a heterogeneous home network. The fault management include diagnosis and recovery from such faults as plug-outs, network and service failures in order to ensure seamless mobility in the heterogeneous home network. The system provides a seamless connection in the network but it needs to be adoptable to different environment.

Access Points (Aps)

An Access Point is a network device capable of creating a communication between a remote wireless stations and a local area network and/or within the network. In Ethernet LANs, acts as a bridge while in remote wireless stations it acts as adaptors. Access Point is made up of a transceiver for signal transmission using spread spectrum transmission which may either be direct sequencing or hoping; and an antenna for receiving signals to and from the remote stations and managed by a WLAN Controller which is responsible for the handling radio frequency and security. The controllers are also responsible for creating a wireless mobility by allowing inter-controller roaming. Also, Access Points may act as a negotiator between devices that can transmit.

An area covered by a single Access Point (AP) is called a cell and can support fifteen to twenty-five wireless stations within the cell at an optimal data rates of 1Mbps to 3Mbps over a distance of about three kilometers (3 Km),(Tulloch & Tulloch, 2002).

Long Term Evolution (LTE)

The LTE standard was first approved in 2007 and designed with the intention of supporting a bi-directional handovers between it and other networks. It is also an all-IP based network and has a cell capacity of more than 200 users at a radius of 5Km at 5MHz.

As LTE evolved from 3GPP to LTE-Advanced as part of 3GPP Release 10 concluded in 2010 improved the LTE radio access in many extents ranging from enhanced spectrum flexibility, and relaying functions of providing a solution for wireless backhauling, among others. The current 3GPP Release 11 added an additional basic functions for coordinating multipoint (CoMP) transmission/reception as well as support for heterogeneous deployments (Astely *et al.*, 2013).

Based on the 3GPP workshop, "Release 12 and Beyond" held in June 2012, addressed the evolution planned to conclude in June 2014 to include: Enhanced local area access; Multi-antenna enhancements; Improved support for machine-type communication (MTC); and Direct device-to-device communication.

Astely *et al.* (2013) provide an overview of the key technology areas /components that are currently considered by 3GPP for Release 12 (Rel-12), including further support for improved local area access by tight interaction between the wide area and the local area layers, signalling solutions for wireless local area network integration, multi-antenna enhancements, improved support for massive MTC, and direct device to device communications.

Hence, it "is a very flexible platform, continuously evolving to address new requirements and additional scenarios" (Astely *et al.*, 2013) including interworking heterogeneous network. This made it an interworking device for the next generation mobile network.

Mobility Management

The roaming between the heterogeneous networks gives rise to the need of a mobility management scheme. Mobility management which is an essential requirement for the provision of network at anytime and anywhere allows access to the network from different locations while maintaining uninterrupted service. Mobility management includes two tasks of handoff management and the user location management. Location management enables a network to discover the current position of the user equipment through registration and paging; while handoff management enables a network to maintain a connection as the mobile node moves from one point to the other either within a cell (Intracell) or between cells (Intercell), and may be performed in two ways: soft and hard.

In the next generation mobile networks, the accessibility can be achieved -through a set of personal devices which gave birth to three high-level mobility types; session, personal and service mobility. Moreover, ad hoc networks also gave birth to more mobility types in term of ad hoc mobility and mode mobility.

Terminal mobility allows a device to roam between different networks with differing technologies while continuing to be reachable for incoming requests and maintaining the existing session during movement across different geographical regions. Adaptive techniques like middleware will provide terminal mobility (Rao *et al.*, 2006).

Personal mobility is a step ahead of terminal mobility in the sense that it is more of the user than device. It is aimed at providing a seamless personal to users without considering the device used by the users.

Session mobility allows continuous enjoyment of a session as the user roams from one device to another, and Service mobility allows users access to service even with changes in network providers.

"In allowing users to access any system at anytime and anywhere, the performance of mobility-enabled protocols is important. While Mobile IPv6 is generally used to support macro-mobility, integrating Mobile IPv6 with Session Initiation Protocol (SIP) to support IP traffic will lead to improved mobility performance" (Nursimloo & Chan, 2005).

Mobility Management consists of all operations required to serve a mobile terminal (users) with services while on the move. There are two types of mobility a network has to support in cellular networks: terminal and personal mobility. Terminal mobility refers to the situation in which a mobile terminal is offered the necessary services for establishing and maintaining access by the network while in personal mobility which is independent of the mobile terminal is a scenario in which the network must offer the necessary services for establishing and maintaining access between the mobile terminal and the user (Küpper, A., 2005).

The operations of mobility management can be divided into two main subsets, namely: location management and handoff management. Location management is the process of discovering a mobile terminal (MT) to enable a network authenticates and updates the location for the establishment of connection. And this can be achieved through location registration (update) and paging. Handoff management on the other hand according to Rao, K.R., Bojkovic, Z.S., and Milovanovic, D.A. (2009) is performed in three steps: initiation, connection generation, and data flow control. This can be either vertical handover (that is, across radio access technologies) or horizontal handover (within a radio access technology). Another way of classifying handoff management is to identify the operation domains which are: inter domain and intra domain handovers (Anderson, K.; 2012).

Rao, Bojkovic & Milovanovic (2006) further classify the mobility of a mobile terminal (MT) in a network into three broad categories: Micromobility (intrasubnet mobility); Macromobility (intersubnet mobility); and Global mobility (interdomain mobility).

In GSM and UMTS, mobility management takes place at the data link layer whereas in a heterogeneous wireless network there is a need for a mobility management at layers above the data-link layer in "order to take advantage of all available technologies at a certain moment and a certain place"(Anderson, K., 2012: 32).

Mobility Protocols

Session Initiation Protocol (SIP)

The Session Initiation Protocol is an application layer signaling protocol designed by IETF between 1996 and 1999 at Columbia University for initiating, modifying, monitoring and terminating internet sessions such as video, messages, online games, etc. it is a negotiating protocols which uses the Real-time Transport Protocol/ Real-time Transport Control Protocol (RTP/RTCP) for transport/control of media and; Session Description Protocol (SDP) for negotiating media.

SIP is used in facilitating PSTN- internet interworking and also to control services that are terminal and network independent. It provides some level of session mobility management support in that the location services and SIP re-negotiation features allow a user to remain in contact even if they change terminals during session (Wisely *et al.*, 2002).

Entities of SIP

SIP, which is a peer-to-peer protocol, defined two major network elements, namely: User Agent (UA) and Network Server. The network server contains the proxy, location, registration, redirect and universal resource locators (URL).

- **User Agent:** The User Agent is an application which contains both the User Agent Client (UAC) and the User Agent Server (UAS) as defined by RFC 2543. The UAC is a client that initiates the SIP request while the UAS is a server that returns a response on the user's behalf. The SIP clients that can function as UA includes: phones and gateways.
- **Network Server:** The network server contains the proxy, location, registration, redirect and universal resource locators (URL). The Proxy Server is an intermediary device that serves as both a client and a server by receiving a request which are either generated internally or by passing them on from a client and forwarding it to other servers. Other functions of the server include interpretation, authorisation, routing, security and network access control. The Redirect Server unlike the Proxy Server which redirects to other servers, accepts a request, record the called party's address and returns to the client with the information regarding the hop to take in order to speak to the UAS. The Registrar Server is responsible for the registration of the client's location by accepting the REGISTER request for the purpose of updating the database.

Operation of SIP

The UAC creates the session by issuing an invitation and the UAS responds by sending a reply message. The SIP request message is made up of the following basic messages: Register, Invite, ACK, Options, Bye and Cancel as shown in figure 1 below.

Figure 1. SIP Session Establishment and Termination between two MTs (User Agents)

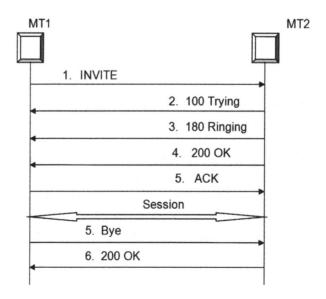

Communication between two User Agents (MT1 and MT2) can be done via two types of messages; namely: Request sent from MT1 to MT2 which contain invitation thereby initiating a call and Response sent from MT2 to MT1 which contain numeric codes that are based on HTTP response code with SDP packet containing the media to be used. Other information contained in the Response message include time(s) the session will be active, information about the bandwidth to be used by the session and the contact information for the MT responsible for the session.

Proxy Mobile Internet Protocol (PMIP)

The proxy Mobile Internet Protocol (PMIP) is an IP mobility management network protocol introduced by IETF in order to assist in the support of IP mobility in a low latency, high data-rate across a heterogeneous network with various access technologies. It gives mobile terminal access to mobility without involvement in the management of their IP mobility signalling (Sanchez *et al.*, 2013) and hence depends on an additional software and hardware implemented on the mobile terminal (Ruckus wireless, 2013).

Mobility management is supported in PMIP by two key elements: the Mobile Access Gateway (MAG) and the Local Mobility Anchor (LMA). The LMA in the mobile core is responsible for maintaining the location of the mobile terminal in the Localized Mobility Domain (LMD) and forwarding the data traffic of the mobile terminal by maintaining an IPv6-in-IPv6 channel with the MAG which is in the core network.

In PMIP, the mobile terminal always maintains its IP address as it moves from one point to within the LMD managed by an LMA. Similarly, "the operation of PMIPv6 does not require the MN to implement any modification or extra software in its layer-3 stack, although it may require the assistance of some layer-2 mechanisms to work more efficiently. These mechanisms are known as link-layer triggers, and are required to quickly detect a change of layer-2 Point of Attachment (PoA)" (Sanchez *et al.*, 2013).

PMIP is one of the technologies that perform localized mobility management which allows a mobile terminal (MT) to move from one access router to another within the same network in a transparent way. It allows for the reduction in mobility signalling traffic and the improvement of handover performance.

Mobility in GSM Networks

Mobility in GSM can realized through the switching capability and data subscription separation. That is, by grouping some PLMNs which provide communication capabilities that the network provider can provide, and passing information among them. The PLMN consist of MSC and GMSC and are not specific to a certain group. The MSC which contain the subscribers' information has a switching capability that may be used by the subscriber using the PLMN and for subscribers' mobility within a network. As far as the mobile terminal is connected to the Base Station (BSS), the information of the subscriber is contained in the MSC/VLR. This information is kept in the MSC even when the mobile terminal is disconnected from the BSS for a certain period of time and when it moves from one MSC to the other, the HLR will instruct the previous MSC to purge the subscription information of the subscriber and send the information to the present MSC (Eberspacher *et al.*, 2009).

Mobility in 3G Networks (UMTS)

The UMTS signal protocol is divided into two strata of access strata (AS) and non-access strata (NAS). The NAS, which is located at the upper layer, is responsible for: Connection Management (CM) for handling circuit-switched calls control, short message services and supplementary services; Session Management (SM) responsible for packet-switched calls; Mobility Management (MM) which handles mobility functions such as location update in the circuit-switched domain; and GPRS Mobility Management (GMM) which is responsible for handling mobility functions such as route update in the packet-switched domain.

The Access Stratum is made up of the physical layer (PHY) in layer 1; Radio Link Control (RLC) and Medium Access Control (MAC) in the second layer; and Radio Resource Control (RRC).

Mobility management in UMTS is mostly done in three major states. The three mobility management states of the mobile terminal (MT) exist. The mobility management states are the detached, connected and idle states.

At the detached state, the mobile terminal is unreachable by the network because it is not attached to the UMTS. In the idle state, the mobile terminal is attached to the UMTS network and mobility management have been established by both the mobile terminal and the SGSN by performing detach/location update and paging procedures respectively. Here, the mobile terminal is tracked by the SGSN at the routing area (RA) level. In the connected state, packet-switched signalling connection is established between the mobile terminal and the SGSN. Unlike in the idle state, the mobile terminal is tracked by the SGSN with precision of the routing area and the serving RNC relocation which is responsible for tracking call-level is executed here.

Mobility in WiMAX

Mobility Management in the WiMAX architecture are designed to achieve minimal handover latency and packet loss. The WiMAX foundation basing on the procedure specified by the IEEE 802.16 standard, has designed network messaging and procedures to provide the network support of mobility.

WiMAX network architecture uses Mobile IP Protocols and special protocols defined by WiMAX NWG to handle mobility. The MIP makes it possible to use off the shelf components such as Home Agents (HA) and the WiMAX specific protocols are used to provide optimization and flexibility in handling mobility. For a given mobile terminal, the MIP HA which resides in the CSN and one or more Foreign Agents resides in each ASN. The mobile terminal's information is transported through the MIP tunnel which ends at the FA in the ASN. On termination of the MIP tunnel at the FA, the data path function (DPF) which is the WiMAX specific protocol takes over and transport the information from the FA to the operating base station (BS) to which the mobile station is attached.

Hence, mobility management in the WiMAX network can be classified as a two-tiered solution: ASN-Anchored and CSN-Anchored. ASN-anchored relates to handover event without the MIP tunnel termination point while the CSN-anchored mobility management are performed on all handover activities and include several localized optimizations such as extending the data path from a previous serving ASN entity to the new ASN, thereby avoiding the effect of Layer-3 handover delays when applicable (Shantidev *et al.*, 2008).

Mobility in TETRA

An optimal mobility management in TETRA will provide a dynamic and critical public safety and disaster relief network will provide a consistent, seamless and secure communication services in cases of emergencies.

Durantini & Petracca (2008), suggest a vertical handover (VHO) solution able to optimize mobility management over a heterogeneous network which is specifically designed to provide public safety and disaster relief organisation using TETRA and TETRA 2 systems with the capability to exploit Wi-Fi and WiMAX broadband access technologies in order to enjoy advanced services.

The concept supports both low-level and high-level mobility by pursuing a cross-layer approach that lets MIP and SIP with SBC collaborate in a complimentary rather than competing way, thus avoiding redundancy. It balances the traffic load among different networks and handles real time traffic with particular respect.

Mobility in Mobile Ad hoc Network

Mobility management in mobile ad hoc network (MANET) takes place in the Local Mobility Anchor (LMA) which will register and update the location of the Mobile terminal inside the Localized Mobility Domain (LMD). The Access Routers (AR) alerts the LMA when a mobile terminal moves from one router to the other in order to update its location. However the access router cannot identify a mobile terminal when they are more than one hop apart because MANET is a multi-hop network (Sargento *et al.*, 2008).

MANET needs an adaptation in order to work in a LMD which relates to the ability of the access router to detect the mobility of mobile terminals. On arrival in a network, the mobile terminal alerts the AR (or gateway) of its location which in turn activates the mobility protocol. Once it is identified by the mobility protocol via bootstrapping, the mobility protocol can operate in the same way than in infrastructure network.

Mobility Management in Heterogeneous Networks

As mentioned earlier, in a heterogeneous wireless network there is a need for a mobility management at layers above the data-link layer in "order to take advantage of all available technologies at a certain moment and a certain place"(Anderson, K., 2012: 32).

Munoz *et al.* (2013) introduce different mechanisms for steering traffic by clarifying the techniques that may adjust mobility parameters and the challenges arising from particular deployment of heterogeneous network including LTE deployment; and propose a fuzzy-based algorithm that enhances network constraints for traffic steering.

In the idle mode, the AP-based cell reselection algorithm indicates that the Aps of the HetNets allows the service providers to control the distribution of users across the network layers. In the connected mode, the inter-RAT HO algorithm on the other hand shows that the adjustment of the associated parameters may depend on the small cell location within the macro cell. Lastly, the SON algorithm which is based on reinforcement learning and fuzzy logic shows that "it can automatically adapt to context variations in order to significantly improve user satisfaction in Heterogeneous networks.

Thakur & Helmy (2013) investigate the capability of existing mobility models by taking into consideration the various aspects of mobility behavior, as well as network protocol performance and then proposed the collective behavior based on realistic aspects of human mobility (COBRA) which attempts to explicitly takes into consideration individual, pair-wise and group mobility.

The model COBRA is capable of spanning the mobility metric space and matches realistic traces with protocol performance, thus reducing "the gap between current models and human behavioral mobility modeling" (Thakur & Helmy, 2013).

Sanchez *et al.* (2013); proposes a network-based integrated mobility framework for wireless optical broadband access network (WOBAN) which is based on the proxy mobile IPv6 (PMIPv6) and IEEE 802.21 (MIH) mobility management protocols. PMIPv6-WOBAN aimed at providing an enhanced the mobility of "users with respect to the overall network resources, both at the wireless access and optical distribution parts; remove the overhead of IP-in-IP tunneling between the PMIPv6 entities, and perform an efficient bicasting during handover process to minimize packet loss"(Sanchez *et al.*, 2013).

The above objectives were achieved by mapping the PMIPv6 framework and IEEE 802.21 MIH services into the hierarchical structure of the WOBAN's Passive Optical Network (PON) by collocating the Local Mobility Anchor (LMA) with the Optical Line Terminal (OLT), and the Mobile Access Gateways (MAGs) with the Optical Network Units (ONUs) which controls a set of heterogeneous wireless Access Points. The OLT-LMA node is able to combine information on mobile mobility and traffic statistics obtained from the ONU-MAGs, thereby initiating handovers of MTs due to ONU and AP overload; hence making the integrated framework provides an enhanced use of resources. Also, the framework contains a number of optimizations that prevent packet loss and providing seamless handover by the single-hop, point-to-multipoint topology of an Ethernet PON (EPON) which avoids the overhead of maintaining tunnels between LMA and its MAGs; and enables the use of multicast EPON bicasting during mobility management. Finally, the PMIPv6-WOBAN framework provides mobility between different networks on the Localized Mobility Domain (LMD).

Distributed Mobility Management (DMM)

Most of the currently standardized IP mobility management protocols such as Proxy Mobile IPv6 (RFC5213) rely to a certain extent on a centralized mobility anchor entity which is in charge of the mobility control and the forwarding of users' data. They offer mobility support at the cost of handling operations at a cardinal point, the mobility anchor, and burdening it with data forwarding and control mechanisms for a great amount of users. As stated in [RFC7333], centralized mobility solutions are prone to several problems and limitations: longer (suboptimal) routing paths, scalability problems, signalling overhead (and most likely a longer associated handover latency), more complex network deployment, higher vulnerability due to the existence of a potential single point of failure, and lack of granularity on the mobility management service (i.e., mobility is offered on a per-node basis, not being possible to define finer granularity policies, as for example per-application). This in turn makes the current mobility protocols prone to several problems and limitations (Chan *et al.*, 2014) [RFC7333] such as single point of failure, routing in a non-optimal route (suboptimal), overloading of the centralized data anchor point due to the data traffic increase, low scalability of the centralized route and context management, scalability problems, signalling overhead (and most likely a longer associated handover latency), more complex network deployment, higher vulnerability due to the existence of a potential single point of failure, and lack of granularity on the mobility management service.

This has prompted researchers and mobile operators to look for different mobility management methods which are more distributed in nature, and that allow to enable mobility on demand for particular types of traffic. This effort brought about what is known as Distributed Mobility Management (DMM) (Fabio *et al.*, 2009).

One of the major requirements for distributed mobility management (DMM) as defined by (RFC7333) is to enable traffic to avoid traversing single mobility anchor far from the optimal path by addressing the scalability issues derived from a centralized mobility management (CMM) deployment and providing mobile nodes with local anchors.

DMM whose concept is based on the distribution of mobility anchors towards the access networks to provide mobile nodes with local anchors and enable optimized routing of traffic above anchor level to any kind of serving point, according to Luca Valtulina (2013) offers to operators a more efficient network deployment driven by a distributed placement of core network entities close to the edge (access) of the network.

Distributed mobility management aims at solving the centralized mobility anchor problems of the traditional mobility management protocol. The benefit of DMM solution is that the data plane traffic does not need to traverse the centralized anchoring point.

Current IP mobility solutions, standardized with the names of Mobile IPv6 [RFC6275], or Proxy Mobile IPv6 [RFC5213], just to cite the two most relevant examples,

The purpose of Distributed Mobility Management is to overcome the limitations of the traditional centralized mobility management [RFC7333] [RFC7429]; the main concept behind DMM solutions is indeed bringing the mobility anchor closer to the MN.

Distributed Mobility Management (DMM) allows network traffic to distribute among multiple mobility anchors which have mobility functions to solve the existing problems in current centralized mobility protocols. There are many DMM approaches extending network-based mobility protocols (e.g. Proxy Mobile IPv6).

In Proxy Mobile IPv6 (PMIPv6), they allow a mobile node to connect to PMIPv6 domain through different physical interfaces.

In DMM scenario, mobility anchors would be deployed in a distributed manner, and as specified in [RFC7333], one of the aims of DMM is to reduce the routing redundancy between mobile node and correspondent node, which means providing a more optimal communication path for application traffic between mobile node and correspondent node. To achieve routing optimization for specific application traffic, the basic idea is to make the traffic using IP address(es) anchored at current anchor, so that downlink traffic from correspondent node to mobile node will go directly to mobile node, but this routing optimization requirement brings a fact that mobile node has to change its IP address as it moving to a new anchor. Some application sessions can cope with the change of IP address either by application layer itself or by the function provided by other layers, e.g. transport layer; but for other application sessions, after IP address changed, the application session would be broken off totally.

So it's reasonable to provide different network layer mobility support according to the need of application.

Cross-Layer Design

Cross-Layer design is a model that allows the flow of information, interaction, coordination and joint optimization across the different layers of a protocol stack in a non-trivial way. Because of the various limitations of the protocol stack (TCP/IP and OSI Models) especially in terms of wireless network performance, cross-layer design is assumed to improve the performance of wireless communications systems (Fotis *et al.*, 2008).

Though, there are many approaches to cross-layer design, they can be classified into strong and weak cross layering. A weak cross-layering, otherwise known as evolutionary approach allows interaction among different layers of a protocol stack while strong cross-layering (also called revolutionary approach) on the other hand, allows joint design of the algorithm implemented with any entity at any level of the protocol stack.

Cross-Layer Signalling Architectures

Researchers have proposed several Cross-Layer Signalling architectures though very few are prototyped and included into current operating systems (Kliazovich *et al.*, 2009). These architectures can be grouped under the following:

- **Inter-Layer Signalling Pipe:** This architecture allows the flow of data in the protocol stack in a bottom-up or top-down manner. This can be achieved via two methods: Packet header which carries the information to the IPv6 header and; packet structure which carries the information into a specific section of the packet structure.
- **Direct Inter-Layer Communication:** It introduces short-cuts out of band performance. For example, CLASS.
- **Central Cross-Layer Plane:** The signalling information in this architecture can be accessed by all the layers of the protocol stack. For example, ÉCLAIR
- **Network-Wide Cross-Layer Signalling:** This method aims at defining cross-layer signalling at different layers of a protocol stack of a system terminal (Kliazovich *et al.*, 2009).

Similarly, cross-layer design can be performed in either a loosely coupled or tightly-coupled cross-layer design. In a loosely-coupled cross-layer design, the optimization is done on one layer without crossing the layers. This can be improved by taking into consideration all the parameters in the protocol layer and transferring the information to the other layers. The information can be utilized in two ways: the algorithm must be changed based on the information from the other layers and; information from the other layers is just as the one in the protocol layer.

In the tightly-coupled cross-layer design in which the information sharing between the layer is not enough and thus the algorithms in different layers are optimized together as one optimization problem (Akyildiz & Wang, 2009).

Cross-Layer Design in 3G (UMTS)

Wang, Q. and Yuan, D. (2010) propose an active ACK control strategy with cross-layer information interaction (CL-AACS) in order to solve the problem of multi-user contention brought by packet scheduling in MAC layer and to improve the performance of TCP in UMTS. The scheme is embedded and placed in the base station to control and return an ACK for the information transferred between the MAC-layer and transport-layer so that all users can have fair TCP throughput and optimized utilization of wireless link resources.

The simulated result shows that the scheme provides fair and effective trade-off for TCP over UMTS.

Cross-Layer Design in WiMAX

In order to close one of the major gaps of inter-layer connectivity between the network and link layer, Neves *et al.* (2008) propose the WiMAX Cross-Layer (WXL) system which is responsible for providing all the required cross-layer services between the WiMAX between the WiMAX MAC layer and the network layers. The system is made up of the middleware layer which is located between the WiMAX technology and the network layer, thus hiding the specific functions of the WiMAX technology from the control plane of the network layer. Interactions with the network layers in the WXL system is provided by a set of dedicated interfaces which consists of the upper and lower interfaces and comprises support for QoS mobility and interactions with link layer technologies respectively.

The test result performed on the test bed indicates a small processing time for QoS reservations, modification and deletions.

Cross-Layer Design in Ad Hoc Network

Gafur *et al.* (2013) present an Enhanced Virtual Carrier Mechanism with a controlled exchange of RTS/CTS for an effective interaction among the protocol layers by sharing valuable information for making the right decision for a realistic response in mobile ad hoc network by enhancing the MAC and network layers. This is done in a way that the elements in one network can be used to improve the other. The scheme will also repair the route within the shortest possible time with less overhead.

Though the simulation result indicates that the scheme overtakes the standard one in different scenarios, but "if the traffic is above a pre-defined threshold no attempt is made for local repairing" (Gafur *et al.*, 2013).

Cross-Layer Mobility Management

To provide a Cross-Layer Mobility Management, Wang & Abu-Rgheff (2003) propose the Cross-Layer Signalling Shortcuts (CLASS) scheme to enable direct communications between arbitrary layers which can be applied in QoS management, power, radio resources, mobility, and in the IP-based next-generation wireless network.

Though CLASS has significant advantages when compared with other methods through a qualitative evaluation, it is yet to be introduced to solve real-world problems and future research is underway to simulate it in a software simulator and implement on I on Linux with kernel modified operating system (Wang & Abu-Rgheff, 2003).

Chiang, Dai & Luo (2012) propose the media-independent pre-authentication redirect tunneling (MPA-RT) which is integrated with media- independent handover (MIH) and session initiation protocol (SIP) to provide a seamless cross-layer handover for SIP applications.

Simulation results indicate that the framework is more efficient to MPA-DB in terms of packet transmission delay and buffer utilization.

Wang, He & Chen (2012) proposes and analyses a cross-layer integrated mobility and service management scheme called DMAPwSR in IPv6 environments with the aim of minimizing the overall cost of mobility and service management. The framework uses smart routers which act as access routers for the MIPv6 systems except that they are capable of processing binding messages from the mobile terminal and storing their location updates in the routing table. The DMAPwSR which is analyzed based on stochastic

Petri net performs better HMIPv6 in terms of network communication overhead which resulted in saving cost of communication per time unit per user because of the selection of best DMAP service area.

The limitations of the DMAPwSR include the minimal functionality of the smart router hence the need for making it feasible for all-IPv6 DMAP- compliant.

Crismani *et al.* (2010) design a MAC scheme which adopts a cooperative physical layer aided cross-layer techniques based on the CoopMAC techniques of Liu et al., "which is improved by improved by facilitating cooperative signal combining at the destination and and employing two relays in the context of a successive relaying technique" (Crismani *et al.*, 2010).

The algorithm for the selection of transmission rate which provided a fixed block error ratio (BLER) when decoding the frame received both at the source and the relay was amalgamated with the efficient likelihood ratio (LLR) combination at the destination of the direct and relayed components. This in turn decreases the probability of outage and raises the throughput of the network.

The framework which is evaluated by the Monte-Carlo simulations investigated the selection and activation of the two relays by the protocol, mitigated the multiplexing loss imposed by the half-duplex constraint of 802.11 stations using a successive relaying protocol relying the two relays. The result indicates that "invoking two relays has the potential of further increasing the network's throughput gain" (Crismani *et al.*, 2010).

Di Caro *et al.* (2006) present a novel design approach based on autonomic components and cross-layer monitoring and control for performance maximization of the WiOptiMo framework which provides a seamless roaming between networks by handling application layer mobility.

The framework which is in its introductory stage is yet to be concluded but it is aimed at presenting an innovative cross-layering and autonomic design for the forth-coming release of next WiOptiMo. From the preliminary results, the researchers intend to include the use of different type of traffic in the wireless network; to monitor other parameters to further boost the response of the scheme and to investigate the use of techniques for efficient smoothing the noisy RSS and to boost the robustness of handover initiation decisions by calculating measures to be used in cross-validation with the RSS.

Wang & Abu-Rgheff (2003) present IP-based multi-layer advanced mobility management architecture to take advantage of the various contributions of the single and cross-combined TCP/IP layers by identifying and abstracting the contribution of each layer to the various functions supporting mobility management. The architecture though supports co-ordinated mobility management of different levels for various types of mobility for heterogeneous networks and also facilitates such functions as fast/seamless handoffs, QoS adaptation due to changes in contexts as a result of mobility; it requires active cross-layer interactions to improve its performance.

MAIN FOCUS OF THE CHAPTER

Motivation

The International Telecommunication Union-Radio Communication sector (ITU-R) in 2008 specified a standard for the 4G (though that of 5G is still on the way) system which is beyond the IMT-2000 called the International Mobile Telecommunication-Advanced (IMT-Advanced) specifications. According to the specifications, 4G wireless technology must support the following criteria: high data rate; high capacity, low cost per bit; low latency; good quality of service (QoS); and mobility support at high speeds, (Seddigh *et al.*, 2010).

The next generation wireless network is devised to accommodate a number of wireless applications, devices and devices. That is, it will be heterogeneous in nature in which a mobile terminal will be able to access the internet anytime, anywhere via the various networks. To provide interaction between the various networks, organisations have developed interworking solutions for heterogeneous networks, (Park, H. *et al.*, 2012). For example, IEEE developed Media Independent Handover (MIH) framework to provide vertical handovers between different networks and suggested Access Network Query Protocol (ANQP) to serve as interface protocol to wireless networks (IEEE Standards, n.d.). 3GPPdeveloped Access Network Discovery and Selection Function (ANDSF) for interworking between 3GPP and non-3GPP networks (3GPP, n.d.). WiMAX also provided solutions for interworking with other networks (WiMAX Forum, n.d.). The heterogeneity of different networks that may have different performance and features requires a middleware which supports mobility adaptation (Cao, Wu & Liu, 2010). The primary objective of a middleware is to facilitate and coordinate the distribution of components, concealing the complexity raised by mobility from applications (Khedo, K.K., 2006). Many researchers have also proffer ways of integrating heterogeneous networks using interworking solutions.

Cao *et al.* (2012) propose SHAWK to provide secure integration of heterogeneous advanced wireless networks. The platform internetworked the various networks by customised mesh routers including 30 (thirty) T902 and twelve (12) T903, and they are interconnected with each other to form a wireless backbone and also to provide access to mobile terminals. Each mesh router consists of three Wi-Fi cards, one for mobile terminal access and the other two for backbone connection.

Nithyanandan & Parthibin (2012) in their paper: vertical Handoff in WLAN-WiMAX-LTE Heterogeneous Network through Gateway Relocation used tightly coupled and loosely coupled integration of the various networks through a gateway with IMS protocol.

Park, H. *et al.* (2012) propose a gateway services provided through gateway function of different network entities by using message encapsulation with MIH protocol header that support cost-effective and efficient integration of heterogeneous network using different interworking solution. It's aimed at discovering of target networks and delivery of various kinds of interworking messages as well as ANQP message.

Pramod, P.J. *et al.* (2012) present the design and development of a heterogeneous network test bed to provide a testing platform in an internetworking environment. The platform comprises of both mobile and stationary terminals with media independent middleware, session based IMS and traffic generation and monitoring devices while MIH was incorporated to support mobility across the different networks. The work is only limited to Bluetooth, WLAN and Ethernet, hence the need to extend it to 4G wireless networks.

Bae, Y-S. *et al.* (2010) propose an adaptive middleware based on the Universal Middleware Bridge that supports adaptive autonomic configuration and autonomous fault management in the middleware layer to provide seamless interconnection and robustness in heterogeneous home networks. Though it provides interoperability, there is still need to apply adaptive middleware to support different networks.

The design of mobility management is a key issue in the next generation heterogeneous mobile network. It is important to provide a seamless service switching for a User Equipment with uninterrupted network service during an IP-based wireless access technologies and the emergence of 4G technologies. Similarly, due to the growing needs of mobility management in the heterogeneous 4G wireless system, many protocols are proposed which operate at the network layer which is responsible for the convergence of the heterogeneous wireless networks. There are also other protocols which operate at other layers. For example, SCTP and SIP at the transport layer and application layer respectively and MIP has been standardized but only for terminal mobility. To provide mobility management in 4G heterogeneous networks, Cao, Wu & Liu (2010) proposed SMART for multimedia streaming applications by providing complete mobility support for both device and user mobility. Handover occurs as the mobile terminal moves from WLAN to 3G, but the quality of the video stream degrades significantly due to the decrease in data rates of transferring the video stream.

Chen, Y-C *et al.* (2011) propose an Advanced Vertical handoff Translation Centre (Advanced VHTC) for heterogeneous wireless networks to serve as a seamless vertical handoff mechanism. The mechanism uses the IEEE802.21 which defines the intermediate layer of MIH between the link and network layers and which through it the network information of the communication protocols in the lower layers can be sent to the MIH user. The major limitation of this mechanism is in the handover processes as the throughput goes down temporarily due to vertical handoff. Hence, a seamless vertical handoff is not achieved.

Magagula, Chan & Falawo (2010) proposed a novel handover coordinator (HC) which utilizes the benefits of different handover approaches and coordinates handovers between various networks in a network-based mobility management environment to further improve handover performance between heterogeneous wireless networks in the next generation wireless network (NGWN). The wider the distance between the MAGs the higher the handover delay and the packet loss, and as Mobile terminal moves from one MAG to another packet start dropping until the MT fully attaches to the new MAG. However, at a certain number of MTs there is a significant increase in packet loss in all scenarios as a result of an increase in the mobility-related messages that must be handled at the same time by the relevant network elements. Hence increases the delay in connection links.

Sargento, S. *et al.* (2008) propose Daidalos II to provide ubiquitous access integrating heterogeneous access networks and providing seamless movement among them by splitting of the mobility management, mobile initiated and network initiated handovers, multihoming, virtual identities and ad hoc and network mobility. The architecture needs to support all functionalities.

The cross-layer design is the important approach for mobility management; the design of mobility protocols is very important for the mobile network and a great importance have being attached to it.

However, a cross-layer design is said to be a violation to the traditional layered protocol and the cooperation of multiple-layers will be a necessity as the single-layer mobility architecture does not give the required mobility and heterogeneity support for the 4G all-IP wireless system. Also, the rare radio resources, the limited power and the emerging short-range networks such as Ad Hoc necessitate cross layer design (Wang & Abu-Rgheff, 2003). Notably, this gives an increasing interest in the adaptation of a cross-layer design system which promises an extended functionality.

Wang & Abu-Rgheff (2003) proposes CLASS (Cross-Layer Signalling Shortcuts) aimed at providing advanced mobility support by enabling cross-layer direct interactions between Non-Neighbouring Layers and decomposing internal/external messages. The CLASS-based architecture is not simulated and its performance not evaluated as compared with single-layer platforms.

Wang, He & Chen (2012) propose a cross-layer integrated mobility and service management scheme called DMAPwSR in Mobile IPv6 environment with the aim to reduce the cost of serving mobile terminals with the various mobility and service management characteristics. The scheme uses smart routers which serve as a dynamic mobility anchor points (DMAPs) to the mobile terminals and to process messages to and from the mobile terminals.

Liu, J. *et al.* (2013) in their paper "Distributed Cross-Layer Optimization in Wireless Networks: A Second-Order Approach" developed a second order algorithm for a special network setting where all links mutually interfere and for general wireless networks where the interference relationship are arbitrary. This is achieved through a double matrix-splitting scheme by distributed Newton's method. Though the framework is a building block, it requires a scheduling scheme.

With all these researches, there is still the need for a systematic scheme that will provide a seamless terminal, session, personal and service mobility support in all-IP heterogeneous mobile networks. This motivates the researcher to design a cross-layer mobility management middleware scheme to provide terminal, session personal and service mobility for all-IP heterogeneous mobile networks.

And to the best knowledge of the researchers, there exist no scheme that integrates SIP and PMIPv6.

Statement of the Problem

The future next generation mobile networks will seamlessly integrate existing and new wireless network systems into an all-IP based network and hence will support a wide variety of wireless terminals which are referred to as heterogeneous terminals. And to support the mobility management requirements in the heterogeneous terminals, cross-layer design/optimization seems to be an interesting candidate.

Wireless networks have the characteristics of been volatile in nature and this resulted to an unstable connections between them (Cao, Wu & Liu, 2010). Mobility management in a heterogeneous wireless network will be determined by the quality of the various networks and sometimes this problem occurs even within a network because the quality of connection varies. Due to the differences in the resources in the various networks, it is not easy for a mobile terminal to roam from one network to another for example, from 2G to WiMAX.

Similarly, the next generation heterogeneous mobile network is expected to accommodate many different mobile terminals (laptops, smart phones, etc.) with different resources such as processing power and technology. Hence, the mobility of such MTs in a heterogeneous network serves as a vital requirement in the design of a 4G heterogeneous network.

Since the heterogeneous network consist of various networks and MTs with different resources, the users are left with the option of selecting the network that best suit their requirements and "how to reflect different requirements of mobile users is not trivial" (Cao, Wu & Liu, 2010).

The traditional TCP/IP protocol stack is designed for fixed terminals and hence cannot support the required mobility in the 4G heterogeneous network. Each layer in the stack has a specific function to perform and depends on the information from the immediate next layer. For example, the transport layer depends on the network layer and does not consider the other layers like the link layer which is responsible for mobility. Hence, the need to devise a cross-layer mobility scheme for next generation heterogeneous network is vital.

The next generation mobile wireless network has the hallmark of heterogeneity and calls for a complete solution supporting all kinds of mobility anywhere and anytime.

The design of the optimized multi-layer mobility management scheme for the heterogeneous network will focus on 2G (GSM), 3G, 4G, WiMAX, TETRA and Ad hoc networks. And also concentrate on the merging of SIP and PMIPv6.

Finally, the research work will interface the mobility management scheme and the real time applications.

Significance of the Chapter

Apart from providing access to the various networks, the proposed cross-layer mobility management middleware will also provide access in situation where the infrastructure based network could not be justified (that is, in bad times).

Because of the seamless coupling of the TETRA and the IP-based networks, the system will also serve as a Next Generation Public Safety Communication System (NG-PCS).

The research work will also serve as a literature for those interested in Cross-Layer mobility management in general and the integration of SIP and PMIPv6 in particular. Hence to the best knowledge of the researcher, this will be the first attempt in the integration of SIP and PMIPv6.

SOLUTION AND RECOMMENDATIONS

The next generation wireless mobile systems is expected to integrate various networks to form a heterogeneous wireless network ranging from 2G, 3G to 4G networks. The provision of a seamless mobility (mobility management) among the various networks in the heterogeneous networks remains a major challenge. Similarly, the protocol stack provided by the current TCP and/or OSI models cannot provide the desired mobility to meet the requirements of 4G; hence the need for a cross-layer design. Though cross-layer design is regarded as the violation of the protocol stack, it is expected to provide the requirement of the next generation wireless network systems.

In view of the above, the researcher will find an answer/solutions to how to integrate 2G, 3G, TETRA, WiMAX and Ad hoc networks to form a next generation heterogeneous mobile network; integrate SIP and PMIPv6 and; finally devise and asses a set of intelligent and workable algorithms for a cross-layer mobility management scheme for an all-IP heterogeneous next generation mobile network system over a real-time test bed applications.

In this chapter, the researchers focuses on modelling the architecture and study of the performance of mobility (which includes terminal mobility, network mobility, personal mobility and session mobility) using a simulation approach based on Riverbed Modeler.

SIP-PMIP Cross-Layer Mobility Management

In this chapter, the Researchers design four scenarios of mobility management, namely: Terminal mobility; Network mobility; Personal Mobility and; Session Mobility in a heterogeneous network which is made up of GSM, UMTS, WiMAX, TETRA and MANET; and their implementation in Riverbed Modeler.

Terminal Mobility

In this scenario, the MT initiates the scanning procedure and links to a new frequency. The MT then starts the authentication process by sending an authentication request frame that informs the new middleware of its identity. The new Middleware responds with an authentication response frame indicating its acceptance or rejection. Once a successful authentication has been accomplished, the MT can send a reassociation request frame to the new middleware, which then response with a re-association response frame containing an acceptance or rejection notice.

Network Mobility

In this scenario, the mobile terminal (MT) changes its connectivity from one middleware to the other (that is from one network to another). Each network have different address prefix, the MT detects new network from the address it obtain as its move from one middleware to another.

Depending on the address obtained by the MT from the new network, it can tell whether it has moved into a new network. The MT which is in the original network has an ongoing end-to-end application with the core network (CN) via a middleware. It then starts moving across the original and reaches the new network. After completion of the network mobility management scheme, the MT resumes the traffic with the CN via the new middleware.

In this design, the Care of Addresses (CoAs) of the MTs are assigned by the middleware. After the completion of terminal mobility, the MT sends a message to the middleware requesting a CoA which is further forwarded to the associated middleware based on the SIP-PMIPv6 protocol. The middleware replies the message with a message containing the CoA. From the CoA received by the MT, it can decide whether it requires network mobility or not. The delay which occurs as a result of sending a CoA request message is called network mobility detection delay.

Session Mobility

In the session mobility scenario, the MT needs to further notify the CN about the new address after its completion of the network mobility. A path discovery procedure between the MT and the CN is needed before sending redirection message. Once the session mobility is completed, all the steps involved in terminal and network mobility in the heterogeneous network are completed.

Personal Mobility

When a user change a device, it can be detected by the log in information that will be sent and received at the Policy/Proxy Server and the server will then notify the middleware to collect the application information from the old device and send it to the new device.

Network Modelling and Results

In this section, we present a result obtained from the simulation and the scenario shown in the figure 2 below is used for the simulation. The simulation was performed using the Riverbed Modeler Academic Edition. Each network (e.g. WiMAX) in the heterogeneous network is modelled as a subnet with all the necessary nodes and parameters as depicted by its architecture.

The figures 2 to 5 above indicate the total mobility management delay using the four proposed mobility as stated in the previous sections. Figures 4 and 5, for video conferencing and voice, respectively, illustrate the Packet end-to-end delay and packet delay variation. Though the packets received and sent are high, as mentioned above, the end-to-end delay and packet variation for both video conferencing and voice are very low and in the ranges of some seconds.

The above results cannot be accepted for real time analysis because the academic edition does not possess the required properties to analyze a heterogeneous network which has a high speed. Also, it doesn't have the capabilities of accepting such networks as WiMAX.

Figure 2. Modelling and Simulation Scenario

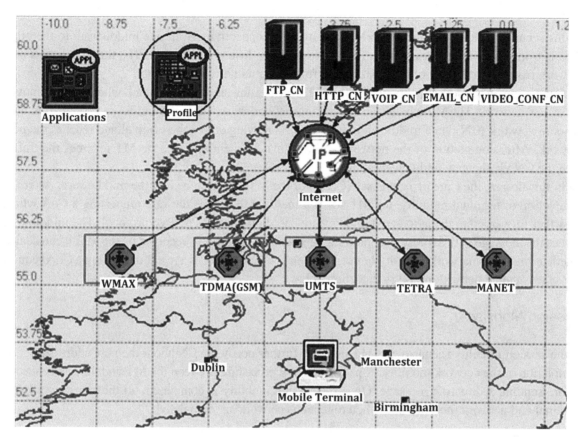

Figure 3. Traffic received (packet/sec) in the heterogeneous mobile network

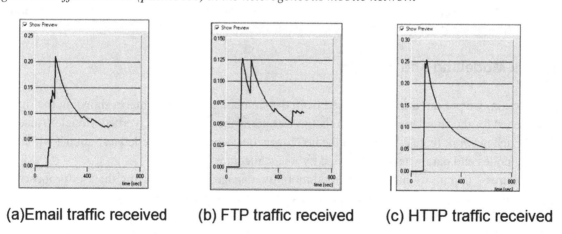

(a)Email traffic received   (b) FTP traffic received   (c) HTTP traffic received

Figure 4. Video conferencing packet flow in the Heterogeneous mobile network

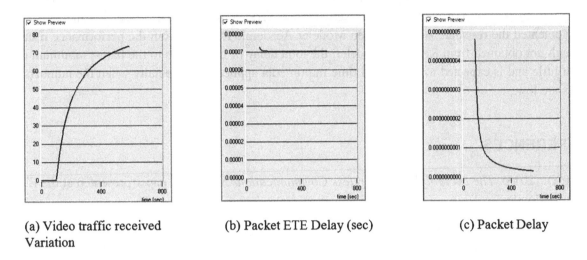

(a) Video traffic received
Variation

(b) Packet ETE Delay (sec)

(c) Packet Delay

Figure 5. Voice packet flow in the Heterogeneous mobile network

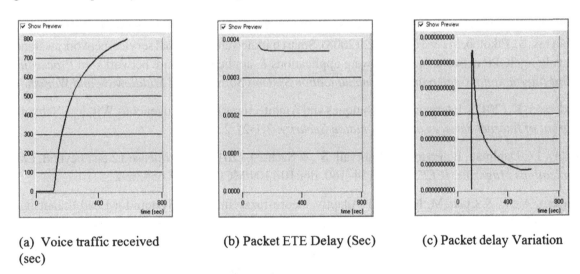

(a) Voice traffic received
(sec)

(b) Packet ETE Delay (Sec)

(c) Packet delay Variation

FUTURE RESEARCH AND DIRECTIONS

In order to analyse the video conferencing properly, there is the need to construct a testbed which is one of the objective of this research which the researcher did not fulfil due to time constraint. Similarly, a better result will be obtain if the Riverbed SteelCentral Network Performance Management.

CONCLUSION

In this chapter, the researchers look at the provision of a seamless mobility management in a heterogeneous wireless network. To provide a seamless and complete mobility support in a heterogeneous network, the researchers proposed a SIP-PMIP Cross-Layer Mobility Management Scheme which provides a seamless mobility support for Terminal, Personal, Network and Service mobility. The researcher modelled and implemented the research using Riverbed Modeler Academic Edition. From the performance results, though not obtained from Riverbed Modeler, the total delay of mobility is to the barest minimum and with little and is expected to give a real time multimedia application especially when the numbers of MTs are low.

REFERENCES

Afif, O. (2013). *The 5G Mobile and Wireless Communications System.* A paper presented at the ETSI Future Mobile.

Aiftimiei, C., Aimary, A., Ceccanti, A., Cecchi, M., Di Meglioy, A., Estrellay, F., . . . White, J. (2012). Towards next generations of software for distributed infrastructures: the European Middleware Initiative. In *Proceedings of IEEE 8th International Conference on E-Science (e-Science).* doi:10.1109/eScience.2012.6404415

Akyldiz, I., & Wang, X. (2009). *Wireless Mesh Networks.* Wiley.

Albayrak, S., Elkotob, M., & Toker, A. C. (2008). Smart middleware for mutual service-network awareness in evolving 3GPP networks network aware applications & application aware networks. In *Proceedings of 3rd International Conference on Communication Systems Software and Middleware and Workshops.*

Anderson, K. (2012). Interworking techniques and Architectures for Heterogeneous Wireless Networks. *Journal of Internet Services and Information Security, 2*(1-2), 22-48.

Astely, D., Dahlman, E., Fodor, G., Parkvall, S., & Sachs, J. (2013). LTE release 12 and beyond. *Communications Magazine, IEEE, 51*(7), 154–160. doi:10.1109/MCOM.2013.6553692

Atayero, A. A., & Luka, M. K. (2012). Adaptive neuro-fuzzy Inference System for Load Balancing in 3GPP LTE. *International Journal of Advanced Research in Artificial Intelligence, 1*(1), 11–16.

Bae, Y.-S., Oh, B.-J., Moon, K.-D., Ha, Y.-G., & Kim, S.-W. (2010, May). Design and Implementation of An Adaptive Middleware Based on The Universal Middleware Bridge for Heterogeneous Home Networks. *IEEE Transactions on Consumer Electronics, 56*(2), 620–626. doi:10.1109/TCE.2010.5505979

Boudriga, N. (2010). *Security of Mobile Communications.* Press.

Cao, J., Wu, W., & Liu, X. (2010). Seamless Mobility Support for Adaptive Applications in Heterogeneous Wireless Networks. In *Proceedings of International Workshop on Mobile Cyber-Physical Systems (UIC-2010 Workshop MobiCPS-2010).*

Cao, J., Zhang, C., Zhang, J., Deng, Y., Xiao, X., Xiong, M., & Yu, Y. et al. (2012). SHAWK: Platform for Secure Integration of Heterogeneous Advanced Wireless Networks. In *Proceedings of 26th International Conference on Advanced Information Networking and Applications Workshops (WAINA 2012).* doi:10.1109/WAINA.2012.118

Chan, H., Liu, D., Seite, P., Yokota, H. & Korhonen, J. (2014). *Requirements for Distributed Mobility Management*. RFC7333.

Chen, Y.-C., Yang, C.-C., Tseng, S.-C., & Hu, Y.-B. (2011) Next Generation Heterogeneous Wireless Networks with QoS Gurantees. In *Proceedings of the IEEE 15th International Symposium on Consumer Electronics*. IEEE.

Crismani, A., Babich, F., & Hanzo, L. (2010). *Cross-Layer Solutions for Cooperative Medium Access Control Protocols*. Academic Press.

Di Caro, G. A., Giordano, S., Kulig, M., Lenzarini, D., Puiatti, A., & Schwitter, F. (2006). A Cross-Layering and Autonomic Approach to Optimized Seamless Handover. In *Proceedings of the 3rd Annual Conference on Wireless On demand Network Systems and Services (WONS)*.

Duan, L., Huang, J., & Walrand, J. (2013). Economic Analysis of 4G Network Upgrade. In Proceedings of IEEE INFOCOM. IEEE.

Durantini, A., & Petracca, M. (2008). Performance comparison of vertical handover strategies for psdr heterogeneous networks. *IEEE Wireless Communications*.

Eberspacher, J., Bettstetter, C., & Vogel, H.-J. (2009). *GSM: Architecture, Protocols and Services*. Chichester, UK: John Wiley and Sons.

Evaluation of Computer and Telecommunication Systems (SPECTS). (2010). Available in http://ieeexplore.ieee.org/stamp/stamp.jsp?tp=&arnumber=5589244&isnumber=5587938

Fabio, G., et al. (2009). *A Hybrid MIPv6 and PMIPv6 Distributed Mobility Management: The MEDI-EVAL approach*. Academic Press.

Fotis, F., Vangelio, G., & Nancy, A. (2008). Cross-Layer Design Proposals for Wireless Mobile Networks: A Survey and Taxonomy. *IEEE Surveys and Tutorials, 10*(1).

Gafur, M. A., Upadhayaya, N., & Syed, A. S. (2013). A Cross Layer Interactive Protocol Mechanism for Manet With a Realistic Response to Network Stimulation. European Scientific Journal, 9(18).

Govil, J., & Govil, J. (2007). *4G Mobile Communication Systems: Turns, Trends and Transition*. Available through IEEE Xplore Digital Library.

3. GPP TS 22.101. (n.d.). *Service principles*. Available in http://www.in2eps.com/3g22/tk-3gpp-22-101.html

3. GPP TS 22.220. (n.d.). *Service requirements for Home Node B and Home eNode B*. Available in http://www.3gpp.org/DynaReport/22220.htm

3. GPP TR 23.829. (2011). *3rd Generation Partnership Project Technical Specification Group Services and System Aspects, Local IP Access and Selected IP Traffic Offload (LIPA-SIPTO) (Release 10)*. 3GPP.

Hongjun, Y., Rong, C., & Zhenjun, D. (2010). Message Oriented Middleware Support for Mobile Ad Hoc Data Sharing. *COMPSAC Workshops 2010*, (pp 305-310).

Huawei. (2014). *5G: A Technology Vision*. Author.

Chiang, W.-K., Dai, H.-J., & Luo, C. (2012). *Cross-layer handover for SIP applications based on media-independent pre-authentication with redirect tunneling. Second International Conference on Digital Information and Communication Technology and it's Applications (DICTAP).* doi:10.1109/DICTAP.2012.6215373

IEEE Standards. (n.d.). *IEEE 802.21™: Media independent handover services.* Available in https://standards.ieee.org/about/get/802/802.21.html

Jayanthiladevi, A., Premlatha, H. M., & Nawaz, G. M. K. (2013). Analysis study of seamless integration and intelligent solution in any situation by the future advanced mobile universal systems 4G-(FAMOUS 4G). *International Conference on Emerging Trends in VLSI, Embedded System, Nano Electronics and Telecommunication System (ICEVENT).* doi:10.1109/ICEVENT.2013.6496551

Katanekwa, N., & Ventura, N. (2013). Mobile content distribution and selective traffic offload in the 3GPP evolved packet system (EPS). *ICOIN, 2013*, 119–124.

Khedo, K. K. (2006). Requirements for Next Generation Middleware Implementations. In Proceedings of International Multi-Conference on Computing in the Global Information Technology. ICCGI.

Kliazovich, D., Michael, D., & Fabriozo, G. (2009). *Formal Methods in Cross-Layer Modelling and Optimization of wireless Networks: State of the Art and future Directions.* IGI Global Publications.

Korhonen, J. (2003). *Introduction to 3G Mobile Communication.* London: Artech House.

Küpper, A. (2005). *Location-based Services: Fundamentals and Operation.* John Wiley & Sons. doi:10.1002/0470092335

Liu, J., Xia, C. H., Shroff, N. B., & Sherali, H. D. (2013). Distributed Cross-Layer Optimization in Wireless Networks: A Second-Order Approach. IEEE INFOCOM 2013. Turin, Italy: IEEE.

Valtulina, L. (2013). *Seamless distributed mobility management(dmm) solution in cloud based lte systems.* Master Thesis. Available in http://essay.utwente.nl/64411/

Magagula, L. A., Chan, H. A., & Falawo, O. E. (2010) PMIPv6-HC: Handover mechanism for reducing handover delay and packet loss in NGWN. In *Proceedings of Global Telecommunications Conference (GLOBECOM 2010).* IEEE. doi:10.1109/GLOCOM.2010.5684108

Monrad, A. (2011). *Core Network migration towards the Evolved Packet Core, Status and Future 3GPP work.* 3GPP Seminar, Moscow.

Mshvidobadze, T. (2012). *Evolution of Mobile Wireless Communication and LTE Networks.* Academic Press.

Munoz, P., Barco, R., Laselva, D., & Mogensen, P. (2013). Mobility-Based Strategies for Traffic Steering in Heterogeneous Networks. *IEEE Communications Magazine*, (May): 2013.

Neves, P., Nissila, T., Pereira, T., Harjula, I., Monteiro, J., Pentikousis, K., Sargento, S., & Fontes, F. (2008). A vendor-independent resource control framework for WiMAX. *Computers and Communications, ISCC 2008.* doi: 10.1109/ISCC.2008.4625750

Nithyanandan, L., & Parthiban, I. (2012), Vertical Handoff in WLAN-WiMAX-LTE Heterogeneous networks Through Gateway Relocation. *International Journal of Wireless and Mobile Networks, 4*(4).

Nursimloo, D.S., & Chan, H.A. (2005). Mobility Management, Quality of Service, and Security in the Design of Next Generation Wireless Network. *African Journal of Information and Communication Technology, 1*(1).

Park, H., Lee, H. H., & Chan, H. A. (2012). Gateway Service for Integration of Heterogeneous Networks using Different Interworking Solutions. In *Proceedings of 15th International Conference on Advanced Communication Technology (ICACT)*.

Pramod, P. J., Malhotra, M., Agarwal, A., Varma, D. P., Jinaga, B. C., & Jain, D. K. (2012). SoIP: An all-IP heterogeneous testbed for SIP-based multimedia services. In *2nd Baltic Congress on Future Internet Communications (BCFIC)*. doi:10.1109/BCFIC.2012.6217951

Rao, K. R., Bojkovic, Z. S., & Milovanovic, D. A. (2006). *Introduction to Multimedia Communications – Applications, Middleware, Networking*. Hoboken, NJ: John Wiley and Sons, Inc.

Ruckus Wireless. (2013). *Interworking Wi-Fi and Mobile Networks – The Choice of Mobility Solutions*. White paper. Author.

Sanchez, M. I. (2013). On Providing Mobility Management in WOBANs: Integration With PMIPv6 and MIH. *IEEE Communications Magazine*.

Sargento, S. & Melia, T. & Banchs, A. & Soto, I. & Moedeker, J & Marchetti, L. (2008). *Mobility through Heterogeneous Networks in a 4G Environment*. Academic Press.

Seddigh, N., Nandy, B., Makkar, R., & Beaumont, J. F. (2010). Security Advances and Challenges in 4G Wireless Networks. In *Proceedings of Eighth Annual International Conference on Privacy, Security and Trust*. doi:10.1109/PST.2010.5593244

Sankaran, C. B. (2012, June). Data offloading techniques in 3GPP Rel-10 networks: A tutorial. *Communications Magazine, IEEE, 50*(6), 46–53. doi:10.1109/MCOM.2012.6211485

Shantidev, M., Venkatachalam, M., & Yang, X. (2008). A Novel Algorithm for Efficient Paging in Mobile WiMAX. In K.-C. Chen & J. R. B. de Marca (Eds.), *Mobile WiMAX*. Chichester, UK: John Wiley & Sons, Ltd; doi:10.1002/9780470723937.ch7

Sharma, P. (2013, August). Evolution of Mobile Wireless CommunicationNetworks-1G to 5G as well as Future Prospective of Next Generation Communication Network. *International Journal of Computer Science and Mobile Computing, 2*(issue. 8), 47–53.

Siddhartha, K., & Madhur, R. N. (n.d.). LIPA: Local IP Access via Home NodeB. *Radisys Whitepaper*.

Tanenbaum, A. S., & Wetherall, D. J. (2011). *Computer Networks*. Pearson.

Thakur, G. S., & Helmy, A. (2013). COBRA: A Framework for the Analysis of Realistic Mobility Models. In *Proceedings of the 16th IEEE Global Internet Symposium*. IEEE.

Thibaut, K. (Ed.). (2014). *5G: A new Philosophy in Connectivity Wireless Protocols on the fly; The End of the Needy Architecture. The European Commission's CONNECT-Community Networks, Control and Technology Directorate – General*. Net Futures.

Tulloch, M., & Tulloch, I. (2002). *Microsoft® Encyclopedia of Networking* (2nd ed.). Redmond, WA: Microsoft Press.

Wang, Q., & Abu-Rgheff, M. A. (2003). Cross-Layer Signalling for Next Generation Wireless Systems. *IEEE Wireless Communications and Networking, 2*, 1084–1089. doi:10.1109/WCNC.2003.1200522

Wang, Q., & Yuan, D. (2010). Effectiveness and fairness tradeoff for TCP using cross-layer design in UMTS system. In *Proceedings of International Symposium on Performance Evaluation of Computer and Telecommunication Systems (SPECTS)*.

Wang, D-C., He, W. & Chen, I-R. (2012). Smart Routers for Cross-Layer Integrated Mobility and Service Management in Mobile IPv6 Systems. *Wireless Pers Commun*. DOI .10.1007/s11277-012-0583-9

WiMAX Forum. (n.d.). Retrieved from http://www.wimaxforum.org

Wisely, D., Eardley, P., & Burness, L. (2002). *IP for 3G: Networking Technologies for Mobile Communications*. John Wiley & Sons, Ltd. doi:10.1002/0470847794

Youssef, S. (2013). *Advanced Mobile Systems*. Lecture Notes Unpublished. Available on VLE at: http://vle.anglia.ac.uk/modules/2013/...../

Zhou, W., Arslan, T., Benkrid, K., El-Rayis, A.O. & Haridas, N. (2013). *Reconfigurable feeding Network for GSM/GPS/3G/WiFi and Global LTE Applications*. Academic Press.

ADDITIONAL READING

Rapooli, S., & Atul, G. (2014). Digital Society from 1G to 5G: A Comparative Study. *International Journal of Application or Innovation in Engineering and Management (IJAIEM)*, Volume 3, Issue 2 of February, 2014. Available at: www.ijaiem.org

Liu, D., Zuniga, JC., Seite, P., Chan, H. & Bernardos, C.J. (2015). Distributed Mobility Management: Current Practices and Gap Analysis, RFC 7429, January 2015. H. Chan, (2011). Problem statement for distributed and dynamic mobility management. Internet-Draft (work in progress), draft-chan distributed mobility- ps-02.txt, Mar. 2011.

Bernardos, C. & Zuniga, J. (2014). PMIPv6-based distributed anchoring, draft-bernardos-dmm-distributed-anchoring-04 (work in progress), May 2014.

BEECube. (2014). Challenges and Solutions in Prototyping 5G Radio Access Network. 5G Whitepaper. Available at: www.beecube.com [Accessed: 13/12/2014].

Eeva, L., & Hao, L. (2013). *Mobile and Wireless Communications Enablers for the twenty-twenty Information Society*. METIS.

David, S. (2013). On the Advanced 5G Network Infrastructure for the Future Internet. A paper Presented at the ICC 2013. Huawei European Research Centre.

Zhao, W., & Xie, J. (2011). OPNET-Based Modelling and Simulation Study on Handoffs in Internet-based Infrastructure Wireless Mesh Networks. *Science Direct Journal of Computer Networks*, 55(2011), pp2675-2688. Available at: www.elsevier.com/locate/comnet

Le, D., Lai, J., & Fu, X. (2007). A New Decentralized Mobility Management Service [-based network.]. *Architecture (Washington, D.C.)*, IPv6.

Nicholas, K., & Ventura, N. (n.d.). *Routing Enhancement for Selectively Offloaded IP Traffic in the Evolved Packet System*.

Compilation of References

3GPP TR 23.829. (2011). *3rd Generation Partnership Project Technical Specification Group Services and System Aspects, Local IP Access and Selected IP Traffic Offload (LIPA-SIPTO) (Release 10)*. 3GPP.

3GPP TS 22.101. (n.d.). *Service principles*. Available in http://www.in2eps.com/3g22/tk-3gpp-22-101.html

3GPP TS 22.220. (n.d.). *Service requirements for Home Node B and Home eNode B*. Available in http://www.3gpp.org/DynaReport/22220.htm

Abolfazli, S., Sanaei, Z., & Gani, A. (2012). Mobile Cloud Computing: A review on smartphone augmentation approaches. In *Proceedings of the 1st International Conference on Computing, Information Systems, and Communications (CISCO12)*.

Abraham, J. (2012). *Generation of mobile communication systems*. Retrieved from: http://www.slideshare.net/jincy-a/generation-of-mobile-communication-systems

Abran, A., Symons, C. R., & Oligny, S. (2001). An overview of COSMIC field trial results. In *Proceedings of the 12th European Software Control and Metrics conference.*

Abran, A. (2015). *Software Project Estimating: The fundamentals for providing high quality information to decision makers*. Hoboken, NJ: John Wiley & Sons.

Acceleo. (2015). *Obeo. Acceleo Generator*. Retrieved April 15, 2015, from http://www.eclipse.org/acceleo/

ACM. (2009). Cloud Computing: An Overview. *ACM Queue, 7*(5). Available at http://doi.acm.org/10.1145/1538947.1554608

ADM. (2015). *Architecture-driven modernization task force*. Retrieved April 15, 2015, from http://www.adm.org

Aepona. (2010). *Mobile Cloud Computing Solution Brief*. White Paper. AEPONA.

Afif, O. (2013). *The 5G Mobile and Wireless Communications System*. A paper presented at the ETSI Future Mobile.

Aiftimiei, C., Aimary, A., Ceccanti, A., Cecchi, M., Di Meglioy, A., Estrellay, F., . . . White, J. (2012). Towards next generations of software for distributed infrastructures: the European Middleware Initiative. In *Proceedings of IEEE 8th International Conference on E-Science (e-Science)*. doi:10.1109/eScience.2012.6404415

Akyldiz, I., & Wang, X. (2009). *Wireless Mesh Networks*. Wiley.

Albayrak, S., Elkotob, M., & Toker, A. C. (2008). Smart middleware for mutual service-network awareness in evolving 3GPP networks network aware applications & application aware networks. In *Proceedings of 3rd International Conference on Communication Systems Software and Middleware and Workshops.*

Amalfitano, D., Fasolino, A. R., & Tremonton, P. (2010). Rich Internet Application Testing Using Execution Trace Data. *Proc. of Second International Workshop on Testing Techniques & Experimentation Benchmarks for Event-Driven Software* (pp. 274- 283). IEEE. doi:10.1109/ICSTW.2010.34

Amalfitano, D., Fasolino, A., & Tramontana, P. (2011). A GUI Crawling-Based Technique for Android Mobile Application Testing. *Fourth International Conference on Software Testing, Verification and Validation Workshops* (pp. 252 - 261). IEEE. doi:10.1109/ICSTW.2011.77

Améndola, F., & Favre, L. (2013). Adapting CRM systems for mobile platforms: An MDA perspective. In *Proceedings of the 2013 14th ACIS International Conference on Software Engineering, Articial Intelligence, Networking and Parallel/Distributed Computing* (SNPD´13) (pp. 323-328), Los Alamitos: IEEE Computer Society. doi:10.1109/SNPD.2013.25

Ames. (2012). *Types of Cloud Computing: Private, Public and Hybrid Clouds*. Retrieved 21 Dec 2014 from http://blog.appcore.com/blog/bid/167543/Types-of-Cloud-Computing-Private-Public-and-Hybrid-Clouds

Ananth, B. (n.d.). *Testing Cloud and Testing using Cloud*. Sonata Software Limited Whitepaper. Retrieved on 25 Dec 2014 from http://www.sonata-software.com/sites/default/files/resources/Cloud_Testing.pdf

Anderson, K. (2012). Interworking techniques and Architectures for Heterogeneous Wireless Networks. *Journal of Internet Services and Information Security, 2*(1-2), 22-48.

Andreasen, M. S., Nielsen, H., Schrøder, S., & Stage, J. (2007). What happened to remote usability testing? An empirical study of three methods. *Conference on Human Factors in Computing Systems*. doi:10.1145/1240624.1240838

Andrews, J. G., Buzzi, S., Choi, W., Hanly, S. V., Lozano, A., Soong, A. C. K., & Zhang, J. C. (2014). What Will 5G Be? *International Journal on Selected Areas in Communications, 32*(6), 1065–1082. doi:10.1109/JSAC.2014.2328098

AndroidDeveloper. (n.d.). Available at http://developer.android.com/training/articles/perf-tips.html

Applause. (n.d.). Retrieved from: https://github.com/applause/applause

Asana. (2015). *Asana*. Retrieved from https://www.asana.com/

Astely, D., Dahlman, E., Fodor, G., Parkvall, S., & Sachs, J. (2013). LTE release 12 and beyond. *Communications Magazine, IEEE, 51*(7), 154–160. doi:10.1109/MCOM.2013.6553692

ASTM. (2011). *OMG Architecture-driven Modernization: Abstract Syntax Tree Metamodel (ASTM)*. Retrieved April 15, 2015, from http://www.omg.org/spec/ASTM

Atayero, A. A., & Luka, M. K. (2012). Adaptive neuro-fuzzy Inference System for Load Balancing in 3GPP LTE. *International Journal of Advanced Research in Artificial Intelligence, 1*(1), 11–16.

AWS. (2015). *What is Cloud Computing?* Retrieved February 18, 2015, from http://aws.amazon.com/what-is-cloud-computing/

Bae, Y.-S., Oh, B.-J., Moon, K.-D., Ha, Y.-G., & Kim, S.-W. (2010, May). Design and Implementation of An Adaptive Middleware Based on The Universal Middleware Bridge for Heterogeneous Home Networks. *IEEE Transactions on Consumer Electronics, 56*(2), 620–626. doi:10.1109/TCE.2010.5505979

Bahar, H. (2013). Islam (2013). Security Architecture for Mobile Cloud Computing. *International Journal of Scientific Knowledge, 3*(3), 11–17.

Bajpai. (2012). Testing as a Service on Cloud. *Igate*. Retrieved on 27 Dec 2014 from http://www.igate.com/iblog/index.php/testing-as-a-service-on-cloud/

Balagtas-Fernandez, F., Tafelmayer, M., & Hussmann, H. (2010). Mobia Modeler: Easing the Creation Process of Mobile Applications for Non-Technical Users. In *Proceedings of the 15th international conference on Intelligent user interfaces* (IUI'10), (pp. 269-272). Hong Kong, China. doi:10.1145/1719970.1720008

Balan, R. K., Flinn, J., Satyanarayanan, M., Sinnamohideen, S., & Yang, H. (2002). The case for cybef foraging. *10th Workshop on ACM SIGOPS European Workshop: beyond the PC*, (pp. 87-92). ACM.

Balan, R. K., Gergle, D., Satyanarayanan, M., & Herbsleb, J. (2007). Simplifying cyber foraging for mobile devices. *5th USENIX International Conference on Mobile Systems, Applications and Services (MobiSys)*, (pp. 272-285). USENIX.

Ban, R., Kaji, K., Hiroi, K., & Kawaguchi, N. (2015). Indoor positioning method integrating pedestrian Dead Reckoning with magnetic field and WiFi fingerprints. In *Eighth International Conference on Mobile Computing and Ubiquitous Networking* (pp. 167–172). doi:10.1109/ICMU.2015.7061061

Bartel, A., Klein, J., Traon, Y. L., & Monperrus, M. (2012). Dexpler: Converting Android Dalvik Bytecode to Jimple for Static Analysis with Soot. *SOAP*, *2012*, 27–38. doi:10.1145/2259051.2259056

Batra & Sharma. (2014). Cloud Testing: A Review Article. *International Journal of Computer Science and Mobile Computing*, *3*(6), 314-319.

Beardsmore, H. (1978). Polyglot literature and linguistic fiction. *International Journal of the Sociology of Language*, *15*(1), 91–102. doi:10.1515/ijsl.1978.15.91

Beck, K. (1999). Embracing change with extreme programming. *Computer*, *32*(10), 70–77. doi:10.1109/2.796139

Belli, F., Budnik, C., & White, L. (2006). Event-based modeling, Analysis and testing of user interactions: approach and case study. Wiley.

Bhalla, M. R., & Bhalla, A. V. (2010). Generations of Mobile Wireless Technology: A Survey. International Journal of Computer Applications, 5(4), 26-32. doi:10.5120/905-1282

Bianco, P., Kotermanski, R., & Merson, P. (2007). *Evaluating a Service-Oriented Architecture*. Tech. Rep. CMU/SEI-2007-TR-015. Software Engineering Institute of Carnegie Mellon University.

Binder, W. (2006). Using bytecode instruction counting as portable CPU consumption metric. *Electronic Notes in Theoretical Computer Science*, 57-77.

Bini, O. (2008). *Fractal programming*. Retrieved January 10, 2015, from https://olabini.com/blog/

Blandford, A., Keith, S., Connell, I., & Edwards, H. (2004). Analytical Usability Evaluation for Digital Libraries: A Case Study.*Joint ACM/IEEE Conference on Digital Libraries* (pp. 27 - 36). IEEE. doi:10.1145/996350.996360

Bluetooth. (2015). *A look at the basics of Bluetooth technology*. Retrieved June 30, 2015 from http://www.bluetooth.com/Pages/Basics.aspx

Boehm, B. W. (1978). *Characteristics of software quality*. North Holland.

Boehm, B. W. (1981). *Software Engineering Economics*. Upper Saddle River, NJ: Prentice Hall PTR.

Borko, F. (2010). *Cloud Computing Fundamentals. Handbook of Cloud Computing*. Springer Science Business Media, LLC.

Boudriga, N. (2010). *Security of Mobile Communications*. Press.

Bowen, J., & Hinze, A. (2011). Supporting mobile application development with model-driven emulation. *Journal of the ECEASST*, *45*, 1–5.

Brambilla, M., Cabot, J., & Wimmer, M. (2012). *Model-Driven Software Enginneering in Practice, Synthesis Lectures on Software Engineering*. Morgan & Claypool Publishers.

Braun, P., & Eckhaus, R. (2008). Experiences on model-driven software development for mobile applications. In *Proceedings of Engineering of Computer-Based Systems,IEEE International Conference and Workshop on the Engineering of computer Base Systems* (pp. 490-493), Los Alamitos: IEEE Computer Society. doi:10.1109/ECBS.2008.50

Brooks, F. (1995). *Calling the Shots. In The Mythical Man-Month: Essays on Software Engineering.* Addison-Wesley.

Brooks, F. P. Jr. (1995). *The Mythical Man-Month.* Boston, MA: Addison-Wesley Longman Publishing.

Bruneliere, H., Cabot, J., Dupé, G., & Madiot, F. (2014). MoDisco: A Model Driven Reverse Engineering Framework. *Information and Software Technology, 56*(8), 1012–1032. doi:10.1016/j.infsof.2014.04.007

Cannasse, N. (2014). *HaXe. Too Good to be True?* GameDuell Tech Talk. Retrieved April 15, 2015, from http://www. techtalk-berlin.de/news/read/nicolas-cannasse-introducing-haxe/

Cao, J., Wu, W., & Liu, X. (2010). Seamless Mobility Support for Adaptive Applications in Heterogeneous Wireless Networks. In *Proceedings of International Workshop on Mobile Cyber-Physical Systems (UIC-2010 Workshop MobiCPS-2010).*

Cao, J., Zhang, C., Zhang, J., Deng, Y., Xiao, X., Xiong, M., & Yu, Y. et al. (2012). SHAWK: Platform for Secure Integration of Heterogeneous Advanced Wireless Networks. In *Proceedings of 26th International Conference on Advanced Information Networking and Applications Workshops (WAINA 2012).* doi:10.1109/WAINA.2012.118

Cariou, E., Le Goaer, O., Barbier, F., & Pierre, S. (2013). Characterization of Adaptable Interpreted-DSML. In *European Conference on Modelling Foundations and Applications* (LNCS), (vol. *7949*, pp. 37–53). Springer. doi:10.1007/978-3-642-39013-5_4

Carroll, A., & Heiser, G. (2010). An Analysis of Power Consumption in a Smartphone. *USENIX annual technical conference*, (pp. 271-285). USENIX.

CASE MDA. (2015). *Committed companies and their products.* Retrieved April 15, 2015, from www.omg.org/mda/committed-products.htm

Cataldo, M., Bass, M., Herbsleb, J., & Bass, L. (2007). On coordination mechanisms in global software development. In *Proceedings of the Second IEEE International Conference on Global Software Engineering.* (pp. 71-80). Munich, Germany: IEEE. doi:10.1109/ICGSE.2007.33

Cataldo, M., Herbsleb, J., & Carley, K. (2008). Socio-technical congruence: a framework for assessing the impact of technical and work dependencies on software development productivity. In *Proceedings of the Second ACM-IEEE International Symposium on Empirical Software Engineering and Measurement.* (pp. 2-11). Kaiserslautern, Germany: IEEE. doi:10.1145/1414004.1414008

Chan, H., Liu, D., Seite, P., Yokota, H. & Korhonen, J. (2014). *Requirements for Distributed Mobility Management.* RFC7333.

Chandgadkar, A. (2013). *An Indoor Navigation System For Smartphones.* Imperial College London.

Charland, A., & Leroux, B. (2011). Mobile application development: Web vs. native. *Communications of the ACM, 54*(5), 49–53. doi:10.1145/1941487.1941504

Cheng-Min, L., Jyh-Horng, L., Chyi-Ren, D., & Chang-Ming, W. (2011). Benchmark Dalvik and Native Code for Android System.*Second International Conference on Innovations in Bio-inspired Computing and Applications*, (pp. 320-323).

Chen, Y.-C., Yang, C.-C., Tseng, S.-C., & Hu, Y.-B. (2011) Next Generation Heterogeneous Wireless Networks with QoS Gurantees. In *Proceedings of the IEEE 15th International Symposium on Consumer Electronics.* IEEE.

Chiang, W.-K., Dai, H.-J., & Luo, C. (2012). *Cross-layer handover for SIP applications based on media-independent pre-authentication with redirect tunneling.Second International Conference on Digital Information and Communication Technology and it's Applications (DICTAP).* doi:10.1109/DICTAP.2012.6215373

Christensen, A. S., Moller, A., & Schwartzbach, M. I. (2003). Precise Analysis of String Expressions.*10th International Static Analysis Symposium (SAS), 2694*, 1-18.

Chun, B. G., Ihm, S., Maniatis, P., Naik, M., & Patti, A. (2011). CloneCloud: Elastic execution between mobile device and cloud. In *Proceedings ACM The European Professional Society on Computer Systems (EuroSys'11).* doi:10.1145/1966445.1966473

Chung, L., & do Prado Leite, J. C. S. (2009). On non-functional requirements in software engineering. In *Conceptual modeling: Foundations and applications* (pp. 363–379). Springer Berlin Heidelberg. doi:10.1007/978-3-642-02463-4_19

Clarke, P. J., Wu, Y., Allen, A. A., Hernandez, F., Allison, M., & France, R. (2013). Towards Dynamic Semantics for Synthesizing Interpreted DSMLs. In *Formal and Practical Aspects of Domain-Specific Languages: Recent Developments.* IGI Global. doi:10.4018/978-1-4666-2092-6.ch009

Combemale, B., Crégut, X., & Pantel, M. (2012). A Design Pattern to Build Executable DSMLs and associated V&V tools. In *Proceedings of the 19th Asia-Pacific Software Engineering Conference (APSEC 2012).* IEEE.

Combemale, B., De Antoni, J., Larsen, M., Mallet, F., Barais, O., & Baudry, B. (2013). Reifying Concurrency for Executable Metamodeling. In *Software Language Engineering* (Vol. 8225, pp. 365–384). Springer. doi:10.1007/978-3-319-02654-1_20

Combemale, B., Deantoni, J., Baudry, B., France, R., Jézéquel, J.-M., & Gray, J. (2014). Globalizing Modeling Languages. *Computer, 47*(6), 68–71. doi:10.1109/MC.2014.147

Commeyne, C. (2014). *Établissement d'un modèle d'estimation a posteriori de projets de maintenance de logiciels.* (PhD thesis). École de Technologie Supérieure, Montréal, Canada.

Common Software Measurement International Consortium & International Function Point User Group. (2015). *Glossary of terms for Non-Functional Requirements and Project Requirements used in software project performance measurement, benchmarking and estimating.* Montréal, Canada: Author.

Common Software Measurement International Consortium. (2010). *Guideline for Sizing Service Oriented Architecture Software.* Montréal, Canada.

Common Software Measurement International Consortium. (2011). *Guideline for the use of COSMIC FSM to manage Agile projects.* Montréal, Canada.

Common Software Measurement International Consortium. (2012). *Guideline for Sizing Real-time Software.* Montréal, Canada.

Common Software Measurement International Consortium. (2014). *Publications.* Retrieved May 20, 2015, from http://cosmic-sizing.org/publications

Common Software Measurement International Consortium. (2015a). Measurement Manual (version 4.0.1). Montréal, Canada.

Common Software Measurement International Consortium. (2015b). *Usage of the COSMIC method.* Retrieved May 20, 2015, from http://cosmic-sizing.org/cosmic/usage/

Constandache, I., Choudhury, R., & Rhee, I. (2010). Compacc: Using mobile phone compasses and accelerometers for localization. In IEEE INFOCOM (pp. 1–9). IEEE.

Corporation, M. (2001). *Microsoft C# Language Specifications*. Microsoft Press.

Costa, P. J., & Cruz, A. M. (2012). Migration to Windows Azure – Analysis and Comparison. In *Proceedings of CENTERIS 2012 - Conference on ENTERprise Information Systems, Procedia Technology*. Elsevier.

Cox, P. A. (2011). Mobile cloud computing: Devices, trends, issues, and the enabling technologies. DeveloperWorks. IBM Corporation. Retrieved from ibm.com/developerWorks

Crane, M. L., & Dingel, J. (2007). UML vs. classical vs. rhapsody statecharts: Not all models are created equal. *Software & Systems Modeling, 6*(4), 415–435. doi:10.1007/s10270-006-0042-8

Crismani, A., Babich, F., & Hanzo, L. (2010). *Cross-Layer Solutions for Cooperative Medium Access Control Protocols*. Academic Press.

Cruz, A. M. (2012). *Mobile Computing – Evolution and Current Status*. Retrieved January 18, 2015, from http://practicalsw.blogspot.pt/2012/08/mobile-computing-evolution-and-current.html

Cruz, A. M. R. (2010). *Automatic Generation of User Interfaces from Rigorous Domain and Use Case Models*. (PhD Dissertation). University of Porto.

Cruz, A. M. R., & Faria, J. P. (2010). A Metamodel-Based Approach for Automatic User Interface Generation. In *International Conference on Model Driven Engineering Languages and Systems* (MODELS 2010) (LNCS), (vol. 6394, pp. 256-270). Springer Berlin Heidelberg. doi:10.1007/978-3-642-16145-2_18

Cuervo, E., Balasubramanian, A. K., Cho, D., Wolman, A., Saroiu, S., Chandra, R., & Bahl, P. (2010). *MAUI: Making smartphones last longer with code offload*. 8th international conference on Mobile systems, applications, and services (ACM MobiSys 10).

Cuervo, E., Balasubramanian, A., Cho, D., Wolman, A., Saroiu, S., Chandra, R., & Bahl, P. (2010). MAUI: Making Smartphones Last Longer with Code Offload. In *Proceedings of ACM 8th Annual International Conference on Mobile Systems, Applications and Services (MobiSys'10)*. doi:10.1145/1814433.1814441

Dai, & Zhou. (2010). A PKI-based mechanism for secure and efficient access to outsourced data. In *Proceedings of the 2nd International Conference on Networking and Digital Society (ICNDS)*, (vol. 1, pp. 640).

Dasnois, B. (2011). *HaXe 2 Beginner's Guide*. Packt Publishing.

De Souza, C. (2005). *On the relationship between software dependencies and coordination: field studies and tool support*. (Doctoral dissertation). University of California, Irvine, CA.

Dead Reckoning System — The NavMote Experience. (n.d.). *IEEE Transactions on Instrumentation and Measurement, 54*(6), 2342–2358. doi:10.1109/TIM.2005.858557

Dehlinger, J., & Dixon, J. (2011). Mobile application software engineering: Challenges and research directions. In *Proceedings of the Workshop on Mobile Software Engineering* (pp. 29-32). Berlin: Springer-Verlag.

Dekkers, C. (2014). *Function Points and Agile Development... Considerations and Opportunities*. Retrieved May 20, 2015, from https://www.linkedin.com/grp/post/2758144-5904564005854285828

Delorey, D., Knutson, C., & Chun, S. (2007). Do programming languages affect productivity? A case study using data from open source projects. In *Proceedings of the First International Workshop on Emerging Trends in FLOSS Research and Development* (pp. 8-8). Minneapolis, MN. doi:10.1109/FLOSS.2007.5

Dhawan, S. (2007) Analogy of Promising Wireless Technologies on Different Frequencies: Bluetooth, WiFi, and WiMAX.*International Conference on Wireless Broadband and Ultra Wideband Communications.* doi:10.1109/AUS-WIRELESS.2007.27

Di Caro, G. A., Giordano, S., Kulig, M., Lenzarini, D., Puiatti, A., & Schwitter, F. (2006). A Cross-Layering and Autonomic Approach to Optimized Seamless Handover. In *Proceedings of the 3rd Annual Conference on Wireless On demand Network Systems and Services (WONS).*

Diaz Bilotto, P. (2015). *Software development for mobile applications through an integration of MDA an HAXE.* (Undergraduate thesis). Computer Science Department, Universidad Nacional del Centro de la Provincia de Buenos Aires, Argentina.

Dinh, H. T., Lee, C., Niyato, D., & Wang, P. (2013). A survey of mobile cloud computing: architecture, applications, and approaches. *Wireless Communications and Mobile Computing, 13*(18), 1587-1611.

Dinh, T., Lee, C., Niyato, D., & Wang, P. (2013). Hong, Chonho Lee, Dusit Niyato, & Ping Wang (2013). A Survey of Mobile Cloud Computing: Architecture, Applications, and Approaches. *Wireless Communications and Mobile Computing, 13*(18), 1587–1611. doi:10.1002/wcm.1203

Doukas, T.. Pliakas, & Maglogiannis. (2010). Mobile Healthcare Information Management unitizing Cloud Computing and Android OS. In *Annual International Conference of the IEEE on Engineering in Medicine and Biology Society (EMBC),* (pp. 1037 - 1040). IEEE.

Do-Xuan, T., Tran-Quang, V., Bui-Xuan, T., & Vu-Thanh, V. (2014). Smartphone-based pedestrian dead reckoning and orientation as an indoor positioning system. In *International Conference on Advanced Technologies for Communications* (pp. 303–308). doi:10.1109/ATC.2014.7043402

Dragert, C., Kienzle, J., & Verbrugge, C. (2012). Statechart-Based AI in Practice. In *Proceedings of the eighth AAAI conference on artificial intelligence and interactive digital entertainment.* AAAI.

Duan, L., Huang, J., & Walrand, J. (2013). Economic Analysis of 4G Network Upgrade. In Proceedings of IEEE INFOCOM. IEEE.

Duffy, T. (2012). *Programming with mobile applications: Android™, iOS, and Windows Phone 7.* Boston, MA: Cengage Learning.

Dunkel, J., & Bruns, R. (2007). Model-driven architecture for mobile applications. In Business Information Systems (LNCS), (vol. 4439, pp. 464-477). Berlin: Springer-Verlag. doi:10.1007/978-3-540-72035-5_36

Dunkel, J., & Bruns, R. (2007). Model-driven architecture for mobile applications. In Business Information Systems (LNCS), (vol. 4439, pp. 464–477). Springer Berlin Heidelberg.

Durantini, A., & Petracca, M. (2008). Performance comparison of vertical handover strategies for psdr heterogeneous networks. *IEEE Wireless Communications.*

Eberspacher, J., Bettstetter, C., & Vogel, H.-J. (2009). *GSM: Architecture, Protocols and Services.* Chichester, UK: John Wiley and Sons.

Ellis, C. A., & Gibbs, S. J. (1989, June). Concurrency control in groupware systems. *SIGMOD Record, 18*(2), 399–407. doi:10.1145/66926.66963

EMF. (2015). *Eclipse Modeling Framework (EMF).* Retrieved April 15, 2015 from http://www.eclipse.org/modeling/emf/

Erl, T. (2009). *SOA Design Patterns.* Upper Saddle River, NJ: Prentice Hall PTR.

Evaluation of Computer and Telecommunication Systems (SPECTS). (2010). Available in http://ieeexplore.ieee.org/stamp/stamp.jsp?tp=&arnumber=5589244&isnumber=5587938

Evans, B., & Verburg, M. (2012). *The Well-Grounded Java Developer: Vital techniques of Java 7 and polyglot programming.* Manning Publications Co.

Fabio, G., et al. (2009). *A Hybrid MIPv6 and PMIPv6 Distributed Mobility Management: The MEDIEVAL approach.* Academic Press.

Fairbanks, G. (2010). *Just-enough software architecture: A risk-driven approach.* Boulder, CO: Marshall & Brainerd.

Falah, Ayadi, & Atif. (2013). Roadmap to Testing the Cloud Techniques, Methodology, and Tools. *IJCSET, 3*(3), 84-89.

Favre, L. (2010). *Model Driven Architecture for Revese Engineering Technologies: Strategic Directions and System Evolution.* Hershey, PA: IGI Global. doi:10.4018/978-1-61520-649-0

Feathers, M. (2004). *Working effectively with legacy code.* Prentice Hall. doi:10.1007/978-3-540-27777-4_42

Fehling, C., & Leymann, F. (2013). *Cloud Computing Patterns Fundamentals to Design, Build, and Manage Cloud Applications.* Tutorial at SummerSoC 2013, Hersonissos, Greece.

Feldman, A. J., Zeller, W. P., Freedman, M. J., & Felten, E. W. (2010, October). SPORC: Group Collaboration using Untrusted Cloud Resources. In OSDI (Vol. 10, pp. 337-350). OSDI.

Fernandes, J. M., & Machado, R. J. (2015). Requirements in engineering projects. Springer. doi: 10.1007/978-3-319-18597-2

Fernando, N., Loke, S. W., & Rahayu, W. (2013). Mobile cloud computing: A survey. *Future Generation Computer Systems, 29*(1), 84-106. 10.1016/j.future.2012.05.023

Fjeldberg, H. (2008). *Polyglot Programming: A business perspective.* (Master's thesis). Norwegian University of Science and Technology, Trondheim, Norway.

Flanagan, C., & Abadi, M. (1999). *Types for safe locking. In Programming Languages and Systems* (LNCS), (pp. 91–108). Springer Berlin Heidelberg. doi:10.1007/3-540-49099-X_7

Fling, B. (2009). Mobile Design and Development – Practical concepts and techniques for creating mobile sites and web apps. O'Reilly Media.

Flinn, J., Park, S., & Satyanarayanan, M. (2002). Balancing performance, energy, and quality in pervasive computing. *22nd International Conference on Distributed Computing Systems.* doi:10.1109/ICDCS.2002.1022259

Flipsen, B., Geraedts, J., Reinders, A., Bakker, C., Dafnomilis, I., & Gudadhe, A. (2012). Environmental sizing of smartphone batteries. *Electronics Goes Green, 2012,* 1–9.

Flora, H. K., Wang, X., & Chande, S. V. (2014). An Investigation on the Characteristics of Mobile Applications: A Survey Study. *International Journal of Information Technology and Computer Science, 11*(11), 21–27. doi:10.5815/ijitcs.2014.11.03

Flores, H., & Srirama, S. N. (2014). Mobile cloud middleware. *Journal of Systems and Software, 92,* 82–94. doi:10.1016/j.jss.2013.09.012

Ford, N. (2006). *Polyglot Programming.* Retrieved January 10, 2015, from http://memeagora.blogspot.fi/

Ford, N. (2008). *Polyglot Programming. In ThoughtWorks Anthology. Essays on Software Technology and Innovation* (pp. 60–69). ThoughWorks, Inc.

Foster, I. (2001). The anatomy of the grid: enabling scalable virtual Organizations. In *Proceedings of the 1st IEEE/ ACMInternational Symposium on Cluster Computing and the Grid*. IEEE.

Foster, I., Zhao, Y., Raicu, I., & Lu, S. (2008). Cloud Computing and Grid Computing 360-Degree Compared. In *Grid Computing Environments Workshop (GCE '08)*. doi:10.1109/GCE.2008.4738445

Fotis, F., Vangelio, G., & Nancy, A. (2008). Cross-Layer Design Proposals for Wireless Mobile Networks: A Survey and Taxonomy. *IEEE Surveys and Tutorials, 10*(1).

Fowler, M. (1999). *Refactoring: Improving the Design of Existing Code*. Academic Press.

Fowler, M. (2010). *Domain Specific Languages* (1st ed.). Addison-Wesley Professional.

Frankel, D. S. (2003). *Model Driven Architecture - Applying MDA to Enterprise Computing*. Indianapolis, IN: Wiley Publishing, Inc.

Gabbard, J. L., Fitch, G. M., & Hyungil, K. (2014). Behind the glass: Driver challenges and opportunities for AR automotive applications. *Proceedings of the IEEE, 102*(2), 124–136. doi:10.1109/JPROC.2013.2294642

Gafur, M. A., Upadhayaya, N., & Syed, A. S. (2013). A Cross Layer Interactive Protocol Mechanism for Manet With a Realistic Response to Network Stimulation. European Scientific Journal, 9(18).

Galorath, D. D., & Evans, M. W. (2006). *Software Sizing, Estimation, and Risk Management*. Boca Raton, FL: Auerbach Publications. doi:10.1201/9781420013122

Gamma, E., Helm, R., Johnson, R., & Vlissides, J. (1994). *Design Patterns: Elements of Reusable Object-Oriented Software*. Pearson Education.

Gao, Bai, & Tsai. (2011). Cloud testing-issues, challenges, needs and practice. *Software Engineering: An International Journal, 1*(1), 9-23.

GEMOC Initiative. (2015). *GEMOC Studio*. Retrieved from http://gemoc.org/studio/

GitHub. (2015). *git*. Retrieved from http://git-scm.com/

Golden, B. (2014). *The New Cloud Application Design Paradigm*. Retrieved from http://www.cio.com/article/2379480/cloud-computing/the-new-cloud-application-design-paradigm.html

Google Inc. (2015). Retrieved from Google Docs: http://docs.google.com

Gottschalk, M., Josefiok, M., Jelschen, J., & Winter, A. (2012). Removing Energy Code Smells with Reengineering Services. Lecture Notes in Informatics, 441-455.

Gouyet, J.-F., & Mandelbrot, B. (1996). *Physics and fractal structures*. Masson.

Govil, J., & Govil, J. (2007). *4G Mobile Communication Systems: Turns, Trends and Transition*. Available through IEEE Xplore Digital Library.

Goyal, S., & Carter, J. (2004). A lightweight secure cyber foraging infrastructure for resource-constrained devices.*6th IEEE Workshop on Mobile Computing Systems and Applications*, (pp. 186-195). doi:10.1109/MCSA.2004.2

Grady, R., & Caswell, D. (1987). *Software metrics: Establishing a company-wide program*. Upper Saddle River, NJ: Prentice Hall.

Graham, P. (2004). *Hackers & painters: big ideas from the computer age*. O'Reilly Media, Inc.

Guetmi, N., Mechaoui, M. D., Imine, A., & Bellatreche, L. (2015). *Mobile Collaboration: a Collaborative Editing Service in the Cloud.* ACM. doi:10.1145/2695664.2696021

Harel, D. (1987). Statecharts: A visual formalism for complex systems. *Science of Computer Programming, 8*(3), 231–274. doi:10.1016/0167-6423(87)90035-9

Harel, D., & Kugler, H. (2004). The Rhapsody semantics of Statecharts (or, on the executable core of the UML). *Lecture Notes in Computer Science, 3147,* 325–354. doi:10.1007/978-3-540-27863-4_19

Harmanen, J. (2013). *Polyglot Programming in Web Development.* (Master's thesis). Tampere University of Technology, Tampere, Finland.

Heitkötter, H., & Majchrzak, T. (2013). Cross-platform Development of Business Apps with MD2. In *International Conference on Design Science Research in Information Systems and Technology* (DESRIST 2013). Springer. doi:10.1007/978-3-642-38827-9_29

Heitkötter, H., Hanschke, S., & Majchrzak, T. A. (2013). Evaluating cross-platform development approaches for mobile applications. *8th International Conference on Web Information Systems and Technologies* (LNBIP), (vol. 140, pp. 120–138). Springer. doi:10.1007/978-3-642-36608-6_8

Herskovic, V., Ochoa, S. F., & Pino, J. A. (2009, April). Modeling groupware for mobile collaborative work. In *Computer Supported Cooperative Work in Design, 2009. CSCWD 2009. 13th International Conference on* (pp. 384-389). IEEE. doi:10.1109/CSCWD.2009.4968089

Herskovic, V., Ochoa, S. F., Pino, J. A., & Neyem, H. A. (2011). The Iceberg Effect: Behind the User Interface of Mobile Collaborative Systems. *J. UCS, 17*(2), 183–201.

Hiya, S., Hisazumi, K., Fukuda, A., & Nakanishi, T. (2013). clooca: Web based tool for Domain Specific Modeling. *MODELS'13 Invited Talks, Demos, Posters, and ACM SRC., 1115,* 31–35.

Hong, J., Suh, E., & Kim, S. J. (2009). Context-aware systems: A literature review and classification. *Expert Systems with Applications, 36*(4), 8509–8522. doi:10.1016/j.eswa.2008.10.071

Hongjun, Y., Rong, C., & Zhenjun, D. (2010). Message Oriented Middleware Support for Mobile Ad Hoc Data Sharing. *COMPSAC Workshops 2010,* (pp 305-310).

Huang, K. (2009). Challenges in Human-Computer Interaction Design for Mobile Devices. In *Proceedings of the World Congress on Engineering and Computer Science.*

Huawei. (2014). *5G: A Technology Vision.* Author.

Huerta-Canepa, G., & Lee, D. (2010, June). A virtual cloud computing provider for mobile devices. In *Proceedings of the 1st ACM Workshop on Mobile Cloud Computing & Services: Social Networks and Beyond* (p. 6). ACM. doi:10.1145/1810931.1810937

Hughes, J. (1989). Why Functional Programming Matters. *The Computer Journal, 32*(2), 98–107. doi:10.1093/comjnl/32.2.98

Hunt, A., & Thomas, D. (1999). *The Pragmatic Programmer: From Journeyman to Master.* Addison-Wesley.

Huth & Cebula. (2011). The basics of cloud computing. *United States Computer.*

IBM Research. (2014). *SaS hub non-functional requirements.* Retrieved May 20, 2015, from https://www.research.ibm.com/haifa/projects/software/nfr/index.html

IDC. (2014). Retrieved from: http://www.idc.com/getdoc.jsp?containerId=prUS24257413

IEEE Standards. (n.d.). *IEEE 802.21™: Media independent handover services.* Available in https://standards.ieee.org/about/get/802/802.21.html

Imine, A. (2009, January). Coordination model for real-time collaborative editors. In Coordination Models and Languages (pp. 225-246). Springer Berlin Heidelberg.

Incki, K., Ari, I., & Sozer, H. (2012, June). A survey of software testing in the cloud. In *Software Security and Reliability Companion (SERE-C), 2012 IEEE Sixth International Conference on* (pp. 18-23). IEEE.

Institute of Electrical and Electronics Engineers Computer Society. (2014). *Guide to the Software Engineering Body of Knowledge (version 3.0).* Washington, DC: IEEE.

International Organization for Standardization. (2007). *Information Technology – Software Measurement – Functional Size Measurement. International Standard ISO/IEC 14143:2007.* Geneva, Switzerland: ISO.

International Organization for Standardization. (2011). *Software Engineering – COSMIC – A Functional Size Measurement Method. International Standard ISO/IEC 19761:2011.* Geneva, Switzerland: ISO.

International Software Benchmarking and Standards Group. (2012). *The Performance of Real-time, Business and Component Software Projects – An analysis of COSMIC measured projects in the ISBSG database.* Balaclava, Australia: ISBSG.

Islam, N., & Want, R. (2014). Smartphones: Past, Present, and Future. *Pervasive Computing, IEEE Computers & Society, 13*(4), 89–92.

Ivanochko, I., Urikova, O., & Gregu, M. (2014). Modern Mobile Technologies for Collaborative e-Business. In *Proceedings of International Conference on Intelligent Networking and Collaborative Systems,* (pp. 515 – 520).

Janssen, C. (2014). *Three-Tier Architecture.* Retrieved May 20, 2015, from http://www.techopedia.com/definition/24649/three-tier-architecture

Jarvenpaa, S. L., & Lang, K. R. (2005). Managing the Paradoxes of Mobile Technology. *Information Systems Management, 22*(4), 7–23. doi:10.1201/1078.10580530/45520.22.4.20050901/90026.2

Jayanthiladevi, A., Premlatha, H. M., & Nawaz, G. M. K. (2013). Analysis study of seamless integration and intelligent solution in any situation by the future advanced mobile universal systems 4G-(FAMOUS 4G). *International Conference on Emerging Trends in VLSI, Embedded System, Nano Electronics and Telecommunication System (ICEVENT).* doi:10.1109/ICEVENT.2013.6496551

Jensen, R. W., Putnam, L. H. Sr, & Roetzheim, W. (2006). Software estimating models: Three viewpoints. *Crosstalk, 2,* 23–29.

Jézéquel, J.-M. (2005). *Model Transformation Techniques.* Retrieved January 13, 2015, from http://people.irisa.fr/Jean-Marc.Jezequel/enseignement/ModelTransfo.pdf

Johnson, L. (2013). *Cloud Computing: Fast Facts.* Retrieved on 10 Dec 2014 from http://www.business2community.com/tech-gadgets/cloud-computing-fast-facts-0386816

Jones, C. (2013). *A short history of the Lines of Codes (LoC) metric.* Retrieved May 20, 2015, from http://namcookanalytics.com/a-short-history-of-the-lines-of-code-loc-metric

Jouault, F., & Kurtev, I. (2005). Transforming models with ATL. In *Satellite Events at the MoDELS 2005 Conference* (LNCS), (vol. 3844, pp. 128-138). Berlin: Springer Verlag. doi:10.1007/11663430_14

Jouault, F., Allilaire, F., Bézivin, J., & Kurtev, I (2008). ATL: A model transformation tool. *Science of Computer Programming, 72*(1), 31-39.

Jouault, F., Allilaire, F., Bézivin, J., Kurtev, I., & Valduriez, P. (2006) ATL: a QVT-like transformation language. In *Companion to the 21ˢᵗ ACM SIGPLAN Symposium on Object-oriented programming systems, languages, and applications* OOPSLA '06 (pp. 719-720). New York: ACM Press. doi:10.1145/1176617.1176691

Juárez-Ramírez, R., Licea, G., Barriba, I., Izquierdo, V., & Angeles, A. (2012). Orchestrating mobile applications: A software engineering view. In R. Aquino-Santos & A. E. Block (Eds.), *Embedded systems and wireless technology: Theory and practical applications* (pp. 41–72). Boca Raton, FL: CRC Press. doi:10.1201/b12298-3

Jureta, I. J., Faulkner, S., & Schobbens, P. Y. (2006). A more expressive softgoal conceptualization for quality requirements analysis.Lecture Notes in Computer Science, 4215, 281–295. doi:10.1007/11901181_22

Kakiuchi, N., & Kamijo, S. (2013), Pedestrian dead reckoning for mobile phones through walking and running mode recognition. In *16th International IEEE Conference on Intelligent Transportation Systems* (pp. 261–267). doi:10.1109/ITSC.2013.6728243

Kamala Ramasubramani, J., & Abran, A. (2013). A survey of Software Test Estimation Techniques. *Journal of Software Engineering and Applications, 6*(10), 47–52. doi:10.4236/jsea.2013.610A006

Kang, W., & Han, Y. (2014). SmartPDR: Smartphone-Based Pedestrian Dead Reckoning for Indoor Localization. *IEEE Sensors Journal, 15*(5), 2906–2916. doi:10.1109/JSEN.2014.2382568

Karaboga & Basturk. (2007). Artificial Bee Colony (ABC) Optimization Algorithm for Solving Constrained Optimization Problems. In Advances in Soft Computing: Foundations of Fuzzy Logic and Soft Computing (LNCS), (Vol. 4529, pp. 789-798). Springer-Verlag. doi:10.1007/978-3-540-72950-1_77

Karaboga, D., & Basturk, B. (2008, January). On The Performance of Artificial Bee Colony (ABC) Algorithm. *Applied Soft Computing, 8*(1), 687–697. doi:10.1016/j.asoc.2007.05.007

Katanekwa, N., & Ventura, N. (2013). Mobile content distribution and selective traffic offload in the 3GPP evolved packet system (EPS). *ICOIN, 2013*, 119–124.

KDM. (2011). *Architecture-Driven Modernization: Knowledge Discovery MetaModel (KDM), versión 1.3*. Retrieved April 15, 2015, from http://www.omg.org/

Kelly, S., & Tolvanen, J-P. (2008). *Domain Specific Modeling: Enabling Full Code Generation*. Wiley-IEEE Computer Society Press.

Kelly, S., Lyytinen, K., & Rossi, M. (1996, may). MetaEdit+ A fully configurable multi-user and multi-tool CASE and CAME environment.*Conference on Advanced Information Systems Engineering*. Springer. doi:10.1007/3-540-61292-0_1

Khalifa, S. (2013). Adaptive pedestrian activity classification for indoor dead reckoning systems. In Indoor Positioning and Indoor Navigation (pp. 1–7).

Khedo, K. K. (2006). Requirements for Next Generation Middleware Implementations. In Proceedings of International Multi-Conference on Computing in the Global Information Technology. ICCGI.

Kiczales, G., & Hilsdale, E. (2001). Aspect-oriented programming. *Software Engineering Notes, 26*(5), 313. doi:10.1145/503271.503260

Kim, H. K. (2008). Frameworks of process improvement for mobile applications. *Engineering Letters, 16*(4), 550-555.

Kliazovich, D., Michael, D., & Fabriozo, G. (2009). *Formal Methods in Cross-Layer Modelling and Optimization of wireless Networks: State of the Art and future Directions.* IGI Global Publications.

Koren, I., & Krishna, C. M. (2010). *Fault-tolerant systems.* San Francisco, CA: Morgan Kaufmann.

Korhonen, J. (2003). *Introduction to 3G Mobile Communication.* London: Artech House.

Kosta, S., Perta, V., Stefa, J., Hui, P., & Mei, A. (2013, April). CloneDoc: exploiting the cloud to leverage secure group collaboration mechanisms for smartphones. In *Computer Communications Workshops (INFOCOM WKSHPS), 2013 IEEE Conference on* (pp. 19-20). IEEE. doi:10.1109/INFCOMW.2013.6970704

Kosta, S., Perta, V. C., Stefa, J., Hui, P., & Mei, A. (2013, June). Clone2clone (c2c): Peer-to-peer networking of smartphones on the cloud. In *5th USENIX Workshop on Hot Topics in Cloud Computing (HotCloud13).*

Kourogi, M., & Kurata, T. (2014). A method of pedestrian dead reckoning for smartphones using frequency domain analysis on patterns of acceleration and angular velocity. In *Position, Location and Navigation Symposium* (pp. 164–168).

Kraemer, F. A. (2011). Engineering android applications based on uml activities. In *Proceedings of the 14th International Conference on Model Driven Engineering Languages and Systems,* (pp. 183–197). Springer.

Kramer, D., Clark, T., & Oussena, S. (2010). MobDSL: A Domain Specific Language for multiple mobile platform deployment. In *International Conference on Networked Embedded Systems for Enterprise Applications* (NESEA). IEEE. doi:10.1109/NESEA.2010.5678062

Kristensen, M. D. (2010). Scavenger: Transparent development of efficient cyber foraging applications. *EEE International Conference on Pervasive Computing and Communications (PerCom).* doi:10.1109/PERCOM.2010.5466972

Ku, Lu, & Gerla. (2014). Software-Defined Mobile Cloud: Architecture, Services and Use Cases. *ICWCM-2014.* IEEE.

Kühne, T. (2006). Matters of (Meta-)Modeling. *Software & Systems Modeling, 5*(4), 369–385. doi:10.1007/s10270-006-0017-9

Kumar, K., & Lu, Y.-H. (2010). Cloud Computing for Mobile Users: Can Offloading Computation Save Energy? *Computer, 43*(4), 51–56. doi:10.1109/MC.2010.98

Küpper, A. (2005). *Location-based Services: Fundamentals and Operation.* John Wiley & Sons. doi:10.1002/0470092335

Lanza, M., Marinescu, R., & Ducasse, S. (2006). *Object-oriented metrics in practice.* Springer.

Ledeczi, A., Maroti, M., Bakay, A., Karsai, G., Garrett, J., & Thomason, C. (2001). The generic modeling environment. *Workshop on Intelligent Signal Processing.*

Lehmann, G., Blumendorf, M., Trollmann, F., & Albayrak, S. (2010). Meta-Modeling Runtime Models. In *Models@ run.time Workshop at MoDELS 2010* (LNCS), (vol. 6627). Springer.

Leontiasis, I., Efstratiou, C., Picone, M., & Mascolo, C. (2012). Don't kill my ads!: Balancing privacy in an ad-supported mobile application market. *12th Workshop on Mobile Computing Systems & Applications.* ACM. doi:10.1145/2162081.2162084

Lettner, M., Tschernuth, M., & Mayrhofer, R. (2012). Mobile platform architecture review: Android, Iphone, Qt. In *Computer Aided Systems Theory EUROCAST 2011* (LNCS), (vol. 6928, pp. 544-551). Berlin: Springer-Verlag.

Li, Wang, Wang, & Li. (2011). Case study of usability testing methodology on mobile learning course. *Advanced Intelligence and Awareness Internet (AIAI 2011).*

Li, H., & Hua, X.-S. (2010). Melog: mobile experience sharing through automatic multimedia blogging. In *Proceedings of the 2010 ACM multimedia workshop on Mobile Cloud Media Computing (MCMC),* (pp. 19-24). doi:10.1145/1877953.1877961

Lind, K., & Heldal, R. (2011). A model-based and automated approach to size estimation of embedded software components. In *Proceedings of the 14th international conference on Model Driven Engineering Languages and Systems (MODELS)*. Wellington, New Zealand: Springer Verlag. doi:10.1007/978-3-642-24485-8_24

Lin, X. (2013). Apply Pedestrian Dead Reckoning to indoor Wi-Fi positioning based on fingerprinting. In *15th IEEE International Conference on Communication Technology* (pp. 206–210).

Liu, J., Xia, C. H., Shroff, N. B., & Sherali, H. D. (2013). Distributed Cross-Layer Optimization in Wireless Networks: A Second-Order Approach. IEEE INFOCOM 2013. Turin, Italy: IEEE.

Liu, F., Shu, P., Jin, H., Ding, L., Yu, J., Niu, D., & Li, B. (2013). Gearing resource-poor mobile devices with powerful clouds: Architectures, challenges, and applications. *Wireless Communications, IEEE, 20*(3), 14–22. doi:10.1109/MWC.2013.6549279

Li, Y. T., Chen, G., & Sun, M. T. (2013). An Indoor Collaborative Pedestrian Dead Reckoning System. In *42nd International Conference on Parallel Processing* (pp. 923–930) doi:10.1109/ICPP.2013.110

Loui, R. (2008). In praise of scripting: Real programming pragmatism. *Computer, IEEE, 41*(7), 22–26. doi:10.1109/MC.2008.228

Madaudo, R., & Scandurra, P. (2013). Native versus Cross-platform frameworks for mobile application development. In *Proceedings of Eclipse-IT 2013 – VIII Workshop of the Italian Eclipse Community*.

Magagula, L. A., Chan, H. A., & Falawo, O. E. (2010) PMIPv6-HC: Handover mechanism for reducing handover delay and packet loss in NGWN. In *Proceedings of Global Telecommunications Conference (GLOBECOM 2010)*. IEEE. doi:10.1109/GLOCOM.2010.5684108

Mahmood & Saeed. (2013). Software engineering frameworks for the cloud computing paradigm. Springer.

Mala, D. J., & Iswarya, R. (2014). A Multi Agent Based Approach for Critical Components Identification and Testing. *International Journal of Systems and Service-Oriented Engineering, 4*(1), 2014. doi:10.4018/ijssoe.2014010102

Mala, D. J., & Mohan, V. (2009). ABC Tester-Artificial bee colony based software test suite optimization approach. *International Journal of Software Engineering, 2*(2), 15–43.

Mala, D. J., & Mohan, V. (2010). Automated software test optimization framework - an artificial bee colony optimization-based approach. *IET Software, 4*(5), 334–348. doi:10.1049/iet-sen.2009.0079

Mala, S., Balamurugan, S., & Nathan, K. S. (2013). Balamurugan, & KS Nathan (2013). Criticality analyzer and tester: An effective approach for critical component identification & verification using ABC. *Software Engineering Notes, 38*(6), 1–12. doi:10.1145/2532780.2532811

Mandelbrot, B. (1983). *The fractal geometry of nature*. W. H. Freeman and Company.

Marchetto, A., Tonella, P., & Ricca, F. (2008). State-Based Testing of Ajax Web Applications.*Proceedings of 2008 Int. Conf. on Software Testing, Verification and Validation* (pp. 121-130). IEEE CS Press. doi:10.1109/ICST.2008.22

Marcu, M., Tudor, D., & Fuicu, S. (2010). A view on power efficiency of multimedia mobile applications. In K. Elleithy (Ed.), *Advanced Techniques in Computing Sciences and Software Engineering* (pp. 407–412). Springer; doi:10.1007/978-90-481-3660-5_70

Marinelli, E. E. (2009). *Hyrax: cloud computing on mobile devices using MapReduce* (No. CMU-CS-09-164). Carnegie-Mellon University.

Marinelli, E. E. (2009). *Hyrax: Cloud Computing on Mobile Devices using MapReduce.* (Master of Science Thesis). School of Computer Science, Carnegie Mellon University, Pittsburgh, PA.

Mark. (2013). *Testing the Cloud.* White Paper. Retrieved on 19 Jan 2014 from www.lightwaveonline.com/content/lw/en/whitepapers/2013/01/testing-the-cloud.whitepaperpdf.render.pdf

Maróti, M., Kecskés, T., Kereskényi, R., Broll, B., Völgyesi, P., & Jurácz, L. (2014, October). Next Generation (Meta) Modeling: Web- and Cloud-based Collaborative Tool Infrastructure. *Multi-Paradigm Modeling, 1237,* 41–60.

Marston, S., Li, Z., Bandyopadhyay, S., Zhang, J., & Ghalsasi, A. (2010). Cloud computing — The business perspective. *Journal Decision Support Systems, 51*(2011), 176–189.

Mateos, C., Zunino, A., Trachsel, R., & Campo, M. (2011). A Novel Mechanism for Gridification of Compiled Java Applications. *Computing and Informatics, 30*(6), 1259-1285. Available at http://www.cai.sk/ojs/index.php/cai/issue/view/CAI-30-2011-6

Mateos, C., Zunino, A., & Campo, M. (2010). m-JGRIM: A Novel Middleware for Gridifying Java Applications into Mobile Grid Services. *Software, Practice & Experience, 40*(4), 331–362.

Mateos, C., Zunino, A., Hirsch, M., & Fernandez, M. (2012). Enhancing the BYG gridification tool with state-of-the-art Grid scheduling mechanisms and explicit tuning support. *Advances in Engineering Software, 43*(1), 27–43. doi:10.1016/j.advengsoft.2011.08.006

Maxwell, K., Van Wassenhove, L., & Dutta, S. (1996). Software development productivity of European space, military, and industrial applications. *Transactions on Software Engineering, IEEE, 22*(10), 706–718. doi:10.1109/32.544349

Mehrotra. (2011). Cloud-Testing vs. Testing a cloud. *Infosys Viewpoint.* Retrieved on 14 Jan 2014 from http://www.infosys.com/engineering-services/white-papers/documents/cloud-testing-vs-testing-cloud.pdf

Mell & Grance. (2009). The NIST definition of cloud computing. *National Institute of Standards and Technology, 53*(6), 50.

Mell, P., & Grance, T. (2011). *The NIST Definition of Cloud Computing.* NIST Special Publication 800 – 145. Computer Security Division, Information Technology Laboratory, National Institute of Standards and Technology, Gaithersburg, September 2011. Retrieved from: http://csrc.nist.gov/publications/nistpubs/800-145/SP800-145.pdf

Memon, A., Banerjee, L., & Nagarajan, A. (2003). GUI ripping: reverse engineering of graphical user interfaces for testing.*Proceedings of the 10th Working Conference on Reverse Engineering* (pp. 260- 269). IEEE CS Press. doi:10.1109/WCRE.2003.1287256

Mernik, M., Heering, J., & Sloane, A. M. (2005). When and how to develop domain-specific languages. *ACM Computing Surveys, 37*(4), 316–344. doi:10.1145/1118890.1118892

Mesbah, A., & Van Deursen, A. (2009). Invariant-based automatic testing of AJAX user interfaces.*Proc. of International Conference on Software Engineering* (pp. 210-220). IEEE CS Press. doi:10.1109/ICSE.2009.5070522

Meyer, B. (2019). *Touch of class: Learning to program well with objects and contracts.* Berlin: Springer.

Miller, J., & Mukerji, J. (2003). *MDA Guide Version 1.0.1.* Object Management Group (OMG). Retrieved from http://www.omg.org/mda/specs.htm#MDAGuide

Min, B.-K., Ko, M., Seo, Y., Kuk, S., & Kim, H.-S. (2011). A uml metamodel for smart device application modeling based on windows phone 7 platform. In Proceedings of TENCON 2011 - 2011 IEEE Region 10 Conference, (pp. 201–205). IEEE.

MMT. (2015). *Model-to-Model Transformation. Eclipse Modeling Framework.* Retrieved April 15, 2015, from https://www.eclipse.org/mmt/

ModAgile. (n.d.). Retrieved from: http://www.modagile-mobile.de

MoDisco. (2012). *Model discovery*. Retrieved April 15, 2015 from http://www.eclipse.org/MoDisco

MOF. (2006). *OMG Meta Object Facility (MOF) Core specification version 2.0*. OMG Document Number:formal/formal/2006-01-01. Retrieved April 15, 2015 from http://www.omg.org/spec/MOF/2.0

MOF. (2008). *OMG. Meta object facility (MOF) 2.0 Query/View/Transformation Specification*. Retrieved April 15, 2015 from http://www.omg.org/spec/MOF/2.0

MOF. (2011). *OMG Meta Object Facility (MOF) core specification version 2.4.1*. OMG Document Number:formal/2011-08-07. Retrieved April 15, 2015 from http://www.omg.org/spec/MOF/2.4.1

MOFM2T. (2008). *MOF Model to Text Transformation Language, Version 1.0*. Retrieved April 15, 2015, from http://www.omg.org/spec/MOFM2T/1.0/

Mohsenzadeh. (2013). Cloud Computing Testing Evaluation. *International Journal of Computational Engineering & Management, 16*(6).

Monitor. (2014). *PowerMonitor*. Available at https://www.msoon.com/LabEquipment/PowerMonitor/

Monrad, A. (2011). *Core Network migration towards the Evolved Packet Core, Status and Future 3GPP work*. 3GPP Seminar, Moscow.

Moritz, F., & Meinel, C. (2010). Mobile web usability Evalution –Combining the Modified Think Aloud Method with Testing Emotional, Cognative Aspects of the usage of web Application. *9th International Conference on Computer and Information Science* (pp. 367 - 372). IEEE.

Mshvidobadze, T. (2012). *Evolution of Mobile Wireless Communication and LTE Networks*. Academic Press.

Mshvidobadze, T. (2012). Evolution mobile wireless communication and LTE networks. In *Proceedings of the International Conference on Application of Information and Communication Technologies*. doi:10.1109/ICAICT.2012.6398495

Munoz, P., Barco, R., Laselva, D., & Mogensen, P. (2013). Mobility-Based Strategies for Traffic Steering in Heterogeneous Networks. *IEEE Communications Magazine*, (May): 2013.

Murray, D., Yoneki, E., Crowcroft, J., & Hand, S. (2010). The case for crowd computing. In *2nd. ACM SIGCOMM Workshop on Networking, Systems, and Applications on Mobile Hand-helds*, (pp. 39-44). doi:10.1145/1851322.1851334

Myers, Sandler, & Badgett. (2011). *The art of software testing*. John Wiley & Sons.

Mylavarapu & Inamdar. (2011). Taking Testing to the Cloud, Future of Work. *Cognizant*. Retrieved on 25 Dec 2014 from http://www.cognizant.com/SiteDocuments/ITIS-Cloud-Based-Testing.pdf

Narula & Beniwal. (2013). Cloud Testing-Types, Service Platforms and Advantages. *International Journal of Computers and Applications, 72*(20).

National Institute of Standards and Technology. (2011). *The NIST Definition of CloudComputing*. Retrieved May 20, 2015 from http://csrc.nist.gov/publications/nistpubs/800-145/SP800-145.pdf

Nayebi, F., Desharnais, J.-M., & Abran, A. (2012). The state of the art of mobile application usability evaluation.*25th IEEE Canadian Conference on Electrical & Computer Engineering* (pp. 1 - 4). IEEE. doi:10.1109/CCECE.2012.6334930

Neves, P., Nissila, T., Pereira, T., Harjula, I., Monteiro, J., Pentikousis, K., Sargento, S., & Fontes, F. (2008). A vendor-independent resource control framework for WiMAX. *Computers and Communications, ISCC 2008*. doi: 10.1109/ISCC.2008.4625750

Neyem, A., Ochoa, S. F., Pino, J. A., & Franco, R. D. (2012). A reusable structural design for mobile collaborative applications. *Journal of Systems and Software*, *85*(3), 511–524. doi:10.1016/j.jss.2011.05.046

NIST. (2011). Cloud Architecture Reference Models. US National Institute of Standards.

Nithyanandan, L., & Parthiban, I. (2012), Vertical Handoff in WLAN-WiMAX-LTE Heterogeneous networks Through Gateway Relocation. *International Journal of Wireless and Mobile Networks*, *4*(4).

Nursimloo, D.S., & Chan, H.A. (2005). Mobility Management, Quality of Service, and Security in the Design of Next Generation Wireless Network. *African Journal of Information and Communication Technology*, *1*(1).

Object Management Group. (2012, Apr.). *Information technology - Object Management Group Unified Modeling Language, Superstructure*. ISO/IEC 19505-2.

OCL. (2014). *OMG Object constraint language (OCL), version 2.4*. Retrieved April 15, 2015, from http://www.omg.org/spec/OCL/2.4

OCLinEcore. (2015) *OCLinEcore Editor*. Retrieved April 15, 2015, from http://wiki.eclipse.org/MDT/OCLinEcore

OMG MDA. (2014). *MDA guide version rev. 2.0 OMG Document ormsc/2014-06-01*. Retrieved 15 April, 2015, from http://www.omg.org/cgi-bin/doc?ormsc/14-06-01

OMG. (2013). *OMG Unified Modeling Language (OMG UML)*. Version 2.5, September 2013. OMG.

Open Group. (2013). Cloud Computing Portability and Interoperability. Document Number: G135. The Open Group.

Oriou, A., Bronca, E., Bouzid, B., Guetta, O., & Guillard, K. (2014). Manage the automotive embedded software development cost & productivity with the automation of a functional size measurement method (COSMIC). In *Proceedings of the Joint Conference of the 24th International Workshop on Software Measurement (IWSM) and the 9th International Conference on Software Process and Product Measurement (Mensura)*. Rotterdam, The Netherlands: IEEE Computer Society Conference Publishing Services.

Ostrand, T., Weyuker, E., & Bell, R. (2005). Predicting the location and number of faults in large software systems. *Transactions on Software Engineering, IEEE*, *31*(4), 340–355. doi:10.1109/TSE.2005.49

Özsu, T., & Valduriez, P. (2011). *Principles of distributed database systems*. Springer Science & Business Media.

Paiva, S. (2015). A domain independent Pedestrian Dead Reckoning System for Tracking and Localization.*IEEE International Conference on Computational Science and Engineering*.

Palmer, N., Kemp, R., Kielmann, T., & Bal, H. (2009, February). Ibis for mobility: solving challenges of mobile computing using grid techniques. In *Proceedings of the 10th workshop on Mobile Computing Systems and Applications* (p. 17). ACM. doi:10.1145/1514411.1514426

Pal, S., & Henderson, T. (2013, September). MobOCloud: extending cloud computing with mobile opportunistic networks. In *Proceedings of the 8th ACM MobiCom workshop on Challenged networks* (pp. 57-62). ACM. doi:10.1145/2505494.2505503

Panyov, A. a., Golovan, A. a., & Smirnov, A. S. (2014). Indoor positioning using Wi-Fi fingerprinting pedestrian dead reckoning and aided INS. In *Int. Symp. Inert. Sensors Systems* (pp. 1–2). doi:10.1109/ISISS.2014.6782540

Parada, A., & de Brisolara, L. (2012). A model driven approach for android applications development. In *Proceedings of the 2012 Brazilian Symposium on Computing Systems Engineering*, (pp. 192–197).

Paradiso, J. A., & Starner, T. (2005). Energy scavenging for mobile and wireless electronics. *IEEE Pervasive Computing / IEEE Computer Society [and] IEEE Communications Society*, *4*(1), 18–27. doi:10.1109/MPRV.2005.9

Pareto, L. (2000). *Types for Crash Prevention*. (Doctoral dissertation). Chalmers University of Technology, Göteborg, Sweden.

Park, H., Lee, H. H., & Chan, H. A. (2012). Gateway Service for Integration of Heterogeneous Networks using Different Interworking Solutions. In *Proceedings of 15th International Conference on Advanced Communication Technology (ICACT)*.

Parkinson, C. N. (1957). Parkinson's law, or the pursuit of progress. Cutchogue, NY: Buccaneer Books.

Park, S., Chen, Q., Han, H., & Yeom, H. Y. (2014). Design and evaluation of mobile offloading system for web-centric devices. *Journal of Network and Computer Applications, 40*, 105–115. doi:10.1016/j.jnca.2013.08.006

PCI Data Security Standard (PCI DSS) Cloud Computing Guidelines. (2013). Cloud Special Interest Group PCI Security Standards Council. Retrieved on 13 Jan 2015 from https://www.pcisecuritystandards.org/pdfs/PCI_DSS_v2_Cloud_Guidelines.pdf

Pearce, M., Zeadally, S., & Hunt, R. (2013, February). Virtualization: Issues, Security Threats, and Solutions. *ACM Computing Surveys, 45*(2), 17. doi:10.1145/2431211.2431216

Pérez Castillo, R., García Rodriguez, I., Gómez Cornejo, R., Fernández Ropero, M., & Piattini, M. (2013). ANDRIU. A Technique for Migrating Graphical User Interfaces to Android. In *Proceedings of The 25th International Conference on Software Engineering and Knowledge Engineering (SEKE 2013)* (pp. 516-519) Boston: Knowledge Systems Institute.

Perez-Castillo, R., & Piattini, M. (2014). Analyzing the Harmful Effect of God Class Refactoring on Power Consumption. *Software, IEEE, 31*(3), 48-54.

Petricek, T., & Syme, D. (2011). *Joinads: a retargetable control-flow construct for reactive, parallel and concurrent programming. In Practical Aspects of Declarative Languages* (pp. 205–219). Springer Berlin Heidelberg.

Petrov, I., & Buchmann, A. (2008). Architecture of OMG MOF-based Repository Systems. In G. Kotsis, D. Taniar, E. Pardede, & I. Khalil (Eds.), *Proceedings of the 10th International Conference on Information Integration and Web-based Applications & Services (iiWAS '08)* (pp. 193–200). New York, NY: ACM.http://doi.acm.org/10.1145/1497308.1497346

Pham, D. T., Ghanbarzadeh, A., Koc, E., Otri, S., Rahim, S., & Zaidi, M. (2005). *Technical Note: Bees Algorithm*. Cardiff, UK: Cardiff University.

Phaphoom, N. & Wang, X. & Abrahamsson, P. (2013). Foundations and Technological Landscape of Cloud Computing. *ISRN Software Engineering*. 10.1155/2013/782174

Prakash & Gopalkrishanan. (2012). Cloud computing solution-Benefits and testing challenges. *Journal of Theoretical and Applied Information Technology, 39*(2), 114–118.

Pramod, P. J., Malhotra, M., Agarwal, A., Varma, D. P., Jinaga, B. C., & Jain, D. K. (2012). SoIP: An all-IP heterogeneous testbed for SIP-based multimedia services. In *2nd Baltic Congress on Future Internet Communications (BCFIC)*. doi:10.1109/BCFIC.2012.6217951

Prasad, G., & Murti, P. R. K. (2012). Mobile Cloud Computing: Implications and Challenges. *Journal of Information Engineering and Applications, 2*(7), 2012.

Priyadharshini & Malathi. (2014). Survey on software testing techniques in cloud computing. *CoRR*.

Putnam, L. H., & Myers, W. (2003). *Five Core Metrics: The intelligence behind successful software management*. New York, NY: Dorset House Publishing.

PyPL. (2013). Available at https://sites.google.com/site/pydatalog/pypl/PyPL-PopularitY-of-Programming-Language

QVT. (2012). *QVT: MOF 2.0 query, view, transformation:Version 1.1*. OMG Document Number: formal/2011-01-01. Retrieved April 15, 2015 from http://www.omg.org/spec/QVT/1.1/SMM

Rackspace. (2013). *Understanding the Cloud Computing Stack: SaaS, PaaS, IaaS*. Retrieved on 16 Dec 2014 from http://www.rackspace.com/knowledge_center/whitepaper/understanding-the-cloud-computing-stack-saas-paas-iaas

Radu, V., & Marina, M. (2013). Himloc: Indoor smartphone localization via activity aware pedestrian dead reckoning with selective crowdsourced wifi fingerprinting. In Indoor Positioning and Indoor Navigation (pp. 28–31).

Rahimi, M. R., Hengmeechai, J., & Sarchar, N. (2008). Ubiquitous Application of Mobile Phones for Getting Information from Barcode Picture. In iCORE 2008.

Rahimi, M.R., Ren, J., Liu, C.H., Vasilakos, A.V. & Venkatasubramanian, N. (2014). Mobile Cloud Computing: A Survey, State of Art and Future Directions. *Mobile Networks and Applications, 19*(2), 133-143.

Rao, K. R., Bojkovic, Z. S., & Milovanovic, D. A. (2006). *Introduction to Multimedia Communications – Applications, Middleware, Networking*. Hoboken, NJ: John Wiley and Sons, Inc.

RCR Wireless News. (2011). *Mobile cloud computing – The value-added role for service providers*. White Paper. Retrieved May 4, 2015, from http://www.rcrwireless.com/20110627/opinion/readerforum/reader-forum-mobile-cloud-computing-8211-the-value-added-role-for-service-providers

Ribeiro, A., & Silva, A. R. (2014). XIS-mobile: a DSL for mobile applications. In *Proceedings of the 29th Annual ACM Symposium on Applied Computing (SAC '14)* (pp. 1316–1323). New York, NY: ACM. http://doi.acm.org/10.1145/2554850.2554926

Rimal, Choi, & Lumb. (2009). A taxonomy and survey of cloud computing systems. In *Proceedings of INC, IMS and IDC, 2009. NCM'09. Fifth International Joint Conference on* (pp. 44-51). IEEE.

Robertson, S., & Robertson, J. C. (2006). *Mastering the requirements process* (2nd ed.). Boston, MA: Addison-Wesley.

Rodríguez, A. V., Mateos, C., & Zunino, A. (2012). Mobile Devices-aware Refactorings for Scientific Computational Kernels. 41 JAIIO - AST 2012, (pp. 61-72).

Rodriguez, J. M., Mateos, C., & Zunino, A. (2011). Are Smartphones Really Useful for Scientific Computing? Advances in New Technologies, Interactive Interfaces and Communicability (pp. 35-44). Springer.

Rodriguez, A. (2011). *Indoor Positioning using Sensor-fusion in Android Devices*. School of Health and Society Sweden.

Roman, G. (1985). A taxonomy of current issues in requirements engineering. *IEEE Computer, 18*(4), 14–23. doi:10.1109/MC.1985.1662861

Ross, M. A. (2005). *Parametric project monitoring and control: performance-based progress assessment and prediction*. Retrieved May 20, 2015, from http://www.dtic.mil/ndia/2005cmmi/wednesday/ross3.pdf

Rott, J. (2011). *Developing green software*. Retrieved from https://software.intel.com/sites/default/files/developing_green_software.pdf

Ruckus Wireless. (2013). *Interworking Wi-Fi and Mobile Networks – The Choice of Mobility Solutions*. White paper. Author.

Sá, M., & Carriço, L. (2011). Designing and Evaluating Mobile Interaction: Challenges and Trends. Foundations and Trends in Human–Computer Interaction, 4(3), 175-243.

Sakuraashe, S., & Warren, L. (2009). Hermes: A tool for testing mobile devices a application. *Software Engineering Conference.*

Salmre, I. (2005). Writing Mobile Code: Essential Software Engineering for Building Mobile Applications. Addison-Wesley.

Salmre, I. (2005). *Writing mobile code: Essential software engineering for building mobile applications.* Boston, MA: Addison-Wesley.

Samimi, F. A., McKinley, P. K., & Sadjadi, S. M. (2006). Mobile service clouds: A self-managing infrastructure for autonomic mobile computing services. In Self-Managed Networks, Systems, and Services (pp. 130-141). Springer Berlin Heidelberg. doi:10.1007/11767886_10

Sanaei, Z., Abolfazli, S., Gani, A., & Buyya, R. (2014). Heterogeneity in Mobile Cloud Computing: Taxonomy and Open Challenges. *IEEE Communications Surveys & Tutorials, 16*(1), 369-392.

Sanchez, M. I. (2013). On Providing Mobility Management in WOBANs: Integration With PMIPv6 and MIH. *IEEE Communications Magazine.*

Sangchul, L., & Wook, J. J. (2010). Evaluating Performance of Android Platform Using Native C for Embedded Systems. *International Conference on Control, Automation and Systems*, (pp. 1160-1163).

Sankaran, C. B. (2012, June). Data offloading techniques in 3GPP Rel-10 networks: A tutorial. *Communications Magazine, IEEE, 50*(6), 46–53. doi:10.1109/MCOM.2012.6211485

Sanou. (2014). *The World in 2014: ICT Facts and Figures.* Retrieved from http://www.itu.int/en/ITU-D/Statistics/Documents/facts/ICTFactsFigures2014-e.pdf

Sargento, S. & Melia, T. & Banchs, A. & Soto, I. & Moedeker, J & Marchetti, L. (2008). *Mobility through Heterogeneous Networks in a 4G Environment.* Academic Press.

Satyanarayanan, M. (2001). Pervasive computing: vision and challenges. *IEEE Personal Communications, 8*(4), 10-17.

Satyanarayanan, M. (2005). Avoiding dead batteries. *IEEE Pervasive Computing / IEEE Computer Society [and] IEEE Communications Society, 4*(1), 2–3. doi:10.1109/MPRV.2005.5

Satyanarayanan, M., Bahl, P., Caceres, R., & Davies, N. (2009, October). The case for VM-Based cloudlets in Mobile Computing. *IEEE Pervasive Computing / IEEE Computer Society [and] IEEE Communications Society, 8*(4), 14–23. doi:10.1109/MPRV.2009.82

Savage, P. (1995). Designing a GUI for business telephone users. *Interaction, 2*(1), 32–41. doi:10.1145/208143.208157

Schmietendorf, A., Fiegler, A., Neumann, R., Wille, C., & Dumke, R. R. (2013). COSMIC Functional Size Measurement of Cloud Systems. In *Proceedings of the Joint Conference of the 23rd International Workshop on Software Measurement (IWSM) and the 8th International Conference on Software Process and Product Measurement (Mensura).* Ankara, Turkey: IEEE Computer Society Conference Publishing Services. doi:10.1109/IWSM-Mensura.2013.15

Sebesta, R. W. (2009). *Concepts of Programming Languages.* Addison-Wesley.

Seddigh, N., Nandy, B., Makkar, R., & Beaumont, J. F. (2010). Security Advances and Challenges in 4G Wireless Networks. In *Proceedings of Eighth Annual International Conference on Privacy, Security and Trust.* doi:10.1109/PST.2010.5593244

Sedgewick, R., & Wayne, K. (2008). *Introduction to programming in Java: An interdisciplinary approach.* Boston: Addison Wesley, Pearson.

Semantics Of A Foundational Subset For Executable, U. M. L.Models (FUML). (2011). Version 1.0. Object Management Group (OMG). Retrieved from http://www.omg.org/spec/FUML/1.0

Shantidev, M., Venkatachalam, M., & Yang, X. (2008). A Novel Algorithm for Efficient Paging in Mobile WiMAX. In K.-C. Chen & J. R. B. de Marca (Eds.), *Mobile WiMAX.* Chichester, UK: John Wiley & Sons, Ltd; doi:10.1002/9780470723937.ch7

Sharifi, M., Kafaie, S., & Kashefi, O. (2011). A Survey and Taxonomy of Cyber Foraging of Mobile Devices.IEEE, 14, 1232-1243.

Sharma, P. (2013, August). Evolution of Mobile Wireless CommunicationNetworks-1G to 5G as well as Future Prospective of Next Generation Communication Network. *International Journal of Computer Science and Mobile Computing, 2*(issue. 8), 47–53.

Sheng, H., Nah, F., & Siau, K. (2005). Strategic implications of mobile technology: A case study using Value-Focused Thinking. *The Journal of Strategic Information Systems, 14*(3), 269–290. doi:10.1016/j.jsis.2005.07.004

Shiraz, M., & Gani, A. (2014). A lightweight active service migration framework for computational offloading in mobile cloud computing. *The Journal of Supercomputing, 68*(2), 978–995. doi:10.1007/s11227-013-1076-7

Siddhartha, K., & Madhur, R. N. (n.d.). LIPA: Local IP Access via Home NodeB. *Radisys Whitepaper.*

Silakov, D. V. & Khoroshilov, A.V. (2011). Ensuring portability of software. *Programming and Computing Software, 37*(1), 41–47. Springer. doi 10.1134/S0361768811010051

Silva, A., & Videira, C. (2008). UML, Metodologias e Ferramentas CASE (vol. 2). Centro Atlântico, Lda. (In Portuguese)

Silven, O. & Jyrkk, K. (2007). Observations on power-efficiency trends in mobile communication devices. *EURASIP Journal on Embedded Systems.* doi 10.1155/2007/56976

Singh, B. & K.S., J. (2012). A Comparative Study of Mobile Wireless Communication Networks and Technologies. *International Journal of Computer Networks and Wireless Communications, 2*(5).

Smith, J. E., & Nair, R. (2005). The architecture of virtual machines. *Computer, 38*(5), 32–38. doi:10.1109/MC.2005.173

SMM. (2015). *OMG Software Metrics Meta-model version 1.0.* Retrieved April 15, 2015 from http://www.omg.org/spec/SMM/1.0

Spielberg, R. F. (2009). *Handbook of reliability, availability, maintainability and safety in engineering design.* London: Springer.

Spiliotopoulos, T., Papadopoulou, P., Martakos, D., & Kouroupetroglou, G. (2010). *Integrating usability engineering for designing the Web experience: Methodologies and principles.* Hershey, PA: IGI Global. doi:10.4018/978-1-60566-896-3

Spriestersbach, A., & Springer, T. (2004). Quality attributes in mobile web application development.Lecture Notes in Computer Science, 3009, 120–130. doi:10.1007/978-3-540-24659-6_9

Sriram, L., & Khajeh-Hosseini, A. (2010). *Research Agenda in Cloud Technologies.* LSCITS Technical Report. Retrieved from: http://arxiv.org/abs/1001.3259

Stahl, T., Voelter, M., & Czarnecki, K. (2006). *Model-Driven Software Development -- Technology, Engineering, Management.* John Wiley & Sons.

Steinberg, D., Budinsky, F., Paternostro, M., & Merks, E. (2009). EMF: Eclipse Modeling Framework (2nd ed.). Addison-Wesley.

Steinberg, D., Budinsky, F., Paternostro, M., & Merks, E. (2008). *EMF: Eclipse Modeling Framework* (2nd ed.). Addison Wesley Professional.

Stern, S., & Guetta, O. (2010). Manage the automotive embedded software development cost by using a Functional Size Measurement Method (COSMIC).In *Proceedings of the 4ᵗʰEmbedded Real Time Software and Systems conference.* Toulouse, France: ERTS2.

Sullivan, K., Griswold, W., Cai, Y., & Hallen, B. (2001). The structure and value of modularity in software design. *Software Engineering Notes, ACM SIGSOFT, 26*(5), 99–108. doi:10.1145/503271.503224

Su, Y. Y., & Flinn, J. (2005). Slingshot: Deploying stateful services in wireless hotspots.*3rd International Conference on Mobile Systems, Applications, and Services*, (pp. 79-92). doi:10.1145/1067170.1067180

Syme, D., Petricek, T., & Lomov, D. (2011). *The F# Asynchronous Programming Model. In Practical Aspects of Declarative Languages* (pp. 175–189). Springer Berlin Heidelberg. doi:10.1007/978-3-642-18378-2_15

Syriani, E., Vangheluwe, H., Mannadiar, R., Hansen, C., Van Mierlo, S., & Ergin, H. (2013). AToMPM: A Web-based Modeling Environment. *MODELS'13: Invited Talks, Demos, Posters, and ACM SRC. 1115.* CEUR-WS.org.

Taboada, G. L., Ramos, S., Exposito, R. R., Tourino, J., & Doallo, R. (2011). Java in the High Performance Computing arena: Research, practice and experience. *Science of Computer Programming*, v.

Taivalsaari, A., & Systä, K. (2012). Cloudberry: An HTML5 cloud phone platform for mobile devices. *IEEE Software, 29*(4), 40–45. doi:10.1109/MS.2012.51

Tanenbaum, A. S., & Wetherall, D. J. (2011). *Computer Networks*. Pearson.

Tang, W.-T., Hu, C.-M., & Hsu, C.-Y. (2010). A mobile phone based homecare management system on the cloud. In *Proceedings of the 3rd International Conference on Biomedical and Informatics (BMEI)*, (vol. 6, pp. 2442). doi:10.1109/BMEI.2010.5639917

Techopedia. (n.d.). *Mobile Cloud Computing (MCC)*. Retrieved May 4, 2015, from http://www.techopedia.com/definition/26679/mobile-cloud-computing-mcc

Testing the Cloud. (2011). *Testing the Cloud: Definitions, Requirements, and Solutions*. Ixia Whitepaper. Retrieved on 14 Dec 2014 from http://www.ixiacom.com/sites/default/files/resources/whitepaper/cloud_testing_white_paper_0.pdf

Testing the Cloud. (2013). *CBR Testing Automation, Special Report*. Retrieved on 10 January 2015 from http://qualisystems.com/wp-content/uploads/2013/08/Testing-the-Cloud1.pdf

Thakur, G. S., & Helmy, A. (2013). COBRA: A Framework for the Analysis of Realistic Mobility Models. In *Proceedings of the 16th IEEE Global Internet Symposium*. IEEE.

Thangarajah, J., Sardi~na, & Padgham. (2012). Measuring plan coverage and overlap for agent reasoning. AAMAS.

The Eclipse Foundation. (2015). *Orion*. Retrieved from http://eclipse.org/orion/

Thiagarajan, N., Aggarwal, G., Nicoara, A., Boneh, D., & Singh, J. P. (2012). Who Killed My Battery: Analyzing Mobile Browser Energy Consumption. *WWW, 2012*, 41–50.

Thibaut, K. (Ed.). (2014). *5G: A new Philosophy in Connectivity Wireless Protocols on the fly; The End of the Needy Architecture. The European Commission's CONNECT-Community Networks, Control and Technology Directorate – General*. Net Futures.

Thompson, C., Schmidt, D., Turner, H., & White, J. (2011). Analyzing Mobile Application Software Power Consumption via Model-Driven Engineering. *Proceedings of PECCS, 2011*, 101–113.

Thompson, S., & Torabi, T. (2007). A process Improment Approach to improve Web From Design and Usability.*18th International Workshop on Database and Expert Systems Applications* (pp. 570 - 574). Regensburg: IEEE.

Tonini, A. R., Beckmann, M., de Mattos, J. C., & de Brisolara, L. B. (2012). *Evaluating Android best practices for performance*. Academic Press.

Trello Inc. (2015). *Trello*. Retrieved from http://www.trello.com

Tucker, A., & Noonan, R. (2007). *Programming languages: principles and paradigms* (2nd ed.). Tata McGraw-Hill Education.

Tulloch, M., & Tulloch, I. (2002). *Microsoft® Encyclopedia of Networking* (2nd ed.). Redmond, WA: Microsoft Press.

Valtulina, L. (2013). *Seamless distributed mobility management(dmm) solution in cloud based lte systems*. Master Thesis. Available in http://essay.utwente.nl/64411/

Van Amstel, M., Bosems, S., Kurtev, I., & Pires, L. F. (2011). Performance in model transformations: experiments with ATL and QVT. In *Proceedings of the 4th international conference on Theory and practice of model transformations* (ICMT'11) (LNCS), (vol. 6707, pp. 198-212). Berlin: Springer-Verlag. doi:10.1007/978-3-642-21732-6_14

van Heeringen, H. S. (2011). Estimate faster, cheaper... and better! In *Proceedings of the 8th Software Measurement European Forum*. Rome, Italy.

van Heeringen, H. S., & van Gorp, E. W. M. (2014). Measure the functional size of a mobile app using the COSMIC functional size measurement method. In *Proceedings of the Joint Conference of the 24th International Workshop on Software Measurement (IWSM) and the 9th International Conference on Software Process and Product Measurement (Mensura)*. Rotterdam, The Netherlands: IEEE Computer Society Conference Publishing Services. doi:10.1109/IWSM. Mensura.2014.8

Van Mierlo, S., Barroca, B., Vangheluwe, H., Syriani, E., & Kühne, T. (2014, oct). Multi-Level Modelling in the Modelverse. In *Proceedings of the Workshop on Multi-Level Modelling*. CEUR-WS.org.

Vaupel, S., Taentzer, G., Harries, J., Stroh, R., Gerlach, R., & Guckert, M. (2014). Model-Driven Development of Mobile Applications Allowing Role-Driven Variants. In *Model-Driven Engineering Languages and Systems,Proceedings of 17th International Conference, MODELS 2014* (LNCS), (*vol. 8767*, pp. 1-17). Springer International Publishing. doi:10.1007/978-3-319-11653-2_1

Verbelen, T., Simoens, P., Turck, F. D., & Dhoedt, B. (2012). AIOLOS: Middleware for improving mobile application performance through cyber foraging. *Journal of Systems and Software, 85*(11), 2629–2639. doi:10.1016/j.jss.2012.06.011

Vidal, A., & Marron, J. J. (2014). Real-time pedestrian tracking in indoor environments. In *Proceedings of IEEE Latin-America Conf. Commun* (pp. 1–6). IEEE.

Vinoski, S. (2008). Multilanguage Programming. *IEEE Internet Computing, 12*(3), 83–85. doi:10.1109/MIC.2008.58

Vogelezang, F. W. (2013a). *The first generation of Functional Size Measurement*. Retrieved May 20, 2015, from http://thePriceofIT.blogspot.nl/2013/01/the-first-generation-FSM.html

Vogelezang, F. W. (2013b). *What is a second generation FSM method*. Retrieved May 20, 2015 from http://thepriceofit. blogspot.nl/2013/02/second-generation-FSM.html

Vogelezang, F. W., & Lesterhuis, A. (2003). Applicability of COSMIC in an administrative environment - Experiences of an early adopter. In *Proceedings of the 13ᵗʰ International Workshop on Software Measurement*. Montréal, Canada: Shaker Verlag.

Wagelaar, D., Tisi, M., Cabot, J., & Jouault, F. (2011). Towards a general composition semantics for rule-based model transformation. In *Proceedings of the 14th International Conference on Model Driven Engineering Languages and Systems, MODELS 2011 Model Driven Engineering Languages and Systems* (LNCS), (vol. 6981, pp. 623-637). Berlin: Springer-Verlag. doi:10.1007/978-3-642-24485-8_46

Wagelaar, D. (2011). A revised semantics for rule inheritance and module superimposit-ion in ATL. In *Proceedings of the 3rd International Workshop on Model Transformation with ATL (MtATL11)* (pp. 62-74).

Wang, D-C., He, W. & Chen, I-R. (2012). Smart Routers for Cross-Layer Integrated Mobility and Service Management in Mobile IPv6 Systems. *Wireless Pers Commun.* DOI .10.1007/s11277-012-0583-9

Wang, Z. (2011). The study of smart phone development based on uml. In *Proceedings of the 2011 International Conference on Computer Science and Service System*, (pp. 2791–2794).

Wang, Q., & Abu-Rgheff, M. A. (2003). Cross-Layer Signalling for Next Generation Wireless Systems. *IEEE Wireless Communications and Networking*, 2, 1084–1089. doi:10.1109/WCNC.2003.1200522

Wang, Q., & Yuan, D. (2010). Effectiveness and fairness tradeoff for TCP using cross-layer design in UMTS system. In *Proceedings of International Symposium on Performance Evaluation of Computer and Telecommunication Systems (SPECTS)*.

Ward, M. (1994). Language-oriented programming. *Software Concepts and Tools*, *15*(4), 147–161.

Warmer, J., Bast, W., Pinkley, D., Herrera, M., & Kleppe, A. (2003). *MDA Explained - The Model Driven Architecture: Practice and Promise*. Addison-Wesley Professional.

Wasserman, A. I. (2010). Software engineering issues for mobile application development.*FSE/SDP Workshop on Future of Software Engineering Research*, (pp. 397–400). doi:10.1145/1882362.1882443

Waugh, R. (2012). Resistance is futile! More Androids are activated every day than babies are born. *Daily Mail*. Retrieved January 18, 2015, from http://www.dailymail.co.uk/sciencetech/article-2086144/CES-2012-More-Androids-activated-day-babies-born.html

Wi-Fi Alliance. (2014). *15 Years of Wi-Fi*. Retrieved June 30, 2015, from https://www.wi-fi.org/discover-wi-fi/15-years-of-wi-fi

WiMAX Forum. (n.d.). Retrieved from http://www.wimaxforum.org

Wisely, D., Eardley, P., & Burness, L. (2002). *IP for 3G: Networking Technologies for Mobile Communications*. John Wiley & Sons, Ltd. doi:10.1002/0470847794

Xia, H., Lu, T., Shao, B., Ding, X., & Gu, N. (2014, May). Hermes: On collaboration across heterogeneous collaborative editing services in the cloud. In *Computer Supported Cooperative Work in Design (CSCWD),Proceedings of the 2014 IEEE 18th International Conference on* (pp. 655-660). IEEE.

Xia, F., Ding, F., Li, J., Kong, X., Yang, L. T., & Ma, J. (2014). Phone2Cloud: Exploiting computation offloading for energy saving on smartphones in mobile cloud computing. *Information Systems Frontiers*, *16*(1), 95–111. doi:10.1007/s10796-013-9458-1

XMI. (2011). *OMG MOF 2 XMI mapping SpecificationOMG*. Document Number: formal/ 2011-08-09. Retrieved April 15, 2015 from http://www.omg.org/spec/XMI/2.4.1

Yang, X., Pan, T., & Shen, J. (2010). On 3G Mobile E-commerce Platform Based on Cloud Computing. In *Proceedings of the 3rd IEEE International Conference on Ubi-Media Computing (U-Media)*, (pp. 198 - 201). IEEE.

Youssef, S. (2013). *Advanced Mobile Systems*. Lecture Notes Unpublished. Available on VLE at: http://vle.anglia.ac.uk/modules/2013/...../

Yumei, W. U., Liu. (2011). A model based testing approach for mobile device. *American Journal of Engineering and Technology Research, 11*(9), 3536-3542.

Zhang, L., Tiwana, B., Dick, R., Qian, Z., Mao, Z. a., & Yang, L. (2010). Accurate online power estimation and automatic battery behavior based power model generation for smartphones.*International Conference on Hardware/Software Codesign and System Synthesis*, (pp. 105-114). doi:10.1145/1878961.1878982

Zhang, X., Kunjithapatham, A., Jeong, S., & Gibbs, S. (2011). Towards an Elastic Application Model for Augmenting the Computing Capabilities of Mobile Devices with Cloud Computing. *Mobile Networks and Applications, 16*(3), 270–284. doi:10.1007/s11036-011-0305-7

Zhao, W., Sun, Y., & Dai, L. (2010). Improving computer basis teaching through mobile communication and cloud computing technology. In *Proceedings of the 3rd International Conference on Advanced Computer Theory and Engineering (ICACTE)*, (vol. 1, pp. 452 – 454).

Zhifangliu, L. B., & Openggao, X. (2009). SOA based mobile application software test framework. *8th international conference on reliability, maintainability and safety* (pp. 765-769). IEEE.

Zhou, W., Arslan, T., Benkrid, K., El-Rayis, A.O. & Haridas, N. (2013). *Reconfigurable feeding Network for GSM/GPS/3G/WiFi and Global LTE Applications*. Academic Press.

Zibula, A., & Majchrzak, T. (2013). Cross-platform development using HTML5, jQuery Mobile, and PhoneGap: Realizing a smart meter application. *Lecture Notes in Business Information Processing, 140*, 16–33. doi:10.1007/978-3-642-36608-6_2

About the Contributors

António Miguel Rosado da Cruz is Invited Adjunct Professor in the Polytechnical Institute of Viana do Castelo. He has a PhD in Informatics Engineering from University of Porto. Has several works published, mainly in the areas of Software Engineering, Model-driven Development, Model Transformation, Software Modeling, Code Generation, User Interface Modeling, Formal Methods, Cloud computing and Metamodels.

Sara Paiva has a PhD in Computer Engineering and has been a teacher at the School of Technology and Management for 10 years. For several years now she is dedicated to the mobile development field (Android and iOS), both for lecturing and research purposes. She has more than 20 publications in journals and conferences and has participated in several research projects. She also accumulates responsibilities as Course Coordinator and as a member of several course committees. Finally, she has a background in the area of neuro-linguistic programming and coaching.

* * *

Fahim Arif has done Bachelors in Telecommunication from College of Telecommunication Engineering (UET Lahore) in 1995 and Master in Sciences in Computer Software Engineering from National University Science and Technology, Islamabad in 2003. He has won NUST Endowment fund scheme scholarship for NUST in 2003 and International Research Support Initiative Program Fund from HEC in 2007. He has completed his PhD degree from National University Science and Technology in 2009. His contribution to international research in recent few years is excellent. He has presented/published numerous research papers in different international conferences including USA and Canada. In addition to his research publications, he is doing as reviewer for various international conferences. He worked as international research scholar in System and Computer Engineering Department, Carleton University, Ottawa, Canada in 2007 and participated in numerous research and academic activities. He is principal investigator (PI) for a project funded by NUST. Recently, his biography has been published by South Asian Publication Who's Who in the World 2008 Edition and awarded with Star Laureate 2008 in recognition to his contributions to knowledge and research. Higher Education Commission of Pakistan has nominated him as their official PhD supervisor in 2010. Currently, he is teaching various academic courses at MCS and supervising PhD and MS/ BE students in their final projects/thesis in NUST. He has organized 2 National conferences (NSEC 2010 and NCIA 2013). Presently is busy in arranging 2nd National Conference on Software Engineering (NSEC 2014) which is scheduled on 11-12 Nov 2014 at MCS, NUST. He presented his research paper in International Conference on Software and Data Engineering held in Dubai from 29-31 Jan 2012. He is authorized consultant for Nexsource Pak (Pvt) Ltd to design and develop a national level project for telemedicine system. He has published more than 35 research papers in international journals and conferences uptill now. His research interests are software engineering, Quality assurance in software, Image processing and remote sensing. 6 PhD and 13 MS students are currently working in his research group.

Franck Barbier (detailed vitæ at www.FranckBarbier.com): (CS) Ph.D. in 1991 (University of Chambéry, France), French higher (CS) Ph.D. (a.k.a. HDR) in 1998 (University of Nantes, France); associate professor from '91 to '98 at the University of Nantes, visiting researcher at the University of Sydney from '98 to '99 and full professor (University of Pau, France) from 2000; Director of the CS Research Department of the University of Pau (LIUPPA) from 2000 to 2004. Deputy Head of the Information and Communication Technologies (ICT) sector at the French Research Agency, a.k.a. ANR (i.e., "French NSF") from 2009 to 2012. Research activities and interests are object/component/service modeling through UML, model driven engineering, software design, test and runtime management for mobile and distributed systems, software adaptation through built-in test, executable models and models at runtime.

Pablo Nicolas Diaz Bilotto received his "Analista Programador Universitario" from UNICEN in 2011, actually seeking his "Ingeniero en sistemas" degree. Actually working for Magic Star - Binbaires since 2012.

Eric Cariou obtained its Ph.D. in computer science from the University of Rennes 1 and Télécom Bretagne in 2003. Then, he got a post-doctorate position at the University of Lille 1. Since 2005, he is associate professor at the University of Pau. His research interests deal with software architecture and model-driven engineering. He worked on software components dedicated to the communication between components and on the integration of component and agent approaches through services. Concerning MDE, he has developed techniques for contract-based verification. They have been applied to verifying model transformations and model execution. He is also working on software adaptation through models@ runtime principles and more precisely on the adaptation of model execution.

Jonathan Corley is a Ph.D. student in the Department of Computer Science at The University of Alabama. His research topic is debugging in the area of Model-Driven Engineering (MDE) with research projects including investigating omniscient debugging for model transformations and empirical research investigating the processes and techniques used during debugging tasks by developers in both General Purpose Language (GPL) and MDE contexts. Jonathan received his B.S. in Computer Science in 2009 at The University of Alabama, continuing on at The University of Alabama to receive his M.S. in Computer Science in 2012.

Huseyin Ergin is a Ph.D. student in the Department of Computer Science at the University of Alabama. His research topic is model transformation design patterns and languages. Huseyin received his B.Sc. in Computer Science and Engineering in 2008 at Yeditepe University, Turkey. Then, he received his M.Sc. in Computer Science in 2011 at Sabanci University, Turkey.

Sheikh Umar Farooq is an Assistant Professor in Department of Computer Sciences at University of Kashmir. He received his PhD from the University of Kashmir. His research interests include Empirical

Software Engineering with Focus on Software Testing Techniques Evaluation and Software Reliability Improvement. He is a Member of many Software Engineering Societies. He serves as reviewer for many top software engineering journals and conferences like Journal of Systems and Software, International Journal of Software Engineering etc. He also served in several program committees like A-Test 2015 etc.

Liliana Favre is a full professor of Computer Science at Universidad Nacional del Centro de la Provincia de Buenos Aires in Argentina. She is also a researcher of CIC (Comisión de Investigaciones Científicas de la Provincia de Buenos Aires). Her current research interests are focused on model driven development, model driven architecture and formal approaches, mainly on the integration of algebraic techniques with MDA-based processes. She has been involved in several national research projects about formal methods and software engineering methodologies. Currently she is research leader of the Software Technology Group at Universidad Nacional del Centro de la Provincia de Buenos Aires. She has published several book chapters, journal articles and conference papers. She has acted as editor of the book UML and the Unified Process. She is the author of the book Model Driven Architecture for Reverse Engineering Technologies: Strategic Directions and System Evolution.

João M. Fernandes is Full Professor at Dept. Informatics / ALGORITMI Research Centre, Universidade do Minho, Portugal. He conducts his research activities in software engineering, with a special interest in software modelling, requirements engineering, and embedded software. As part of his research and teaching activities, his work is focused on the methodological and technologic aspects related with the use of a multi-perspective, model-driven approach for developing software systems. Within his research and teaching activities, he maintains regular collaborations with the industry. He was invited professor/researcher at U. Bristol (UK, 1991), Abo Akademi (Turku, Finland, 2002--03), ISCTEM (Maputo, Mozambique, 2003), U. Algarve (Faro, Portugal, 2004--06), U. Aarhus (Denmark; 2006--07), and UFSC (Florianópolis, Brazil; 2013). He has authored more than 100 scientific publications published in journals, books and conference proceedings and is co-editor of the book "Behavioral modeling for embedded systems and technologies: applications for design and implementation" (IGI Global, 2010). João is member of the Editorial Review Board of the Journal of Information Technology Research, IGI Publishing, since Jun/2007. He has been involved in the organisation of various international events, including ACSD 2003, DIPES 2006, GTTSE 2009, PETRI NETS 2010, ACSD 2010, the MOMPES workshops series (2003-2012), and ICSOB 2015. He is a regular reviewer for scientific journals and conferences. He also regularly serves as a member of the program committees of international conferences and workshops. For more information, please access www3.di.uminho.pt/jmf.

André L. Ferreira's research is mainly focused on Experimental Software engineering, where he tries to study models for improving the software process. He has studied in detail the integration of benchmarked and analytic based process improvement models. Currently, he's an Invited Assistant Professor at Universidade do Minho, Department of Informatics.

Olivier Le Goaër is an assistant professor at the University of Pau. His research interests focus on software evolution and metamodeling. His technological watch includes web and mobile software development. He received his PhD in computer science from the University of Nantes.

Nadir Guetmi received the state engineer degree in Computer Science from University of Badji Mokhtar Annaba, Algeria. Currently, PhD student in the LIAS / ISAE-ENSMA laboratory of Poitiers, France. His research interests focus on collaboration software and multi-agent systems.

Juhana Harmanen is a shareholder and a member of executive board in a fast growing startup company ADA Drive Ltd, Helsinki. As a member of executive board he is responsible for operational management in accordance to the company strategy decided by the Board of Directors reporting to the CEO. He is responsible for the organization and prioritization of the product development, as well as for the commercialization of a significant innovation into a profitable business in conjunction with other members of the executive board. His responsibilities as a CTO, a software architect, and a team leader are to enforce the best practices and coding conventions in product architecture and infrastructure as well as to provide guidance and leadership in a team environment. He received his BSc IT and MSc IT from Tampere University of Technology including studies completed at National University of Singapore. Mr. Harmanen pursues for knowledge both in the industry and in leadership, as well as in the development of new business and strategy, and he is currently taking MSc IEM at Aalto University in Strategy and Venturing.

Abdessamad Imine received MSc and PhD degrees in Computer Science from University of Sciences and Technology of Oran (USTO), Algeria, and University Henri Poincaré of Nancy, France, respectively. He is currently Associate Professor at Lorraine University and senior researcher at INRIA-LORIA center of Nancy. His research interests include optimistic protocols, security for collaborative systems, social networks and formal methods.

Muhammad Laminu (Student Member, IEEE and IET) received his National Diploma and Bachelor of Engineering Degree from Ramat Polytechnic Maiduguri and University of Maiduguri, Nigeria in 1995 and 2008 respectively. He just graduated from Anglia Ruskin University, Chelmsford with MSc. Mobile Telecommunications. He is a lecturer in the department of Electrical and Electronic Engineering at Ramat Polytechnic and his research interests are Cross-Layer Design, Mobility Management, Ad-hoc networks, Embedded Systems, and Electronic Systems Modelling.

Mathias Longo is a teacher assistant at Universidad Nacional del Centro de la Provincia de Buenos Aires (UNICEN) and a member of Instituto de Sistemas Tandil (ISISTAN) and has a PhD grant of Argentinian National Council for Scientific and Technical Research (CONICET). His research areas include mobile computing, service-oriented computing.

D. Jeya Mala has a Ph.D. in Software Engineering with Specialization on Software Testing and is Associate Professor in Thiagarajar College of Engineering, –a leading educational and philanthropic institution in Tamil Nadu, India. She had been in the industry for about 4 years. She has a profound teaching and research experience of more than 12 years. She has published a book on "Object Oriented Analysis and Design using UML" for Tata McGraw Hill Publishers. She has published more than forty (40) papers about her research works at leading international journals and conferences such as IET, ACM, Springer, World Scientific, Computing and Informatics etc. As a researcher, Dr. Jeya Mala had investigated practical aspects of software engineering and object oriented paradigms for effective software development. Her work on Software Testing has fetched grants from UGC under Major Research

Project scheme. Her dissertation has been listed as one of the best Ph.D. thesis in the CSIR – Indian Science Abstracts. She is a life member of Computer Society of India (CSI-India) and Indian Science Congress Association (ISCA) and a member of ACM-India, and iSoft. She forms the reviewer board in Journals like IEEE Transactions on Software Engineering, Elsevier – Information Sciences, Springer, World Scientific, International Journal of Metaheuristics etc. She has completed certification on Software Testing Fundamentals, Brain bench certification on Java 1.1 programming, IBM certification as Associate Developer Websphere Application Studio. She is a proud recipient of several laurels from industries like Honeywell, IBM and Microsoft for her remarkable contributions in the field of Software Development and Object Orientation.

Cristian Mateos received a Ph.D. degree in Computer Science from the UNICEN in 2008. He is a full time Teacher Assistant at the UNICEN and member of ISISTAN-CONICET. His main research interest are parallel/distributed programming, Grid middlewares and Service-oriented Computing.

Tommi Mikkonen (MSc 1992, Lic. Tech. 1995, Dr. Tech 1999, all from Tampere University of Technology, Tampere Finland) works on software architectures, software engineering, web and mobile systems, and open source software development. Over the years, he has written a number of research papers, and supervised theses and research projects on software engineering. At present, he is working as the head of the Department of Pervasive Computing at Tampere University of Technology.

Luís Pereira was born in 1994, in Braga, Portugal, and hold a Degree in Computer Science. During his academic time he developed a few mobile applications (Android and iOS), like the management track, where the main idea was to focus on Geocoding and Fused Location Provider. He is one of the authors of "A Domain Independent Pedestrian Dead Reckoning System Solution for Android Smartphones".

João Paulo Quintão is a Computer Science student for three years, having his degree completed in July 2015. Born in 1994, in Braga, this computer engineer puts his effort and expertise in the development of some smartphone applications, for both Android and IOS. As an example, he has management track, which is mainly focused on Geocoding and Fused Location Provider. João is one of the authors of "A Domain Independent Pedestrian Dead Reckoning System Solution for Android Smartphones".

Ana Rodriguez is a teacher assistant at Universidad Nacional del Centro de la Provincia de Buenos Aires (UNICEN) and a member of Instituto de Sistemas Tandil (ISISTAN) and has a PhD grant of Argentinian National Council for Scientific and Technical Research (CONICET). Her research areas include mobile computing, service-oriented computing.

Jorge Amadeu Alves Pereira da Silva has a BSc degree in Computer Engineering (Engenharia Informática) and in Biology (Biologia). Sudent of the Master of Software Engineering in IPVC.

Eugene Syriani is currently an assistant professor in Computer Science at the University of Montreal. He was formerly an assistant professor at the University of Alabama until 2014. He received a Ph.D. in Computer Science in 2011 and holds a B.Sc. in Mathematics and Computer Science since 2006, both at McGill University. Affiliated to McGill, Eugene also pursued postdoctoral research on model transformation in the Canada-wide NECSIS project on model-driven engineering for automotive systems.

Eugene's main research interests are in model-based design, in particular model transformation design and verification, model-driven methodology, simulation-based design, and application of MDE in non-computer science domains. He serves on the program committee and organizes several international conferences and workshops. Eugene is also a reviewer for journals in modeling and simulation.

Simon Van Mierlo is a PhD Student at the University of Antwerp.

Frank Vogelezang is Manager of the Pricing Office of Ordina. Doing empirical research on what IT services should and can cost. The "should cost" involves cost calculation, benchmarking and productivity improvement. The "can cost" involves pricing benchmarks, pricing strategy models and value based pricing initiatives.

Sufian Yousef is the creator and Director Telecommunication Engineering Research Group (TERG) at Anglia Ruskin University Chelmsford, UK since 2003. He is well known for his outstanding Academic Leadership in teaching and research in the fields of IT and Telecommunication Engineering with over 32 years lecturing and course development experience in Jordan Telecommunication College and Anglia Ruskin University. He has won the award of Royal Academy of Engineering for sabbatical to Marconi Research Centre in Great Baddow to carry out military research on ATM.

Alejandro Zunino is an adjunct professor at Universidad Nacional del Centro de la Provincia de Buenos Aires (UNICEN) and a member of Instituto de Sistemas Tandil (ISISTAN) and the Argentinian National Council for Scientific and Technical Research (CONICET). His research areas include grid computing, service-oriented computing and mobile computing. Zunino has a PhD in computer science from UNICEN.

Index

Become an IRMA Member

Members of the **Information Resources Management Association (IRMA)** understand the importance of community within their field of study. The Information Resources Management Association is an ideal venue through which professionals, students, and academicians can convene and share the latest industry innovations and scholarly research that is changing the field of information science and technology. Become a member today and enjoy the benefits of membership as well as the opportunity to collaborate and network with fellow experts in the field.

IRMA Membership Benefits:

- **One FREE Journal Subscription**
- **30% Off Additional Journal Subscriptions**
- **20% Off Book Purchases**
- Updates on the latest events and research on Information Resources Management through the IRMA-L listserv.
- Updates on new open access and downloadable content added to Research IRM.
- A copy of the Information Technology Management Newsletter twice a year.
- A certificate of membership.

IRMA Membership $195

Scan code to visit irma-international.org and begin by selecting your free journal subscription.

Membership is good for one full year.

Printed in the United States
By Bookmasters